AFGH

M000228998

AFGHANISTAN

The Taliban Years

S. IFTIKHAR MURSHED

BENNETT & BLOOM

First published
in 2006 by
BENNETT & BLOOM
www.bennettandbloom.com

PO Box 2131
London W1A 5SU
England

© S. Iftikhar Murshed 2006

Typeset and designed by Desert♥Hearts

Printed and bound by
Newton Printing, London, England

British Library Cataloguing in Publication Data
A catalogue record for this book is available from the British Library

ISBN 1-898948-94-1 • 978-1-898948-94-0 (paperback)
ISBN 1-898948-93-3 • 978-1-898948-93-3 (hardback)

Contents

I

The emergence of the Taliban

I WAS WORKING at Pakistan's Board of Investment when, on 5 November 1996, I was asked by foreign secretary Najmuddin Shaikh to meet him urgently. As soon as I entered his office, he told me that I had been appointed additional foreign secretary responsible exclusively for Afghanistan. My assignment entailed shuttle missions between the warring Afghan factions. The purpose was to narrow their differences and bring them to the negotiating table so that sustainable peace, which had eluded Afghanistan for almost twenty years, could be restored.

That was a tall order not only because the Afghans are fiercely independent and stubborn but also for the reason that the country's decade-long struggle against Soviet occupation had been a decentralized conflict, fought in many theatres of war through the length and breadth of approximately 647,500 square kilometres of rugged Afghan territory. There had been no central figure around whom the people could rally. The nationalist upsurge that normally accompanies a successful freedom struggle was, therefore, absent from Afghanistan. Local commanders, who had fought against the Soviet occupation army, established themselves in their respective areas. Peace therefore did not return to the country. The conflict that followed transformed itself from a heroic war of liberation to an ugly contest for power among the leaders of the factions who had previously constituted the Afghan resistance against the Soviets.

I had been the director general in charge of Afghanistan from 1988-90, a period which coincided with the Soviet withdrawal from that country and the resistance against the Moscow-installed Najibullah government. But several years had passed since then. I was out of touch with the transformed ground realities in Afghanistan. The Pushtun-dominated Taliban movement had risen from obscurity to control 75 percent of the territory and had captured the country's capital, Kabul, on 27 September 1996. The remaining 25 percent of Afghanistan was in the hands of a coalition of unlikely bedfellows, the Shura-e-Aali-e-Difa-e-Afghanistan—the Supreme Council for the Defence of Afghanistan—more commonly known as the Northern Alliance. The latter represented minority ethnic groups who, despite their hatred of each other, were united by their fear of the Taliban. Afghan society had thus become dangerously polarized along ethnic fault lines.

Through history, Afghanistan has seldom known peace. Its ethnic heterogeneity and, to an extent, its topography, geographical location and the extremity of its climate with bitterly cold winters and scalding summers, have shaped and influenced its violence-ridden past. Peaceful coexistence among the ethnic groups led by the Pushtuns, who account for about 50 percent of a population of 16.48 million, and the Tajiks (22.9 percent), Hazaras (12 percent), Uzbeks (6.25 percent) and other small groups such as the Turkmen and Aimaks has been alien to the Afghan experience. The ethnic map of the country, with the groups separated and confined to clearly defined areas, has also militated against national unity. The Hindu Kush range, which translates as the "slayer of Hindus", has served as the rough divide.

In the historical context, the term "Afghan" was probably first used in the fifteenth century during the reign of Mahmud of Ghazni, a ruler of Turkish descent, while the name of the country, "Afghanistan," was coined in the sixteenth and seventeenth centuries by the Moguls. History contains no record of an Afghan state before 1747. Eastern Afghanistan formed part of the Mogul Empire while its west was controlled by the Safavids of Iran. Kabul became the capital of Mogul territory west of the Indus.

The second major Afghan town, Kandahar, was contested between the Mogul and Persian empires up to the time when it was taken by the latter during the reign of the Mogul emperor, Shah Jahan. The shahs of Iran continued to treat Afghanistan a province of their empire until the nineteenth century.

The quest for national cohesion in a heterogeneous population defines the Afghanistan problem. The difficulties are compounded because the disparate groups of the country were brought together, through the centuries, more by accident rather than any shared desire to live together. The urge for unity was absent from Afghan society because one group, the Pushtuns, imposed itself on the others. The ethnic minorities were subjugated and treated as second-class citizens. The Pushtuns monopolized economic and political power with the encouragement of imperial Britain in the nineteenth and early twentieth centuries. Thus uni-ethnic rule in a multi-ethnic society, and its attendant backlash, unleashed violence among a people who had never wanted to be united into a single nation.

I asked myself whether this had changed. After all, the Afghan people had united to resist the Soviet occupation of their country in the 1980s as they had in the years preceding that event to oppose the communist reforms foisted on their traditional tribal society by the People's Democratic Party of Afghanistan (PDPA). Or were these mere aberrations? Were the Taliban willing to make concessions to the non-Pushtuns? Did the minority ethnic groups of the Northern Alliance want national unity or did they envisage that their interests would be better served by the fragmentation of their country? Was outside interference responsible in considerable measure for the continuation of the turmoil? To what extent was the Afghan concept of Islam responsible for the Taliban's obscurantist world view? How was I to bring the Afghan groups to the negotiating table if they were still influenced by the tragic events of their short history and what was the real story of their past?

The Great Game

In 1747, Ahmed Shah Abdali founded the Kingdom of Afghanistan and extended it up to Kashmir as well as the Punjab, Sindh and Baluchistan of present day Pakistan. He was conferred the title Durr-i-Durran (Pearl of Pearls) and from this his tribe, which was to play so a prominent role in Afghan history, became known as the Durrani. After Abdali's death in 1773, the empire fragmented into independent city states and spurred rivalry between the British and the Russians for dominance of the country.

The emergence of Afghanistan as a state in the last two centuries owed itself more to Britain's imperial ambitions than any desire among its peoples to forge national identity. British writers claimed that their country had contributed significantly to give "a national unity to that nebulous community which we call Afghanistan (which the Afghans never called by that name) by drawing a boundary all round it and elevating it into a position of buffer state between ourselves and Russia".[1] External compression was, therefore, applied by the advancing empires of Britain and Russia to foster effective cohesion among the Afghan groups.[2] The conflicting interests of the two imperial powers did not permit either to establish itself in Afghanistan. The alternative to an armed clash over the territory was to transform it into a buffer state. It was also in their interest, if Afghanistan was to play this role, to ensure that chaos and anarchy did not prevail in it. A strong ruler was, therefore, needed in the country. Britain and, to an extent, Russia feared chaos in a leaderless Afghanistan more than the unfriendliness of an Afghan ruler.[3] The British were also conscious that there was nothing to guarantee Afghanistan's continued existence as a buffer between England and Russia as no other country cared about its survival.[4] This generated a disproportionate British interest in Afghanistan which played itself out as the "Great Game" in the nineteenth century. The attempt to incorporate Afghanistan in the British sphere of influence led to two Anglo-Afghan wars from 1839 to 1842 and 1878 to 1880. The first resulted in defeat for the British while the second enabled them to control Afghanistan's foreign policy and annex sizeable territory. These lands, stretched from the Indus to the Durand Line, which demarcates the present-day border between Pakistan and Afghanistan. The result was the delimitation of the frontiers of Afghanistan in the west, south and east by the British, and in the north by the Russian and British governments.

After bringing Afghanistan into existence, the need for a strong ruler, or amir, to hold the country together thus became of paramount concern to the British who, on occasions, played a decisive role in the selection of the amir. So deep was their involvement that British support became essential to ensure any particular amir's continued occupation of the Afghan throne. They provided him the subsidies and weapons to build an army and consolidate power. Furthermore, the subjugation of the ethnic minorities by the Pushtun amirs was carried out with the encouragement and support of the British. In the words of a Russian historian "after 1849 Dost Muhammad turned to the conquest of non-Afghan peoples living north of the Hindu Kush [Uzbeks, Tajiks, and Turkmen] with the support of the British India Company".[5]

With British subsidies, Amir Abdur Rahman, who ruled from 1880 to 1901, sought to establish an absolute monarchy. He was succeeded by his son, Habibullah, who was assassinated in 1919. Habibullah's son, Amanullah Khan, then became the amir but later changed this title to 'king,' and during his ten-year rule, tried to modernize the country. He won Afghanistan's independence in the third Anglo-Afghan war in 1919 but lost the subsidy as a consequence of which he failed to establish a resource base or build a reliable army. An insurrection supported by extremist clergy ensued and Kabul was taken by the rebels in January 1929. An ethnic Tajik rebel ruled for the next nine months when the capital fell, yet again, in October 1929 to the Pushtun tribes led by Nadir Khan, a member of the royal family.

As was perhaps inevitable under the circumstances, the power base in Afghanistan has constantly remained extremely narrow. Its exercise has been the privilege of the Pushtuns (or Pathans), within the Pushtuns that of the Durranis, and within the Durranis of the Barakzais. For almost half a century during which power rested with the Mohammadzai branch of the Barakzai clan, Afghanistan was controlled by an inner cabinet consisting of key members of the royal family and a few of their trusted associates. Command positions in the army were invariably held by members of the royal family and, in some instances, by staunch supporters of the monarchy. The successful coup by Sardar Muhammad Daud Khan in July 1973 against his cousin, King Zahir Shah, merely ended the monarchy but did not result in any diffusion of power. In effect, power was transferred from the former oligarchy to a single individual.

These factors which included the imperial rivalry of Britain and Russia, geographical separation of the Afghan ethnic groups and a traditionally narrow power base, combined to prevent the peaceful growth of Afghanistan into a state in the true sense of the word. Founded, as it was, as a loose confederation of Pushtun tribes under Ahmad Shah Abdali, the Afghan national identity became synonymous with Pushtun nationalism. Despite the presence of other ethnic groups, Afghanistan has been a country run by the Pushtuns and for the Pushtuns. The other groups have, with considerable justification, been described as "the victims of an internal colonisation".[6] Afghan governments have been generally preoccupied with exclusively Pushtun issues such as the Afghan irredentist campaign and the advancement of Pushtu as the state language. The latter has included "the required learning of Pushtu in the schools, support for research in Pushtu literature, and the enshrining of Pushtu as the national language in article 35 of the 1964 constitution".[7] Without exception, Afghan cabinets have been dominated by Pushtuns completely out of proportion to the population ratio. For instance, in a cabinet of sixteen, the number of non-Pushtuns hardly exceeded one and very rarely two. Even this meagre representation was not always ensured. Pushtuns were appointed governors in most provinces, even where the population was predominantly of other ethnic groups "but a non-Pathan [Pushtun] has never been appointed governor of a Pathan province".[8] It is, therefore, interesting that when the Taliban were in control over the major part of Afghan territory from 1996 until the end of 2001, they appointed eleven non-Pushtuns as governors, some of them in Pushtun provinces, and included four or five members of the minority ethnic groups in the cabinet.

Economic development was equally unbalanced. Practically all development projects were concentrated in the Pushtun areas. Agricultural programmes were to be found in Khost and the Helmand Valley, forestry schemes at Ali Khel, hydroelectric power generation and irrigation in Nangarhar—all Pushtun provinces. Even when development took place in regions where other groups were dominant as with cotton ginning and processing in the north at Kunduz and along the Oxus, it was "often in an area with a Pushtun settler population dating from the government's deliberate shifting of Pathans to these areas before the Second World War".[9] Similarly, the great majority of Afghan industrial workers were "often members of those families who were moved into the non-Pushtun provinces and were never quite able to fit happily into the local community".[10] Thus the growing industrial elite was as Pushtun-dominated as was the administrative elite.

The process of Pushtun domination

The most comprehensive accounts of Pushtun subjugation of the Tajiks, Uzbeks, Turkmens and the Hazaras of Afghanistan are mainly to be found in the works of Soviet historians. This process, which involved conquest followed by persecution and ethnic cleansing, reached its peak under Amir Abdur Rahman who is often described as the Bismark of Afghanistan.[11] The enormity of the Afghan tragedy, both historical as well as contemporary, cannot be overstated. It raises fundamental questions such as whether the people of Afghanistan can, and in particular the minority groups, be expected to forget the past and begin a process of genuine reconciliation, or will the legacy of interracial disharmony and hatred continue to define the country's post-Taliban future?

The Tajiks lost their state with the fall of the Samanids, but continued to fight stubbornly to preserve their independence. It was only in the eighteenth and the first half of the nineteenth centuries that the Afghan feudal lords defeated the Tajik peasants of the Kabul, Kandahar and Ghazni regions. In the 1830s a bitter struggle between the Tajiks and the Pushtuns began, which culminated in the 1880s when Abdur Rahman succeeded in finally breaking the Tajik resistance. The establishment of Pushtun authority in the Tajik areas was accompanied by the confiscation of land from the local aristocracy, the forcible seizure of small holdings from the peasantry, and the transfer of unworked lands to the state. The vast state holdings thus acquired were distributed among the Pushtun immigrants who formed military colonies in these areas. The indigenous population was strangulated economically through the imposition of exorbitant taxes from which the Pushtuns were exempted. Crippled economically and ostracized politically, a sizeable number of local Tajiks were forced to move to Turkestan in search of a living.

The process was repeated with the Uzbeks. In the first half of the nineteenth century the Uzbeks, who were settled in northern Afghanistan, constituted the feudal khanates of Kunduz, Mazar, Shibberghan and Maimena. They were dependent to a greater or lesser degree on the amir of Bukhara. However, as early as the accession of Dost Muhammad, the Afghan government began to conquer southern Turkestan including the Uzbek khanates. The bloodshed continued for several decades until Abdur Rahman was able to capture all the territory between the Amu Darya (the Oxus) and the Hindu Kush. Again excessively high taxes were imposed on the local population forcing them to migrate. Their land holdings were proclaimed state property and an intensive process of Pushtun colonization of the area commenced.[12]

The Turkmen experience was no different. At the dawn of the nineteenth century, the greater part of their principalities had become vassals to Bohkara and it was not until the conquest of Andkhoi, Shibberghan and Maimena by Abdur Rahman that these areas were assimilated into Afghanistan. This was in fact facilitated by the Russo-English demarcation of 1885-1887. Property was again confiscated from the local population thus making them wholly dependent on the mercy of the Pushtun aristocracy. Many reverted to nomadic ways while others became shepherds and herded the flocks of the new landowners.[13]

However, it was the Hazaras who suffered the most because, as Shia Muslims, they were detested not only by the Pushtuns but also by the other ethnic minorities. This sectarian bias against them has always been and continues to be one of the most shameful aspects of Afghan society. Jealousy and envy also played a role because, unlike the other ethnic groups, the Hazaras had guarded their independence and did not submit for a prolonged period to any outside power for six centuries. The people of the "Hazarajat" accepted only their own leadership until the 1890s when they were finally subjugated, after a long and fierce conflict lasting several decades, by Abdur Rahman. Not only did they lose a considerable portion of their land to the Pushtun feudal lords but also suffered persecution, the barbarity of which has few parallels even by Afghan standards. The heads of slaughtered Hazaras were placed on pillars along the highways as a warning to those contemplating rebellion. The bazaars of Kandahar and other major towns were filled with Hazara prisoners who were sold at cheap prices as slaves. A foreigner who happened to be in Kabul in the 1890s observed that "a short while ago a Hazara baby was bought for half a crown, and the purchaser got the mother for fifteen shillings".[14] On other occasions, prisoners were traded for guns, ammunition and horses. The possession of Hazara slaves became a status symbol for prosperous Pushtuns.[15] Even after slavery was abolished by King Amanullah, the Hazaras continued to live as outcasts possessing neither wealth nor any rights.

In the 1960s, a second infiltration of the Hazara areas took place when about sixty thousand Pushtuns from the plains were settled in the Hazarajat. The local population meekly accepted this as they were too weak to offer any resistance. In this period they also became the victims of wealthy Pushtuns who lent them money at interest rates that verged on extortion.

Seldom have minority communities in any society suffered so much. This aspect of Afghan history will continue to cast a shadow on the prospects of sustainable peace in the country. But the problem is far more complicated because the ethnic minorities also distrust and even despise each other as the tragic tale of Afghanistan has so frequently demonstrated.

Afghan political structure and non-Pushtun groups

After their "colonization", which was completed by Abdur Rahman, the non-Pushtuns became mere bystanders as their country underwent political change. They were unable to even express their grievances. Their subdued anger at Pushtun political, economic and social predominance became increasingly pronounced and instilled parochial rather than national loyalties. The indignities and the persecution that the Hazaras suffered made them particularly bitter.

The subjugation of the ethnic minorities of Afghanistan was, in a sense, also a conflict between Pushtun tribesmen and the non-Pushtun urban population. The conquest of the towns, which had previously been controlled by merchants and artisans, resulted not only in the loss of urban political influence, but also in "the collapse of organization, skills, and economic activity. Their markets constricted and they suffered from plundering and heavy taxation imposed by tribally and rurally oriented rulers . . . The picture presented until the late nineteenth century was that of dying urban communities. The subsistence orientation of the peasant and the nomad made them virtually independent of the towns economically, while their numbers and organization gave them political control in both town and countryside."[16]

Contemporary writers have described the effects of the "rapacity" of the victorious Pushtun Barakzai forces. The burden of their demands fell mainly on the Tajik section of the population with the result that "in the immediate vicinity of towns no human voice greets or curses the visitor. Once rich vineyards are dried up and all around is desolation. This is specially the case in the Qandhar district where every fresh change of rulers has only brought increased taxation, until the population has been decimated and tax gatherers, enraged at not being able to squeeze money out of the mud walls, seized and sold into slavery the last inhabitants of once prosperous towns and villages."[17]

The urban centres of eastern and southern Afghanistan, rather than the Afghan tribes, were the worst sufferers of the two Anglo-Afghan wars of the nineteenth century as well. While the country's meagre economy as a whole was undoubtedly damaged seriously, the urban population was badly hit by inflation and the scarcity of basic commodities. The population and the economy of Kabul and of the Kandahar regions declined sharply; the province of Herat also suffered enormous material losses.

No relief was in sight for the non-Pushtuns because the amirs of Afghanistan faced difficulties of their own. The consolidation of power was never an easy task for them. The threat to their position came mainly from their own kinsmen or other Durrani chiefs. Amir Habibullah Khan and King Zahir Shah have been the only two rulers to ascend and occupy their thrones (the latter for four decades) without a challenge. Whenever the throne was contested, which was generally the case, the issue was decided by the Pushtun tribesmen. In the conditions prevailing at the time, involvement in these dynastic contests represented the only form of political activity in the country. The non-Pushtuns were in no position to play any role in these contests and had no influence on their outcome. Thus they were denied all means for political advancement.

Furthermore, the evolution of Afghanistan's international personality also militated against the interests of the ethnic minorities. With the demarcation of Afghanistan's international frontiers and the guarantee of its territorial integrity by Britain and Russia, the Afghan rulers became relatively free from worries about foreign intervention and they used this breathing space to deal with their people. The amirs had always suspected Persia of irredentist designs in the western part of Afghanistan, and Russia of expansionist interests in the north. In the perception of the Afghan rulers, these were the two areas most vulnerable to foreign ingress. To an extent, they could now count on British support in containing these threats. Despite this, the amirs were unable to break away out of a mindset that the country's neighbours were inherently hostile and sought to annex Afghan territory. They, therefore, deliberately chose an isolationist foreign policy as that would not only reduce external threat but also enable them to pursue vigorous domestic measures. This helped them in particular to insulate the non-Pushtun areas in the north and the west, and consolidate their grip on these regions. This could not have been achieved without the help of the Pushtun tribesmen. Thus, the authority of the state was identified with the rule of the Pushtuns and opposition to it with the ethnic minorities. The latter were, therefore, to remain suspect in the eyes of the Pushtun rulers of Afghanistan.

Reform measures

The Afghan political structure has undergone fundamental changes since 1747. Though the amir has always been at the top of the power pyramid, his support base has varied under different rulers. Ahmed Shah Abdali's "election" represented tribal consensus and his kingdom was, in essence, a Pushtun tribal confederation. Incessant dynastic struggles and internecine warfare within the Durranis and between them and other Pushtun tribes, particularly the Ghilzais, dominated events in Afghanistan after Abdali's death until amir Dost Muhammad Khan finally succeeded in uniting the country. He was able to rally national support largely because of the British invasion and occupation of Afghanistan from 1839-1842. However, after his death internal conflict resurfaced and continued with ferocity until Abdur Rahman seized Kabul and declared himself amir in 1880. It was during his reign, which lasted until 1901, that Afghanistan began to acquire the semblance of a nation state.

Until his ascension the central government was dependent on support, in descending order of importance, from the Pushtun tribes, the religious leaders, the settled population in both rural and urban areas and the economic interest groups. Abdur Rahman took consequential measures to alter the power structure by trying to make the government less dependent on tribal support. Besides keeping the tribes under control, he institutionalized the bureaucracy, the army and the monarchy. Till then, provincial governments were primarily organized along tribal lines with each tribe ruling in its own area autonomously. Whatever little control the government was able to exercise was usually through the army. To strengthen central authority, Abdur Rahman demarcated provincial boundaries that cut through tribal territory and doubled the number of provinces. Subsequent rulers stabilized the new system so that pure tribal government was done away with. Abdur Rahman further weakened the authority of the tribal chiefs by appointing them to seemingly important but innocuous posts in Kabul.

Claiming to rule by divine right, Abdur Rahman virtually eliminated the influence of the religious leaders by incorporating them into government service and appropriating their endowments. On a parallel track, measures were taken to establish a professional army loyal to the central government and insulated from tribal influence. This experiment was entirely new to the Afghan experience. The tribal levies, who constituted the backbone of the army, were encouraged to pledge fealty to the amir rather than their own tribes. Abdur Rahman also introduced Western military technology and organization. The modernization process was continued by his son, amir Habibullah, who set up a military academy for the officer corps.

These efforts were only partially successful because tribal rather than national loyalty continued to be the dominant impulse within the army. This was evident from the successful revolt against Amanullah, which was led by the Shinwaris of eastern Afghanistan, while his successor, King Nadir Shah, was able to capture Kabul only with the assistance of the Wazirs and the Mahsuds from the British-India side of the frontier. Thus the supremacy of the tribes had never really been diminished.

The new rulers, the Muhammadzais, were conscious of the influence of the tribes and also recognized the need for eliminating the dependence of the government on tribal military support. They understood only too well that a well-equipped and disciplined army, which could protect the state from the tribes, was desperately required. However, such a force was eventually only to emerge, with Soviet military assistance, during Sardar Muhammad Daud Khan's first tenure as prime minister from 1953 to 1963. Thus for the first time in Afghan history, the central government had acquired the capability to respond decisively to any tribal or religious insurrection.

Two primary elements are identifiable in the complex relationship between the government in Kabul and tribesmen on the east. First, urban economic weakness and the autocratic and feudal character of the monarchy itself made the Afghan amirs increasingly dependent on the Pushtun tribes for the defence of the country and the preservation of their dynasty. The tribes were also the only obstacle in the way of British incursions into Afghanistan. Thus those in the British-India side of the frontier not only played a decisive role in determining who among the various Durrani contestants was to hold power in Kabul, but also provided the surest guarantee of Afghanistan's territorial integrity. The amirs, therefore, wanted to at least influence, as they could not control, the movement and direction of tribal enterprise. Second, despite the support that they derived from the tribes, the amirs, conscious of their own weakness, did in fact welcome British control over the tribesmen as that provided them the opportunity to consolidate internally without tribal interference. With the departure of the British from South Asia, Afghan rulers feared that the attention of the tribesmen east of the Durand Line would be diverted towards Kabul.

Managing the relationship with the tribesmen in British-India was a major preoccupation of the rulers in Kabul. The process for the imposition of the central government's authority over the tribal chiefs, which was started by Abdur Rahman, ended during the first premiership of Sardar Muhammad Daud Khan. The changed political structure was incorporated into the Afghan constitution of 1964. Article 2 of the constitution, which abolished tribal territory, stated: "All territories and localities which are under the sovereignty of the king constitute a homogeneous whole, and in no respect can any distinction be made between parts of the country." Article 9 was directed against the membership of tribes and read "all persons residing within the kingdom of Afghanistan are to be treated as Afghan subjects". Article 13 proclaimed the equality of all Afghan subjects. Article 26 dismantled tribal administration and forbade the collection of duties or taxes by anybody except the government. The methods introduced by Abdur Rahman were used for the implementation of these constitutional provisions. Tribal chiefs were appointed to harmless posts in the executive, the upper house of the legislature or the judiciary. In other instances, they were made governors of provinces far from their own regions. Tribal administration was replaced by new regional organizations under government-appointed officials. This process started at the top of the tribal hierarchy and stretched down to the smaller administrative units. However, in the more remote and smaller centres the administration was left to the local chiefs.

The modernization efforts were primarily focused on the armed forces. However, the military reforms spilled over into other sectors and contributed to the establishment of a bureaucracy, an educational system and a few basic political institutions. In time, the bureaucracy was restructured and expanded to play a more assertive role in Afghan society. The civil servants exercised a liberalising influence. Like them, the intellectual elite which included teachers, doctors and college students also gave voice to the need for political liberalization, broadening of the base of government, and the establishment of an egalitarian socio-economic system. Thus modernists were pitted against traditionalists and the former became more influential after Daud Khan's retirement 1963. Through all this, the most significant political force to emerge was the military. It became the only organization in the country capable of acting effectively on a nationwide scale. Its command positions were, however, held by members of the royal family and by its most loyal and trusted supporters. But that was as far as the reforms were intended to go.

To an extent the reform programme of the Afghan rulers was helped by the influence of Islam on Afghan national life. Though the disparate Afghan groups had little in common, the sense of community and brotherhood instilled by Islam provided a much needed unifying force. It was used by the Afghan rulers to mobilize opposition first against the Sikhs and later the British. However, although the principles of Islam permeated the 1964 constitution and it was declared the state religion, official policy emphasized nationalistic rather than religious ideology. Unfortunately, the former continued to be equated with Pushtun supremacy. In the early 1950s, King Zahir Shah declared publicly that "the strength of the Muslim faith did not necessarily guarantee stability and national unity".[18] As a result, the country's traditional institutions were progressively secularized through the years.

It was not till the early 1970s that employment opportunities in government were opened up for non-Pushtuns as a measure to promote national unity. Though recruitment into the armed forces was mainly from the Pushtun tribes, representatives from other ethnic groups were also gradually taken into the military. Conscription helped to bring persons from different communities together and contributed to the lowering of barriers between them.

Simultaneously, even economic development projects were initiated in various non-Pushtun regions. Substantial investments were made in industry and agriculture north of the Hindu Kush and in areas far away from the capital such as Herat. A special effort was made to improve the overall infrastructure particularly the upgrading of roads and modernization of communications.

The Afghan dilemma

Well into the twentieth century, the framework within which the rulers of Afghanistan tried to promote unity before the communist revolt was a combination of two major but contradictory principles. The first was encouraging the gradual growth of a national Afghan, rather than as in the past, a Muslim identity. This was to be achieved by overriding ethnic and linguistic divisions, through legal and administrative reforms and by increasing the participation of non-Pushtun groups in the government and bringing economic development to their regions. The second was preserving the strength of traditional forces, in other words, respecting Pushtun domination.

Pushtun dominance continued to be equated with national and cultural unity, and in this sense there was no change from the past. The army, modernized and equipped with the latest weapons, remained the principal instrument for imposing national unity and maintaining the authority of the central government. However, it was totally under the control of the Pushtun leadership. There was also no change in the approach towards the cultural autonomy of the other groups. In fact, for the first time in the basic law of the country itself, Pushtu was declared the national language. It was made compulsory in schools and proficiency in the language was required for appointment to senior government positions. The Pushtun Academy and Afghan Historical Society were set up to sponsor research in Pushtun history and culture. Although Dari (Persian) was also the official language, Pushtu was allowed to develop at its expense.

Only limited reforms were thus carried out through a modernized bureaucracy and military but these did not have any impact on the political power structure. The reforms were imposed from above and did not originate from the masses. Political activity was generally suppressed or at best severely restricted as the formation of political parties was prohibited. After the promulgation of the 1964 constitution, a political parties bill was passed by parliament. King Zahir Shah, however, withheld his consent on the ground that political parties would emerge from the ethnic groups and militate against national unity. Thus the continuance of Pushtun domination could only be ensured if the other ethnic groups were kept away from any organized political activity. The irony is that the absence of legitimate party organizations encouraged parochial loyalties and by the 1970s resulted in the formation of political parties along ethnic lines.

The rivalry between the imperial powers of the earlier centuries, the cruel process of Pushtun domination and the superpower rivalry in the Cold War period ensured that peace and stability would elude Afghanistan. The turmoil of today has its roots in the past. Previously, external powers were to an extent responsible for the chaos, but in the contemporary era the Afghans themselves are mostly to blame. The competition for power and wealth between the Pushtuns and the ethnic minorities continued to generate violence in Afghan society and became alarmingly pronounced by the time the Taliban captured Kabul in September 1996. How then were efforts to proceed in order to promote reconciliation among a people who refused to be reconciled?

THE FOUR PHASES OF RECENT AFGHAN HISTORY

AT ANOTHER LEVEL, religious extremism coloured by the conservative traditions of tribal Afghanistan has always been resistant to change and at variance with contemporary values. Thus the socialist Afghanistan of the People's Democratic Party of Afghanistan encountered domestic violence for attempting to transform the country through progressive reforms from 1978 up to 1992 while the Taliban, during their rule from 1996 to 2001, faced international condemnation for clinging senselessly to tribal customs which were often far removed both from civilized conduct as well as from the spirit and the true teachings of Islam.

Centuries of conflict, internal upheavals and dislocations thus brought unparalleled misery to the Afghan people who, it seemed, had become accustomed to suffering. Would they be willing to listen to neighbouring Pakistan to change their ways? Was it possible to overcome a mindset that had become so deeply entrenched among them or could this only be achieved gradually? But was the transformed and impatient post-Cold War world willing to wait for Taliban-dominated Afghanistan to come to terms with itself?

Four distinct phases in recent Afghan history had also singly and collectively contributed towards the unending turmoil in the country. The first, the coup by the PDPA on 27 April 1978; the second, the Soviet invasion and occupation from 29 December 1979 to February 1989; the third, the prolonged resistance against the Moscow-installed Najibullah regime until 28 April 1992 and; the fourth, the emergence and rise of the Taliban. The influence of these phases, particularly the last, is still evident in post-Taliban Afghanistan.

Phase one: after the PDPA coup

Zahir Shah succeeded his assassinated father, Nadir, as king of Afghanistan in 1933. He ruled for almost forty years until his overthrow in 1973 by prince Daud. In 1953 Daud, then prime minister, launched a modernization programme that was later to prove consequential, albeit, in the negative sense. Daud resigned in 1963, prompting Zahir Shah to promulgate a new constitution that sought to encourage political freedom and envisaged an elected consultative parliament. With the ouster of Zahir Shah, Daud abolished the monarchy, established a republic and proclaimed himself president. He was assassinated on 27 April 1978 by the same officers who were behind him in the 1973 coup. However, this time they handed over power to the Marxist-Leninist PDPA. With Daud ended two hundred and thirty-one years of rule by the Durranis of Kandahar.

The cause of Daud's downfall lay in his own reforms. He depended heavily on assistance from the United States and the Soviet Union without developing domestic consensus. This phase in Afghanistan's history saw the development of the infrastructure, the strengthening of the army and the expansion of education. The elite went to the academic institutions of the West, the military officers were sent to the Soviet Union while the Islamists were trained in Egypt's Al-Azhar University. This was to bring about a transformation of the country's political structure. Previously, the struggle for autonomy by ethnic minorities had dominated Afghan politics. The Persian-speaking Tajiks and Hazaras as well as the Turkic-speaking Uzbeks and Turkmen had been equally active to rid themselves of Pushtun domination. Actual power even among the Pushtuns, however, vested only with the tribal elite and this resulted in a loose unity of the underprivileged. The marginalized and frustrated intellectuals thus joined radical groups ranging from the Marxists to the Islamists. The stage was thus set for a power struggle between the two which led to the Soviet invasion of Afghanistan. The conflict that ensued would hasten the collapse of the Berlin Wall and bring the Cold War era to an end.

The PDPA was created in January 1965 in Kabul at the residence of Nur Muhammad Taraki. Its thirty-three founding members elected Taraki, a Pushtun, as secretary general and Babrak Karmal, a Persian-speaking Kabul resident, as his deputy. Serious differences, however, developed between the Taraki-led Khalq (Masses) faction and the urbanized Persian-speaking group, the Parcham (Flag), under Karmal. By 1967 the party had split.

Though both factions were staunchly pro-Soviet, Moscow was partial to the Parcham which it found more pliable and receptive to advice. The Khalqis were considered self-opinionated and unpredictable. Ideologically, they were orthodox Marxist-Leninists representing the economically and socially under-privileged Pushtuns. Taraki, himself a tenth-grade drop-out, was projected by his group as a man of letters because he spoke English which he had learnt in the early 1930s while working for an Afghan merchant in Bombay. In contrast, many among the Parchamis, with their upper-class backgrounds, had received higher education abroad while Karmal, the son of an army general, had graduated from Kabul University's faculty of law and political science.

The next twelve years saw the rift between the Khalq and Parcham factions widen into pervasive enmity. The former derided the Parchamis as bourgeois and therefore unfit to represent the proletariat. During his days in parliament, Karmal was said to have had connections with the king and thus all Parchamis were described by their rivals as "royal communists". In turn, the latter looked upon the Khalqis with ill-disguised contempt because of their low social standing, lack of education and their inability to comprehend the intricacies of statecraft.

To pre-empt the Khalq-Parcham tensions from exploding into street violence, the Communist Party of the Soviet Union intervened in May 1977. The two factions were merged and Taraki once again became secretary general and Karmal his deputy. The new thirty-member unified central committee was divided equally between the two groups.

However, this new-found PDPA unity was cosmetic and proved short-lived. Each faction acted independently of the other. They recruited their own men to the army and police, a task which the Khalq entrusted to the ruthlessly ambitious US-educated Hafizullah Amin and the Parcham to Mir Akbar Khyber.

The April 1978 coup was spearheaded by military officers sympathetic to the Khalq faction of the PDPA. They moved swiftly with a mix of air and armoured attacks on Daud's headquarters, the defence ministry, the telecommunications network and other strategic centers. Daud loyalists within the military were not only taken by surprise but completely demoralized. In the build up to the coup, the Khalqis and in particular Hafizullah Amin had sought out a substantial number of disgruntled Pushtun officers in the armed forces and the secret police. This gave the Khalq faction, in which Amin emerged as the second most powerful man, effective control of the military and a decisive advantage over the Parcham group. Amin's rise undid the feeble Soviet attempt of the previous year to restore PDPA unity. Karmal, as the party's deputy secretary general, became increasingly sidelined. Amin claimed that the coup had been masterminded and executed by the officers that he had recruited; therefore, Karmal was not entitled to occupy the number two slot in the new dispensation. For the same reason, he also rejected, with the support of the newly established Khalq-dominated Revolutionary Council, Karmal's demand that cabinet posts and key military positions be shared equally between the two factions.

The Soviets attempted yet again to restore PDPA unity. In April 1978 a high-level KGB delegation led by Vladimir Khrychov arrived in Kabul and persuaded Amin to accept equal Khalq-Parcham representation in the cabinet. The trade-off was that Taraki would be invested with the office of president and prime minister. Karmal was thus relegated to the backwaters and appointed deputy president of the Revolutionary Council. Amin became foreign minister and the first deputy prime minister.

Even this arrangement did not last long. With Taraki's support, Amin secured the approval of the PDPA Politburo to send Karmal and six of his close associates to ambassadorial exile. On Moscow's request, Karmal was assigned to Prague. However, despite this, tension between the Khalq and Parcham groups continued to simmer beneath the surface until August when the Parchami defence minister and two generals were arrested on charges of plotting a coup that was to have taken place on 4 September.

The purge of the Parchamis thus began with a vengeance. They were dismissed from government and hundreds were imprisoned. Orders were issued to Karmal and the other recently appointed ambassadors to return home immediately to face trial. As expected, they sought political asylum. Karmal continued to live in Prague until October 1979 when he moved to Moscow. Thus the Parchamis were, at least temporarily, sidelined.

Like the Taliban, the Khalqis did not take easily to enlightened educated opinion particularly of those who had attended academic institutions of the west. They went even further and persecuted men of learning, whom they looked upon as counter-revolutionaries. Intellectuals were hounded on flimsy pretexts and even the possession of an English dictionary was enough to invite the wrath of the Establishment. Educated Afghans, especially those who were not members of the PDPA prior to the coup, were branded anti-proletariat and excluded from government. Amin, Mansoor Hashmi and Salim Masudi were the only US-educated ministers in the first communist cabinet. The rest, barring three who had studied in Soviet institutions, were either graduates of the Kabul University or had merely completed high-school education. Abdul Karim Mesaq, the finance minister, had only attended primary school.

The semi-literate and inexperienced Khalq government then embarked on ill thought-out reforms that were to have disastrous consequences. These socialist measures were far removed from the religious beliefs, customs and traditions of the Afghan people and generated a violent reaction. Thus, even those whom the reforms were meant to benefit turned against the government.

The starting point of the reform process was the implementation of the "Basic Lines of the Revolutionary Duties of the Democratic Republic of Afghanistan", a thirty-point programme, that had been announced a fortnight after the coup. Its stated purpose was to "transform traditional Afghan society into a new flourishing one based on the principles of socialism and equality". Towards this end, eight revolutionary decrees were hastily issued. Of these, three—the sixth, seventh and the eighth—dealt with social and economic reforms. Decree six had two aims. The first provided debt relief to peasants by exempting them from repayment of loans incurred prior to 1974. The second sought to restore mortgaged land to owners in return for a small payment. Contrary to expectations, these measures led to resentment among the peasants because the repayment of debt is obligatory in Islam. Furthermore, those in desperate need of money could not even secure a small loan. Decree seven, promulgated in October 1978, aimed at the emancipation of women. Taraki proudly announced: "Afghan women from now are free in the real sense of the word and have equal rights with men." Despite its progressive spirit, the decree contained clauses that alienated not only the conservative elements of society but also, surprisingly, women.

Feminists were embittered by article three, which fixed the maximum amount for dowry or *mahr* at a mere three hundred Afghanis (the exchange rate of the Afghani plummeted between 1979 and 1983 from 39 to 99 Afghanis to one US dollar). The article read: "The girl or her guardian shall not take cash or commodities in the name of the dowry in excess of ten dirhams according to Shariat." In Islamic traditions *mahr* is the money that the husband pledges to the wife, not her father. One third is paid either after or before the marriage while the remainder becomes due if the husband divorces his wife. The decree also gave the right of divorce to women. The result was that the stability of the family structure in this traditional society was ruined while women were deprived of financial security in the event of divorce. Article four of the same decree permitted women, contrary to Afghan traditions, to terminate their engagements if they so decided. This dealt a further body blow to the family unit.

The social reforms also obliged Afghans to send their women to the newly established adult literacy institutions. This caused commotion in many parts of the country, notably Herat where it was first introduced. In March 1979, massive demonstrations were held in the streets of the city and resulted in two weeks of violent clashes with the law enforcement authorities, particularly the army.

Thus, apparently well-intentioned reforms ignited rebellion because of the perception that they were contrary to tribal Afghanistan's obscurantist interpretation of Islamic doctrines. The Khalq regime came down with a heavy hand. Disappearances, torture, custodial killings and summary executions were carried out with abandon by Amin's secret police which was controlled by his nephew and son-in-law Assadullah Amin. This intensified the resistance, forcing the regime to move even closer to the Soviet Union. The latter's presence in government became all pervasive. In December 1978, a treaty of friendship and cooperation was concluded with the Soviet Union under which Moscow was to provide assistance to Kabul in the event of internal instability or external threat.

Though the resistance to the Khalq regime in Kabul was inspired by the single objective of restoring an Islamic government in Afghanistan, it was divided into seven Sunni Muslim groups based in Peshawar, Pakistan, and eight Shia parties headquartered in Iran. The latter were united, under Iranian pressure, into the Wahdat-e-Islami (later to be known as the Hizb-e-Wahdat) while the former continued to operate individually as distinct groups. These parties were to have a profound impact on subsequent events in Afghanistan.

Among the seven Peshawar-based parties four were fundamentalist and three moderate. The former consisted of:

—Jamiat-e-Islami: a Tajik party formed by Burhanuddin Rabbani, the subsequent leader of the Northern Alliance, in 1970. Ahmed Shah Masood was, until his assassination on 9 September 2001, the head of its military component known as the Shura-e-Nazar.
—Hizb-e-Islami (Hikmatyar Group): a Pushtun-dominated party created by Gulbadin Hikmatyar. It sought to initiate an Iranian-style revolution and to establish a one-party fundamentalist state (Hikmatyar was subsequently associated off and on with the Northern Alliance).
—Hizb-e-Islami (Khalis Group): a splinter group of the Hizb-e-Islami (Hikmatyar Group) established by Yunis Khalis in 1979. Most of its fighters later joined the Taliban.

—Itehad-e-Islami: a Saudi-backed party, again primarily Pushtun, formed in 1980 by Professor Abdul Rasool Sayyaf (he is also associated with the Northern Alliance and is said to have brought Osama Bin Laden back to Afghanistan during the four years that the Rabbani regime controlled Kabul).

The moderates included:

—Harakat-e-Inqilab-e-Islami: a Pushtun-dominated party founded by Muhammad Nabi Muhammadi in 1978. It also included a sizeable number of Uzbeks. It advocated free elections, agricultural reform and non-alignment.

—Mahaz-e-Milli: emerged in 1979 under Pir Syed Ahmad Gillani. It was Pushtun-dominated and monarchist (Gillani was represented by his son Hamed at the UN-sponsored meeting of Afghan groups in Bonn and he signed the agreement of 5 December 2001 establishing an interim post-Taliban administration under Hamid Karzai).

—Jubba-e-Nijat-e-Milli: a Pushtun party established in 1978 by Professor Sibghatullah Mujaddadi. It favoured representative government based on Islamic principles and Afghan traditions. It did not oppose the participation of the monarchists in any future government.

The fundamentalists were inspired by the political teachings of Hasanul Bana and Sayyid Qutb of Egypt as well as Maududi of Pakistan. Their objective was to restructure Afghan society in accordance with Quranic injunctions and the Sunna or Islamic traditions. They were anti-West and, in particular, anti-United States because of its support for Israel. Though they received American assistance for their fight against Soviet and Afghan communism, they did not conceal their hatred of Washington. Hikmatyar, who was later to be associated with the anti-Taliban Northern Alliance, refused to meet President Reagan when he was in New York in 1986 to address the UN in his capacity as the president of the resistance alliance. The moderates, in contrast, were conservative nationalists who favoured a role for the monarchy and whose objectives included the safeguarding of national independence and the defence of Islam. They were inclined to establish a strong relationship with the West, particularly the United States.

The fundamentalists and the moderates remained apart throughout the war against the Soviet occupation forces, despite attempts to bring them together. Their differences contributed to the chaos that engulfed Afghanistan long after the communists were ousted from Kabul.

The repression of the Afghan people by the regime in Kabul resulted not only in the intensification of the resistance but also led to divisions within the PDPA. Taraki and a number of PDPA leaders, encouraged by the Soviets, wanted to slow down the pace of reforms and to also include non-communists in the government. This was, however, staunchly opposed by Amin.

Because of his independent approach, Amin alienated the Soviet Union. He not only rejected Moscow's advice on slowing down the reforms but also blocked further Soviet involvement with the running of the secret police and the military. The Kremlin began to suspect him of pro-Washington leanings because of his American educational background.

During Taraki's meeting with Soviet leader Leonid Brezhnev in Moscow on 10 September 1979, it was widely believed that he was asked to eliminate Amin. Taraki lost no time in carrying out the assassination plan on his return to Kabul the following day. He summoned Amin to the presidential palace but the latter refused to comply because he had been forewarned by his protegé Taroon, Taraki's aide-de-camp. Amin was, however, prevailed upon to change his mind on being assured of his personal safety by Ambassador Pazanov of the Soviet Union. On reaching the palace there was a shoot-out resulting in several deaths. Amin, however, escaped but Taroon, who shielded him during the firing, was killed. Shortly afterwards Amin returned to the palace with his supporters, arrested Taraki and later strangled him despite reported appeals from Brezhnev to spare his life. The stage was thereby set for the Soviet invasion of Afghanistan and thus began the second phase of the Afghan conflict.

Phase two: the Soviet Invasion

On 27 December 1979, the Soviet Union invaded Afghanistan with an initial eighty-five thousand troops. Amin was killed and Babrak Karmal, whom they had brought from exile in Moscow, was installed in his place.

The anti-Khalq insurgency which had spread to the entire country rapidly transformed into a full-fledged war of liberation. A jihad or holy war was declared. Moscow justified its incursion into Afghanistan by declaring that it was "entirely defensive" and designed to provide security to a friendly neighbouring Marxist regime as well as to protect its southern flank from Islamic fundamentalists and American imperialism. Karmal's mission was to slow down the pace of the Amin-Taraki reforms, to correct the mistakes of the past, to broaden the political base of the regime and to reorganize the armed forces and the secret police with the active involvement of the Soviets.

To fulfil his mission, Karmal initiated several measures. One of his first acts was the release of all political prisoners who numbered in the tens of thousands. He also announced the abolition of all anti-democratic and anti-human rights regulations, declared a ban on arrests and persecution, decreed respect for Islamic principles and freedom of conscience, promised the protection of lawful property, upheld the right of individual and collective security and guaranteed the restoration of peace to Afghanistan.

On advice from Moscow, Karmal also pledged not to change Afghan society rapidly, and to broaden the base of his government by including non-communists. He proclaimed a provisional constitution entitled "The Fundamental Principles of the Democratic Republic of Afghanistan" in April 1980. It defined the rights and duties of the citizens as well as the functions of the branches of state. In the face of the Islamic resistance, the constitution guaranteed "complete freedom in the performance of Islamic religious rites". Drafted by the Soviet advisers, translated by their Tajik specialists and refined by the Legislative Department of the Ministry of Justice, the provisional constitution was in form and substance similar to those of the Soviet republics of Central Asia.

Another Karmal initiative was the creation of the National Fatherland Front (NFF) in 1981 which, his regime claimed, was a coalition of "nationalist, patriotic, democratic and progressive forces". Its primary objective was the mobilization of support against the opposition and it was projected as "an important step to give the masses of the people a say in running the affairs of the country". The provincial branches of the NFF tried to establish offices in the countryside but no one dared come near them for fear of reprisal by the Islamic resistance.

A sizeable public sector-led economic revival programme involving an investment of about thirteen billion Afghanis was also launched. The major part of the funding was to come from the Soviet Union and the rest from its East European allies.

These economic and social measures further intensified the determination of the Afghan people to resist the occupation and the communization of their country. Except for Kabul, the provincial capitals and a handful of centres in some of the provinces, the country was now under the control of the resistance. Militarily, the Soviets employed all the might at their disposal short of using nuclear weapons to eliminate the opposition.

Moscow soon realised that the deeply entrenched hatred among the masses for communism was reinforced by their determination to free their country from foreign occupation which no amount of military force could defeat. Accordingly, pressure on Karmal to fulfil his promise of broad-basing the regime was increased. His reluctance to deliver prompted the Soviets to oust him and to establish a government which was not outwardly communist. This, they felt, would also give an impetus to the Geneva proximity talks which had begun in June 1982 because Karmal was considered the symbol of the Soviet occupation of Afghanistan.

Furthermore, by the mid-1980s the Soviets had realised that their intervention into Afghanistan had been a major blunder. They wanted a way out but Karmal would not hear of it and this provided yet another reason to get rid of him. Thus, six years after he was installed as the general secretary of the Communist Party of Afghanistan, he was replaced on 4 May 1986 by Dr Najibullah, the chief of the notorious secret police. The latter also had the advantage of belonging to the majority Pushtun community.

Najibullah was instructed to facilitate the withdrawal of Soviet forces from Afghanistan by including non-communists in the government. Dr Hassan Sharq was accordingly appointed prime minister and other non-communists were also included in the cabinet.

Najibullah also launched a programme of national reconciliation. He invited the leaders of the opposition to join the PDPA in a coalition government and made concessions to the armed groups operating in different parts of the country. Only an insignificant few took the bait. Otherwise these overtures had no impact on lessening the strength of the resistance. To appease the feudal elements in the opposition, Najibullah suspended land reforms. This again was of little consequence as the reforms had had no significance in the face of the conflict and chaos that had gripped the entire country.

Thus Najibullah failed to restore peace to Afghanistan which continued to bleed from the lashes of internal turmoil. Nothing had changed with the replacement of Karmal. The resistance continued to control almost the entire countryside. All the highways except the one from Kabul to the north were inoperative. The Soviets and their protegés controlled, as before, only Kabul and the provincial capitals as the resistance became progressively strong. Soviet losses were heavy and there was also the financial crunch. Thus the only option available was to withdraw from Afghanistan. This process began under the Geneva Accords in the summer of 1988 and was completed by 15 February 1989.

According to one estimate, the Soviet misadventure in Afghanistan cost them US$29 billion. In addition, approximately 26,000 Soviet soldiers had died and 1,200 aircraft and helicopters and tens of thousands of armoured vehicles were destroyed.

The Islamic resistance was vigorously supported by the US, the West and moderate oil-rich countries of the Islamic world, particularly Saudi Arabia. In addition to Afghans, thousands of Arabs, including Osama Bin Laden, were indoctrinated in madrassas, or religious schools, in Pakistan and provided military training by the CIA and Pakistan's Inter Services Intelligence (ISI). They were regarded by all, including the west, as the Mujahideen or holy warriors who were waging a "heroic" jihad to rid their country of foreign occupation and the "ungodly" communists who controlled Kabul. After the defeat of the Soviet forces, the world abandoned Afghanistan and forgot its people who had struggled so valiantly and sacrificed so much in the cause of the free world. Pakistan was left alone to deal with more than three million refugees on its soil and thousands of highly motivated and militarily trained Islamic extremists.

The Geneva Accords on Afghanistan signified the end of the Brezhnev and the Reagan doctrines that had dominated the final years of the Cold War. The former sought to protect neighbouring communist regimes while the latter was built around support to insurgencies against such governments. In Geneva the Soviets undertook to end their presence in Afghanistan in support of the Najibullah regime while the US agreed to end its assistance to the Mujahideen.

Phase three: after the Soviet withdrawal

The Geneva Accords were flawed inasmuch as the Afghans were left out of the proximity talks which had dragged on for years. Therefore no agreement was reached on a successor government in Kabul.

In mid-1988, I was working as director of foreign secretary Abdul Sattar's office. Sattar was to subsequently become foreign minister when General Pervaiz Musharraf took over the government in October 1999. During his tenure as foreign secretary, Sattar had become close to Prime Minister Junejo who tried to assert himself against President Zia-ul-Haq's Afghanistan policy of disproportionate support to Gulbadin Hikmatyar. As a consequence, Junejo was dismissed and Sattar was sent as Pakistan's ambassador to Moscow. He was replaced as foreign secretary by Dr Humayun Khan and I was promoted director general for Afghanistan.

The Soviets were soon to begin their withdrawal from Afghanistan but continued to support Najibullah for whom they left behind huge quantities of weapons and ammunition for the fight against the Mujahideen. In this period there were frequent Afghan Scud missile attacks on the North West Frontier Province (NWFP) of Pakistan. It became almost routine for me to summon the Soviet ambassador to lodge strongly worded protests which he invariably rejected.

The seven Peshawar-based Mujahideen parties, who had resisted the Soviet occupation of Afghanistan, formed an anti-Najibullah interim government in exile with Pakistan's backing and encouragement. The most powerful person in this set-up was Gulbadin Hikmatyar. It was Islamabad's hope that the leaders of the Mujahideen parties would sit together and work out the modalities for establishing a post-Najibullah government in accordance with the wishes of the Afghan people.

Pakistan, which was under the military rule of General Zia-ul-Haq through the decade-long Soviet occupation of Afghanistan, was staunchly supported by the US-led west and became the third largest recipient of American economic and military assistance after Israel and Egypt. Islamabad's clandestine nuclear weapons development programme and the reality that the country was under a military dictatorship were ignored. The conclusive defeat of communism was considered far more important than pious concerns about non-proliferation and democracy.

In the second week of August 1988, the US ambassador in Islamabad, Arnie Raphel, invited my wife Ismet and me for dinner along with others associated with Afghanistan. Though the US felt that Islamabad was inclining too far towards Hikmatyar and his fundamentalist approach, Pakistan was lauded by Raphel and the other guests for its support in defence of the free world.

Up to this point all assistance to the Afghan Mujahideen groups had been channelled by the ISI through the leadership of the resistance parties. This enabled Pakistan to maintain control on them. However, the United Nations High Commissioner for Refugees, prince Sadruddin Aga Khan, decided to provide assistance directly and ignore the existing mechanism. The assessment in Islamabad was that this had probably been done on advice from the Americans who were not happy with Pakistan's partiality towards the hardliners in the Afghan interim government. Zia-ul-Haq was furious.

Prince Sadruddin, who was on a visit to Islamabad, was invited by the president to lunch on 16 August. Foreign secretary Humayun Khan and I were among the guests and were treated to a graphic description, in choice four-letter words, of what Zia thought of the prince prior to the latter's arrival. We were told to keep a tight leash on the UN, its agencies and all non-governmental humanitarian organizations as they were working against Pakistan's objective of installing a friendly Islamic government in Kabul. When Sadruddin appeared, Zia was cold and aloof and bluntly told him that under no circumstances must the UN establish direct contact with the Mujahideen commanders. All assistance to the Afghans was to be channelled through the Pakistan government and the leaders of the Afghan resistance factions.

The next morning, Zia and the top military leadership flew in a Pakistan Air Force C-130 transport plane to Bahawalpur, a city in southern Punjab, to witness a firepower demonstration of battle tanks which the Americans wanted to sell to Pakistan. Ambassador Raphel also went to Bahawalpur but in his own aircraft. For the return journey Zia invited Raphel to travel with him. The C-130 took off and, after a few minutes, crashed killing all on board. The cause of the tragedy remains one of the unsolved mysteries of Pakistan's eventful history. It was difficult for me to believe what had happened. Barely twenty-four hours back, I was lunching with Zia, and earlier in the week Ismet and I had spent a delightful evening with Arnie Raphel and his wife. The incident was a sad reminder of the transient nature of life and the uncertainty of the future.

In accordance with Pakistan's constitution, the chairman of the senate, Ghulam Issaq Khan, took over as president. Elections were held and Benazir Bhutto became prime minister.

The ageing Ghulam Issaq Khan, who had started his career as a bureaucrat, was one of the few leaders that I have come across who read his brief thoroughly and had a special flair for detail. He, along with Bhutto, co-chaired monthly government meetings on Afghanistan which were attended by the army chief of staff, the heads of intelligence agencies, the ministers of foreign affairs, defence and the interior as well as the relevant officials from the foreign office. For such meetings, I was required to circulate a working paper among the participants. Our efforts in this period aimed at making the Afghan interim government more flexible had come to naught. In my paper for one of these meetings I had written that the "Afghan interim government was as rigid and as inflexible as a corpse". This infuriated Army Chief of Staff General Mirza Aslam Beg who said that the foreign office had no respect for the "heroes" who had defeated the Soviet occupation forces. The paper was staunchly defended by Tanvir Ahmed Khan who had replaced Humayun Khan as foreign secretary a few weeks earlier. He was supported by Prime Minister Bhutto who said that the working paper was entirely accurate because the Mujahideen leadership was stubborn and refused to make any political compromise. President Ghulam Issaq Khan, who was known for a subtle sense of humour, intervened and in his Pushtun accent declared: "The working paper is flawed because a corpse is never rigid for a long time—rigidity appears only briefly during rigor mortis!"

In early 1990, I was given the additional charge of director general of Foreign Minister Sahibzada Yaqub-Khan's office with the further responsibility for policy planning. On 6 August 1990, the first Benazir Bhutto government was dismissed by Ghulam Issaq Khan, who had a special interest in Afghanistan. Yaqub-Khan continued as foreign minister in the caretaker government of Prime Minister Ghulam Mustafa Jatoi and was, in effect, one of the most influential men in Pakistan as he was not only relied upon by the all-powerful president but also commanded the respect of the armed forces because of his military background. In that period Yaqub-Khan had left Afghan policy in my hands and I used to report directly to Ghulam Issaq Khan. The president and I were working on an election plan for Afghanistan which we hoped to present to the Afghan interim government.

With the Soviet withdrawal from Afghanistan, the expectation was that the Najibullah government would collapse and, to hasten this, the Mujahideen intensified their attacks against the regime. Their first target was Jalalabad, the capital of the eastern province of Nangarhar. It was expected that the city, which is near the Pakistan border, would be captured with ease. Some seventy soldiers of the regime defected to the Mujahideen who, instead of receiving them with open arms, slaughtered them and mutilated their bodies which they sent back to Jalalabad in sacks. The barbarity convinced the city's defenders that they would meet the same fate and strengthened their resolve to fight. The Mujahideen laid siege to the city which continued for three months and ended in their defeat. This boosted the morale of the regime which launched counter-offensives in which the Mujahideen suffered further setbacks.

The fortunes of the Najibullah regime continued to rise until an abortive coup attempt in March 1990 by General Tannai, the Khalqi defence minister. Thus the old rivalry between the Khalqis and the Parchamis surfaced again. Several Khalqi officers subsequently fled Kabul and many of them sought and were given asylum in Pakistan.

There were two immediate consequences of the abortive coup. Najibullah could no longer trust the Khalqis regardless of whether they had been associated in the coup attempt. They were accordingly purged from the army. This created confusion in the defence forces and destabilized the regime even further. The second consequence was that it prompted the Karmal loyalists who were furious at his ignominious ouster to resume their intrigues against the regime. Kabul thus became a hotbed for intrigue and tension which was to continue until the capture of the city by the Taliban.

General elections were held in Pakistan in the autumn of 1990, as a consequence of which Nawaz Sharif became prime minister on 1 November of that year. Around that time, I left for a five-year ambassadorial assignment in Seoul.

In Afghanistan, Najibullah's position became progressively weaker. His principal supporter, the Soviet Union, was on a steep nosedive to elimination and so he could no longer count on Moscow's military and economic assistance. The powerful ethnic Uzbek warlord Rashid Dostum, who had hitherto extended support for purely selfish reasons, also abandoned him. Whereas previously Najibullah had been willing to take non-communists into the government, he was now ready to step down and transfer power to the Mujahideen. Accordingly, in April 1992, he informed the UN of his intentions and the latter devised a mechanism for the transition. It envisaged an interim dispensation consisting of a fifteen-member committee of non-controversial Afghans, living in the US, Europe, the Middle East, Pakistan and Afghanistan. The committee, in turn, would transfer power to the Mujahideen within six months. In mid-April 1992, the UN asked the committee members to assemble in Pakistan from where they were supposed to move into Afghanistan.

Most of the committee members thus gathered in Islamabad and were about to proceed to Kabul when on 18 April a coup, backed by Ahmed Shah Masood and Abdul Rashid Dostum, was staged by Karmal loyalists. A number of Najibullah's supporters, including the minister of national security, were killed. Najibullah, however, managed to escape and took asylum at the UN office in Kabul. The organizers of the coup, all of whom were Persian-speaking Parchamis, requested Masood, who was at the time in Charikar sixty-five kilometres to the north of Kabul, to take over. Masood instead asked the seven leaders of the Mujahideen factions, who were in Peshawar evaluating the committee's nominees, to form a government in Kabul. The leaders, however, could not agree on its composition or even what the next step should be.

The Peshawar Accord: To facilitate the formation of the government, Pakistan intervened. Prime Minister Nawaz Sharif went to Peshawar on 24 April 1992 and invited the Afghan leaders for talks at the governor's house. Six Mujahideen groups, led by Mujaddadi, Rabbani, Sayyaf, Gillani, Nabi Muhammadi and Yunis Khalis, attended. The proceedings were, however, boycotted by Hikmatyar who was considered the most important of the resistance leaders because of his military strength and his extensive control of Afghan territory.

The talks nevertheless resulted in an agreement which provided a mechanism for a peaceful political transition in three phases. Under the first phase, Mujaddadi, the head of the weakest Mujahideen party, became president for two months from 28 April. In the second phase Mujaddadi was to be succeeded on 28 June by Rabbani who was to remain in office for four months. Phases one and two were successfully implemented albeit with difficulty. The third phase envisaged the drafting of a constitution to be followed by elections in the six-month combined presidential terms of Mujaddadi and Rabbani. If the interim government failed to accomplish these tasks within the stipulated timeframe, Rabbani was to step down and hand over power to a "jihadi council" consisting of the leaders of the seven resistance parties.

Hikmatyar was furious that minor leaders had been chosen to lead Afghanistan in the six-month interim period. He also suspected—and in hindsight he was not mistaken—that Rabbani would not relinquish power when his term expired. He therefore entered Kabul, captured key positions including the presidential palace and the interior ministry. Masood retaliated by immediately attacking the capital with a combined force of his own men, the remnants of the communist elements and Dostum's Uzbek militia. Hikmatyar was driven out of Kabul but he established himself in Charasiab, a district some twelve kilometres to the south of the capital. Charasiab was to remain his headquarters until it fell to the Taliban two years later. Thus began another sad and violent episode of Afghan history.

Hikmatyar's expulsion from Kabul enabled Mujaddadi to move to the capital on 28 April 1992, four days after the conclusion of the Peshawar Accord, to become the first president of the Islamic Republic of Afghanistan. The replacement of the communist regime with an Islamic government was a cause for which the Afghan people had fought for fourteen long years. The cost was enormous. More than a million and a half people were killed, half a million were maimed, a third of the population became refugees and about two hundred thousand faced even more hardship as internally displaced persons. Thousands more were to die from the land mines planted by the Soviet occupation forces. The infrastructure of Afghanistan had been completely destroyed. There was hardly a building that had not been hit during the brutal conflict. There was no longer any irrigation system and agricultural production, the mainstay of the economy, was at a standstill. The tragedy had few parallels in human history. The violence, which was now being inflicted on the country by the Afghans themselves, continued. With the collapse of the Soviet Union, the Cold War came to an end amid hopes that the new world order would be underpinned by peace and stability. Afghanistan, however, continued to be ravaged by conflict.

The government in Kabul existed only in name. The state structure had broken down. The institutional collapse was demonstrated by the disappearance of the army virtually overnight. Huge quantities of weapons which included tanks, aircraft, armoured personnel carriers and massive ammunition dumps were left by the departing Soviet forces for their protegés. In the eastern zone alone, Najibullah's corps commander abandoned 633 tanks and thousands of vehicles. Weapons, therefore, were never to be in short supply for the power-hungry Afghan factions.

The authority of the interim government did not extend beyond Kabul as the warlords established their own centres of power in the provinces. The Tajik Ismail Khan, of Rabbani's Jamiat-e-Islami, governed eight south-western provinces from Herat. Dostum, who had previously supported Najibullah with his Uzbek militia, established himself in the six northern provinces with headquarters in Mazar-e-Sharif. Haji Qadeer, a Pushtun, ruled the three eastern provinces adjacent to Pakistan. Hikmatyar was entrenched in Charasiab. Other local commanders were dominant in Kandahar and the southern provinces. The Shias, in turn, became the masters of Bamyan and a few central regions. The warlords accepted neither instructions nor advice from the feeble coalition in Kabul and they administered their areas as personal fiefdoms. This was accompanied by a countrywide breakdown of law and order. Rape, brigandage, theft and murder brought yet more suffering to ordinary Afghans. The commanders, from the warlords right down to the local chiefs, ruled as though by divine right. Each was a law unto himself.

During his two-month tenure, Mujaddadi tried but failed to have his term of office extended. Rabbani's assumption of power on 28 June 1992 began with intense shelling of Kabul by Hikmatyar on the pretext that remnants of the communist army including those loyal to the famous Parchami general Baba Jan as well as Dostum were in control of the city. This was hotly denied by Masood and Rabbani.

Severe sectarian violence soon erupted in Kabul. Ali Mazari's Shia Wahdat-e-Islami, based in the western part of the city, and the Saudi-backed Ittehad-e-Islami of Professor Sayyaf attacked each other. This resulted in thousands of deaths and the destruction of the western part of the capital.

As Hikmatyar had anticipated, Rabbani refused to step down at the end of his four-month tenure and had his term extended for a further two years through a council he convened on 29 December 1992 with the support of Nabi Mohammadi, Sayyaf and Pir Gillani—the three principle leaders of the Mujahideen coalition. It was claimed that the council was attended by 1,335 delegates from all over Afghanistan and was, as such, genuinely representative. This was roundly rejected by Hikmatyar and other non-partisan Afghans. Radio Message of Freedom, run by the Hizb-e-Islami of Hikmatyar, described the proceedings as a "declaration of war against the nation". Hikmatyar resorted to intense rocket attacks on Kabul and the regime retaliated by strikes against Charasiab. This continued for two months resulting in thousands of civilian deaths and the complete destruction of the southern and eastern part of the capital. Tens of thousands fled the city to take refuge in camps established by the UN in the eastern province of Nangarhar.

Hikmatyar, who had earlier rocketed Kabul on the flimsy pretext of the presence of communist remnants in the armed forces, now had an excuse to resume his attacks. He claimed with good reason that Rabbani had fraudulently usurped power through a non-representative council and vowed to oust him through military means.

The Islamabad Accord: Pakistan intervened again. Prime Minister Nawaz Sharif invited Hikmatyar, Rabbani and the other leaders to Islamabad and the talks resulted in a power-sharing agreement on 7 March 1993 under which Rabbani continued as president and Hikmatyar was appointed prime minister. The new arrangement was to last until July 1994 and in this period the regime was to draft a constitution, hold parliamentary and presidential elections and create a national army and police force. The leaders went to Mecca and, in front of Islam's holiest shrine, the Kaaba, they pledged to honour the agreement. However, shortly afterwards, differences broke out between Hikmatyar and Rabbani on the formation of the cabinet and the distribution of ministries.

During this period, Pakistan, which had been preaching the need for political stability to the Afghans, was itself in chaos. President Ghulam Issaq Khan dissolved the national and provincial assemblies on 18 April but the decision was overturned by the Supreme Court and Nawaz Sharif was reinstated on 26 May, only to be dismissed again by the president on 18 July for reasons of corruption. Moin Quershi, who had served for many years in the World Bank, headed the interim government until Benazir returned to power for her second term on 19 October 1993. Her government was, in turn, dismissed by President Farouk Leghari three years later and Nawaz Sharif became prime minister again, with a huge parliamentary majority, in February 1997.

The Jalalabad Accord: The inability to form a government under the Islamabad understanding led to a resumption of fierce fighting in the weeks leading up to 29 April 1993, when the leadership of nine mujaheeden groups, including Rabbani and Hikmatyar, met in Jalalabad at the initiative of the Nangarhar shura (council) led by governor Haji Abdul Qadeer. After protracted negotiations and under pressure of the Nangarhar shura an accord was signed on 20 May which involved some modifications to the Islamabad understanding.

The government thus formed included each of the seven Peshawar-based Sunni parties and the Shia groups. However, despite being the new prime minister, Hikmatyar did not dare enter Kabul as he feared that he would be killed by his arch-enemy Ahmed Shah Masood, who had become defence minister. He therefore established himself in Charasiab and ministers were thus obliged to shuttle between the two cities. Cabinet decisions were never implemented. Hikmatyar soon realised that he was prime minister only in name and that actual power lay with Rabbani and Masood. He initially remained silent but when Rabbani refused to endorse a cabinet recommendation that an agreement with Russia under which the latter printed the national currency be abrogated, he reacted sharply and the ill-disguised tensions within the government came into the open.

At this point Hikmatyar, who barely eighteen months earlier had rocketed Kabul on the mere presumption that Dostum was in the city, reconciled his differences with the latter. The two seemingly implacable ideological enemies thus became allies and forged an anti-government alliance which also included the Shia Wahdat party of Ali Mazari and the Islamic National Liberation Front of Mujaddadi. The new alliance, which was called the Shura Hamahangi (the Supreme Coordination Council of the Islamic Revolution of Afghanistan), thus started a war against the Rabbani regime on the first day of 1994 which continued sporadically until February 1995, when the Taliban overran Hikmatyar's headquarters at Charasiab.

Rabbani was to hold office until July 1994. However, he secured a decision from the Afghan supreme court, while the chief justice was out of the country, extending his term to December 1994. Even this decision was not respected by the president and he continued in office until the Taliban takeover of Kabul in September 1996.

The impression that Pakistan was partial to Hikmatyar in this period is not borne out by the extent of financial support disbursed by Islamabad to the individual Mujahideen factions. For instance, between 1990 and April 1992, the largest recipient of this assistance was in fact Burhanuddin Rabbani's Jamiat-e-Islami. He was paid 460 million rupees (the value of the rupee was approximately thirty to the US dollar) for the Jamiat, while Ahmed Shah Masood, who headed the military wing of the party, received 142 million rupees. Thus the total assistance given by Pakistan to the Jamiat was 602 million rupees. Younis Khalis's Hizb-e-Islami was given 496 million rupees. Next in line was Gulbadin Hikmatyar, whose party was provided with 366 million rupees, while Professor Sayyaf was paid 244 million, Pir Gillani 241 million, Nabi Mohammadi 240 million, Mujaddadi 160 million, and Mohseni 60 million. During the period of Soviet occupation of Afghanistan five to ten times this amount was paid to the factions annually in addition to weapons, ammunition and other supplies. This was, of course, in coordination with the US, Saudi Arabia and other countries who had supported the Mujahideen in their struggle against the communists.

Phase Four: Emergence and rise of the Taliban

The Taliban movement was a reaction to the prevailing anarchy after the Soviet withdrawal from Afghanistan and the subsequent misrule of the Rabanni regime (*tâlibân* is the plural of the word *tâlib* which means "student"). The assumption that they first emerged in the summer of 1994 is erroneous. The Taliban are the product of the madrassas or seminaries that have existed in Afghanistan since the coming of Islam into that country. In Afghan history, students from these seminaries have always risen at the time of national crises either to fight invaders or to oppose unpopular regimes within the country. The core of the resistance to the British during the Afghan wars of the nineteenth century was from the Taliban of the time. Similarly, the struggle to rid the country of Soviet occupation through the 1980s was spearheaded by the Taliban, and, in the second half of 1994, it was again the students from the madrassas who set forth to restore order in the country. In previous times the

Taliban had always returned to their seminaries after achieving their objectives. This was not to be so after 1994, because, on defeating the local warlords, they decided to form a government themselves.

In the last week of August 1994, Mulla Omar Akhund set out with forty-five followers from a madrassa in Maiwand, Kandahar, to punish a commander who had molested a local family. It was neither ideology nor religious fervour that accounted for their subsequent success. It was the war-weariness of the populace that made them welcome any force which could deliver them from the hands of brigands. They hungered for the restoration of peace and the semblance of an honest administration, no matter how harsh its system of justice.

Local warlords had created fiefdoms owing nominal loyalty to one political leader or the other, but imposing in fact their own arbitrary fiat in the areas that they controlled. In Kandahar, the main road to Herat on the one hand and to Chamman in Pakistan on the other had toll posts and barriers at virtually every kilometre, where local commanders exacted "fees" and whatever other extortions they decided upon on any passing traffic. The lives and honour of ordinary citizens were at their mercy.

Initially even Rabbani sought to use the Taliban to eliminate his opponents and to quell the unrest that had been generated by his failure to abide by the Islamabad Accord. He offered them assistance and there is sufficient evidence to show that his emissaries frequently contacted the Taliban to offer financial and other support. Rabbani is on record as saying: "The Taliban and some Mujahideen from Kandahar asked us to help them to open roads and improve law and order in their province. We supported them."[19]

The Taliban, however, did not need such assistance. The local commanders who surrendered brought with them substantial quantities of weapons and ammunition. With each success the ranks of the Taliban swelled with veterans who had fought against the Soviets. However, it was not through force of arms but the persuasiveness of their message that the Taliban were able to triumphantly sweep first the eastern and then the western part of Afghanistan. This was accompanied by surprisingly few casualties.

By late October 1994, the Taliban movement gained victories one after another in their war against the Mujahideen and, within a short time, captured the whole province of Kandahar, from where they spread their influence to the other parts of the country. During this phase, the Taliban were loosely allied to Dostum who controlled six provinces in the north, Hikmatyar who was positioned in a small area in eastern Afghanistan, the

Hazara Shias who were predominant in central Afghanistan and also other small groups who had little control of territory. Rabbani declared jihad against Dostum and persuaded the grand mufti of Saudi Arabia to issue a fatwa, or religious injunction, against him.

The Afghan situation in mid-1994 was very different from what Pakistan had expected after the collapse of the communist regime in Kabul and the disintegration of the Soviet Union. The peace accords between the resistance factions attempted by Islamabad had come to naught and Afghanistan remained in the grip of turmoil and factional fighting. Islamabad was understandably anxious to see the centuries old trade routes to the resource-rich Central Asian region reopen. Soon after the establishment of the Mujahideen government in Kabul, Pakistan sent a survey team to examine the possibility of reactivating the Kabul-Salang Pass-Hairatan road to Uzbekistan. However, this route was found to be unfeasible because of the fighting between the Afghan groups. The other route available, the Quetta-Kandahar-Herat-Ashgabat highway, was considered more viable. A delegation headed by General Naseerullah Babar, the minister of interior in Benazir Bhutto's second government, embarked on a journey along this route on 21 September 1994 and completed its travel via Ashgabat, Tashkent, Almaty, Kashghar and Gilgit on 5 October. Special security arrangements were made by Amir Imam, a retired army colonel who was serving as Pakistan's consul general in Herat. This task was assigned to him because he was known to most of the Mujahideen commanders. He claimed that he had trained about eighty thousand of them during the Soviet occupation of Afghanistan.

The entire route inside Afghan territory that Babar used was under the control of warlords. The delegation was able to confirm that there was an absence of central authority except in Herat where commander Ismail Khan, who was loyal to the Rabbani regime in Kabul, controlled the road from Dilaram onwards. The delegation met all the major power groups who assured safe passage. Colonel Imam's assessment, which was rejected by Babar, was that it would be difficult to use this route on a regular basis because of the war lords.

Immediately after returning to Islamabad, Babar decided to send a goodwill caravan which would deliver medical supplies to hospitals along the route. He wanted the caravan to reach Ashgabat in time for Benazir Bhutto's visit to Turkmenistan from 30-31 October 1994 for that country's independence day celebrations. What Babar did not realize was that the situation had completely changed since his own transit through

Afghanistan the previous month. Kandahar was about to be captured by the Taliban. The convoy consisting of thirty five-ton military trucks was delayed and was only able to leave Pakistan on 31 October. The journey was hazardous and the convoy was captured on several occasions by local warlords only to be rescued by the Taliban who had taken Kandahar around the time that the caravan reached the city.

The despatch of the convoy was an ill-advised decision by the publicity-hungry Babar. The drama and fanfare that went into the whole episode was for no better motive than to project this foolhardy venture as an achievement of the Bhutto government. The lives of the caravan members were unnecessarily risked and their safe return to Pakistan can only be attributed to luck. The same gifts to the four south-western provinces of Afghanistan could have been sent through the traders and would have earned enormous goodwill. Furthermore, the sending of a military convoy at a time when the Taliban were ascendant was interpreted as support for the movement. The erroneous belief that emerged was that the Taliban were a Pakistan-created entity. Islamabad was never able to live down this ill-founded reputation. Babar's visit to the area just thirty days before Kandahar fell to the Taliban lent further credence to the assumption that they were sponsored by Pakistan. Babar also did little to dispel the rumours at the time that the Taliban owed their existence to him. In actual fact, Babar had never met the Taliban and was surprised to learn about their emergence. His reference to them as "our boys" after their initial successes fuelled vicious and unrelenting propaganda against Pakistan and resulted in regional tension which was to last several years. Lastly, though the Rabbani regime had long outlived its legality, it was still recognized by Pakistan. However, Babar did not think it necessary to obtain Kabul's permission for sending the convoy. This was clearly a violation of Afghanistan's sovereignty and was justifiably resented by the Rabbani government.

In 1994 and 1995 there were several international initiatives aimed at promoting a political settlement in Afghanistan. Pakistan supported the idea of proximity talks which was proposed during 7th Islamic Conference of Foreign Ministers (ICFM) in Islamabad from 7-9 September 1994. The first round of such talks was held during the ICFM between the different Afghan groups and the secretary general of the Organization of the Islamic Conference (OIC). This was followed by a second round in Tehran from 29 November to 7 December in which Pakistan, Iran and the UN participated. These meetings, like so many others, achieved nothing.

In March 1995, Mehmoud Mestiri, the UN secretary general's special envoy for Afghanistan proposed the establishment of a council to discuss the modalities of a peace settlement. He envisaged that the council would consist of two representatives from each of Afghanistan's thirty-two provinces and, to balance its composition, also include fifteen to twenty eminent personalities both from inside as well as outside Afghanistan. The proposal remained on the drawing board and never got off the ground. Rabbani, however, visited Pakistan from 13-15 March to attend a summit meeting of the Economic Cooperation Organization.[20] The participants did nothing more than take "serious note" of the situation in Afghanistan and unanimously agreed to support a UN-sponsored peace process.

On 10 March 1995, Pakistan's ambassador to Afghanistan, Qazi Humayun, assumed charge of his post but the mission was temporarily relocated to Jalalabad the following day because the embassy had been ransacked by the Rabbani regime the previous year. The mission finally reopened in Kabul on 3 May 1995. Around this time, the unrepresentative nature of the Rabbani regime was acknowledged by Mehmoud Mestiri, when he declared: "General Masood, Professor Rabbani and others associated with him have been arguing that by pushing the Taliban out of Kabul they have achieved victory all over Afghanistan. In fact, the reality is that the base of the government has become narrower and could be said to represent only the Tajik ethnic group. The Pushtuns, Uzbeks and Hazaras have been alienated. These three ethnic groups represent about 60 percent of the population of Afghanistan."[21]

The special representative on Afghanistan of the OIC secretary general, Ibrahim Saleh Bakr, visited Pakistan from 11-12 June 1995 and proposed the formation of a group of a hundred persons representing all the provinces of Afghanistan as well as representatives of political parties and neutral personalities which would meet in Jeddah, Saudi Arabia, to discuss the establishment of a transitional government. This proposal was preceded by a visit to the region by prince Faisal Al-Turki, the Saudi minister for intelligence services (several years later he became ambassador to Britain), in the last week of May. Again, like the Mestiri proposal, it was a non-starter.

General Abdul Wali, the son-in-law of ex-king Zahir Shah, arrived in Pakistan on 29 June 1995 for a six-week visit. He proposed the convening of a grand assembly, known in Afghan tradition as a "loya jirga", for the transfer of power to a transitional government. The proposal for such an assembly has been made time and again, as well as after the 11

September 2001 terrorist attacks in New York and Washington, to resolve the problems of Afghanistan. However, the three requirements for a loya jirga are that it can only be convened by a head of state recognized by all Afghans, it can only be held on Afghan soil and it is only called at a time of grave national crisis. The first of these preconditions posed a serious problem as, for the past several decades, the country did not have a leader acceptable to all segments of Afghan society.

On 6 September 1995, the Pakistan embassy in Kabul was set ablaze by a mob of three thousand instigated by the ruling junta. A Pakistan-based sanitary worker, who the crowd mistook for Amabssador Humayun, was killed. The ambassador, the defence attaché, other diplomats and embassy personnel received serious injuries. The defence attaché was stabbed several times and left bleeding on the floor because it was thought that he was dead. Despite this, which was the second attack on the embassy in a year, Pakistan did not break off diplomatic relations with the Rabbani regime. Islamabad's policy has always been to recognize the entity that controlled Kabul. Thus Pakistan recognized the previous regimes including that of Rabbani long after the latter had lost its legitimacy and even after it had ransacked and burnt the embassy. The reason is Pakistan's porous and more than two thousand kilometre-long border with Afghanistan, makes it impossible not to have dealings with any regime in Kabul, no matter how hostile. In the case of the Taliban, however, Pakistan withheld formal recognition for nine months, even though the movement had taken Kabul and was in control of most of Afghanistan. The reason for this was that Islamabad hoped to encourage the Taliban to include all other ethnic groups in its government using the bait of recognition to achieve such an outcome. Nevertheless, regular contact and day-to-day dealings with the Taliban continued unhindered.

In the winter of 1995-96, the Tajik-dominated regime took a strategic decision to broaden its base by inviting other leaders to join it. In January, Rabbani's representative, Dr Abdul Rahman, met Hikmatyar in Sarobi, Dostum in Mazar-e-Sharif and the Shia opposition groups in Bamyan. These initial meetings achieved nothing. Instead, in February, all the opposition groups with the exception of the Taliban established a ten-member council for negotiating with Kabul.

In the interim, the other groups began to gravitate towards Kabul. On 27 March the council of the Hizb-e-Islami gave Hikmatyar the power to negotiate a power-sharing agreement with Kabul. By the first week of May, approximately one thousand Hikmatyar troops arrived in the capital to help in its defence against the Taliban. On 26 June, Hikmatyar entered Kabul to assume the post of prime minister and his party was given nine portfolios in the new coalition. The same day the Taliban launched a massive rocket attack on the capital in which sixty-one people were killed and more than a hundred injured.

The political breakthrough induced Rabbani to visit Jalalabad in an endeavour to persuade its shura, which controlled the three eastern provinces, to abandon its policy of neutrality and to join his government. Rabbani offered to step down in favour of any moderate leader and proposed a meeting of all Afghan groups to elect a new head of state.

On a parallel track, negotiations were intensified with Dostum while Masood kept the Taliban at bay outside Kabul. Through December 1995, Dostum came under considerable Iranian pressure—which included financial inducements—to reconcile with Rabbani. The Iranian expert on Afghanistan, deputy foreign minister Alaeddin Broujerdi, visited Dostum several times during the month to persuade him to receive Rabbani in Mazar-e-Sharif.

Dostum was in two minds. He was half inclined to meet Rabbani through Iranian good offices because he had been promised financial support but feared that such a move might not be in his interest. Rabbani, he felt, was isolated and this militated against any compromise with him. On the other hand Dostum also thought that he could gain political mileage if Rabbani came to Mazar-e-Sharif to apologize to him for the Saudi fatwa and the declaration of the jihad. Iran's efforts achieved some success as Dostum agreed to a truce at the end of August 1996 and the Salang highway connecting Kabul to the north was opened for civilian traffic for the first time in over a year. However, Dostum refused to join the government until greater autonomy was guaranteed to the provinces.

There were also problems within the Shia Hizb-e-Wahdat which had split into two factions headed respectively by Karim Khalili and Akbari. Broujerdi, therefore, visited Bamyan in December 1995 and established a commission to reconcile the differences between Khalili and Akbari. Iran's obvious objective was to get the ethnic minorities to unite under the Shias and the Persian-speaking groups of the north in support of Rabbani.

For their part, the Taliban refused to negotiate with anyone nor did they come forward with any power-sharing proposal of their own. They adamantly insisted on the overthrow of the Kabul regime and convened a meeting of more than a thousand notables in Kandahar on 20 March 1996 to chalk out the future strategy while they continued to shell and rocket Kabul. The meeting, which ended on 4 April, nominated Mulla

Omar as "amirul momineen" ("commander of the faithful") and the undisputed leader of the jihad against the Rabbani regime. This confirmed that the Taliban had no intention of returning to their seminaries after achieving their objectives because the amirul momineen, like absolute monarchs, continues in office for his entire life unless he becomes mentally or physically incapacitated.

In April 1996 alone the Taliban fired 866 rockets on Kabul killing 180 civilians and injuring an estimated 550. Their onslaught resulted in the fall of Jalalabad with less than twenty casualties. In Sarobi, where Rabbani and Masood had sent their own commander to strengthen its defence and mine the approaches, the local Ahmadzai tribe joined the Taliban, and the commanders around Sarobi either surrendered immediately or fled to Kabul. It had been claimed that the capital could sustain a siege for more than a year but its surrender came virtually overnight on 27 September 1996 with only 200 casualties. Almost immediately after entering Kabul, the Taliban killed Najibullah and kept his body hanging for several days in the centre of the city.

The capture of Kabul by the Taliban and the retreat of the Rabbani government north of the Hindu Kush resulted in the formation of the Northern Alliance and threw Dostum into prominence. He emerged as the strongman and the leader of the minority ethnic groups. The factions within the Northern Alliance decided to set aside their differences which, nevertheless, continued to simmer beneath the surface as subsequent events would demonstrate. Their immediate priority was to work out a joint political and military strategy against the Taliban. On 4 December 1996, a parallel government was set up in Mazar-e-Sharif by the Northern Alliance. Though it consisted of many parties, the alliance was dominated by three elements which, in descending order of importance at the time, included Dostum's Uzbek Jumbish-e-Milli, the Tajik Jamiat-e-Islami led by Burhanuddin Rabbani, and the Shia Hizb-e-Wahdat headed by Karim Khalili.

The main elements of the Northern Alliance

Some Afghan Pushtuns believe that the underlying impulse behind the creation of the Jamiat-e-Islami in 1970 was to replace more than two-and-a half centuries of Pushtun rule by that of the Tajiks who constitute the largest ethnic minority. It tried to achieve this during the Soviet occupation of Afghanistan by concentrating its efforts in the Tajik majority areas and subsequently through its control of Kabul during the four-and-a-half year presidency of Burhanuddin Rabbani. Consequently, it was the only resistance party that did not have any representation in the powerful council of eastern Afghanistan which emerged after the fall of the communist regime and lasted until 11 September 1996 when the Taliban captured Jalalabad, the headquarters of the council.

Prior to his involvement in the Islamic movement of Afghanistan, Rabbani was well known for his anti-Pushtun views. He was one of the four founding members of an organization which styled itself a movement against national oppression. This group consisted only of Tajiks from northern Afghanistan and dedicated itself to redress the persecution which the ethnic minorities had suffered from centuries of Pushtun rule. Rabbani, however, left the movement because of differences between him and its leader, Tahir Badakshani, on tactics and strategy. After breaking away from this organization, he associated himself with Islamists at the faculty of theology at the Kabul University where he was teaching.

When Rabbani succeeded Mujaddadi in accordance with the provisions of the Peshawar Accord in June 1992, he removed Pushtuns from key positions in the administration and the army and replaced them with Tajiks. All his close aides were Tajiks and there was not a single Pushtun in the army division that controlled the important air base at Baghram.

Meanwhile Dostum's Jumbish-e-Milli, like the Hizb-e-Wahdat, wanted Afghanistan to be a federation with maximum autonomy for the provinces. The Hizb-e-Wahdat came to prominence when Iran merged the eight Shia factions of Afghanistan into a single party. The organization was initially led by Ali Mazari and when he was killed under mysterious circumstances, allegedly by the Taliban, Karim Khalili became its leader. The Hizb-e-Wahdat had a three-point agenda which it wanted to incorporate in any future constitution. Firstly, the Shias were to be given semi-independent status for which the country would have to become a federation. One of the states within the proposed federation would be exclusively for Shias and would be called "Ghugistan" with Bamyan as its capital. Secondly, the Shia Jafferia school of thought would be one of the two principle religious doctrines of the country; the other one being the Sunni Hanafi school. All official transactions would be based on the doctrines of both schools and all litigation involving Shias would be in accordance with Jafferia tenets even when the case was being heard in a non-Shia province. Finally, a third of all posts in the federal administration, judiciary and the military would be reserved for Shias.

As opposed to the objectives of the minority groups, the Taliban goal was the unification of the country under a strong central leadership and the establishment of an Islamic system based on Hanafi law. The first of these goals clashed with those of the ethnic minorities which wanted greater autonomy while the second was vigorously resisted by the Shias which insisted that only Jafferia law should be applied to them.

Initial international reaction to the Taliban

The reaction of the US to the Taliban soon after they had taken Kabul was one of cautious support. The first formal American pronouncement on them came on 18 November 1996 during a UN conference in New York of countries with interest in Afghanistan. Three elements in the statement of the US delegate, assistant secretary Robin Raphel (the first wife of Amabssador Arnie Raphel, who died in the Bahawalpur air crash along with President Zia-ul-Haq), were particularly interesting. She observed that the Taliban were purely an indigenous movement, that their success had little to do with military prowess (implying that they were preferred by the Afghan people to the chaos that had been prevailing), and that some of the policies pursued by the Taliban were extreme but this could be moderated by engaging with them.

The Russians also wanted to establish contact and develop relations with the Taliban. Deputy foreign minister Mamedov, who attended the same UN conference as Raphel, requested the Pakistan delegate, Najmuddin Shaikh, to facilitate a meeting between senior Taliban functionaries and representatives of the Russian government. Moscow had earlier told Washington that it would never again repeat the mistake it had made in 1979 of intervening in Afghanistan. Russia had no problems with Taliban control of Kabul and 75 percent of Afghan territory so long as the movement did not advance north along the borders of Uzbekistan and Tajikistan—because Moscow feared the export of extremists religious ideology, the influx of refugees and the spill-over of the conflict into these Central Asian states.

Tehran alone was bitterly opposed to the Taliban. One of the reasons for this was that the Sunni minority lived in areas contiguous to Afghanistan. Iran feared that the Taliban might instigate a Sunni uprising on its territory. This apprehension turned to hysteria after the capture of Herat by the Taliban. Furthermore, Tehran considered the Taliban an impediment to its own ambitions in Afghanistan.

Perhaps the greatest initial external success that the Taliban met with, due to no effort of their own, was the decision of the OIC to adopt the vacant seat formula in respect of Afghanistan. This entailed the expulsion of the Rabbani regime from the OIC where Afghanistan would not be represented until an internationally recognized government was in place in Kabul.

After their capture of the Afghan capital, the Taliban leadership repeatedly affirmed that their agenda was purely domestic and that they posed no threat to any country and in particular their neighbours. For their part, they expected external powers not to interfere in Afghanistan's internal affairs. This was never to be because some countries were determined to replay the Great Game of the nineteenth century in order to carve out their respective areas of influence inside Afghanistan. The next five years would prove to be eventful.

2
The sequential settlement formula

THE DAY I took over my new Afghanistan assignment, I had my first, somewhat comical, encounter with the Taliban.

President Farouk Leghari had just dismissed the second Benazir Bhutto government amid scandals. Her brother Murtaza had been gunned down in Karachi the previous month and her husband, Asif Ali Zardari, was arrested amid reports about his complicity in the murder. Yaqub-Khan was reappointed foreign minister in the caretaker administration of Prime Minister Meraj Khalid. So often had he held this post since the time of General Zia-ul-Haq that the world record for being appointed foreign minister under various governments was probably his, as he would jokingly tell me. Elections were to be held within ninety days and the speculation was that Yakub-Khan would again become the next government's foreign minister. It was Yakub-Khan who insisted that I should again head the foreign ministry's sensitive Afghanistan department because he preferred known faces or, as he put it in rather unflattering Shakespearean terms, it is "better to bear the ills we have than fly to others that we know not of".

I was talking with Yakub-Khan in his office in the evening when foreign secretary Najmuddin Shaikh stormed into the room to say that Mulla Ghaus, the acting Taliban foreign minister, was waiting outside and wanted to meet us.[1]

"Let him come in," said Yakub-Khan.

"Okay, but I warn you he's going to kiss you," replied Najmuddin.

"Do I have to kiss him back?" asked an obviously worried Yaqub-Khan.

At this point, Ghaus walked in unannounced, hugged the startled Yaqub-Khan and kissed him on both cheeks. I was next in line. He was a short fair-skinned man with an untidy black beard which did little to hide his protruding teeth and receding gums. Thick small-lensed dark glasses concealed his eyes, one of which had been injured some years earlier during the fighting against Soviet occupation forces. I was later to discover that he had a subtle sense of humour.

The brief conversation with Ghaus was about a sequential settlement of the conflict in Afghanistan starting with a cease-fire and ending with the formation of a political commission that would work out the modalities for a permanent broad-based government. This proposal had been evolved by the United Nations Special Mission for Afghanistan (UNSMA) and considerable work had already been done on it. Mulla Ghaus brushed aside the idea of an immediate cease-fire on the grounds that the opposition would use the lull in the fighting to regroup and attack Kabul. This was the first glimpse that I had of the difficulties that would be confronting me in the coming months.

Shibberghan

My first visit to Afghanistan was on 7 December 1996, a little more than a month after the meeting with Ghaus, when we flew to Shibberghan, the capital of the northern province of Jowazjan, for talks with General Rashid Dostum.

Our delegation was led by Najmuddin Shaikh and included other foreign ministry colleagues as well as Aziz Ahmad Khan who had been urgently recalled a few weeks earlier from his diplomatic assignment in Kuala Lumpur to be appointed ambassador at large for Afghanistan. He had not been designated resident ambassador in Kabul in order to avoid the impression that we had extended diplomatic recognition to the Taliban. Specifically, the purpose of our visit to Shibberghan was to build upon the progress made by UNSMA on its sequential settlement idea.

We assembled at the Chaklala air force base in Rawalpindi at 7am. It was cold and misty. We all wore woollen kurtas and shalwars (knee-length shirts with baggy pyjama-style trousers) and heavy winter jackets. The suave Najmuddin, who was not accustomed to such apparel, also donned a white chitrali cap that made him look like a confused, beardless Afghan tribesman who had misplaced his rifle.

The plane was a Fokker Friendship that had been acquired by the Pakistan Air Force in the 1960s. As we boarded the aircraft, I noticed a circular metal device attached to one of the wheels which, as I was to learn subsequently, was meant to deflect missiles that could be fired at us en route. The fuselage was divided into two sections. The front was like any ordinary passenger plane with regular seats arranged in rows. The rear was fitted out as a drawing room with two armchairs on one side facing each other and separated by a centre table. There was a telephone that connected with the cockpit on the window side of one of the chairs. The other side of the aisle had comfortable sofas that faced the two armchairs. Little did I realize at the time how often I would be flying to Afghanistan in this aircraft. On a midsummer night some seven months later when I was returning to Islamabad after talks with Ahmed Shah Masood, it almost crashed into the Hindu Kush due to a mechanical breakdown.

Some three hours later we landed at Shibberghan airport. It was bright and sunny though bitterly cold. In a rare departure from established practice, Dostum was at hand to receive the delegation. Pakistan's consul general in Mazar-e-Sharif, Ali Sherzai, who had become close to Dostum, was also present. The protocol extended to us was embarrassing. It almost seemed that Dostum had forgotten that Najmuddin Shaikh was only a senior diplomat of the Pakistan foreign service and not an Arab sheikh from the oil-rich Gulf region. The governor of Shibberghan and the leaders of the Northern Alliance were lined up to greet us. There was a guard of honour and we were presented bouquets by little children. We drove in a motorcade escorted by motorcycle outriders to the city where people had obviously been forced to assemble to welcome us.

Gazing out of the car window, one was struck by the poverty which no amount of meaningless pomp and ceremony could disguise. Misery born out of deprivation and want had left its imprint on the faces of people. However, the scars of war, that had ravaged Afghanistan for the past eighteen years, were absent from Shibberghan. The buildings were intact and there was no visible sign of destruction. This was because the resistance against the Soviet occupation forces and the civil war that followed was mainly confined to the Pushtun areas south of the Hindu Kush. During the years of Soviet occupation of the country, the major Mujahideen commander in the north was the much touted "Lion of the Panjsher", Ahmed Shah Masood. In the early 1980s, Masood had concluded a secret agreement with the Soviets under which he gave them free passage to the Pushtun areas south of the Hindu Kush in return for financial and material assistance. Russian military engagement in the north was, therefore, confined mainly to small pockets of Pushtun resistance.

This was to be my first and last meeting with Dostum. He was a burly man whose deportment exuded authority. Dostum's career began as a worker in a gas field near Shibberghan. He joined the communist party and subsequently entered the army where he was trained by the Soviets. He rose quickly in the military to command ten thousand men. His force was organized and disciplined which made it one of the most effective fighting units in the country. After the Soviet withdrawal, Najibullah was able to remain in power only so long as Dostum supported him. When this powerful ethnic Uzbek changed sides, Najibullah fell.

Dostum's well-known weakness for women and wine, as Ali Sherzai told me, often found expression in drunken orgies. He was as feared as he was respected. A man of strong likes and dislikes, Dostum was capable of extreme brutality as well as generosity. On more than one occasion he is known to have had his opponents skinned alive. A Pakistani columnist recalls the blood-soaked courtyard of Dostum's office building in Mazar-e-Sharif which he had entered for a meeting with him. He asked one of the guards whether a goat had been slaughtered but was horrified when he was told that barely an hour earlier, a soldier had been killed for stealing. The man was tied to the wheels of a tank which drove around the courtyard as Dostum and his officers watched.

From the Shibberghan airport it took us about half-an-hour to reach Dostum's palace, for it was nothing short of that, reflecting as it did opulence to the same extent that the streets of Shibberghan mirrored poverty. Crystal chandeliers hung from high ceilings. Expensive carpets and rugs adorned the floors. Imported European furniture filled the rooms. We walked up a winding marble staircase to a lounge that was large enough to accommodate a hundred people. It was here that the meeting with Dostum was held.

Dostum spoke in Dari while his deputy General Malik interpreted along with Ali Sherzai. Here again we were able to witness how terrified people were of him. Barely six months earlier, he had masterminded the murder of Malik's brother, Rasool Pahlawan. Yet Malik dared not look him in the eye and sat obsequiously with bowed head in his presence. At that time one could hardly have imagined that a few months later, Malik would engineer Dostum's ouster in alliance with the Taliban.

Dostum's delegation consisted of all the component elements of the Northern Alliance notably Dr Abdur Rahman and Younis Qanooni of the Jamiat-e-Islami, Ustad Mohaqiq of the Hizb-e-Wahdat and Syed Agha Mansur Naderi who represented the Ismaili community of Afghanistan.

Dostum recalled his earlier help to the Taliban against General Ismail Khan when his aircraft had bombed Herat and Shindand. After the fall of Kabul to the Taliban, he had established contact with them. However, this overture had been rebuffed and he had received an ultimatum from Kabul demanding access to the north. The Taliban were therefore entirely to blame for the ongoing hostilities. He had been left with no option but to fight back even though he firmly believed that there could

be no military solution to the Afghanistan problem. In an obvious reference to Burhanuddin Rabbani's misrule, Dostum said that the last six
years had clearly demonstrated that even the control of Kabul could not
guarantee peace. A political process was the only way out of the
Afghanistan quagmire.

Najmuddin told Dostum that an understanding had already been
reached, through the good offices of UNSMA, on a cease-fire as well as
the exchange of prisoners and dead bodies to be monitored by a commission of six representatives from each side of the Afghan political divide. It
was, therefore, imperative that the process should now move forward and
that discussions should be held on the formation of a political commission.
There had been differences on the composition of the commission as also
on that of the neutral or joint force that could provide security and preserve law and order in Kabul. Dostum was then asked whether he had any
proposals on the political commission and the demilitarization of Kabul.

The Uzbek asked for a short adjournment for consultations with his
delegation. When the negotiations resumed after an hour, the following
proposals in sequential order were read out by Dr Abdur Rahman:

1. A political commission should be established consisting of four
   representatives from the Taliban and six from the Shura-e-Aali-
   e-Difa-e Afghanistan (Supreme Council for the Defence of
   Afghanistan). (When questioned about this, Dostum explained
   unconvincingly that the Taliban represented only some of the
   Pushtuns while the Shura-e-Aali-e-Difa included many ethnic
   groups such as the Tajiks, Uzbeks, Turkmen, Hazaras, Ismailis as
   well as Pushtuns.)
2. A cease-fire commission should be constituted under the joint
   auspices of the UN and the OIC.
3. Implementation of the cease-fire.
4. Demilitarization of Kabul which would entail the withdrawal of
   troops and heavy weapons to a radius of fifty kilometres from the
   city.
5. Exchange of prisoners and dead bodies.
6. Joint security of Kabul by a force selected on proportionate representation from the provinces.

We explained to Dostum that logically a cease-fire agreement would
have to precede any agreement on a political commission. It was unreasonable to expect the creation of a commission through agreement

among the Afghan groups without a cease-fire. While we understood his rationale for the composition of the commission, it would be better if it consisted of representatives from all the provinces of Afghanistan as that would also ensure the participation of all ethnic groups. Furthermore, proposals aimed at ensuring representation of the north and the south could perhaps be less effective than agreeing on proportionate representation for all ethnic groups.

On demilitarization and withdrawal of troops and heavy weapons from Kabul to a specific distance, it was explained that the objective should be to make the capital a safe city no matter how subsequent events unfolded. This could be achieved through two mutually reinforcing measures. First, a neutral or joint security force in which all provinces would be represented (the Dostum proposal on this was reasonable in so far as it provided that bigger provinces should have a larger representation). The second step was the removal of heavy weapons. Whether this was to a distance of fifty kilometres or less was immaterial since it would only mean that bringing them back would take five rather than three hours. Another flaw with the fifty-kilometre idea was that it clashed with the idea of a comprehensive cease-fire. In other words, troops of the two sides were free to engage in combat outside the fifty kilometre demilitarized zone.

To our surprise these modifications were accepted by Dostum who explained that by putting the formation of the political commission as the first step, he only wanted to emphasize that this was the issue to which his side attached the highest priority. He insisted, however, that all elements including the cease-fire must be part of one single agreement. What, therefore, emerged was a verbal understanding, which Dostum agreed to confirm to us in writing within a day or two, along the following lines:

1. A cease-fire to be supervised under UN and OIC auspices by a commission with six members from each side.
2. The exchange of prisoners and dead bodies (implicitly this too would be handled by the cease-fire commission).
3. The formation of a political commission in which all ethnic groups would have proportionate representation (the composition of the commission would be negotiated by the Taliban and the Shura-e-Aali-e-Difa-e Afghanistan).
4. The political commission would:
   (a) discuss and agree upon a broad-based interim government in which all ethnic groups would be represented and which

would propose state structures and arrange, through elections or a loya jirga, a permanent political settlement in Afghanistan;

(b) agree upon the withdrawal of heavy weapons from Kabul;

(c) agree upon the induction into Kabul of a joint security force which would include units from all the provinces—the size of each unit would be determined by the population of the province; and

(d) agree upon the time-frame for the implementation of the various elements and tasks assigned to the commission.

From the tenor of the discussions it was clear that Dostum was anxious to have a cease-fire. We felt that this was probably because he was, according to field reports, under pressure in Badghis province. Furthermore, we had also learnt that the Taliban were planning an offensive into Faryab province for which they had mobilized support from the Pushtuns of Kahsair—a small town on the way to Maimena, the capital of Faryab. Only Dr Rahman of the Jamiat-e-Islami, in which differences between Burhanuddin Rabbani and Ahmed Shah Masood were emerging, was reluctant to see the talks move ahead along the lines eventually agreed. He insisted that the demilitarization of Kabul should be given the same primacy as a cease-fire. In effect he was saying that the Taliban should voluntarily give up their ground successes even before the peace process got underway.

After the talks, Dostum hosted a lunch for us that was more like a banquet fit for kings. Sibghatullah Mujaddadi, the leader of the Jubba-e-Nijat-e-Milli, who happened to be visiting Shibberghan, was also invited. I had known Mujaddadi since 1989 during my tenure as director general for Afghanistan at the foreign office. When Najmuddin told him that I would be shuttling between the Afghan groups in the coming months to promote the peace process initiated by the UN, Mujaddadi joked that I was the "murshed" or the spiritual guide of Afghanistan. I responded that far from being a "murshed" I was only a "murid" or a disciple of the spiritual guide who had to emerge from the Afghans themselves.

In Afghan traditions, gifts are always presented to visitors which the latter has to reciprocate. Dostum gave each member of the delegation a hand-woven Bukhara carpet. Unfortunately, we had forgotten to bring presents with us when we left Islamabad. Dostum smiled when he sensed our embarrassment and declared that we had given him the most precious of all gifts by visiting him. We left Shibberghan for Islamabad the same evening with reason to be satisfied on the outcome of the negotiations. Early next morning we were scheduled to leave for Kandahar where a meeting had been lined up with the reclusive leader of the Taliban, Mulla Muhammad Omar Akhund.

Kandahar

As we approached the runway at Kandahar airport, we saw the wreckage of several warplanes, helicopters and tanks that had been destroyed during the fighting. Unlike Shibberghan the previous day, our reception at Kandahar was simple and without ceremonies. We were received by senior Taliban representatives and officials of our consulate. The twenty kilometre drive from the airport to the city took forty-five minutes because of the appalling condition of the war-damaged road which was pockmarked with large potholes. We were, therefore, forced to drive along its side for a good part of the journey on soil that had only recently been cleared of land mines. There was hardly any traffic along the route.

Kandahar city with its adobe huts and houses told another tale. It was a sad tale; a tale of devastation and destruction. A large number of the houses had gaping holes caused by artillery fire. The bullet-scarred walls of the buildings, as we drove into the city, were reminders of the intensity of the fighting. People lived in whatever was left of their half-destroyed homes. One did not fail to notice that many in the streets were without a limb or an eye. We passed by the tomb of Ahmed Shah Abdali. Little did he know, when he assumed the throne in 1747, how his country would bleed from war and self-inflicted wounds in the subsequent centuries.

As we still had an hour before our meeting with Mulla Omar, we were taken to our consulate general where we were served refreshments and given a briefing. Amir Imam, of General Babar's convoy fame, had come to Kandahar from Herat for this purpose. We were told that complete peace and security prevailed in the 75 percent of Afghan territory controlled by the Taliban. There was no longer any theft, murder or molestation of women and young boys. The most conspicuous, perhaps the only achievement of the Taliban, was the deweaponization of their society. On our way from the airport, we had observed that no one carried a gun. This was certainly remarkable as a firearm was almost a part of the Pushtun tribal attire and as natural to them as the wearing of a necktie is to males in Western societies.

Imam said that a few days earlier a fruit vendor in Herat had told him that one night he had gone to sleep in a place near to his fruit cart which he had covered with a plastic sheet. Next morning he noticed that some of the fruit was missing. This surprised and disappointed him because he thought that theft had been eradicated with the coming of the Taliban. However, his confidence was restored when he found money in one corner of his push cart. Apparently a Taliban night patrol had taken the fruit and, in the absence of the vendor, had left the money being absolutely sure that it would not be stolen.

Yet another incident indicative of the hopes and expectations that were later to be shattered by the Taliban's obscurantist world view was a conversation that our Kandahar consulate officials had with a mechanical engineer whose monthly take home pay was equivalent to a paltry $20. The man said that he was not in the least bitter about his inadequate emoluments because his leaders were even poorer than he was. The reason for this was that the Taliban were a volunteer movement and none of its members—down from Mulla Omar to provincial governors, ministers and its fighters—received any pay.

Several months later, I asked Mulla Wakil Ahmad Mutawakil, who had become foreign minister, how he managed to survive without a regular salary. He replied that he and his other colleagues in government were supported by other members of their families, most of whom either managed a small income from agriculture or from trading. Around this time, I also recall a conversation in my office in Islamabad with UN assistant secretary general Angela King who had visited a women's prison in Kabul a week earlier. She said that the prisoners were in a pitiable condition and suffering from chronic malnutrition and disease. On return to New York however, King lashed out at the Taliban in her report for violation of human rights, particularly gender discrimination.

Our meeting with Mulla Omar took place at eleven that morning in a large dilapidated building which housed the secretariat. The contrast with Dostum's palace in Shibberghan was stark. We entered a large room and were asked to sit on the carpeted floor. A plate of fruit, consisting mostly of the famed Kandahari pomegranates, and a glass of milk were placed before each one of us. Taliban officials were already present. Opposite me, with his back against the wall, squatted Mulla Ghaus, who smiled and asked why our foreign minister, Sahibzada Yaqub-Khan, had not come to Kandahar. Within a few minutes of our arrival, Mulla Omar walked in, greeted us briefly and then sat down in front of Najmuddin Shaikh.

Omar had an impressive personality. He was dressed in a dark kurta and shalwar with a traditional Afghan chador, or shawl, over it as if to conceal the mending patches on his worn-out clothes. Like his comrades, he had a long beard which was as black as his turban. Tall, fair and lean, Omar looked at us with his single piercing green eye—the other had been lost in combat as a Mujahid against the Soviets. When I was introduced to him, he seemed a trifle perplexed. Many months later, I was told by the Taliban ambassador in Islamabad that when the authorities in Kandahar had learnt about my appointment they thought that my surname Murshed signified that I was some kind of a spiritual leader, and that he had expected that like them I would be bearded.

Omar welcomed us in a voice so soft that he was almost inaudible. Had it not been for the interpretation into Urdu we would not have been able to take in a word of what he was saying. Omar recalled all that Pakistan had done for Afghanistan during the decade-long Soviet occupation of the country. Pakistan, he said, continued to host millions of Afghan refugees long after the Soviet withdrawal because of the chaos and turmoil that had been created by the power-hungry warlords and the ousted Rabbani regime. The Afghans would never be able to redeem the debt that their entire nation owed to Pakistan.

We were the first official delegation to be received by Omar. He came across as an extremely shy and reticent person who was never at ease with outsiders. The meeting lasted ninety minutes out of which he spoke for only five. The rest of the time was taken by Najmuddin Shaikh who insisted on explaining UNSMA's sequential settlement formula with all its nuances. He also gave a blow by blow account of our meeting with Dostum the previous day. I doubt whether Omar understood most of what was conveyed to him leave alone the finer points. Out of politeness he responded that he had come to know a number of things about the sequential settlement formula that he had been unaware of until then. The proposal would be examined by the Taliban shura and a response would be given to us in a few days.

The promised response never came and I was to learn later that whenever the Taliban leadership told a visitor that a particular proposal would be discussed in their shura it meant that they were not interested. This saved them the embarrassment of rejecting outright the initiatives taken by their friends and well-wishers.

Najmuddin congratulated Omar for the Taliban's success in bringing peace and security to the major part of Afghanistan which they controlled. There had also been a noticeable reduction in narcotics trafficking in these areas. However, Omar was told that there were also some negatives, albeit exaggerated, but which nevertheless had impacted adversely on the Taliban image. Of these the perceived mistreatment of women was particularly important. The Taliban needed to take remedial measures if they wanted representation in international organizations such as the United Nations. It was, therefore, advisable that they should send a representative to the UN in New York at the earliest, as well as to other capitals. Furthermore, they should also overcome their hesitation in talking to countries which they considered hostile, for instance Iran and Russia. The misgivings that these countries had about the Taliban had to be assuaged.

Omar, who was getting thoroughly bored with the proceedings and also a little irritated with the sermonizing, suddenly perked up to say that he was very happy that trust and confidence between Pakistan and the Taliban were growing. He then suggested that we should discuss the issues flagged by Najmuddin with his colleagues. Subsequently, discussions were held with Mulla Muhammad Hassan, who was then the head of the shura in Kabul, Mulla Muhammad Hassan Rahmani, the one-legged governor of Kandahar, and other important functionaries of the Taliban. Here Najmuddin spoke in even greater detail. He stressed the need for the Taliban to realize that far more important than their military "jihad" was the political jihad. The Taliban seemed to believe that military conquest was all that mattered. This was an erroneous presumption because international political acceptability was vital if they wanted to consolidate their ground successes.

Furthermore, the Taliban had to realize that they were internationally isolated and that only Pakistan and, to an extent, the US spoke on their behalf as was evident from the New York conference on Afghanistan organized by the UN the previous month. However, this situation could be reversed if the Taliban effectively presented and explained their perspectives in international forums and addressed the security concerns of some of their neighbours, who felt threatened by their policies. All this could be done without compromising on any of the principles of Islam. What was needed was flexibility so that an intra-Afghan dialogue could be initiated. The urgency for Taliban representation in the UN was again emphatically reiterated, as also, the importance of opening a few schools for girls and allowing women the right to work in some ministries where separate work places could be established.

Mulla Hassan maintained that they had discussed these matters in detail with the UN agencies. The Taliban considered peace and security to be foremost among human rights and did not want a return to the old days when the honour, lives and property of the citizens were in constant jeopardy. If the UN did not recognize this as a major contribution towards the preservation of human rights, the fault was not on the side of the Taliban. He stated that the Taliban desired peace and wanted international cooperation and assistance but if this entailed a departure from Islamic principles they would rather die.

Our assessment was that while the Taliban had given no immediate indications of flexibility, it was possible that they could consider our advice and perhaps act upon it if we offered them economic incentives. One immediate result, however, was that the delegation was given a letter of appointment signed by Mulla Omar nominating Abdul Hakim Mujahid as the Taliban representative to the UN in New York. We were told that initially they considered appointing Hamid Karzai, who on 22 December 2002 became the head of the interim post-Taliban dispensation, but had eventually decided on Mujahid.

We thought that the meeting was over when Mulla Jalil, the deputy foreign minister, walked in. He had been with Mulla Omar and had been instructed to tell us that the opponents of the Taliban were receiving massive military and economic assistance from Russia and Iran. The Taliban were in need of some heavy weapons but it was entirely up to Pakistan to decide whether it was willing to provide such help. While Islamabad thought this through, the Taliban would welcome food and fuel supplies, assistance for road repair as well as for the rehabilitation of the electricity transmission system from the Kajakai dam to Kandahar. Jalil also informed us that the Taliban wanted to move ahead with railway and gas pipeline construction projects and that for the latter an understanding had been reached with the Argentinean company Bridas.

As we had no intention of providing any military assistance, contrary to the myth that the ground success of the Taliban was due to weapons and training provided by the ISI, Mulla Jalil was merely told that the request had been noted. He was informed that on road construction we were prepared to extend cooperation; on the electricity transmission grid, we would examine how we could provide the equipment and expertise when details were made available to us; on the railway project we suggested, and Jalil agreed, that the Taliban should write either to the Spanish company ICEX or to the Korean conglomerate Daewoo, as both wanted to carry out a preliminary survey; on the gas pipeline project Mulla Jalil was told that according to our information, the American company UNOCAL was interested in leading the construction consortium.

The sequential settlement formula

We returned to Islamabad the same day. The verbal understanding on the sequential settlement reached with Dostum was given in written form by our consuls general at Mazar-e-Sharif and Kandahar to the Shura-e-Aali-e-Difa-e-Afghanistan and to the Taliban leadership respectively. We were under no illusion that the latter would respond promptly. However, the written reply that we subsequently received from the Shura-e-Aali-e-Difa completely undermined all that had been agreed upon during our talks with them in Shibberghan. Dostum and his allies reversed the sequence of the settlement process by going back to their original proposal that had been read out to us by Dr Abdur Rahman on 7 December with minor modifications.

In their response, the Shura-e-Aali-e-Difa again insisted that Kabul should be demilitarized immediately after a cease-fire which would be supervised by a commission consisting of six members from each side. Their concept of demilitarization was merely the withdrawal of forces and heavy weapons to a distance of fifty kilometres from Kabul within a time-frame that was to be negotiated. After this a political commission would work out the modalities for the establishment of a broad-based government which would include national political and social personalities within and outside the country. Only when the broad-based government was in place would there be an exchange of prisoners and dead-bodies which would be followed by the establishment of a joint security force on the basis of proportionate representation from the provinces. This force would "be brought into being under the supervision of the United Nations and the Organization of the Islamic Conference".

We were, therefore, back to square one. All that we thought we had achieved during the 7 December meeting with Dostum had been undermined. The proposal was a recipe for chaos. All groups would retain their weapons which were to be withdrawn to fifty kilometres from a demilitarized Kabul. The power vacuum would certainly result in fighting for control of the capital as no joint security force was envisaged until the very end of the proposed sequential process. In effect, the Taliban were being asked to surrender the capital and to give up at the negotiating table all they had achieved on the ground. The exchange of prisoners and dead bodies, which was an important confidence-building measure and was given the highest priority by the Taliban, came towards the end of the sequential measures. It became clear that peace was not what the Shura-e-Aali-e-Difa wanted.

The next that I heard about the sequential settlement formula was in Tehran during a regional conference on Afghanistan organized by the Iranian government from 25-26 January 1997. Only Turkey and

Pakistan, which I represented, attended the meeting which was conspicuous by the absence of Dostum representatives, Karim Khalili of the Hizb-e-Wahdat and Pir Gillani. The Taliban, who were only invited a day prior to the conference could not possibly have attended even if they had wanted to. UNSMA was represented by its chief, Dr Norbert Holl, a somewhat crude Arabic-speaking diplomat of the German foreign service.

Sibghatullah Mujaddadi lashed out at Burhanuddin Rabbani, who had been invited by the Iranians as "the President of Afghanistan". Mujaddadi said that all Afghan leaders should repent and ask God's forgiveness for they, and they alone, were responsible for Afghanistan's continuing tragedy. It was hypocritical to blame neighbouring countries for the turmoil that had gripped the country in the past several years. In an obvious reference to Rabbani's refusal to step down long after his term of office had expired, he said that the Afghan leadership were selfish and only wanted to perpetuate themselves in power. Even at this late stage matters could be set right as he had secured the concurrence of Mulla Omar for a settlement beginning with a cease-fire, the exchange of prisoners and the establishment of a political commission which would take steps to establish a credible broad-based government. Mujaddadi said that he had conveyed this to Dostum but was yet to receive a reply as the latter was then in Moscow.

With this revelation, I made a short statement recalling that Dostum and the Shura-e-Aali-e-Difa had agreed to the same sequential process during a meeting with us in Shibberghan only the previous month. Without disclosing that subsequently Dostum had reneged on that understanding, I said that Mujaddadi's confirmation of Mulla Omar's acceptance of the idea provided a sound basis for an Afghan peace process. Surprisingly, Rabbani did not dispute my statement as he seemed to be disinterested in the proceedings. He had been received by the Iranians as a head of state and that was all that mattered to him. It was the same Rabbani who had told us in the early 1990s how much he detested the Iranians because of their sectarian bias in favour of the Hazaras. He had declared that the only problem he had during his prayers was that Iran was in the way as he faced the Kaaba in Mecca.

The hastily convened, ill-planned and badly organized Tehran meeting turned out to be an unmitigated failure. Mujaddadi and the Nabi Muhammadi representative refused to sign the conference declaration since it referred to the Rabbani faction as the government of Afghanistan.

Reopening the Pakistan embassy in Kabul

A few days after our visits to Shibberghan and Kandahar, it was decided that Amabssador Aziz Ahmad Khan should proceed to Kabul to set up the Pakistan embassy. To mitigate the hardship of living in Afghanistan, Aziz and I agreed that he and his staff would return to Pakistan by rotation for ten days after spending three consecutive weeks in Kabul. Aziz and his staff normally travelled to and from Afghanistan by road and his first journey in the third week of December 1996 was a stark reminder that by crossing the frontier one was not only travelling to another country but was moving backwards in a time tunnel to a bygone age.

Aziz and his team crossed into Afghanistan from the border post of Torkham. The local Taliban commander, a kind man, genuine in welcome and warm in hospitality greeted them and offered tea. For the onward journey to Jalalabad, a pick-up truck loaded with Taliban, armed with grenade launchers, provided escort. The road was bumpy due to decades of disrepair. As the pick-up in front of the Pakistani officials bounced on the road so did the weapons in the hands of the Taliban who were already dozing. The barrels were pointing towards Aziz and his group and the foremost thought in their minds was the consequence of an accidental firing or a faulty trigger mechanism.

Mid-way between Torkham and Jalalabad the road improved considerably. Even in the earlier part only a small section was badly damaged but the rest could be restored to normal through patchwork if the resources were provided to the Taliban as had been promised by us to Mulla Jalil. Aziz and his colleagues were impressed by the fertile land and the rich agricultural fields near and around Jalalabad. The countryside was beautiful, even the barren patches had a distinctive character with the backdrop of high mountains and the Kabul river in the distance on the right as they moved towards Jalalabad.

Before reaching the city they crossed the airport which consisted of a small ramshackle terminal building. On one side of the runway, partially hidden by plants, was an Ariana propeller aircraft, which had crashed some months earlier. The story was that the pilot detected engine trouble as he took off from Kabul, but instead of returning he decided to carry on to Jalalabad relying on fate which, unfortunately, failed him and the hapless passengers about half a kilometre short of the runway. When I heard about this, I could not help commenting that stupidity accounted in good measure for the bravery that distinguished the Afghan people.

Jalalabad turned out to be a squalid, congested, noisy small town like any in Pakistan's North West Frontier Province (NWFP) and thus our embassy officials felt at home! They were to spend the night at our consul general's residence and move on to Kabul the next morning. Aziz took the opportunity to call on the governor of Nangarhar and overall in-charge of the eastern provinces, Mulla Kabir. Like many of the senior Taliban officials he was in his twenties. Kabir was warm and effusive in his welcome and his body language exuded a confidence remarkable for someone holding such a responsible position at so young an age.

Early next morning, Aziz left for Kabul so as to get there in time for lunch. Prior to the Soviet invasion of Afghanistan, the two-lane Jalalabad-Kabul highway had been of extremely high quality—better than most roads in Pakistan. What Aziz and his team were travelling on in December 1996 was a road without any macadam surface and, like the one from the Kandahar airport to the city, full of pot-holes which gave the ride a rollercoaster effect. Here again, war had taken a heavy toll. The journey, quite naturally, was slow and uncomfortable.

Aziz recalls that along the entire route there were many destroyed tanks and armoured personnel carriers from the time that the Soviets were in Afghanistan. The number of these wreckages had decreased considerably over the years as they had been dismantled and sold as scrap in Pakistan by the local population who desperately sought to survive through whatever means their war-devastated country could provide.

The embassy team were surprised that the only checkpoints they encountered during their journey were at the outskirts of Jalalabad, Sarobi and Kabul. Equally conspicuous was the absence of armed patrols. The inspections at each check-post were carried out by wild-looking but polite men whose primary concern was the confiscation of weapons and, ridiculously, music cassettes which the Taliban considered un-Islamic. The ribbons of destroyed audio and video cassettes were prominently displayed as if to advertise the triumph of good over evil. The extent to which Taliban-controlled Afghanistan had regressed in so short a time became painfully apparent.

Previously, during the period of Burhanuddin Rabbani's misrule, there were twenty-nine check-posts along the same route. Each used to be manned by different warlords who extorted as much as they could in cash and in kind from every passing vehicle. With the Taliban take-over of the area, only those transporting exports paid the usual *octroi* and taxes.

The small sleepy villages along the road from Jalalabad to Kabul reflected normalcy. It was difficult to believe that this had been the scene of fierce factional fighting barely four months earlier. So all-pervading was the sense of security that Aziz insisted on doing without the armed escort for the remainder of his maiden journey to the Afghan capital. He told me later he felt much safer without the grenade launchers being pointed at his vehicle by the clumsy Taliban escort.

As Aziz and his colleagues entered the outskirts of Kabul they were awed by the devastation. The entire military cantonment and the industrial area on the fringes of the city had been razed to the ground. Kilometre after kilometre of half-destroyed buildings lined the road. The Microyan, a large complex of apartment buildings built by the Soviets, reflected the ravages of war. Plastic sheets substituted for glass windows and, as we had seen in Kandahar a few weeks earlier, the walls of almost every building were pockmarked by bullets and shrapnel. The artillery shell-cratered roads testified to the intensity of the fight for Kabul which began after the withdrawal of the Soviets and the fall of the Najibullah regime. It is ironic that it was the Mujahideen and not the Soviet occupation forces who had destroyed Kabul, Kandahar, Herat and other Afghan cities. How right Mujaddadi was when he accused Burhanuddin Rabbani and the Afghan leadership, during the Tehran meeting on Afghanistan in January 1997, of being entirely responsible for the suffering of the Afghan people. Ahmed Shah Masood, Hikmatyar, Ali Mazari, Sayyaf, Dostum and others were all ambitious men whose thirst for power brought nothing but ruination to their country. The Taliban were no less to blame. Their movement, however, was merely a reaction to the prevailing anarchy caused by Rabbani's refusal to honour the Peshawar, Islamabad and Jalalabad accords as well as the solemn pledge made by all factional leaders at the Kaaba.

On entering Kabul, Aziz and his staff were met at the roadside in the city centre by the Taliban chief of protocol. Present also was the defence attaché of the Pakistan embassy, brigadier Ashraf Afridi, who had been stabbed and left for dead when the Rabbani regime ransacked and burnt the Pakistan embassy in 1995. Aziz and his officials were then taken by the Afghan protocol to brigadier Afridi's house which had, in happier and more peaceful days, been the residence of the Austrian ambassador. Subsequently, the building was taken over by the Rabbani regime and was used by Ahmed Shah Masood as his guest house. After a lunch of traditional Afghan meats and pulao rice, Aziz proceeded to the former German Club which was to serve as his temporary residence.

The next day Aziz explored the city at leisure and the extent of damage inflicted by the Mujahideen became even more shockingly clear. An entire suburb near Kabul University had been totally destroyed. The Dar-ul-Aman palace, which had once basked in majestic splendour from its hillside location, was irretrievably damaged. At the foot of the palace, across the road, was the ruin of the famous National Museum with its priceless treasures looted and smuggled to various corners of the world. The once beautiful city, so rich in culture, lay in ruins because of the murderous power struggle among the Mujahideen. Its population had been reduced to utter destitution.

The plight of ordinary people was made even worse because of the strict enforcement of the Taliban's erroneous interpretation of Islam. The religious police, the Amr-bil-Maroof, patrolled the streets and those thought to be violating Islamic tenets were often publicly punished. But it was the women who suffered the most. The few that dared venture outside their homes walked in fear. A religious police stalwart administering the whip (a two-inch broad two-foot long leather belt with a handle) on non-conforming women was not an unusual sight. The one-eyed, one-legged justice minister of the Taliban, Mulla Turabi, who along with defence minister Mulla Obaidullah surrendered to the authorities in post-Taliban Kandahar in January 2002, was particularly notorious for the ruthless implementation of the social code that was inflicted on the Afghan people, especially women.

The Taliban proudly claimed, as Najmuddin was repeatedly told in Kandahar, that they had restored peace and security to the country and that this was the most fundamental of all human rights. Kabul, as indeed other cities of Afghanistan, were peaceful. The thefts, murders, rapes, so common during the period that the Mujahideen were in power had virtually disappeared. Unfortunately, this achievement was marred by the misbehaviour of the overzealous religious police.

Aziz's first call on the Taliban leadership was on Mulla Nane who was deputizing for Mulla Rabbani, the acting chairman of the Council of Ministers. The meeting was at ex-king Zahir Shah's former palace, Arg, which presented a rather forlorn and unkempt appearance. Several cabinet ministers were also present on the occasion and it was quite obvious that the Taliban leadership were very pleased with Pakistan's decision to appoint an ambassador albeit an ambassador-at-large. This was construed by them as an indirect recognition of their supremacy in Afghanistan. Even after Pakistan's recognition of the Taliban regime in May 1997 we neither requested nor received any *agrément* for Aziz. Thus he became the only ambassador in diplomatic history to be accredited without *agrément*, without a formal letter of credence and without presenting credentials to the head of state. Up to the end of his assignment in mid-2000, Aziz remained the sole ambassador in Kabul.

After the meeting, Mulla Nane hosted a lunch which was held in the royal dinning room. Waiters who had served in the palace for decades were in attendance. The food was typical Afghan fare, rich in meats and served in huge quantities. Nane, a "jihadi" commander who had lost a leg fighting the Soviets, appeared quite ill at ease at the dining table and being confronted with an assortment of cutlery. He ignored the formalities and disarmingly let his tribal culture take over. He tucked into the food with his fingers as did the other Afghans. The only concession they made to their guests from Pakistan was to remain at the dining table though they would have much rather preferred to sit on the floor.

When Aziz visited the office of the governor of Kabul the place was teeming with people. There was a total absence of formality normally associated with the office of such a senior person. It was more like the house of a village elder where people freely came and went bringing with them both complaints and greetings.

In all government offices it was more than apparent that the Taliban were trying to come to grips with their new responsibilities. They had no experience of running a bureaucracy and were suspicious of those who had served in the ministries of the previous regimes. It was an unenviable situation. They needed experienced people but were wary of fifth columnists. The absence of a state structure was to remain the main impediment in the way of efficient governance.

A few days later Aziz returned to Pakistan as he was recalled from Malaysia at short notice and had yet to pay his farewell calls in Kuala Lumpur. He decided, that instead of taking the Kabul-Jalalabad-Torkham route, to return via Gardez, bypassing Khost and entering Pakistan at Parachinar from the border post at Kharlachi.

Aziz, brigadier Afridi and a few embassy officials left Kabul early in the morning. The drive up to Gardez was fairly comfortable as the road was in a much better condition than the one to Jalalabad. At Gardez, a small town with mostly ruined structures, Aziz dropped in unannounced at the governor's office. The latter was in Kabul so he was received by the deputy governor, a young Talib of Tajik descent from Badakhshan, who spoke only broken Pushto. It was interesting to see a non-Pushtun serving in this position in a Pushtun province. It demonstrated that the Taliban, unlike the Afghan amirs of the past, had no problem with including representatives of other ethnic groups in the government. Their emphasis was on enforcing their own obscurantist ideology through any means even if this meant that they would have to rely on the ethnic minorities.

From Gardez towards the border there was only a dirt road along a stream. At places even that disappeared and Aziz and his companions had to drive in the shallow waters of the stream. The route was through a narrow valley flanked by mostly barren mountains and it took about seven hours to travel the eighty odd kilometres to the Pakistan border.

When the group reached Kharlachi they were told by the Taliban border guards that the post had been closed for the past several months and no crossings were allowed. Aziz protested that it would be impossible to return to Gardez because the sun had set and soon it would be dark. Finally the leader of the guards suggested that the embassy officials should speak to the commandant whose camp was a couple of kilometres away. Aziz requested that he should be allowed to talk to the commandant on the wireless but was informed that the set could only be used for receiving calls. In order to get the commandant to call the border post, the leader of the contingent devised an ingenious method. He told Aziz that he would fire his machine gun and this would definitely induce the commandant to establish contact with him. The Talib then fired a long burst into the evening sky and, sure enough, within minutes his wireless handset crackled and he explained the reason for firing. Shortly afterwards the commandant arrived, greeted the travellers courteously and listened patiently to what Aziz had to say. He finally agreed to let the group cross the border provided the Pakistan side had no objection because the post had been closed to traffic through an understanding between the Taliban and the Pakistani authorities. Aziz informed the commandant that officials across the border had already been informed and were awaiting his arrival. On hearing this, the commandant escorted the embassy team to the crossing point but only allowed them to move into Pakistan after he had satisfied himself that officials on the other side were indeed waiting for the group.

After spending the night in the comfort of a well maintained Pakistan army mess in Parachinar, Aziz proceeded to Islamabad. When he entered my office, I was taken aback to see that he had grown a beard. He said that he had done so to make himself less conspicuous in Taliban-controlled Afghanistan. Without a beard, he explained, he would have felt like a delegate who had decided to address the UN General Assembly attired in Bermuda shorts.

Till this point it was clear that neither the misguided mullas of Kandahar nor the corrupt leaders of the minority ethnic factions in the Northern Alliance were in any mood to negotiate a peaceful settlement of the Afghan crisis. The stalemate after the Taliban capture of Kabul on 27 September 1996 became increasingly tense. The spring and early summer of 1997 were marked by Byzantine political intrigues within the component elements of the Northern Alliance and in particular the Jumbish-e-Milli. This was to erupt into ferocious fighting towards the end of May the consequences of which were as dramatic as they were far-reaching.

3
Recognition
of the Taliban

IN THE period January-May 1997, I had several meetings with Mulla Ghaus. He was a shrewd negotiator and would persistently insist that Pakistan should extend diplomatic recognition to the Taliban. The reply he invariably received was that this was unimportant. What mattered was that we were dealing with the Taliban as a government. Furthermore our ability to take up their cause with other countries and in international forums would be impaired if we recognized their government at this critical stage. They controlled most of Afghanistan and had demonstrated their staying power. Recognition would follow as soon as peace was restored in all of Afghanistan and the Taliban had got the other ethnic groups and factions on board. They had the advantage of being able to negotiate from a position of strength and should, therefore, talk to their enemies.

Such responses must have been irritating for Ghaus. On one occasion, he said that he was willing to do much more than merely talk to his enemies. Gulbadin Hikmatyar, he observed with caustic humour, was a very generous man who readily gave his daughters in marriage. He was willing to offer his services as a Hikmatyar son-in-law if that would help in the restoration of peace.

At times Ghaus gave me the impression that he was not entirely happy with the Taliban leadership. There were reports that it was Ghaus who had actually started the Taliban movement in 1994. However, after the fall of Kandahar, Mulla Omar was selected as the leader for the reason that he belonged to a bigger tribe. Another report suggested that it was Mulla Rabbani who had launched the movement.

Tensions within the Northern Alliance
Soon after our visit to Shibberghan in December 1996, the fissures within the Northern Alliance became more pronounced. Tensions emerged not merely between the component elements of the Alliance but also

within the individual parties. Interference from neighbouring countries in support of one group against the other increased.

Useful information was provided to us by Consul General Ali Sherzai from Mazar-e-Sharif. He reported that Dostum visited Moscow in December 1996 and on 11 January 1997, a Russian delegation headed by Lieutenant General Kazhnikov, deputy chief of border security, arrived in Shibberghan to assess the military requirements of the Jumbish-e-Milli. Dostum was promised ten helicopter gunships, ten fighter aircraft, a hundred T-62 tanks, two hundred Russian-made missiles similar to the US Stingers and a huge quantity of heavy weapons. By 18 January the helicopter gun-ships and the aircraft reached Mazar-e-Sharif along with the heavy weapons.

In the meantime the economic situation in Northern Afghanistan went from bad to worse. There was galloping inflation. Officials stopped going to work as they were not paid salaries. Discontent was widespread and people blamed the Jumbish-e-Milli for the situation. In mid-January 1997, Ali Sherzai reported that the chances of any improvement in the state of affairs was slim and the possibility of a mass uprising could not be ruled out.

Bitterness and rifts among the Jumbish-e-Milli leadership began to surface. The animosity between Dostum and the family of the late Rasool Pahalwan came into the open. Rasool Pahalwan, General Malik's brother, had been emerging as a possible rival to Dostum and was believed to have been assassinated by the latter's cohorts in June 1996. A showdown between Malik and Dostum was imminent. Dostum removed some of his important commanders such as Majeed Rozi and Immamuddin from their posts as he doubted their loyalties. To strengthen his personal security, he appointed his brother Qadir Dostum, the garrison commander of Mazar-e-Sharif.

Strains also appeared in the Hizb-e-Wahdat (Khalili Group). The Commander of the Hizb-e-Wahdat forces, General Hashmi, spoke against Karim Khalili and indicated to Ali Sherzai, that he was ready to cooperate with the Taliban if he was helped logistically and provided financial assistance.

The situation in Badghis province was tense. The morale of the Jumish-e-Milli forces was low. Its commanders faced a threat not only from the Taliban but also from the forces loyal to Rasool Pahlawan. To reinforce his forward positions, Dostum rushed 3,500 troops and some eighty tanks along with sufficient quantities of diesel and petrol to Faryab in mid-January 1997.

Simultaneously, the differences between Dostum and Ahmed Shah Masood became acute. During a meeting on 15 January 1997 in Salang, the two blamed each other for their defeat in Baghram and Charikar. Members of the Jamiat-e-Islami, and in particular those in Ahmed Shah Masood's Shura-e-Nazar, held Dostum both in contempt as well as fear because of his ruthlessness. To demonstrate his strength, Dostum dispatched fresh reinforcements to his troops in the Salang sector on 16 January 1997 for launching a major offensive against the Taliban.

On 1 February 1997, Ali Sherzai had an exclusive meeting with General Malik, who was also director of foreign affairs of the Northern Alliance. He disclosed that Russia and Iran were exerting pressure on Dostum to declare the independence of the territories controlled by the Northern Alliance and assured him that they would extend immediate recognition to his government. Uzbekistan had also agreed to do so. The Turkish government, according to Malik, had also been consulted but had advised Dostum against taking any step that would lead to the dismemberment of Afghanistan. Malik advised that Pakistan should initiate a peace process that would keep Dostum involved in a dialogue with the Taliban. At the same time, in order to isolate Dostum, the Taliban should intensify their propaganda against him through the media and declare him a communist and an infidel. As BBC radio broadcasts in Pushtu were listened to and taken seriously by a majority of Afghans, the Taliban should use this channel to declare that they had nothing against the people of the north and that Dostum was the only problem. This would hasten the latter's downfall. He should be singled out for being responsible for the killing of innocent civilians and imposing a tyrannical and dictatorial rule on the people of Afghanistan. Malik counselled that the Taliban might be advised not to launch any attack on Badghis for the time being as that would put him (Malik) and his family in a very difficult position vis-à-vis Dostum. The morale of the Jumbish-e-Milli forces was extremely low and Dostum would eventually be willing to compromise with the Taliban. The economy of the north was on the verge of collapse and people were finding it difficult to have even a single meal a day. Violence could erupt at any moment. Malik requested Sherzai for a mobile satellite telephone as all his lines were bugged—it was for this reason that he had been unable to establish direct contact with Pakistan.

The following day Ali Sherzai met Dostum at Qila Jangi in Mazar-e-Sharif. The latter professed friendship for Pakistan and reiterated his resolve for peace stating that he would move ahead with the peace process even if Ahmed Shah Masood and Rabbani did not go along with him. Sherzai felt that Dostum was desperate, demoralized and broken from within. His differences with Ahmed Shah Masood had become even sharper and verged on hostility. On a parallel track, anti-Dostum elements within the Jumbish-e-Milli were growing stronger. Sherzai felt that Dostum's professed desire for peace was a hoax and was aimed to buy time to wipe out the opposition from within his own party as well as to shore up his finances and defence capabilities.

Both Dostum and Malik sought Pakistan's help to advance their respective ambitions. This was rejected by us as we knew only too well that any form of interference in Afghanistan's internal affairs would be counterproductive. Our single objective was the restoration of durable peace in Afghanistan as no other country had suffered more than Pakistan from the continuation of the Afghan turmoil.

Sherzai reported on 3 February 1997 that, in a tactical move, Ahmed Shah Masood had shifted his headquarters from Panjsher to Andrab in Baghlan province with the intention of trapping the Taliban in the Panjsher valley and then launching an offensive from the rear of the Salang through the Tajik-populated areas.

Despite all that Dostum had told Sherzai about wanting peace, he moved his entire air force to Shibberghan for the purpose of strikes against Herat and Badghis. Alongside this, a trusted Dostum commander, Zainuddin, popularly known as Zainy Pahlwan, was sent to Badghis along with twenty tanks and 1,500 troops to attack Taliban positions in the province. Dostum also sent two saboteurs to Kandahar with orders to assassinate Mulla Omar and other important Taliban leaders.

In the meanwhile, foreign military assistance to the Northern Alliance, particularly from Iran and Russia, continued to pour in. Five SU22s from Russia were expected within a few days while a fully loaded train carrying long-range guns, missiles, rockets and other arms, and ammunition from Iran was on its way to Shibberghan through Turkmenistan.

It became increasingly apparent that the divisions within the Northern Alliance were no less profound than their hatred and fear of the Taliban. Though both Masood and Dostum had mobilized for action against the Taliban, their hatred of each other intensified. The extent of anti-Dostum feelings found expression in the jamming of the Jumbish air force radar system by his enemies within the Northern Alliance. Similarly, the missiles mounted on the aircraft were also made unserviceable. Badghis itself was teeming with Dostum haters. Thus the

Taliban felt that, instead of attacking the province, they should come to some sort of understanding with these elements as that would enable them to reach Shibberghan without much resistance.

Ali Sherzai had another tête-à-tête with General Malik on 18 February 1997 during which the latter disclosed that Dostum had had a secret meeting with a high-level delegation from Russia in Tirmiz, Uzbekistan, the previous day to chalk out a strategy for launching a two-pronged attack on Herat. Malik disclosed that commander Zainuddin along with three thousand troops had been sent to Mashhad (or Meshed) from where, in coordination with the Iranian government, an offensive against Herat was to be launched. The Jumbish-e-Milli troops would launch their attack from the Badghis side. Malik also revealed that an Indian cargo aircraft, which was offloaded in Tirmiz, had brought arms and ammunition for Dostum on 15 February. Pakistan, Malik said, had become a passive bystander and this enabled Dostum to strengthen his economic and military position through massive infusions of assistance from Iran, Russia and India. He emphasized that the anti-Dostum elements were in desperate need of financial help as well as a satellite telecommunications system. Malik told Ali Sherzai that he could topple Dostum if only he was sure of support from Pakistan. This was conveyed to Sherzai time and again in several earlier meetings. Our response was that we had no desire to interfere in Afghanistan's internal affairs. Sherzai was shortly afterwards transferred from Mazar-e-Sharif as we felt that he was becoming too closely involved in the internal intrigues that typified the Afghan power struggle. He was to be replaced by Ayaz Wazir, the Pakistan foreign office director responsible for Afghanistan, in May 1997.

Malik launched an uprising against Dostum which began on the night between 18-19 May 1997. The insurrection spread like wildfire across the northern provinces thereby bringing into the open the latent animosities within the Northern Alliance. On 20 May our consulates general in Herat, Kandahar and Mazar-e-Sharif informed us that the Taliban had publicly declared their support for Malik and that the rebellion had started from Malik's home province, Faryab, where his forces and those of his brother Gule Pehlwan had gained control. The initial reports indicated that the rebels were about to gain control of the provinces of Samangan, Sar-e-Pul and Baghlan. General Ismail Khan, the former governor of Herat, who had joined forces with Dostum, was arrested in Faryab along with one thousand of his troops by elements loyal to Malik. The Taliban were reported to have moved forward to the Masood-controlled Salang area and also to the Shibber pass in the Hizb-e-Wahdat-dominated province of Bamyan. Dostum's whereabouts were not immediately known. He was variously reported to be in Shibberghan, Tirmiz or Tashkent.

Our acting consul general in Mazar-e-Sharif (Ayaz Wazir was yet to take up his new assignment) reported on 19 May that the situation in the north had become abruptly volatile after the cold-blooded assassination of the important Jumbish-e-Milli commander, A. R. Haqqani, along with five of his bodyguards at his residence in Mazar-e-Sharif, allegedly by Dostum loyalists. This instigated the anti-Dostum forces within his own substantial military establishment to rebel. The Northern Alliance's 511 Division deployed in Faryab attacked the Jumbish border division and captured its commander, Zainuddin Pahlawan. Malik also prevailed upon General Ghaffar Pahlwan of the 510 Division, whose son was killed by a Jamiat commander in 1995, to join hands with him against Dostum. His cousin, Juma Gul, commanding a brigade of the 53rd Division of General Qadir Dostum at Andkhoi also joined Malik and raised the white flag of the Taliban in the city. Malik took down portraits of Dostum as well as his emblems from all buildings in Faryab and replaced them with the Taliban standard. Commander Fatehullah of the 511 Division deployed at Tashqurghan in Samangan province, with the assistance of Harkat-e-Islami forces, took over the entire city. The supporters of the slain Haqqani captured the area up to Chashma-e-Shafa twenty-five kilometres short of Mazar-e-Sharif and raised Taliban banners. All roads to and from Mazar-e-Sharif were blocked and, for security reasons, our consulate personnel shifted from their homes to the office building.

On 20 May the acting consul general reported that the situation in Mazar-e-Sharif had become even more tense. The revolt against Dostum which started in Faryab had engulfed the entire provinces of Badghis and Saripul and parts of Jauzjan, Balk and Samangan.. The Taliban attacked pro-Dostum elements in Bamyan. Men from the Hizb-e-Islami of Gulbadin Hikmatyar in the north joined the anti-Dostum forces and had captured some villages and were advancing towards Mazar-e-Sharif. An unannounced curfew prevailed in the city. Among the Central Asian republics, Turkmenistan, because of its policy of neutrality, had maintained close contact with the Taliban as well as the Northern Alliance. The assessments provided to us by Ashgabat were, therefore, generally balanced and based on the prevalent ground realities. Our ambassador in Turkmenistan at the time, Tariq Osman Hyder, was told on 20 May by the commander of the Turkmen border guards, General Kabulov, that the reason for the revolt of General Malik and Gule

Pehlwan was the assassination the previous year of Rasool Pehlwan. Kabulov had attended the latter's funeral and was sure that Malik and Gule Pehlwan would soon avenge the murder of their brother who had always considered himself equal, and not subservient, to Dostum. They hated Dostum for good reason but also despised him because of his low origin as a petty worker in a gas field near Shibberghan. In this sense the Afghans, no matter which ethnic group they may belong to, are class-conscious. Family background is important and a person is often introduced as the son or relative of a notable or by his profession.

Kabulov confirmed the information that had been provided to us by our consulates in Afghanistan and his assessment was that the defection of the 511 Division in Faryab had dealt a crippling blow to Dostum. Although the Taliban were yet to move, there was nothing to stop them advancing across the Murghab to Badghis and Faryab. On 19 May some representatives of the Taliban had entered Mauchack, a village on the Afghan side of the border with Turkmenistan, and had asked the population to keep calm and not to flee into Turkmenistan. Till that time there had not been any exodus into Turkmenistan. Kabulov also said that there had been reports that Dostum aircraft had bombed Maimena and Andkhkoi in Faryab. According to him, General Ismail Khan had not been captured (this was later proved incorrect) although some of his senior officers had been taken into custody including the Chief of Staff of the Second Division, Zinullah Khan. Kabulov said that the position on the Afghan-Turkmen border was completely stable because of his country's policy of neutrality.

Our assessment in Islamabad was that it was not possible to forecast the future turn of Afghan events with accuracy. Loyalties in the country had always been fickle, allies frequently became foes and, as in the present instance, sworn enemies often cooperated with each other in order to achieve immediate objectives. Malik's rebellion had merely demonstrated that the Dostum-led Northern Alliance had received a severe setback from which it would be difficult to recover. If the Taliban and General Malik, an Afghan Uzbek, could forge a durable alliance, then the initial semblance of a broad-based dispensation could emerge. Ahmed Shah Masood had been isolated and might even decide to cooperate with the Taliban if he felt that this would serve his interests.

By 22 May the provinces of Badghis, Faryab and Sar-e-Pul had fallen to Malik. Dostum loyalists continued to maintain a tenuous hold over Jowzjan and Balkh—his own whereabouts remained a mystery. The expectation was that Shibberghan would be taken by the rebels within a day or two. Should this happen, then Mazar-e-Sharif, the capital of neighbouring Balkh, would capitulate within hours. Fighting was reported to have erupted in the province of Samangan and the Shibber Pass area of Bamyan. In the provinces controlled by Ahmed Shah Masood relative calm prevailed in Takhar and Badakshan whereas there had been some fighting in Kunduz and Baghlan. The Taliban flag had been raised in all places captured by Malik.

The Afghanistan situation had thus undergone a radical transformation. The stalemate since the Taliban capture of Kabul on 27 September 1996 had ended. The Jumbish-e-Milli, which was militarily the most powerful element of the Northern Alliance had crumbled. General Malik, who was now in league with the Taliban, had replaced Dostum as the new leader of the Afghan Uzbeks. Burhanuddin Rabbani had paled into insignificance and his pretensions as the president of Afghanistan stood exposed. Ahmed Shah Masood was waiting in the wings to decide on his next step. With the virtual disappearance of the Northern Alliance, the Hizb-e-Wahdat no longer had the support of the other factions. The Taliban were clearly ascendant and their ability to cooperate with other ethnic groups had been demonstrated.

On 23 May we evacuated our personnel from Mazar-e-Sharif for security reasons with the assistance of the UN. On the morning of 24 May I had a detailed meeting with Mulla Ghaus in Islamabad at the conference room of the foreign ministry. He again asked me when Pakistan was going to recognize the Taliban now that they had got Malik on board. I told him they still had to reach out to the other ethnic groups. He disclosed that they were already doing this. The Hizb-e-Wahdat had sent a delegation to Kabul for talks with the Taliban that very day. Ahmed Shah Masood had also telephoned Mulla Omar to say that he wanted to negotiate an honourable surrender. Omar had accordingly designated Mulla Obaidullah, the Taliban defence minister, and Masood had nominated General Faheem (later defence minister in Karzai's interim cabinet which assumed office at the end of 2001) to talk about the terms of the surrender. This was evidence enough, according to Ghaus, to demonstrate that all the major ethnic groups of Afghanistan were either in alliance with the Taliban or were in the process of joining them. Pakistan's reluctance to extend formal recognition was, therefore, incomprehensible. I responded that this was not enough. The time for recognition would come when all groups had actually joined the Taliban.

When the meeting ended at about noon, I went downstairs to see Ghaus to his car when he received a call on his mobile phone. He spoke for a couple of minutes and then with a broad smile told me that

Shibberghan, the capital of Dostum's home province Jowzjan, had been captured by the Taliban. After seeing Ghaus off, I rushed to inform foreign secretary Shamshad Ahmed (he had replaced Najmuddin Shaikh when Nawaz Sharif took office as prime minister) about the new ground situation in northern Afghanistan. Ahmed was about to leave his office for a flight to Abu Dhabi with President Farouk Leghari and I told him I would keep him informed in Abu Dhabi about further developments.

That evening at around 8pm I received a phone call from General Rana, the director general of Inter Services Intelligence, to inform me that Mazar-e-Sharif had been captured by the joint forces of the Taliban and General Malik. Rana told me that he had already informed Prime Minister Nawaz Sharif who had given clearance for recognition of the Taliban after the foreign office had been consulted. I replied that the decision would have to be held in abeyance for a few hours until foreign minister Gohar Ayub Khan (Yaqub-Khan's successor in the second Nawaz Sharif government), who was returning from a visit to Washington early the next morning, had spoken to the prime minister himself. I informed Shamshad accordingly in Abu Dhabi.

As foreign minister Gohar Ayub had been travelling the whole night, I decided not to disturb him until after 10am. However, when I phoned I was told that he had already left for his ancestral village in Haripur some two hours driving distance from Islamabad. I spoke to him as soon as he reached Haripur and requested him to contact Nawaz Sharif. A short while later, I received a message from him to say that he would be returning to Islamabad in the afternoon and that I should arrange a press conference during which he would announce our formal recognition of the Taliban.

I drafted the statement to be made by the foreign minister and in the afternoon of Sunday 25 May 1997, he announced Pakistan's recognition of the Taliban government. In his statement, Gohar Ayub said that the government of the Islamic State of Afghanistan fulfilled the criteria for recognition—it was in effective control of most of the territory of Afghanistan and was being supported by other ethnic groups in that country.

Prior to the announcement, I took the initiative of separately briefing the Saudi, Turkish, Russian and Iranian ambassadors as well as the chargé d'affaires of the US and China about our intention. A collective briefing was given to the Kazak ambassador and the Uzbek chargé d'affaires. The ambassador of Turkmenistan was not available. The gesture of taking the envoys into confidence in advance was appreciated by all sides.

Recognition of the Taliban

In my briefing to the envoys I said that the Taliban now controlled all of Afghanistan. It could no longer be said that they represented only the Pushtuns. A majority of the Uzbeks were fully behind them and there were indications that the Tajiks and the Hazaras would be falling into line within a day or two. What I did not tell them was that Karim Khalili of the Hizb-e-Wahdat had already contacted General Malik and the Taliban for arriving at a settlement while the ethnic Tajiks in Takhar and Baghlan had also risen in support of the Taliban. I explained that the areas so far controlled by the Taliban had witnessed complete peace and security and it was hoped that with the extension of their control the entire country would enjoy the peace and stability that had eluded it for almost two decades. The Taliban had on several occasions held out the assurance that their agenda was entirely domestic and that they posed no threat to any other country. It was stressed that withholding recognition of the Taliban, now that they controlled almost the entire country and had broad-based support, was unfair and discriminatory. The Taliban were anxious to start the process of the reconstruction and rehabilitation of Afghanistan and expected the whole-hearted support of the international community. In our view such assistance would make the Afghan parties realize the benefits of peace.

The Russian ambassador was surprisingly positive. He expressed full understanding of our decision and expressed the view that the developments in Afghanistan could turn out "to be a blessing in disguise". He said that his country could live with a Taliban-dominated Afghanistan provided they did not destabilize the neighbouring Central Asian republics. He stated that the Russian deputy foreign minister, Viktor Pasuvaluk, would be in Islamabad on 7 June for talks with me on Afghanistan during which he hoped to be able to meet Mulla Ghaus.

Similarly, the Iranian ambassador's reaction was also one of understanding. He stated that Pakistan and Iran should coordinate closely on Afghanistan. He said that foreign minister Velayati had extended an invitation to Gohar Ayub Khan to visit Tehran from 31 May to 1 June and that this would provide yet another valuable opportunity to discuss Afghanistan and bilateral relations at a high level.

The US chargé d'affaires simply noted our decision and asked whether the Taliban would moderate some of their policies in the future. I told him that the way to bring about moderation was to engage with them as had been stated by assistant secretary of state Robin Raphel during the UN conference on Afghanistan in November 1996.

The Saudi ambassador expressed understanding and said that he would revert to us after consulting his government. Saudi Arabia was to follow our lead by also recognizing the Taliban. The Turkish ambassador took copious notes on what I had to say and cryptically remarked "we wish you the best of luck". The Kazakh ambassador and the Uzbek chargé d'affaires did not express any opinion. The Uzbek chargé d'affaires welcomed the consultations that Aziz Khan and I would be having in Tashkent with foreign minister Abdulaziz Kamilov in a few weeks. The Chinese chargé d'affaires, while expressing understanding of our decision was non-committal. He said that he would get back to me after informing his government.

As I had not been able to brief the ambassador of Turkmenistan, a meeting was arranged between Tariq Osman Hyder and the country's president, Saparmyrat Niyazov, on 26 May. Prior to the meeting, Shikhmuradov—the Turkmen foreign minister who resembled the film star Walter Matthau and who fell out with Niyazov in 2000 to join the Turkmen opposition—told Hyder that Kazakh foreign minister Kasymzhomar Tokayev had proposed an emergency special session of the Commonwealth of Independent States to discuss the events in Afghanistan. President Askar Akayev of Kyrgyzstan, who was overthrown in March 2005 through a popular uprising known as the 'Tulip Revolution,' had supported this idea and had requested Russian assistance for the Central Asian states. Moscow had responded that it would send three special battalions to Kyrgyzstan despite its distance from Afghanistan. Russia was also consulting closely with Uzbekistan on the rapidly changing Afghan situation. When Hyder asked whether Ashgabat would recognize the Taliban, Shikhmuradov responded that, in principle, President Niyazov was in favour but did not want to be amongst the very first to take such a step in order to avoid criticism from Russia and the other Central Asian republics.

Niyazov, or "Turkmenbashi" as he styles himself, is a flamboyant head of state with absolute powers whose picture adorns all offices both in the government as well as in the private sector. The problem is that he changes the colour of his hair every now and then necessitating a massive national effort to replace the photographs on display. During their meeting, Niyazov told Amabssador Hyder that developments in Afghanistan had moved in the right direction. Without a strong central authority in Kabul the turmoil would continue. Dostum had destroyed himself through his internal intrigues despite massive Russian and Uzbek material support. His own people were miserable. He had been betrayed by his closest associate which demonstrated that he lacked the capacity to lead. Niyazov disclosed that he had warned Turkey's president, Suleyman Demirel, during the Economic Cooperation Organization summit held earlier in Ashgabat that Turkey had made a mistake in supporting Dostum alone. Demirel had simply replied that his country had no other option but to support a Turkic leader.

Niyazov said that a visiting Russian minister had told him that a high-level meeting would be held in Moscow under the chairmanship of Prime Minister Viktor Chernomyrdin to evolve a Russian response to the advance of the Taliban north of the Hindu Kush. Niyazov claimed to have told him that the Russian government should desist from painting an unrealistic picture of a security threat to the Central Asian republics from the Taliban. Turkmenistan's considered opinion was that there was no such threat and, as such, a process should be initiated through the UN for the recognition of the Taliban, who controlled 90 percent of Afghan territory.

Niyazov felt that Russia was playing the Taliban card for its own interests. It had yet to reconcile itself to its diminished stature in the world and wanted to retain its influence in the Central Asian republics. That was the reason for Moscow's unneeded presence in Tajikistan. It had a strategic interest in keeping alive the non-existent threat from a Taliban-dominated Afghanistan.

Niyazov then said that Turkmenistan fully understood and respected the position adopted by Pakistan and its recognition of the Taliban the previous day. This was in Islamabad's security interest. Turkmenistan, because of its policy of neutrality, was in a delicate position. It could not be among the first to recognize the Taliban. However, Ashgabat would lobby for recognition of the Taliban, particularly through the UN, and in ten or fifteen days the process would undoubtedly yield results. The Turkmen consulates General in Mazar-e-Sharif and Herat would continue to function as usual. He said that he needed a week for consultations before finalizing Turkmenistan's position on the recognition issue. The establishment of Taliban control over most of Afghanistan, he felt, would accelerate the gas pipeline project from Turkmenistan, through Afghanistan and onto Pakistan.

Our decision to recognize the Taliban had put our future initiatives on Afghanistan in a completely different perspective. In the past we had repeatedly, and with all sincerity, called for the establishment of a broad-based government through an intra-Afghan peace process. Our recognition of the Taliban therefore implied that a broad-based government was emerging but not through an intra-Afghan dialogue as we had envisaged but through a change of loyalties in keeping with the traditional internal dynamics of power in Afghanistan.

The support that the Taliban had received from the disparate ethnic groups implied the supremacy of nationalistic impulses over centrifugal tendencies based on ethnic diversity. The territorial integrity of the country had been ensured which, we thought, would gather further strength as cooperation between the Taliban and the others increased.

Our assessment was that as the new broad-based entity that was emerging demonstrated its staying power, other countries would also extend recognition to the government in Kabul. Within days it became clear that this assumption was wishful thinking.

Rout of the Taliban in Mazar-e-Sharif

Aziz Khan, accompanied by consul general Ayaz Wazir, a few consulate officials and a team of journalists, both foreign as well as Pakistani, left for Mazar-e-Sharif on 26 May aboard a special aircraft. The purpose was to reopen the consulate general and to assess the situation. The plane touched down at 11am. The delegation was received warmly at the airport and escorted to the consulate. From there Aziz and Ayaz were taken to General Malik's office which was located in a small building that functioned both as the local foreign ministry as well as a guest house. The place was surrounded by Malik's bodyguards which was an indicator that matters were not as they should have been. For all his efforts which had resulted in the ouster of Dostum and the Taliban control of the north after a nine-month stalemate, Malik had been offered the post of deputy foreign minister. He was disappointed and bitter.

Malik, nevertheless, greeted Aziz and Ayaz warmly in the presence of media representatives form the BBC, VOA, APP and others. Just as the officials were about to be seated, a typical tribal mullah with a bushy beard walked into the room. He did not bother to introduce himself or greet the guests. This was none other than Mulla Abdul Razzaq whom the Taliban had appointed as leader of the north.

Ayaz Wazir walked over to him, shook hands and introduced himself as the new consul general of Pakistan in Mazar-e-Sharif. Razzaq did not reciprocate the greeting and instead stormed out of the room yelling that the Taliban had come to Mazar-e-Sharif for serious business but Malik only wanted to project himself through the media. He stared menacingly at the cameras which the journalists were carrying and screamed that taking of photographs was un-Islamic. To avoid further public scenes,

Aziz requested the pressmen to leave quickly. For his part, Ayaz ran after Razzaq to bring him back as the break-up of the meeting in this manner would have been disastrous. Razzaq had already got into the vehicle waiting for him. Ayaz shouted after him requesting him to listen to what he had to say if only for a minute. Razzaq did not respond. Ayaz implored him again and this time it worked because he invoked Pushtun traditions under which it is incumbent to listen to what a visitor, particularly a fellow Pushtun, has to say. Razzaq came out of his jeep and walked back to the meeting venue with Ayaz. The latter took care to speak to Razzaq in Kandahari Pushtu, which softened him further.

After the talks, during which nothing substantive was discussed, Malik hosted a lunch which was attended by about fifty people. Twelve of the guests were seated at the table while the rest sat on the floor in accordance with Afghan traditions. Razzaq was at the head of the table, flanked by Aziz to his right and Malik to the left. There was initially a pin-drop silence which further increased the tension. Razzaq then asked Ayaz Wazir which tribe he belonged to. Ayaz replied that, as his name implied, he was a Waziri. Razzaq suddenly turned to Aziz and asked when Islam would be enforced in Pakistan. Aziz was taken aback and nudged Ayaz, who was seated next to him, to tackle the situation. As a tribesman himself, Ayaz decided to handle the rude and abrasive Razzaq in a typical tribal way. He jokingly reminded Razzaq that Afghanistan had emerged in 1747 but it had taken the Taliban two hundred and fifty years to introduce their version of Islam and, if Pakistan followed the Afghan example, its people would have to wait for another two hundred years since the country had achieved its independence only fifty years ago. The guests burst into laughter. This gave Aziz pause to recollect himself and he curtly told Razzaq that Pakistan was already an Islamic republic and this had been incorporated into its constitution.

In order to reduce the tension further, Ayaz asked Razzaq his age, to which the latter responded that he was thirty-two. Ayaz then said that had he grown a beard, as Razzaq had done, then more than half of it would have been grey as he was almost fifty. He was, therefore, much older than Razzaq and, in accordance with Pushtun traditions, younger persons need the permission of elders before they speak. Razzaq should, therefore, behave himself and ask permission before he said anything. There was more laughter. By this time Razzaq was completely deflated but Ayaz, true to his tribal instincts, did not leave matters at that. Sensing that the other Afghans were on his side, he reminded the baffled Razzaq that a little while earlier he (Razzaq) had objected to the presence of the print and electronic media. When Razzaq nodded, Ayaz informed him that even the grand mufti of Saudi Arabia had allowed the taking of photographs for passports, visas and other essential documents. Razzaq acknowledged this but tried in vain to explain his behaviour through faulty religious arguments and then kept quiet for the rest of the meal. This, rather amusing, conversation demonstrated that despite the changes that Afghanistan had undergone in the past several years, it had never really moved away from "Pakhtunwali", or the code of the Pushtuns, one of the central planks of which is respect for elders.

After lunch, Aziz and Ayaz took leave of Malik assuring him that they would work closely together in the days ahead. At this point, Malik whispered to Aziz that he wanted to meet him separately. The meeting took place later in the afternoon during which Malik said that some days earlier he had concluded an agreement with the Taliban the stipulations of which were: joint operations against the opposition (i.e. Dostum elements); formation of a military council with the Taliban in the north; non-interference by the Taliban in the Jumbish-controlled north until the formation of a central government after elections in the whole country (the procedure would be in accordance with the sharia); and the establishment of a political commission which would decide on the composition of the central government on the basis of proportionate representation.

By appointing Razzaq in charge of the north, the Taliban had derailed the agreement. Malik complained that after all that he had done to help the Taliban, they had made him deputy foreign minister instead of entrusting him with the responsibility of administering the north. He said that the Taliban were trying to impose their culture and their version of Islam on the north which would never be acceptable to the other ethnic groups. He warned that if the Taliban did not modify their policies quickly, violence and unparalleled bloodshed would erupt. He appealed to Pakistan to use its influence with the Taliban in the interest of peace and security in Afghanistan. Aziz told him that Pakistan's only objective in Afghanistan was the restoration of sustainable peace and stability in that country and it would use whatever limited influence it had to persuade the Taliban to honour the agreement with Malik.

After this meeting, Aziz proceeded straight to the consulate general, took a round of the building and had a cup of tea before giving an interview to the foreign media on the sprawling lawns of the consulate. He then flew back to Islamabad leaving Ayaz Wazir and the consulate staff in Mazar-e-Sharif. He came straight to my office to say that the situation was explosive. The Taliban had misbehaved and a severe backlash was inevitable. What was worse was that the people in the north were blaming Pakistan for imposing the Taliban on them.

When Malik saw that he could no longer control the situation, he telephoned the Taliban ambassador in Islamabad to ask Kandahar to send peace emissaries to defuse the situation. A small group of mediators which included foreign minister Ghaus and Ehsanullah, the governor of the Afghan Central Bank, were accordingly sent to Mazar-e-Sharif.

On the morning of 27 May, Ayaz received a message from General Malik requesting for an urgent meeting. He rushed to Malik's office and on the way noted that heavily armed Taliban and Malik's Uzbek militia literally seemed to be waiting for a signal to begin hostilities. On entering Malik's office building he was alarmed to see about thirty Taliban elders led by Mulla Ghaus in one room and an equal number of Malik supporters in another. This was a clear indication that the simmering tensions in the north had further exacerbated and could erupt into violence. Ayaz was escorted to Malik's office and found him to be extremely agitated.

Malik went straight to the point and requested Ayaz to convince Mulla Ghaus to honour their earlier agreement. The Taliban had also started disarming the people of the north which was resented by them. Razzaq had left no doubt in their minds, if any now existed, that they would be under Taliban tutelage just as the minority ethnic groups had been dominated by the Pushtuns through Afghanistan's tragic history.

Malik said that the Taliban should stay out of the city and leave the administration to him. He would do exactly as they wanted. As if to prove this point, he stated that after declaring his allegiance to the Taliban he had closed girls schools and colleges and was even growing a beard. The Taliban, he said, might have succeeded in disarming the people from Kandahar to Kabul but these were their fellow Pushtuns. The ethnic Uzbeks, however, would never surrender their weapons to the Taliban nor would they rely on the Pushtuns for protection. He implored Ayaz in a typical Pushtun way by touching his chin (Malik's mother was Pushtun) to convince Mulla Ghaus not to insist on running the administration and disarming the Uzbeks. By the time Ayaz came out of Malik's office it was time for the mid-day prayer. He saw a group of people gathering for the service in the adjacent room and joined them. However, he noticed that not a single Uzbek was in the congregation. They prayed separately although they belonged to the same Sunni sect as the Taliban. This demonstrated the extent of hatred between the two groups as Islamic prayer is not only an act of worship but also symbolizes fraternity, unity and the absolute equality of all believers before God. It is unthinkable that people assembled in the same building should pray in separate congregations.

After prayers Ayaz told Ghaus that the tension in the north had heightened and even a small incident could ignite conflict. A wrong decision on the part of the Taliban would cost them dearly. As an important leader who was also foreign minister, he (Ghaus) could salvage the situation by taking the Taliban out of the city and letting Malik run the administration in accordance with the written agreement between them. Furthermore, Mazar-e-Sharif was encircled by the Taliban and it was impossible for Malik to do anything against their interests. Ayaz also pleaded that Malik and his followers should not be disarmed.

Ghaus brushed this aside and pontificated that all Afghans were equal fellow Muslims and brothers. They could not be treated differently on the basis of ethnicity. Islam did not believe in such divisions. Ayaz reminded him that during the prayers the ethnic Uzbeks and the Taliban had prayed separately and this was proof enough, if any were required, of the depth of hatred and disunity between the Pushtuns and the people of the north. Ghaus would have none of this and insisted that he was in the right. There could be no compromise and Malik's requests were summarily rejected. The pieces were, therefore, in place for the impending disaster.

After informing Malik about his futile efforts to persuade the Taliban to be reasonable, Ayaz left for the consulate which was some five minutes driving distance from Malik's office. He told me later that this was the longest drive of his life. Those five minutes seemed like the whole day. The hatred in the eyes of the local Uzbeks as they saw the consul general's vehicle with the Pakistan flag was unforgettable. So intense was their anger that Ayaz thought that he would be killed there and then. He heaved a sigh of relief on reaching the consulate.

An hour after Ayaz arrived at the consulate at around 4pm there was a sudden burst of Kalashnikov fire interspersed by the sound of rocket launchers. It was uncertain who was fighting whom. All consulate personnel had gathered within the premises and the gates were immediately closed. They felt that they would be the first and most obvious targets. Fortunately the telephone lines were still working and the officials were able to establish contact with some of their local friends. The initial reports were that the fighting, which the Taliban had tried to quell, was between two groups of the Hizb-e-Wahdat. As evening fell, the firing increased in intensity. The most plausible explanation, at the time, for the fighting was that Malik's bodyguards had resisted the Taliban attempt to disarm them.

Later at night, Ayaz received a telephone call from a person who professed to be Mulla Ehsanullah, the Taliban State Bank Governor. The latter asked him to convey a message to Kandahar not to send more troops through the Salang Pass area. Ayaz had seen Ehsanullah briefly but had never spoken to him and was, therefore, unable to recognize his voice and, as such, was not sure whether the person at the other end was really Ehsanullah. This could have been a ruse by the Jumbish or the Hizb-e-Wahdat to implicate the consulate personnel for siding with the Taliban. Ayaz, wisely, did not respond. At all events, contact with Kandahar under the circumstances would not have been possible.

The fighting continued through the next day and our immediate concern was the safety of the consulate officials. I spoke to them every half hour. Ayaz told me that they could see dead bodies in front of the consulate and all officials were now sleeping in the basement.

Another version of how the fighting broke out was that in the early hours of 27 May, elements of the Hizb-e-Wahdat fired on the grave of the slain Shia leader, Ali Mazari, so that the impression among their own community would be that the Taliban had carried out this act. The immediate consequence was a fierce Hizb-e-Wahdat attack on the Taliban. During the course of my several telephone conversations with Ayaz Wazir, I was told that there was a rumour that Mulla Razzaq and Malik had again joined forces and were planning a combined operation against the Hizb-e-Wahdat. This later proved totally incorrect.

The foremost problem for us at this point in time was the evacuation of the consulate personnel. All flights to Mazar-e-Sharif had been suspended because of the heavy fighting. The only way to get our people out of Afghanistan was a perilous two-hour road journey north to the border town of Hairatan and then into Tirmiz in Uzbekistan from where they would be picked up by an aircraft sent from Islamabad. For the journey to Hairatan they would require an armed escort which only Malik could provide.

The firing tapered off by about 8pm on 28 May. The silence of the night was, however, constantly broken by the sound of heavy guns. On the morning of 29 May a local employee of the consulate brought the news that the Taliban had been killed by the thousands and their bodies were scattered all over the city. Most of them were unarmed pilgrims who had come to Mazar-e-Sharif when the city was taken by Malik and the Taliban, to pray at what they believed to be the tomb of Ali, the fourth Caliph of Islam. The city was completely new to them and they did not know where to take shelter or in which direction to run for safety when the fighting started.

At around 10am the consulate's security guard came running to Ayaz to say that General Fauzi, Malik's military commander, was waiting outside and wanted to talk to him. The consulate officials felt that this was the end and if Fuazi entered the premises with his men they would all be killed. However, there was no option. If Fuazi was not allowed in he would attack the building. The consulate officials had a few Kalashnikovs which they loaded and then stationed themselves at the windows of the first floor which overlooked the front yard. Ayaz slipped a pistol into his pocket and with his finger on the trigger walked to the gate to meet Fauzi. He was mentally prepared for the worst.

Fauzi, however, entered the consulate premises without his men, to the relief of the Pakistani officials. The purpose of the visit was to ask whether Ayaz knew anything about Mulla Ghaus who was missing—he was seen by some people in a pick-up heading towards Kabul. Ayaz responded that he knew nothing. The last time that he had met Ghaus was in Malik's office on 27 May. Ayaz enquired about Mulla Razzaq and was told by Fauzi that he was in "safe custody". There was suddenly a huge bomb blast about a hundred yards away followed by heavy firing. Everyone, including Fauzi, ran for shelter. When the fighting died down, Fauzi left. Ayaz and the other consulate personnel told me later that the probable purpose of Fauzi's visit was to kill them all on the pretext that they were sheltering Ghaus. It was the bomb blast and the subsequent firing that had saved them because Fauzi believed that Taliban remnants were nearby and that Ghaus was in the consulate.

In the evening the fighting stopped and Malik phoned Ayaz to come to his house. Ayaz said that it would not be possible for him to leave the consulate without proper security arrangements. Malik, therefore, sent his air force chief who escorted Ayaz to his residence. Malik told Ayaz Wazir that the violence had started after a fatwa was declared by the religious leaders of the north declaring a jihad against the Taliban for reneging on the agreement that had been signed earlier. Furthermore, the overbearing and intrusive attitude of Mulla Razzaq had made any form of cooperation impossible and had resulted in the fatwa. Malik then asked Ayaz to convey a message through Islamabad to the authorities in Kandahar and Kabul that he was still ready to work with the Taliban provided they honoured the agreement they had signed with him. He offered the use of his aircraft for this purpose.

Ayaz thanked him but politely declined the offer of the plane. He told Malik that the Pakistan government would send an aircraft to Tirmiz to take him and the consulate officials to Islamabad. All that was required of Malik was an armed escort to take them to the border town of Hairatan from where they would cross into Uzbekistan. Malik agreed, but on condition that Ayaz should travel alone. The sudden departure of the entire consulate would send the wrong signals to his supporters. Ayaz refused to leave his staff behind and Malik finally decided to allow all the personnel to leave together on condition that they would return soon. The presence of the Pakistani consulate officials was vital to his own credibility.

Fierce fighting again resumed on 30 May. Ayaz and his team set out for Hairatan at around noon. Malik kept his promise and provided the armed escort. I was now completely out of touch with them and would only know whether they were still alive if they succeeded in crossing the infamous "Friendship Bridge" over the Amu River into Tirmiz. The Pakistan embassy in Tashkent sent an official to Tirmiz to facilitate the entry of our personnel into Uzbekistan.

That evening I received a call from Ayaz Wazir only to be told that they had to make the hazardous journey back to Mazar-e-Sharif because the Uzbek border officials had not received authorization from Tashkent to allow their entry into Uzbek territory. A second attempt would be made to leave Afghanistan the following day. I gave a piece of my mind, without mincing words, to the Uzbek ambassador in Islamabad and also asked our ambassador in Tashkent to make a strong demarche to the local foreign office. Luckily, the second attempt succeeded and our personnel reached Islamabad safely on the evening of 31 May. They had undergone tremendous pressure and had witnessed the execution of a thief who had stolen the camera of a BBC correspondent that day en route to Hairatan.

The silver lining to this otherwise bleak situation was that Malik was still willing to cooperate with the Taliban if they abided by their undertaking not to interfere in the north. We were also able to confirm that Mulla Razzaq, as had been conveyed to Ayaz by General Fauzi, had been arrested by Malik. The whereabouts of Mulla Ghaus and his team of mediators remained a mystery. A disturbing report that we received was that they were attempting to leave Mazar-e-Sharif when the fighting erupted and had mistakenly driven to the area of the city controlled by the Hizb-e-Wahdat and had been killed. Another unconfirmed report was that they had been captured by Malik.

In this period, the United Arab Emirates and Saudi Arabia had joined Pakistan in extending recognition to the Taliban. By 31 May, the ground situation in the north remained fluid. Malik had been able to regain sole control of the provinces of Faryab, Jowzjan, Sar-e-Pul, Balkh and Samangan, inflicting considerable losses on the Taliban. Ahmed Shah Masood also took the opportunity to launch attacks against Charikar, Baghram, Jablus Siraj and Pul-e-Khumri, near the Salang highway, but was repulsed by the Taliban.

In the next few days Mazar-e-Sharif would witness carnage unparalleled in its barbarity. The Taliban as well as the innocent pilgrims who had come from the south were massacred. About seven thousand were taken prisoner by Malik and a few days later they were slaughtered and thrown into mass graves. UN investigators and forensic experts confirmed several months later that most of them had their hands tied behind their backs and were machine-gunned down. There was not a whimper of protest from international human rights activists who, it seemed, were only concerned about highlighting the many and unpardonable acts of cruelty perpetrated by the Taliban and, in particular, by their religious police.

In time the Taliban were pushed back south of the Hindu Kush although some of their fighters continued to maintain a presence around Mazar-e-Sharif. The ground situation in Afghanistan reverted to what it was after 27 September 1996 with the Taliban in control of 75 percent of Afghan territory and the balance under the opposition. Dostum, the so-called strongman of the north, had been ousted by his own deputy, Malik. The latter was just not strong enough to control the situation in the north and came increasingly under the influence of the Jamiat-e-Islami and in particular of Ahmed Shah Masood.

Pakistan, which had extended recognition to the Taliban in the mistaken belief that they would be able to get the rival factions on board, was severely criticized both at home and abroad. However, I have always felt that the criticism was for the wrong reason. Pakistan, I believe, was at fault for not recognizing the Taliban much earlier, especially as they had demonstrated their staying power after capturing Kabul. We had violated our traditional Afghan policy of recognizing and dealing with any entity that controlled Kabul. Yet we waited nine months before extending recognition to the Taliban. We kept insisting that they should get the power-hungry factions, and not representatives of other ethnic groups, to join them. We had forgotten, or deliberately ignored, that unlike other Afghan governments of the past, non-Pushtuns already held important government positions in the movement. Aziz's meeting with the Tajik deputy governor of Gardez on his return to Pakistan after his first visit to Kabul was just one example. We had turned a blind eye to the reality that several non-Pushtuns had been made governors of Pushtun provinces, that some of the ministers of the Taliban government belonged to the minority ethnic groups and that ideology and not ethnicity was the driving force behind the Taliban movement. In effect what Pakistan was insisting on was that the Taliban should include the warring factions as against the minority groups in their dispensation. None other than the leaders of these factions were entirely to blame for the civil war in the country after the Soviet-installed Najibullah regime had been toppled.

For their part, the Taliban were not willing to do business with the leaders of the factions until the latter surrendered their weapons and repented the misery they had brought to the people of Afghanistan. Some months later, Mulla Omar reminded me that the factional leaders had not only destroyed but also looted the country. How else, he asked, could Dostum, an obscure worker in a gas-field near Shibberghan, have become the owner of the Balkh airline besides possessing several palaces? How did Ahmed Shah Masood acquire the ownership of the Pamir airline? Where had Professor Sayyaf got all his wealth from? Haji Qadeer and his brothers—including Abdul Haq who was killed by the Taliban when he entered Afghanistan to incite a tribal rebellion against them after the US bombing against Taliban and Al Qaida targets started on 8 October 2001—had become owners of shopping malls abroad. Who had financed them? All of these leaders, according to Omar, were accountable to the people of Afghanistan.

With this background, Pakistan should have realized that the Taliban would never agree to share power with those whom they considered responsible for the tragedy of Afghanistan. They were willing to include other ethnic groups in their government but not the leaders of the factions. Had Pakistan extended recognition and provided some economic assistance to the Taliban soon after the latter took Kabul, it would have been able to develop influence and leverage over them.

Our unceasing efforts to persuade Kandahar to move towards a political settlement meant nothing to Mulla Omar. The Taliban did not owe Pakistan anything. Contrary to the propaganda that was churned out by some countries, Pakistan did not provide any military assistance to the Taliban. There were no Pakistani soldiers directing the military operations. There were no ISI personnel anywhere in Afghanistan advising the Taliban. Not a single bullet went into Afghanistan from Pakistan. The country was already saturated with weapons left over from the period of Soviet occupation and it was the flow of these from Afghanistan to Pakistan and not vice versa that was to become problematic for us. The Taliban were an indigenous movement and their success had little to do with their military prowess, as the US assistant secretary of state, Robin Raphel, had informed the UN in November 1996. Moderation would have been brought to some of their policies had the world engaged with them as she had advised. However, the international community chose instead to isolate them and this brought only suffering to the Afghan people.

The ill-advised decision of the Benazir Bhutto government to send the trade caravan through southern Afghanistan in September 1994, without the permission of the Rabbani regime which we recognized, and her interior minister's foolish reference to the Taliban as "our boys" convinced many countries, in particular Iran and Russia, that the Taliban were indeed created, nurtured and supported by Pakistan with the help of Saudi Arabia and the United States. The reaction of both Tehran and Moscow to the events of May-June 1997 was indicative not only of their main objectives in Afghanistan but also showed how the Afghan tragedy was likely to unfold because of their interference in the next five years.

Iran's reaction to the fall of Mazar-e-Sharif

The capture of Mazar-e-Sharif by the Taliban in May 1997 came at a time when Iran was preoccupied with presidential elections. The authorities in Tehran were literally caught unawares and their immediate reaction was muted. On 25 May, the day when Pakistan announced its recognition of the Taliban, the spokesman of the Iranian foreign office reiterated the standard line that there was no military solution to the Afghan crisis and those who presumed that they could settle the "Afghan plight" through intervention (the reference to Pakistan was obvious) were committing a mistake. The only way to resolve the Afghan problem was through the establishment of a government comprising the representatives of "different factions".

President Hashemi Rafsanjani expressed similar concern during an interview to international and Iranian correspondents over "the way Afghanistan's affairs were being currently handled". He emphasized that Iran had always pursued a policy of non-interference in the internal affairs of other countries and affirmed that any attempt to impose a military settlement in Afghanistan was a mistake.

Recognition of the Taliban

To questions about Iran's recognition of the Taliban now that they had taken Mazar-e-Sharif and controlled most of the country, Rafsanjani replied that it was Tehran's consistent policy to follow the UN insofar as recognizing a government was concerned. Till then the Rabbani regime was represented in the world body and Iran, he added, would "await future developments".

The reaction in the Iranian media, reflecting the government position, was interesting inasmuch as the primary concerns spelled out were the protection of Shias in Afghanistan, American ingress into the region and oil and gas pipelines to and from Central Asia. The commentary in the *Iran News* of 26 May, entitled "Fall of Mazar-e-Sharif sets Alarm Bell Ringing", emphasized the need for the Iranian government to draw the attention of the international organizations to the security of the Shia minority community in the Hazarajat and Bamyan regions in order to protect them from "religious bias". The newspaper also asked the Iranian government to take all measures for the safety and security of the Iranian border with Afghanistan.

Iran News maintained that "the latest military and political adventurism" of the Taliban was for the economic and political objectives of other countries, the focal point being UNOCAL plans to export natural gas from Turkmenistan to the Asian and European markets via Karachi. It asserted that the US objective was to block Iran's entry to the lucrative Asian markets. The paper alleged that the defections from Dostum's forces were the result of "immense bribery" by the Taliban and that "monetary and weaponry cards" were used by the US through UNOCAL and Saudi Arabia with the help of "certain influential factions" in Pakistan to ensure a Taliban victory. The Iranian daily, *Jamhouri Islami*, in its usual vein, repeated the allegation that the US, Saudi Arabia and Pakistan were the main supporters of the Taliban. It raised the spectre that the Shias of Afghanistan would be liquidated by the Taliban "at their leisure".

The Iranian media also gave prominent coverage, but without immediate comment, to Pakistan's recognition of the Taliban. It was apparent that: (a) the developments in northern Afghanistan had been too sudden and come at an odd time for the Iranians; (b) the initial reaction in Tehran was subdued and measured inasmuch as there was no excessively harsh language either against Pakistan or the Taliban; (c) Rafsanjani's comments indicated that Tehran could come to terms with having to deal with the Taliban; and (d) Iran was evaluating the situation and its actual policy would emerge when the ground situation stabilized.

An Islamic Republic News Agency (IRNA) report of 26 May quoted deputy foreign minister Alaeddin Broujerdi as saying that only a broad-based government was the solution to the ongoing conflict in Afghanistan. If the different ethnic groups in that country were ignored it would only alter the features of the crisis but not resolve it. He reaffirmed that any development inside Afghanistan was its internal affair, and stated that Iran would continue its policy of helping achieve peace in Afghanistan by forging understanding among all the warring factions and providing humanitarian assistance. Tehran was closely monitoring the ground events and would oppose any elements that endanger the security of the region. Broujerdi's comments were undoubtedly moderate and indicated a reluctant acceptance of the altered ground realities.

Meanwhile, the Iranian press carried agency reports that Russia and the Central Asian countries were alarmed at the "ascent of Taliban fundamentalism" and had placed their border security forces, particularly the Russian troops in Tajikistan, on alert. The local media in Iran was, in fact, more engrossed in the crisis arising from the Turkish military action against the Kurdish PKK (Kurdistan Workers' Party) in Iraq. All newspapers carried the report that the Turkish chargé d'affaires in Tehran had been summoned to the foreign ministry to receive an official protest. Most of the editorials were highly critical of Turkey and there was little or no comment about the events in Afghanistan.

However, after the Taliban rout in Mazar-e-Sharif, the statements of the Iranian government and the media became more strident. Pakistan's ambassador in Tehran, Khalid Mahmood, was hurriedly called to the Iranian foreign office on 2 June and told by Director General Mir Mahmood Musavi that about two hours earlier the Taliban had summoned the Iranian chargé d'affaires and handed over a *note verbale* demanding the closure of the embassy in Kabul and the withdrawal of all diplomats within forty-eight hours. The embassy was accused of anti-Taliban activities, details of which would be revealed, according to Musavi, only after the text of the note verbale had been received. He added that Iran knew what was going on in Afghanistan. Despite Pakistan's declaratory policy that it was not supporting the Taliban in "the intra-Afghan fighting," Tehran had "its own views". It was clear "from the beginning" that the Taliban were carrying out their activities against other Afghan groups with the support of "some sources in Pakistan". Iran had always been a good friend of Pakistan in words and deeds. There had been differences between the two countries but these had never created serious problems. However, all that had changed. Pakistan's support to the Taliban was creating "problems and difficulties for Iran's security and its interests in the region".

Against this background, Iran had the right to expect Pakistan to change its policy of support to the Taliban and to immediately contact the latter to reverse their decision on the closure of the Iranian embassy. Mahmood was asked to convey the Taliban response to the Iranian foreign office within twenty-four hours. Musavi, who claimed to be speaking on behalf of foreign minister Velayati, repeated the standard Iranian propaganda line that "Pakistan is the creator and supporter of the Taliban" and wielded enough influence with them. He recalled the reference to the Taliban as "our boys" by "their godfather, who was none other than the interior minister of Pakistan in the Benazir Bhutto government".

Mahmood did not allow himself to be provoked by these wild accusations and coldly asked whether there had been any incident that could have precipitated the closure of the Iranian embassy. Musavi, who was not sophisticated enough to understand the implication of this loaded question, admitted that there had been demonstrations in Dasht Borji, the Shia quarters of Kabul, which the Taliban had quelled. This had resulted in the deaths of twelve Shias and the arrests of many more.

I called the Afghan ambassador to the foreign office on 3 June and conveyed the gist of the Iranian demarche to him. I tried to make him understand that Iran was a major regional country and it was important to keep the channels of communications open with them. The ambassador replied that he would convey Tehran's message to Kabul. However, he continued, there was incontrovertible evidence that the Iranian embassy in Kabul had for a long time been indulging in subversive activities against the Taliban. For instance, the recent trouble in Dasht Borji had been instigated by Tehran. The Taliban, therefore, had no alternative but to close down the Iranian embassy temporarily. As and when conditions improved, Kabul would consider allowing Tehran to re-establish its diplomatic presence in the Afghan capital. As if to prove the point that the Taliban had not severed all connections with Tehran, the ambassador added that the Iranian consulate in Herat had not been closed down.

This was immediately conveyed to the Iranian ambassador in Islamabad who requested our cooperation in the evacuation of three Iranian embassy personnel still in Kabul. He also asked Pakistan to look after Iranian interests in the Afghan capital. I assured him of our maximum help in the evacuation but, as for looking after Iranian interests, I reminded him that we had a very thin presence in Kabul. After our own evacuation from Mazar-e-Sharif, the consulate general was being looked after by locally recruited staff and perhaps Iran could make similar arrangements in Kabul. Furthermore, under the Vienna Convention on Diplomatic Relations, the concurrence of the receiving state would be required to enable us to look after Iran's interest in Afghanistan.

On 2 June, the Iranian foreign minister, Ali Akbar Velayati, wrote to the UN secretary general to draw his attention to the "bleak situation in Afghanistan". The Iranian foreign minister called for immediate "political intervention" by the UN, including "exertion of pressures on the warring factions and their foreign supporters to prepare the ground for national conciliation and lasting peace in Afghanistan". He observed that the recent "operations by certain armed groups in the relatively calm northern Afghanistan" were indicative of "war-mongering and monopolization of power" which were aimed at depriving a substantial part of the Afghan population from participation in national politics and power sharing. He emphasized that there was no military solution to the Afghan problem and reiterated the need for the establishment of a broad-based government. Velayati also wrote that the "continuation of foreign intervention and support to intransigent factions" involved great perils and would lead to the further expansion of the crisis and aggravate the human tragedy. He reaffirmed Iran's support to the UN endeavours in Afghanistan. A similar letter was addressed to the Organization of the Islamic Conference secretary general, Ezzedin Laraki.

In separate telephone conversations, Velayati discussed the Afghanistan situation with Prime Minister Inder Kumar Gujral of India and the foreign ministers of Turkmenistan, Kazakhstan and Kyrgyzstan. He drew their attention to foreign intervention in Afghanistan and urged them to extend humanitarian assistance to northern Afghanistan.

The phone call to Gujral was intended as a warning to Pakistan that unless it reversed its Afghanistan policy, Iran would be compelled to ask India to play an active role in the settlement of the Afghan conflict. According to the Iranian media, Velayati and Gujral took note of the negative fallout of the Afghanistan crisis for regional security. They agreed that there was no military solution to the Afghan issue, that foreign interference would further complicate the situation, and that the long standing conflict could only be resolved through negotiations between the Afghan parties and ethnic groups.

Meanwhile, the Iranian permanent representative to the UN in New York, during an interview with IRNA, urged that "the mediating countries" should take into account the interest and future of the Afghan people instead of promoting their own strategic and economic interests. He described the decision of Pakistan, Saudi Arabia and the United Arab Emirates to recognize the Taliban as "hasty".

In a new development, Gulbadin Hikmatyar, who had been living in Tehran since his positions were overrun by the Taliban in 1996, met the Iranian intelligence chief Ali Fallahian to review the latest developments. During the struggle to oust the Soviet-installed Najibullah regime, Hikmatyar considered Iran his foremost enemy after Russia while Tehran despised him because of his contempt for the Afghan Shias. However, realpolitik had its own compulsions and Hikmatyar and his new-found Iranian friends decided to set aside their past differences and unite in a common endeavour to get rid of the Taliban. This was no more than an alliance of convenience. In February 2002, barely two months after the Taliban had been replaced by Hamid Karzai's interim administration, the authorities in Tehran asked Hikmatyar to close his offices in Iran and subsequently expelled him.

After his meeting with Fallahian, Hikmatyar criticized Pakistan publicly for the first time in an interview which appeared in the *Iran News* of 3 June. He had refrained from such criticism the previous month despite provocative questions, obviously planted by the Iranian authorities, during a press briefing. He alleged that the new Nawaz Sharif government, which professed neutrality towards the Afghan groups, was helping the Taliban even more than the previous Benazir Bhutto administration. He lashed out at Islamabad for closing down the Hizb-e-Islami's only mouthpiece, the Peshawar-based newspaper *Shahadat*. All this was music to Iranian ears as they believed that Hikmatyar had always been a protegé of Pakistan's military intelligence. Furthermore, he was particularly important for the Iranians at the time because the defeat of a sizeable Taliban contingent under siege in Pul-e-Khumri depended on support form the Hizb-e-Islami.

After it became clear that the Taliban had suffered a severe setback in Mazar-e-Sharif, the subdued comments in the Iranian media were replaced by virulent criticism of Pakistan, Saudi Arabia and the US. The *Iran News* editorial of 31 May, reminded Pakistan what had happened to earlier "foreign stooges" in Afghanistan such as Hafizullah Amin, Taraki, Babrak Karmal and Najibullah before concluding that the fate of the Taliban was not going to be any different as they were also "the most obedient servants of Pakistan, Saudi Arabia and the United States". The advice given to Islamabad was that it should "listen to the voice of reason" and "force the Taliban to sit at the negotiating table along with their compatriots".

In a stinging commentary, the *Jamhouri Islami* of 28 May lamented that the positive statements made by Prime Minister Nawaz Sharif soon after his election victory promising a review of Pakistan's Afghanistan policy had not been carried through. It was alleged that "the Nawaz Sharif government has drawn the sword and wants to exterminate all those opposed to the Taliban and stifle their voices". The Iranian media also gave extensive coverage to the losses sustained by the Taliban with graphic, almost gleeful, accounts of how a large number of them were killed, wounded and captured by the forces of General Malik, the Hizb-e-Wahdat and the "Mujahid Ahmed Shah Masood".

The *Tehran Times* of 31 May repeated much of the same self-serving propaganda. It also expressed the view that the Taliban were routed in the north because the people were urbanized and less susceptible to the fanatic dogma of the Kandaharis than the rural populace of the south. Furthermore, it was all too obvious that the Taliban were controlled by foreigners and supported by the Pakistan army which had not only provided weapons but also personnel who had fought alongside their puppets from the religious seminaries.

By the second week of June, Iranian media comments against Pakistan became increasingly venomous. The bottom line was that the defeat of the Taliban in the north had conclusively demonstrated that no single group could impose itself on the Afghan nation and that the "foreign funded Taliban" should have learnt from their rout in Mazar-e-Sharif that the Afghans, irrespective of their ethnicity, were fiercely independent and would never submit to foreign domination. Editorials claimed that several Pakistani army officers were among the prisoners that had been taken by the "defenders of the north". It was alleged that thousands of religious students, Afghans as well as Pakistanis, had been indoctrinated "to fight the communists" and had left their madrassas for this purpose. However, the only lesson they had learnt from the seminaries in Pakistan was "to slaughter fellow Muslims and distort the image of Islam". The Nawaz Sharif government was described as ineffective and totally under the control of the Pakistan army and the ISI who were funding terror in Afghanistan. Islamabad needed to understand that its policies would destabilize the entire region and if Afghanistan fragmented, the immediate fallout would be on Pakistan itself which was no more than a patchwork of tension-ridden ethnic areas where narrow sectarian and tribal interests could ignite violence unprecedented in its proportions.

This media broadside against Pakistan, with the approval and the encouragement of the Iranian government, continued unabated. Yet not a shred of corroborative evidence was ever produced to prove that the Pakistan military was providing material and personnel support to the Taliban. The army officers said to have been captured by the forces of Malik, Masood and the Hizb-e-Wahdat were never shown on television nor did their photographs ever appear in the print media. Similarly, not a single bullet or weapon from Pakistan was ever shown to the public. All that the Iranian media could do was to persist with unsubstantiated allegations of Pakistan's military support to the Taliban in the Afghan civil war.

When we protested, the foreign office in Tehran expected us to believe that they had no control over the press which, they claimed, was free. We were reminded that there had been no public criticism of Pakistan by the Iranian government and the grievances that Tehran did have against Islamabad were conveyed to us through quiet diplomatic channels.

Thus the occurrences of May 1997 had cast a shadow on Pakistan-Iran relations and the Afghanistan-related differences between the two countries became the main cause of tension until the ouster of the Taliban. Without naming Pakistan, Iranian officials called for the end to "foreign intervention" in Afghanistan. Any doubt as to the nature of this "intervention" was eliminated by the officially prompted media in its diatribe, which reached new heights, against Pakistan. Velayati's telephone call to Gujral and the statement by the Iranian ambassador in New Delhi to the Indian media in mid-June—despite denials to us by the foreign office in Tehran—equating the Taliban to Kashmiri freedom fighters was a clear indicator that Iran would not have any hesitation in undermining Pakistan's core security concerns unless Islamabad revised its perceived policy of support to the Taliban.

The short-lived triumph of the Taliban in Mazar-e-Sharif on 24 May and their ignominious defeat a few days later demonstrated that Iran was ready to make tactical adjustments to its overall Afghan-policy in accordance with the prevailing ground realities. Tehran was willing, albeit reluctantly, to deal with the Taliban so long as the latter, along with General Malik, controlled the north. Its immediate core concern was protecting the interests of the Shia community in Afghanistan and its own security. An altogether new situation emerged when the Taliban's high-handedness ended their alliance with Malik and resulted in disaster for them. The reversals suffered by the Taliban brought great relief to Tehran. A Taliban-controlled Afghanistan would have dealt a major, perhaps irreversible blow, to Iran's strategic, political, economic and sectarian agenda in Afghanistan and beyond. Policy makers in Tehran had never forgotten that Afghanistan was once considered a province by imperial Persia and the dream of a greater Khorasan, which once incorporated within the Persian empire parts of Afghanistan, Tajikistan, Turkmenistan and Uzbekistan, even if it meant the fragmentation of Afghanistan, remained an unstated objective.

The Taliban's advance to the north, howsoever brief, shocked Iran and resulted in a grudging acceptance that the Taliban were a reality and could not be wished away. This necessitated a change in Iran's operational policy. Instead of offensive posturing against "the Taliban rebels" the emphasis became the formation of a broad-based government in which the Dari (Persian)-speaking minorities of the north and, in particular, the Shias would have a disproportionate share. Support for the ethnic minorities of the north, but for altogether different reasons, also constituted Russia's Afghanistan policy and resulted in close coordination between Moscow and Tehran.

Russia's reaction to the events of May 1997

The Taliban capture of Mazar-e-Sharif on 24 May caused deep concern to the Russian government. Though Dostum's ouster had been widely predicted, the speed with which his downfall came startled the Russian leadership. Their first official pronouncement was: "The situation in Afghanistan's provinces adjacent to the CIS southern border has sharply deteriorated. Internal clashes between the various groups and clans of local leaders are taking place. Reports indicate that the armed units of the Taliban movement may take advantage of the situation. This endangers the security of the CIS countries, primarily Uzbekistan and Tajikistan. The Russian leadership declares that if the CIS border is violated, the mechanism of the CIS Collective Security Treaty will immediately be activated. Instructions have already been issued to the corresponding agencies." Though the statement was strongly worded, it precluded CIS action against Afghanistan unless their borders were violated. It also sent a signal to the CIS member countries not to take any unilateral action as this could have serious consequences.

Pakistan's ambassador in Moscow at the time, Mansur Alam, was called to the Russian foreign office by the deputy director of the Third Asia Department, Konstantin Viktorovich Shuvalov, who expressed appreciation that I had informed the Russian ambassador in Islamabad before we announced our recognition of the Taliban. Shuvalov explained that his government was watching the developments in Afghanistan very closely and their assessment was that the situation was still fluid and unclear. Moscow's first reaction was to express concern over the possible threat to the CIS borders. Till then the situation had not worsened but this could change and the Central Asian republics could be confronted with a massive influx of refugees. Russia wanted the Taliban to understand these concerns and act in a responsible manner. The actions of the Taliban would have a bearing on their future relations with the Russian Federation. Shuvalov hoped that Pakistan would bring this to the notice of the Taliban. He was at pains to explain that his government was following a policy of strict neutrality and non-interference and considered the dramatic new developments as Afghanistan's internal affair. The time was not yet opportune for the Russian Federation to take a decision on recognizing the Taliban. Moscow would take all aspects of the radically transformed situation in Afghanistan into consideration. Thinking aloud, Shuvalov added that no country in the world could feel secure in an unstable region. The leaders of Afghanistan must therefore understand the importance of international laws, norms and principles. The international community would judge them on that basis alone. He emphasized that the process of dialogue between Pakistan and Russia was now more critical than ever.

Paradoxically, the rise of the Taliban initially helped strengthen, rather than weaken, Pakistan-Russia relations because of the latter's perception that Islamabad wielded influence over the Taliban. Moscow needed Pakistan's help to establish initial contact with Kandahar.

Our assessment had always been that Moscow did not want a settlement in Afghanistan because a continuation of the conflict would deny the landlocked Central Asian republics a transit corridor through Afghanistan. This, in turn, would perpetuate their dependence on Russia for their exports and strengthen Moscow's influence in its "Near Abroad". To consolidate its presence in the region, there were already an estimated thirty thousand Russian troops in Tajikistan on the pretext that the rise of the Taliban would derail regional stability.

However, the Americans thought differently. They believed that the Russians had modified their policy and were ready to deal with the Taliban. Robin Raphel told Najmuddin Shaikh during their meeting in New York at the UN conference on Afghanistan in November 1996 that Moscow genuinely desired peace in Afghanistan but had expressed concern over "unilateral initiatives by Pakistan" as was evident from the trade caravan of Nasirullah Babar. A similar impression was conveyed to me by Ibrahim Al-Bakr, the OIC special envoy on Afghanistan, on 21 November 1996.

The information provided to us by the Americans was corroborated at the UN conference on Afghanistan during Najmuddin's meeting with G. E. Mamedov, who until his appointment as ambassador to Canada in 2004, was one of Russia's several deputy foreign ministers. Mamedov said that Moscow wanted peace in Afghanistan and had no intention of interfering in that country a second time. He also described Pakistan as a key player without whom a solution of the Afghanistan problem would not be possible.

Significantly, Mamedov requested Pakistan's assistance in facilitating Russian contact with the Taliban on the understanding that this should not be considered by the latter as weakness. He elaborated that the Russians wanted to meet a person of authority. Najmuddin suggested that either he or the Russian ambassador in Islamabad could meet Mulla Ghaus. In the course of my meeting with Ghaus on 18 December, I suggested that he should establish contact with the Russian ambassador. This, however, did not materialize because Ghaus asked the Russian envoy to come to the Afghan embassy while the latter insisted that the venue of any meeting should be his own mission.

Despite its declaratory policy of wanting a peaceful settlement in Afghanistan, Russia continued to supply weapons on a substantial scale to the Northern Alliance. Dostum visited Moscow in mid-January 1997 and was able to secure firm commitments of military assistance. By the first week of March of that year, Kulyab in southern Tajikistan had become a major base from where the Russians supplied military equipment and food to the forces of Ahmed Shah Masood in the hope of persuading him to launch an offensive in spring against the Taliban. It was believed that this would relieve the pressure on the forces of Dostum and the Hizb-e-Wahdat in central Afghanistan as they needed the time for regrouping and reinforcing their defences.

In this period, I had a series of frank and detailed Afghanistan-related discussions with Alexander Alexeyev, the Russian ambassador in Pakistan who became deputy foreign minister in 2004. The latter insisted that the reason for the continuation of the Afghan turmoil was the supply of weapons by Pakistan to the Taliban. I asked him for the proof which he was unable to provide and then I told him bluntly that it was Russia and Iran that were prolonging the conflict by supplying weapons to the

Northern Alliance. I could give him documentary evidence of the daily flights to Shibberghan and Mazar-e-Sharif bringing in huge quantities of Russian and Iranian weapons. Alexeyev went on the defensive and conceded that he could not rule out the possibility of Russian military hardware being sold to the Northern Alliance by elements within the Russian armed forces in Tajikistan because the soldiers had not received any pay for the past several months.

Thus Russia, like Iran, was completely taken aback by the spectacular capture of Mazar-e-Sharif by the joint forces of Malik and the Taliban. Again, like Tehran, Moscow was willing to come to terms with ground realities and have dealings with Kandahar. The subsequent reversals suffered by the latter convinced Russia that the control of all of Afghanistan by the Taliban was not inevitable. The Northern Alliance had, therefore, to be provided full support in close coordination with Iran. An unwritten understanding thus emerged between Moscow and Tehran the central purpose of which was to ensure that the Taliban would not be able to vanquish the ethnic minorities of northern Afghanistan. The assessment of several analysts was that for Russia this had the twin benefit of enabling it to maintain its presence on the southern borders of the former Soviet republics of Central Asia and, at the same time, by stoking the conflict, denying these countries the trade routes as well as the oil and gas pipeline projects through Afghanistan to the warm waters of the south. In time an entente between Russia, Iran and India emerged while the rest of the international community became increasingly disillusioned by the absurd obscurantist policies of the Taliban.

The dramatic capture of Mazar-e-Sharif by the Taliban was the outcome of the intrigues and disunity within the Northern Alliance. It demonstrated nevertheless that cooperation between Kandahar and the minority ethnic groups was not an impossibility. The Taliban had forged an alliance, albeit short-lived, with the Uzbek, General Malik, while the Tajiks and the Hazaras were in contact with them. The prospect however er of achieving a durable political settlement received a severe setback because of the despicable behaviour of the Taliban in Mazar-e-Sharif. Their subsequent rout was entirely due to their arrogance.

After the events north of the Hindu Kush in May, the Northern Alliance, or the Supreme Council for the Defence of Afghanistan (Shura-e-Aali-e-Difa-e-Afghanistan) as it grandiloquently styled itself, existed only in name. Dostum was never to recover his former stature as the strongman of the north and power shifted to the ethnic Tajik-dominated Jamiat-e-Islami and more particularly to Ahmed Shah Masood. It was against this backdrop that our quest for a political settlement began. The ethnic groups had shown that they were willing to negotiate with each other as at the end of May 1997 and this gave us a feint glimmer of hope that the shuttle mission that we were about to begin could succeed.

4
The search for a political settlement, 1997–1998

IN EARLY June 1997, the chief secretary of Pakistan's North West Frontier Province, Rustam Shah, conveyed an urgent message to me from Ahmed Shah Masood. The latter said that he wished Pakistan well and could not possibly be hostile to it. After all, his father was buried in Peshawar. He wanted to meet a senior Pakistan official on neutral soil, preferably Dubai. The meeting should be kept secret.

It was accordingly decided by the government that Rustam Shah and I would proceed to Dubai. No one else was to know of the meeting and foreign office colleagues were told that I had gone to Lahore for three or four days to attend a family marriage. Mulla Omar and the top Taliban leadership in Kandahar were, however, informed as I would ultimately be required to convey Ahmed Shah Masood's message to them.

We reached Dubai on the afternoon of 18 June and met the delegation sent by Ahmed Shah Masood the same evening at the Forte Grand Hotel where they were staying. The Northern Alliance team was led by Younis Qanooni of the Jamiat-e-Islami. He was a finance minister when the Burhanuddin Rabbani regime controlled Kabul and subsequently became a minister in December 2001 in the interim administration of Hamid Karzai. He resigned to contest the presidential election on 9 October 2004 but was defeated by Karzai. The other members of his delegation included Ustad Fazl, the head of the Hizb-e-Wahdat's political division, and a person who was introduced to us as Hamid from the Jumbish-e-Milli.

We were warmly welcomed by Qanooni at the lobby of the hotel and conducted to a small conference room. He invited me to begin the talks. I told him that I was in Dubai to listen to any new ideas that he might have about bringing the Afghan conflict to an end. For its part, Pakistan stood for the restoration of durable peace and stability in Afghanistan. It was against outside interference and fully supported Afghanistan's unity and territorial integrity. There could be no military solution and it was important for all the Afghan groups to work towards a negotiated political settlement. All parties should adopt a positive approach as the future could not be built on the wounds of the past.

Qanooni replied that there had been a complete change in the Afghan situation and this was what had prompted his leadership to request for the meeting. He expressed the hope that it would lead to greater understanding between Pakistan and Afghanistan which, in turn, would benefit the entire region. Like most Afghan leaders I have met, whether from the Taliban or the Northern Alliance, he was lavish in his praise for the help that Pakistan had rendered to the Afghan people in their jihad against the Soviet occupation forces. His prayer was that God might give the Afghans the opportunity to repay this debt that they all owed to Pakistan. Qanooni continued that Pakistan and Afghanistan were indistinguishable. They had everything in common and should work in unison in international forums such as the UN. The two countries should supplement each others' efforts. If things were in place, Pakistan could play an effective role in Central Asia. Pakistan and Afghanistan would be able to re-establish broad and deep economic collaboration. Unfortunately, the convergence that had brought Pakistan and Afghanistan together during the struggle against the Soviets had disappeared. His colleagues had hoped that this convergence would continue to inspire the relationship between the two countries after the jihad. However, these hopes had been shattered and what existed was an unsavoury stalemate. Wrong policies had been pursued "somewhere", as a consequence of which, the two countries now had to start from scratch. At all events, the Afghan people would never forget the help that Pakistan had given them in their hour of greatest need.

Qanooni said that despite the strains in the relationship between Pakistan and Afghanistan, the countries must not look back. They should build upon their commonalities. The two peoples had similar perceptions. Afghanistan had always welcomed dialogue with Pakistan. Numerous delegations had been exchanged but, unfortunately, to no avail. The time had come to be frank and forthright with each other. Future changes in Afghanistan should not be brought about by military means but through dialogue and negotiations. Welcoming my emphasis on non-interference by external powers in the internal affairs of Afghanistan, Qanooni said that the continuation of the conflict was detrimental to Afghanistan's neighbours. Pakistan had suffered immeasurably. The violence in Afghanistan had resulted in millions of deaths and had devastated the country's infrastructure, its culture, and its entire national system. His leadership would not wish to prolong the conflict even by one hour. It must be brought to an immediate end. However, if pushed against the wall, the Northern Alliance would be left with no option but to meet force with force. The conditions prevailing inside Afghanistan were deteriorating rapidly and it was important to move fast towards peace. Pakistan and Iran should evolve a new strategy to bring this about. The two countries had to move in unison. They should identify their enemies and friends both at the regional as well as the international levels. There must be a rapprochement between them so that they could work together for peace. The Afghans had come to Dubai with an open and positive mind. The presence of the Pakistan delegation symbolized the determination of the Nawaz Sharif government to move towards a settlement.

Qanooni's emphasis that Pakistan and Iran needed to move in tandem to resolve the Afghanistan conflict left me in no doubt that this so-called "secret" meeting was with the approval of Tehran. Qanooni's brief had obviously been cleared by the Iranian government.

I told Qanooni that Pakistan was impartial towards all the Afghan groups. This was demonstrated by its non-recognition of the Taliban for nine months though they controlled Kabul and two-thirds of the country. Our neutrality was again illustrated by Prime Minister Nawaz Sharif's meeting with Professor Rabbani the previous month during the ECO summit in Ashgabat.

There should be no doubt that Pakistan had a vital interest in the restoration of durable peace in Afghanistan as no other country had suffered more from the continuation of the conflict. However, a permanent settlement could only emerge from the Afghans themselves for which a meaningful dialogue among the Afghan groups was essential. Qanooni had been present when we visited Shibberghan on 7 December 1996. He could not have forgotten that Dostum, in the presence of the other leaders and representatives of the Northern Alliance, had agreed to a sequential settlement beginning with a cease-fire, the exchange of prisoners, the creation of a political commission that would deliberate upon the modalities leading to the establishment of a broad-based government. Finally, the methodology for the demilitarization of Kabul was to be determined. Subsequently, at the conference on Afghanistan convened by Iran at the end of January 1997, Sibghatullah Mujaddadi had announced that he had met Mulla Omar in Kandahar a few days earlier and that the latter had accepted these proposals. The main elements for a permanent settlement were, therefore, in place. The Afghan parties were now within negotiating range and a serious attempt for a dialogue had to be made.

I reminded Qanooni that the events in Mazar-e-Sharif in May had clearly shown that the Afghan factions were perfectly capable of establishing cooperation with each other irrespective of their ethnic diversity or political differences. General Malik and Mulla Ghaus had signed a written agreement on 19 May, on 24 May Ahmed Shah Masood had indicated that he wanted to negotiate an honourable surrender, and on the same day Karim Khalili of the Hizb-e-Wahdat had sent a delegation to Kabul for talks.

The building blocks for the creation of sustainable peace were in place and it was for this reason that Pakistan had been working towards convening an intra-Afghan dialogue in Islamabad. We envisaged that countries bordering Afghanistan would be invited as observers or even guarantors should an agreement among the Afghan parties emerge. Our initial soundings with Iran, Turkmenistan and Uzbekistan indicated that they were favourably disposed to the idea. While we spoke, the new foreign minister of Pakistan, Gohar Ayub Khan, was visiting Tajikistan and the other Central Asian republics to develop this concept further. Perhaps even the United States and Russia could be invited to the meeting which should be held under UN auspices. This was a concept I had developed during a visit to Moscow in the first week of April. I did not, however, tell Qanooni that I had already discussed this with the Russians and they were enthusiastic about taking part in the process. The idea subsequently emerged as the "Six Plus Two Group".

Qanooni welcomed the concept of an intra-Afghan dialogue though he had reservations about Islamabad as the venue. Furthermore, there appeared to be a contradiction. On the one hand, Pakistan claimed to be for conciliation among the Afghan groups and, on the other, it had been trying to unseat the Rabbani government at the United Nations. He was already aware of the sequential settlement proposal which he felt had been overtaken by events. Similarly, the agreement between the Taliban and Malik was no longer valid. The central issue was the establishment of a broad-based government and he wanted to know whether the Taliban were willing to move towards such a dispensation.

We decided to adjourn the meeting to the following day when we would first discuss the broad principles of policy and then the procedure for the adoption of that policy.

The second meeting with Qanooni was held at 10.30am at the Avari

Hotel where I was staying. I told Qanooni that the gist of our discussion the previous evening had been conveyed to Islamabad. Because of the positive nature of the discussions, Pakistan had decided that it would reopen its consulate general in Mazar-e-Sharif. We expected the Northern Alliance to give full protection to our consul general and his staff. Qanooni said that he too had briefed his leaders about our earlier talks. They were happy with the outcome and had asked him to convey their complements to the Pakistan delegation. He had been instructed to carry the negotiations through to its ultimate success.

Qanooni expressed delight at our decision to reopen the Mazar-e-Sharif consulate general and assured me the personnel and premises would be given full protection. He then added: "Please ensure that there are more people from the ministry of foreign affairs and less from Inter Services Intelligence" and then quickly explained that this remark had only been made in jest and that I should not take it seriously.

Qanooni asked me advice on the principles of policy and the procedures that should be followed to bring about a settlement of the Afghanistan problem. I replied that this was an internal Afghan issue and I, as an outsider, had no right to tell them how they should conduct their own affairs. Qanooni said that I should not be diplomatic with him. He was convinced of the sincerity of the Pakistan delegation and he only wished to hear my views. I replied that the principles of policy should be the restoration of durable peace and stability through an intra-Afghan peace process; the cessation of outside interference in the internal affairs of Afghanistan; and commitment to the unity and territorial integrity of Afghanistan. The procedure for the initiation and implementation of these principles should be through an intra-Afghan dialogue in Pakistan to which countries with common borders with Afghanistan would be invited as observers and even possible guarantors should an agreement emerge. The US and Russia could also be invited. The conference should be held under UN auspices. The intra-Afghan dialogue would deliberate upon various proposals leading to the establishment of a broad-based government.

Qanooni agreed with this enunciation of the principles of policy and procedures and asked about specific proposals that could be discussed in an intra-Afghan meeting. I replied that these could include a number of options such as:

(i) the president and the prime minister could be from the Taliban while the other factions would appoint ministers;

(ii) the Northern Alliance could appoint the president, the Taliban the prime minister and the ministries could be divided proportionately based on the population of the respective regions;

(iii) the president could be appointed by the Taliban and the prime minister by the Northern Alliance with ministries again being divided proportionately to the population under the control of each group;

(iv) neither the Taliban nor the Northern Alliance would appoint the president or the prime minister. In this case the leader could be a neutral figure acceptable to all Afghan groups;

(v) an interim government consisting of neutral personalities could be formed to conduct elections to a shura;

(vi) the disbandment of all private armies and the establishment of a national police or army consisting of personnel from all provinces. The force thus created would collect all heavy weapons. This would be followed by the establishment of a shura to draft a constitution and to hold elections for a parliament after which the shura would be dissolved. The parliament would elect the president and the prime minister; and

(vii) stoppage of hostilities immediately followed by exchange of prisoners and leading to the formation of an interim council which would, in turn, work out the modalities for an interim broad-based government.

It was made plain to Qanooni that I was merely thinking aloud and what I had said should not be construed as proposals from the government of Pakistan.

Qanooni replied that the Northern Alliance would extend whole-hearted support for our initiatives aimed at a negotiated settlement. The future government had to be broad-based. The Northern Alliance recognized the Taliban as a major force. They had never suggested that any government should be formed without the Taliban. The cause of the conflict in Afghanistan was foreign interference. It would help if outside powers remained neutral. He expressed the hope that the intra-Afghan talks would commence soon and made the following proposals:

(i) establishment of a joint commission consisting of representatives of the Taliban and the Northern Alliance. It would discuss the formation of a broad-based government;

(ii) the commission would work under a time frame which should be specified now;

(iii) the scenarios outlined by me would be discussed by the commission;

(iv) the government of Pakistan would be consulted on the formation of the commission. Pakistan would also be consulted on the issues to be brought before the commission;

(v) the commission would meet in Kabul for which the city would have to be demilitarized;

(vi) the security of Kabul could be achieved either through a joint security force or through a neutral force;

(vii) the outcome of the commission's deliberations would be guaranteed by the countries bordering Afghanistan; and

(viii) the commission would meet under UN auspices.

I responded that while I held no brief for the Taliban, I was sure that they would not agree to the demilitarization of Kabul. In effect they were being asked to give up all that they had achieved on the ground at the negotiating table. In the past when the demilitarization of Kabul had been discussed with them, they had asked whether such a demand had been made in the four years that Burhanuddin Rabbani was in control of the capital. By the same logic, the Northern Alliance now would never agree to the demilitarization of Mazar-e-Sharif. I told Qanooni that he should only make proposals that were likely to be accepted. It was for precisely this reason that I had suggested that the venue for the meeting should be Islamabad. In this way the contentious issue of the demilitarization of Kabul could be finessed. To my question about the time frame that was envisaged for the commission to complete its work, Qanooni replied that it should be no more than two weeks. He also said that though the Northern Alliance was not too pleased with the performance of Dr Norbert Holl, they were still inclined to believe that the commission should meet under UN auspices.

Qanooni suggested that I should visit Mazar-e-Sharif as early as possible after consulting the leadership in Kandahar about his proposals. I stressed that in the meantime it was important for the two sides to take confidence-building measures such as a cease-fire and the exchange of prisoners. It was unrealistic to expect the commission to meet without a cease-fire.

During our meeting that morning the talks were interrupted many times to enable Qanooni to receive telephone calls from General Malik, Karim Khalili and Ahmed Shah Masood. We decided to meet again at 6pm for a final session. The evening session was short. Rustam Shah and I presented a draft summation of our discussions and the points of convergence which Qanooni felt was far too elaborate. He was not in favour of a signed written document as the consultations were informal. He then listed the following as his final proposals:

(i) the Afghan conflict should be brought to a close through mediation;

(ii) to bring this about it was necessary to have a broad-based government;

(iii) it was essential to have a mechanism for a broad-based government. This mechanism would be a political commission consisting of representatives of the Taliban and the Northern Alliance. Pakistan would be consulted on the composition of the commission as well as on its agenda;

(iv) the political commission would make arrangements for a broad-based government (a cease-fire and exchange of prisoners would be discussed by the commission). The commission should take no more than fifteen days to establish a broad-based government after which it would be dissolved;

(v) the commission would convene and operate under UN auspices;

(vi) the neighbouring countries would support and guarantee the formation of the commission as well as its deliberations;

(vii) the commission would meet in Kabul which would be demilitarized (it was clearly understood that this idea was tentative and subject to acceptance by the Taliban); and

(viii) the negotiations between Pakistan and the Northern Alliance should continue. The next round would be in Mazar-e-Sharif after Pakistan had consulted the Taliban.

Qanooni concluded the meeting by saying that the Northern Alliance had its own political and military agenda for Afghanistan. The programmes they were pursuing would not await the outcome of the proposals that had just been made. It was, therefore, vitally important that an agreement should emerge at the earliest. It was necessary that Pakistan should immediately put these proposals across to the Taliban. If the views of the Taliban were conveyed to the Northern Alliance early, the latter would review their own political and military agenda accordingly.

The shuttle mission

On our return to Islamabad, Rustam Shah and I briefed Prime Minister Nawaz Sharif about our meeting with Younis Qanooni in Dubai. Nawaz Sharif, who obviously did not understand the complexity of the issues involved, turned to me and said that I should solve the Afghanistan problem within one week! For this purpose I was free to travel to Kandahar, Mazar-e-Sharif or any other place in Afghanistan without obtaining the approval of the government as was required under our procedures. Two planes—the Pakistan Air Force Fokker which we had used for going to Shibberghan and Kandahar in December 1996, and a four-seater Falcon jet, also belonging to the air force—were at my disposal.

Sharif seriously believed that the conflict in Afghanistan could be resolved within days. He never read the briefs and position papers that the foreign office sent him. He had no patience for detail as he was in a hurry to win political laurels in the early months of his second tenure as prime minister. He was, therefore, completely unaware that it was a different Afghanistan from the early 1990s when his first administration had brokered the Peshawar and Islamabad accords. He considered these accords, which brought chaos to Afghanistan, as significant achievements. He did not realize that Pakistan no longer had influence in Afghanistan. We had no leverage on the Taliban because we had done nothing to help them and we were hated by the Northern Alliance who held us responsible for their ouster from Kabul.

It became apparent later that, contrary to what the Iranian media were saying about him, Sharif disliked the Taliban and was partial to Burhanuddin Rabbani. The latter was among the first to congratulate Sharif on his re-election as prime minister with a landslide majority earlier in the year.

I proceeded to Kandahar on 26 June along with Rustam Shah, Aziz Khan and Ayaz Wazir. Abdul Majid, a retired ISI brigadier who was working with me at the Afghanistan desk at the foreign ministry, also accompanied us. This group constituted our core negotiation team for the duration of the shuttle mission. Majid was an asset as he had been closely associated with Afghanistan for the past several years and knew virtually everyone of any importance on both sides of the Afghan political divide. In a sharp departure from the usual practice, I decided to take along journalists from the print and electronic media for shuttle-related travels to Afghanistan.

The talks in Kandahar were held with Mulla Rabbani, the head of the Taliban government, and with deputy foreign minister Mulla Jalil. Rabbani was a quiet, gentle, unassuming man. It was difficult to imagine that this person was the equivalent of the prime minister of Taliban-controlled Afghanistan. He had taken part in the resistance in the 1980s against the Soviet occupation forces and was seriously injured in the fighting. Mulla Rabbani was moderate in his views and could have brought Afghanistan out of its isolation. However, he was completely overshadowed by Omar who, as "amir-ul-momineen" ("commander of the faithful"), took all the decisions. What I did not know at the time was that Mulla Rabbani also had a sly sense of humour. Several months later, when the Monica Lewinski scandal had captured the headlines, he told Aziz Khan during a lunch at the Pakistan embassy residence in Kabul that Clinton must be a very strong president to be able to cope with so many women. He then asked if Aziz knew what Clinton ate as that was surely the reason for the latter's virility.

Qanooni's proposals were discussed in detail during the talks with Rabbani and Jalil. As we had anticipated, they insisted that the peace process should commence with a cease-fire and exchange of prisoners. Rabbani asked how anyone in his right senses could expect talks to take place, and that too in Kabul, without a cease-fire. He explained that the exchange of prisoners was important for the Taliban because they were a volunteer movement. No one, not even he as the head of the government, received any pay. The men who were at the front had risked their lives not because of money but for the reason that they believed in the cause. The least the Taliban leadership could do for those who had been captured was to secure their release. If these two conditions were met, he had no objection to the subsequent formation of a political commission which, he felt, should convene in Islamabad for reasons of security.

Rabbani said that the leadership of the Northern Alliance were unreliable as was evident from their track record of broken promises and pledges. Malik had invited the Taliban to the north and had used them to oust Dostum as well as to eliminate his rivals even within his own party, the Jumbish-e-Milli. When his purpose had been achieved he turned upon the Taliban. This treachery had resulted in the slaughter of thousands of people from the south. The Taliban, at Malik's request, had sent their foreign minister, Mulla Ghaus, and central bank governor, Mulla Ehsanullah, as emissaries to remove misunderstandings. Even these unarmed envoys had been arrested in complete violation of all norms of civilized conduct. The Taliban, therefore, just did not trust Malik and his accomplices. If the Northern Alliance were sincere about negotiations they should, as a first step, unconditionally release the peace emissaries. We did make it a point to tell Rabbani that Ghaus, whom Ayaz Wazir had met in Mazar-e-Sharif on 27 May, had been completely unreasonable and had done nothing to reduce the tensions. Rabbani replied that emissaries could not be arrested—I wondered how he had come to know about the principle of diplomatic immunity.

After the talks we went to another room for lunch. In accordance with Afghan customs we all sat on the floor and partook of the meal which consisted of roasted mutton, chicken, salad and the traditional whole wheat bread. The only non-Afghan items were cans of Coca-Cola and Seven Up that were consumed with great speed, interspersed with loud burps and with unmistakable relish. The drivers and servants also joined us for lunch and there was no seating protocol—a practice the Taliban considered an absurdity of Western etiquette. I tried to continue the discussion on the initiation of a peace process. Mulla Rabbani politely told me that I should talk about lighter matters while eating as politics should not be discussed at lunch or dinner. This mild reprimand was well-deserved as I had forgotten that politics and religion are considered inappropriate topics for the dining table and particularly so in sophisticated circles in the West.

When lunch was over we resumed the talks on the Qanooni proposal. Neither Rabbani nor Jalil had anything new to add so I decided that I should draw our hosts' attention to the appalling international image of the Taliban particularly on gender discrimination. Jalil was obviously getting bored. He yawned and used the visiting card I had given him earlier as a toothpick. Rabbani, on the other hand, listened attentively. The other members of our delegation were visibly nervous as they were not sure what I would say and how it would be received by the Taliban leadership.

I bluntly told Rabbani that I did not agree with their interpretation of Islam which had brought a bad name to this moderate and modern religion. Furthermore, the Taliban should stop describing their struggle against the Northern Alliance as a "jihad". It was anything but a jihad as they were killing fellow Muslims for no better reason than the achievement of political supremacy. All human beings were answerable to God. Life was finite and death inevitable. How would the Taliban leadership account for themselves for waging war against their own countrymen? Wars of aggression were proscribed by the Quran, only those in self-defence were allowed. Aggression was anathema to Islam. Moreover, jihad had a far broader meaning and implied a struggle that man must wage against himself and on behalf of himself. The important aspect of jihad was the eradication of poverty and ignorance. Rabbani agreed with this but said that it was the Northern Alliance that was the aggressor. The Northern Alliance had usurped power and had no legitimacy. The regime of Burhanuddin Rabbani had brought death and devastation to

Afghanistan for more than four years. The only objective of the Taliban was to defeat the power-hungry warlords and restore durable peace to their country.

I then reminded Rabbani that after the Taliban takeover of Kabul on 27 September 1996, the international community was willing to accept them, despite such barbarous acts as the killing of Najibullah and then hanging his corpse for several days in Kabul. The Americans, who had been initially supportive, had turned against them because of their mistreatment of women who had been denied employment and education opportunities. This again was totally repugnant to the teachings of Islam.

I asked Mulla Rabbani to answer simply either "yes" or "no" whether Islam, which did not believe in the concept of original sin, placed men and women on an absolutely equal footing and that the Quran had repeatedly emphasized this to the extent that in one of its verses gender equality had been reiterated ten times. Rabbani unhesitatingly answered in the affirmative. He also agreed that: the first convert to Islam was a woman (the Prophet Muhammad's wife, Khadija); the first martyr in the cause of the religion was a woman (Summaya); the Prophet Muhammad's youngest wife, Aisha, had led an army of men into battle; women in Islam were actually at an advantage because their husbands had no right on their property and earnings—but men were, on the contrary, required to provide for their wives regardless of how rich or poor either spouse was; and the greatest emphasis in Islam was in the acquisition of knowledge and the banishment of ignorance both by men as well as women. Rabbani went a step further and said that one of Islam's most important law-givers was a woman, namely Muhammad's wife Aisha. She had authenticated several of the Prophet's sayings (hadiths) which, after the Quran, constitute the most important source of Islamic law.

Rabbani explained that, as Muslims, the Taliban had no problem with the education and employment of women but this had to be in accordance with the Afghan tradition of segregation. At present, the Taliban were fighting a war and had neither the money nor the resources to even provide for the education of males let alone females. Education for women would be made available if they had the funds. What Rabbani did not tell me—perhaps because he was unaware of it—was that several hundred schools for girls were already functioning in the Taliban-controlled areas of Afghanistan. This was discovered by a Swedish NGO that was working in Kandahar and other provinces in the south of the country.

We left Kandahar with the promise that in the next few days, we would impress upon the Northern Alliance that the release of the peace envoys was absolutely essential for starting a dialogue between them and the Taliban.

We flew to Mazar-e-Sharif on 1 July and first had a meeting with Burhanuddin Rabbani. This was followed by detailed talks with General Malik who led the Northern Alliance team. The gist of the discussions in Kandahar was conveyed to them. Malik responded that I had brought nothing new. The Taliban sought the military subjugation of the northern provinces and had reneged upon the written agreement that he had signed with them. He said that the Taliban only wanted the release of prisoners. In the past when prisoners had been released, they had resumed hostilities.

I emphasized to Malik that confidence-building measures were urgently required. There was merit in the Taliban demand for the release of their unarmed emissaries. This would generate goodwill and give an impetus to the peace process. Malik responded that Ghaus and Ehsanullah were with the Northern Alliance as their "guests" and were being well looked after. He would consult other members of the Alliance to determine whether they should be "allowed" to return to Kandahar or Kabul and then get back to us within a few days.

As regards the cease-fire, Malik asserted that the Taliban were responsible for the hostilities and if they stopped attacking the Northern Alliance there would automatically be an end to the fighting.

On 8 July, our negotiating team assembled at the Chaklala air force base again and flew to Kandahar. Four hours of intensive discussions were held, this time, with deputy foreign minister Jalil, the affable one-legged governor of Kandahar Mulla Hasan, and Mulla Wakil Ahmad Mutawakil, the adviser to Mulla Omar who was subsequently to become foreign minister. The Taliban were persistent in their demand for confidence-building measures, the most important of which was the release of their peace emissaries and were dismissive of the proposed formation of a political commission. On our insistence, they finally agreed to give the idea a "positive and quick consideration" subject to the prior release of their peace envoys. Their perception of a political commission was a mechanism that would organize a cease-fire, arrange an across-the-board exchange of prisoners and only then discuss the formation of a government in which all the ethnic groups, but not necessarily the present leadership of the Northern Alliance, would be represented.

Surprisingly, the leadership in Kandahar were less critical of General

Malik. Earlier, during our visit to Kandahar on 26 June, they had blamed him squarely for the setback that they had received. Our delegation was now told that Malik was not a free agent and that he probably acted at the behest of powerful elements within the Northern Alliance. The Taliban were, therefore, willing to deal with him provided he demonstrated sincerity.

Our next visit to Mazar-e-Sharif, four days later, was to be eventful. Ahmed Shah Masood sent a message that he wanted to meet me personally. He would send a helicopter to take me from Mazar-e-Sharif, when I visited the city next, to a place in Takhar province which would be specified later. Although the Taliban had been expelled from Mazar-e-Sharif, fierce fighting was continuing in other areas in the north especially in Takhar. We reached Mazar-e-Sharif aboard the Pakistan Air Force Fokker at 11am on 12 July. I was told in Islamabad, prior to our departure, that I would first be meeting Masood over lunch and then return to Mazar-e-Sharif for follow-up talks with the other leaders of the Northern Alliance. However, the programme was changed as Masood was still on his way from the battlefront to Farkhar, the summer resort of ex-king Zahir Shah, which had been selected as the venue for the meeting. At the Mazar-e-Sharif airport, I was informed that Masood had accordingly "instructed" Burhanuddin Rabbani and General Malik to have quick short meetings with me after which I was to be flown to Farkhar.

On the way from the airport to Burhanuddin Rabbani's residence, the chief of protocol, who was in the car assigned to me, made some interesting revelations. He said that a day earlier, General Malik had made a public statement acknowledging Ahmed Shah Masood as his leader. This was resented by the ethnic Uzbeks and, in particular, the Jumbish-e-Milli. They had tauntingly started referring to Malik as "Mrs Ahmed Shah Masood". This confirmed what Mulla Jalil had told us in Kandahar on 8 July that Malik had been eclipsed by other leaders of the Northern Alliance. The chief of protocol, who was an ethnic Uzbek, whispered to me to be gentle with Malik as he was under enormous pressure and even feared for his life. Words of assurance from me would boost Malik's morale. He said that Masood was now the most powerful man in the north and even "President" Burhanuddin Rabbani, who disliked him, was taking instructions from the "Lion of the Panjsher".

The meeting with Rabbani was more in the nature of a courtesy call. He told me that as soon as he had heard of Nawaz Sharif's re-election he had offered special thanks-giving prayers. Sharif, he said, was committed to the restoration of sustainable peace in Afghanistan and could be certain of the complete support of all the groups within the Northern Alliance. I thought to myself that what Rabbani really wanted was a replay of 1992 and 1993 so that he could be installed in Kabul again, with Pakistan's help, as the president of Afghanistan. As we were taking leave from Rabbani to go to Malik, one of the local officials walked into the room to say that Masood had reached Farkhar and had conveyed instructions that we should proceed there immediately.

We were rushed to the airport at breakneck speed and then made to board Masood's helicopter which was in such a state of disrepair that I could scarcely believe it could fly. Within a minute after take-off it suddenly lurched to one side and the shuttle team as well as the Pakistani journalists who had accompanied us thought that we would crash. However, the pilot managed to stabilize the helicopter and we gradually gained height. We flew over the provinces of Samangan and Kunduz before entering Takhar. Our flight route was close to the Afghan border with Uzbekistan and Tajikistan. At a distance we could see the Oxus river, or the Amu Darya, which had played so important a role in defining the course of Afghanistan's sad history. Everything seemed peaceful on the ground and it was difficult to believe that we were actually flying over an area where fierce fighting between the Taliban and the Northern Alliance was raging.

The journey took us a little more than seventy minutes and we landed at a makeshift heliport some five kilometres from Farkhar. The scenery was breathtakingly beautiful with emerald-green fields through which a bubbling stream meandered. Although it was midsummer the weather was refreshingly mild. At the heliport, which was no more than a circular cemented patch on the grass, we boarded four-wheel drive vehicles to be taken to Farkhar. We had to drive through the shallow waters of the stream in many places where the fruit-tree-lined dirt track disappeared. We noticed huge piles of weapons and ammunition at several points. Most of the crates had Persian slogans, written in bold ink, which read *"Marg bar Amrika!"* "Death to America!" It was not difficult to imagine where these massive quantities of munitions had come from.

We reached Farkhar in about fifteen minutes. It was obvious why the former kings of Afghanistan had chosen this charming little village as their summer resort. Ahmed Shah Masood greeted us with warmth and escorted us to a building which, we were told, had once served as the royal resort. This was to be Pakistan's first official contact with Masood in three years. Little did I know at the time that it would also be our last meeting with him.

Masood professed friendship for Pakistan and recalled our support for the Afghan struggle against the Soviet occupation of their country. In his assessment, Pakistan appeared to look upon certain Afghan groups as its friends and others as enemies. He emphasized that this was an erroneous presumption because all Afghans were aware of the help given to them by Pakistan and, as such, could not possibly be hostile. His impression was that Pakistan was following an ambivalent policy towards Afghanistan. The hardliners in Islamabad were in favour of the military option whereas others sought the promotion of a political process. He affirmed his preference for dialogue with the Taliban rather than conflict.

Masood was obviously implying that elements within the Pakistan government were against him. Brigadier Majid told Masood that he should be the last person in the world to entertain such misgivings as he had been one of the main recipients of Pakistani financial assistance in the early 1990s. I intervened to say that Pakistan had only one policy towards Afghanistan and this was the restoration of durable peace through an intra-Afghan dialogue. The purpose of the shuttle mission was to promote this objective and we were determined to persevere with our efforts. This point was conceded by Masood, who said that our sincerity could be gauged by the number of visits I had made to Kandahar and Mazar-e-Sharif in the last two weeks.

It was emphasized to Masood that for the peace process to get underway it was essential for the Northern Alliance to take the immediate confidence-building measure of releasing the Taliban peace emissaries. He claimed to know nothing about this as he had been away from Mazar-e-Sharif. He would, however, intercede with Malik on behalf of the envoys. A similar assurance was given to us by the Itehad-e-Islami's Sayyaf who was present for the second half of the meeting.

Masood was obviously being insincere as we knew only too well that Malik was totally subservient to him. A simple telephone call to Malik was enough for the peace envoys to be freed and the only impediment in the way of a dialogue between the Taliban and the Northern Alliance would have been removed. It was obvious that Masood had his own political and military agenda as Qanooni had made clear to me during our meeting in Dubai. Nothing short of the demilitarization of Kabul would have induced the Northern Alliance to come to the negotiating table. They were merely buying time for more weapons supplies from Iran and also testing the waters to determine whether the Taliban had been sufficiently demoralized after their debacle in Mazar-e-Sharif to agree to the demands of the Northern Alliance. The next day Masood made a statement bitterly criticizing Pakistan.

After the meeting we returned to the heliport for the journey back to

Mazar-e-Sharif. However, ten minutes after take-off we were told by the pilot that the helicopter was running out of fuel and we would have to make an emergency landing at Taloqan, the capital of Takhar. We landed on a gravel strip which served as the runway for the Taloqan airport. Wireless contact was established with Masood who sent us an Antonov-32 to fly us on to Mazar-e-Sharif.

On our return to Mazar-e-Sharif, a meeting was held with Malik who was assisted by other Northern Alliance officials including Qanooni. Malik seemed nervous and it was obvious that he was not sure of himself. I told him that the Taliban were willing to consider the early formation of a political commission provided their peace emissaries were released. He was evasive and responded that they were in the process of forming a government and that the issue would be discussed when the coalition was in place. At this point I began to suspect foul play and there was a lurking suspicion in my mind that both Ghaus and Ehsanullah might have been killed.

The meeting with Malik was short because he could not tell us anything new without the approval of Ahmed Shah Masood. Furthermore, the captain of the Fokker had insisted that we should take off well before sunset in order to clear the mountains before it became dark because the plane could not fly at a high altitude and was not equipped for night flying over such mountainous terrain. We reached the airport about forty minutes before sundown and were told by the crew that we would barely be able to cross the mountains before nightfall. We took off immediately and after an hour it was pitch dark. A little while later the captain came over to me and whispered that the plane had developed an engine problem and the radar system was also not functioning properly. He had, therefore, taken the decision to return to Mazar-e-Sharif but the problem was that he could not establish contact with the control tower. To make matters worse, the runway lights at the Mazar-e-Sharif airport were off. The alternative was to fly to Uzbekistan and try to land at Tirmiz. However, we had no flight clearance and the aircraft could be shot down.

We circled for about ten minutes above Mazar-e-Sharif and then all of a sudden the plane literally dived towards the ground because the runway lights had suddenly and unexpectedly come on. We managed to land safely. We were told by the Northern Alliance officials on duty that they had tried to establish contact with our plane but in the absence of a response, they were sure that it was a Taliban aircraft and had activated their missiles. The countdown had begun and our plane would have been shot down within the next five or six seconds. Apparently the runway lights had been accidentally turned on by a nervous and inexperienced ground technician.

We were taken to a guest house where we spent the night. The local officials refused to provide us police protection because they claimed that authorization would be needed from Malik. Despite frantic efforts, we were unable to establish contact with the general. We were therefore left at the mercy of a hostile population which considered us enemies since we were perceived as the main backers of the Taliban. We did not even have a pistol to defend ourselves. Fortunately, a member of the delegation had a satellite telephone and we were able to establish contact with Islamabad. We were told by the control tower at the Chaklala air force base that there had been panic there as it was believed that we had either crashed or been shot down when contact with us could not be made. We were also able to phone our homes and assure our families that we were safe. The rest of the night passed without incident.

The next morning a team of technicians flew in from Islamabad and repaired the plane. By mid-afternoon we were on our way home.

We continued to receive conflicting signals about the fate of the peace envoys and Mulla Razzaq. As early as the second week of June, foreign minister Shikhmuradov of Turkmenistan was told in Tehran by Velayati, his Iranian counterpart, that Ghaus and Razzaq had been executed in Mazar-e-Sharif. Shikhmuradov responded that this conflicted with his own information and that such a development, if true, would torpedo all hopes for a negotiated political settlement of the conflict. A few days later, Shikhmuradov received Malik's emissary Khudai Kuli Khan, who said that Ghaus and Razzaq were alive and that he had met them three days before his arrival in Ashgabat. The message brought by him was that Malik respected Turkmenistan's policy of neutrality and his group would never create any difficulties for the government in Ashgabat. Malik was also ready for a round table discussion on Afghanistan to promote a political process.

In mid-July 1997, Shikhmuradov informed us that he had instructed the head of Afghan desk of the Turkmen foreign office, who was then in Mazar-e-Sharif, to pressure Malik to release Ghaus and Ehsanullah. Malik said that both had been slightly wounded during an air raid but had recovered and were safe in Maimena. He was ready, in principle, to release the Taliban leaders but if he did so at that stage it would deprive him of an important bargaining chip. Thus the envoys, if they were really alive, were being used as hostages.

Malik also urged Turkmenistan to persuade Pakistan and the Taliban to come to an understanding with him. It was vitally important that the Taliban should not repeat their earlier mistakes and should guarantee him the autonomy to govern his areas in the north. Shikmuradov then corroborated our own information that Malik's influence had been eroded and that it was Masood who was actually calling the shots. The apparent importance being given to Malik was mere window-dressing to enable Masood to consolidate his grip in the north. Three of Masood's commanders, who had previously never been allowed to enter Mazar-e-Sharif during Dostum's time, were then in the city. To counterbalance Ahmed Shah Masood's growing influence, Malik informed the Turkmen desk officer for Afghanistan that he had even released some of Dostum's commanders from jail.

On 31 July Shikhmuradov met Malik in Kirki near the Afghan border. The latter lied that the morale of the Northern Alliance, even without Dostum, was high and that its leaders were cooperating with each other. Malik wanted friendship with Pakistan and had been pleased to meet me. It was unfortunate that he had been forced to throw the Taliban out when they reneged on the agreement under which control of the north was to be left to him. Malik was ready to compromise with moderate and rational elements of the Taliban leadership. However, the problem—which Pakistan knew only too well—was that hardliners were more influential in Kandahar and that they refused to make any concessions. The Taliban would never be able to achieve their objectives militarily by subjugating the people of the north who had a different way of life. The latter would resist any form of domination and the conflict would, therefore, be perpetuated.

Malik claimed to have been assured by Masood that he did not intend to take Kabul. The latter had also recently met President Emomali Rahmonov of Tajikistan twice. The two had discussed the measures they would take to stem Uzbek interference in their respective regions. Later events would show the extent of hatred between Uzbekistan and Tajikistan. Shikmuradov told us on more than one occasion that a principal reason for the continuation of the turmoil in Afghanistan was that the latter's northern Central Asian neighbours were fighting their turf wars on Afghan soil. The Taliban, he said, did not have an external agenda and neighbouring countries should stop interfering in Afghanistan. He explained that there were many ethnic Afghans of Turkmen origin but his government had always considered them to be nationals of Afghanistan for whom Ashgabat had no responsibility. Uzbekistan and Tajikistan, however, thought differently as both countries treated Afghans of Uzbek and Tajik origin as their own countrymen. Thus they arrogated to them-selves the right to interfere in Afghanistan's internal affairs which had contributed, in no small measure, to the continuation of the turmoil.

Malik said that he had paid a useful visit to Tehran where he had met President Rafsanjani, foreign minister Velayati as well as representatives of the Iranian military and secret service. Although his impression was that Iran would continue to support the Northern Alliance, he had also noted that there were signs of better Iranian understanding of the poli-cies of Pakistan and Saudi Arabia which were indispensable for moving towards an Afghanistan settlement. Malik also claimed to be in contact with the Russians and hoped for "practical results to follow". As for the Taliban envoys, Malik said that it was difficult for him to release them without meaningful dialogue with Kandahar.

Shikhmuradov's assessment of this meeting with Malik was that the latter and the other Northern Alliance leaders were ready to hold pre-liminary working-level talks with the Taliban in Turkmenistan. Ashgabat and Islamabad would also participate in the meeting which could discuss the modalities for a subsequent intra-Afghan dialogue in Pakistan as had been suggested by us to Qanooni in Dubai.

The shuttle mission and Turkmenistan's efforts to promote a peaceful resolution of the violence in Afghanistan yielded nothing. Intrigue and low-intensity conflict were to define the future course of events.

Conflict and political initiatives

Shortly afterwards, the Northern Alliance announced the formation of a government and declared Mazar-e-Sharif the temporary capital of Afghanistan. A similar, but abortive, experiment had been tried earlier when Taloqan was designated the capital. The fissures within the Northern Alliance deepened even further. Malik had become discredited and was regarded with suspicion even within his Jumbish-e-Milli. There were also divisions in the Hizb-e-Wahdat as well as within the Jamiat-e-Islami of Burhanuddin Rabbani. At another level, the three main par-ties of the coalition were distrustful of and in competition with each other.

Since the Taliban blitzkrieg leading to the fall of Mazar-e-Sharif to them on 24 May 1997 and their subsequent rout a few days later, the ground situation in northern Afghanistan had turned full circle. However, by the September of that year, the Taliban were in control of twenty-five of Afghanistan's thirty-two provinces and, despite the revers-es of May, seemed to be supremely confident.

Rather than embark on any new military manoeuvre, the Taliban adopted a strategy of consolidation. After recapturing the Mazar-e-Sharif airport, they made a tactical retreat to the heights a few kilometres south of the airport which, therefore, came within their artillery range. Hairatan was retaken by them, which implied that their presence along the frontiers of the three bordering Central Asian republics had been re-established. They were in control of Kunduz, which is adjacent to Tajikistan, Hairatan at the border with Uzbekistan, and Herat, Badghis and areas of Faryab along the frontiers of Turkmenistan. Darra-e-Suf which lies between Bamyan and Mazar-e-Sharif was also captured by pro-Taliban commanders thereby denying the Hizb-e-Wahdat access to Mazar-e-Sharif. Ahmed Shah Masood's move towards the Kunduz airport was not only blunted but he also lost ground to Taliban elements in Nahrin as result of which about 250 of his men along with ten to twelve of his tanks were captured. These battlefield successes of the Taliban in the early autumn of 1997 were almost entirely due to the support given to them by the local commanders. This implied that they had considerable support in the Tajik, Uzbek and Turkmen areas of Afghanistan. Another reason was the presence of a sizeable Pushtun population north of the Hindu Kush as a result of the re-settlement policies pursued by the amirs of Afghanistan in the nineteenth and the first part of the twentieth centuries.

In the second week of September 1997, we were informed by the Turkmen authorities that, according to Russian and Uzbek sources, Dostum, who was until then in Turkey, had reached Tirmiz and was reportedly on his way to Mazar-e-Sharif via Shibberghan. A number of Dostum loyalists were still in place including Majid Durdi who would probably join him. The assessment of the Turkmen government was that if Dostum, who would be supported by Russia and Uzbekistan, reasserted control it would create a threat and a problem for the Taliban. However, Khalili and his Hizb-e-Wahdat, who dominated Mazar-e-Sharif, and who were fully backed by Iran, would be opposed to the return of Dostum. If pressure on Malik continued to mount, he could well form a fresh alliance with the Taliban.

Dostum's return to Afghanistan further weakened the already fragile Northern Alliance. There were reports of a reconciliation between him and Malik. Even if it were true, it would only be a short-lived marriage of convenience as the hatred between the two was far too intense. For all practical purposes, the Jumbish-e-Milli had been marginalized. Dostum claimed that he had been asked to return by Burhanuddin Rabbani, Ahmed Shah Masood and Karim Khalili. This was publicly denied by Rabbani.

We also received reports that the tensions within the Hizb-e-Wahdat had become even more acute. The known differences between its leader Karim Khalili, a Shia nationalist, and the party's pro-Iranian Mohaqiq had further increased. The Shias—who had always lived on the fringes of Afghan society and had been the victims of Afghan, particularly Pushtun, racial prejudice—in the meantime had been disproportionately built up by Iran as a result of which they alone controlled Mazar-e-Sharif soon after the Taliban had been expelled from the city. This was bitterly resented by the other minority ethnic leaders, particularly Ahmed Shah Masood.

The Jamiat-e-Islami had become even more divided as the animosity between Burhanuddin Rabbani and Ahmed Shah Masood came into the open. Despite these divisions within and between the component elements of the Northern Alliance, it continued to claim being the legitimate government of Afghanistan. This farce was endorsed by the international community which refused to adopt the vacant seat formula, as the OIC had done, in respect of Afghanistan's seat in the United Nations.

On 9 October, Malik arrived in Ashgabat from Tehran via Mashhad and again met Shikhmuradov. He repeated the usual refrain that the Taliban could not win through military means and they must be persuaded to settle their differences with the other Afghan groups at the negotiating table. He was also extremely unhappy with Turkey and Uzbekistan for their support to Dostum. The latter's return to Afghanistan had been a mistake as it had considerably weakened the Northern Alliance. According to Malik, Dostum did not have even a slight chance to re-establish his former supremacy in the north.

In October 1997, the Taliban, after their tactical retreat to the heights near the Mazar-e-Sharif airport retook it and encircled the city except to the south. This gap had been left in order to allow the forces of the Northern Alliance to withdraw to Bamyan. The Taliban advance towards Mazar-e-Sharif was deliberately slow as they wanted to avoid pitched battles since that would have only unnecessarily resulted in the further loss of lives. Huge quantities of arms, ammunition and food supplies were captured by them at Hairatan, which remained in their control in spite of several attempts by the forces of Dostum, Masood and the Hizb-e-Wahdat to retake it. As in the previous weeks, the local commanders in the north continued to switch their loyalties to the Taliban. Around this time, there were rumours that Malik and his close aides had been poisoned by Dostum during their reconciliation meeting in the latter's stronghold, Shibberghan. Though this rumour later proved to be unfounded, it nevertheless illustrated the degree of mistrust and the internal dissensions within the Northern Alliance.

By November, as the conflict in the north was about to go into the usual winter freeze, the ground situation was weighted heavily in favour of the Taliban with their control established over more than 80 percent of Afghan territory. Simultaneously, the fissures within the Northern Alliance became chronic and verged on violence.

The attempt by the Northern Alliance leadership to bring about a Dostum-Malik reconciliation failed and skirmishes took place between the two in Malik's own stronghold of Faryab. Key positions were taken by Dostum's forces and Malik was rumoured to have fled first to Kulyab in Tajikistan and then to Panjsher from where Ahmed Shah Masood was trying to broker a truce between the two.

Ever the political chameleon, Malik tried without success to reach another agreement with the Taliban. Dostum, on the other hand, released 135 Taliban prisoners and indicated that he was willing to set more free. This was publicly appreciated by the Taliban and, for a while, there seemed to be a possibility of a political understanding emerging between them and the Dostum-led Jumbish.

Ahmed Shah Masood's prominence within the Northern Alliance received a setback with Dostum's return. Earlier, as we had learnt during our visit to Mazar-e-Sharif on 12 July, Malik had publicly acknowledged Masood as the leader of the north to the consternation of the ethnic Uzbeks. Now Masood had to contend for supremacy in the area with Dostum. The pieces were, therefore in place for rivalry between the two.

By December 1997, the Taliban/Jumbish-e-Milli contacts yielded result and a significant exchange of prisoners took place between the two. The Taliban released 120 Dostum troops and, as a special gesture, provided their own aircraft to fly the men to Shibberghan. Three Jumbish-e-Milli pilots were among the prisoners released by the Taliban. For his part, Dostum set free some two hundred Taliban fight-ers and promised to release even more. This initial confidence-building measure resulted in telephone contact between Dostum and Mulla Omar. Dostum also deputed his representative Mulla Abdul Baki Turkestani to Kandahar for talks. The latter told me that Dostum was trying to consolidate his position among the ethnic Uzbeks after the damage that had been done by Malik's treachery. He resented the dis-proportionate strength of the Hizb-e-Wahdat in and around Mazar-e-Sharif which he considered his own area. To reverse this, Dostum was trying to raise a force of between eight to ten thousand. The purpose was not to militarily confront the Hizb-e-Wahdat but to demonstrate his own strength. Turkestani also told me that Dostum was appalled at the systematic and cold-blooded extermination of the Taliban by Malik. He regarded this as a blot on the honour of the ethnic Uzbeks which they would never be able to live down.

Around this time, Mulla Omar and Ahmed Shah Masood also established telephone contact as a result of which the latter released a number of Taliban prisoners. Despite this, there were serious clashes between the forces of the two. On 5 December, the Taliban captured the strategically important Bangi bridge, the gateway to Taloqan. Masood suffered considerable losses in men and material.

It was probable that in the event of a Dostum-Taliban understanding, the Hizb-e-Wahdat would fall into line as its leader Karim Khalili was partial to Dostum during the latter's confrontation with Malik. This would, in turn, isolate Ahmed Shah Masood whose survival would then depend on cooperation rather than confrontation with the Taliban.

By March 1998, the Afghanistan situation seemed to be defined more by hatred among the Northern Alliance components for each other than by any concerted military action on their part against the Taliban. There was complete chaos in the north which was further compounded by fighting among the alliance factions. The previous month the forces of Dostum and Ahmed Shah Masood clashed in Samangan while Masood loyalists captured some strongholds of their own Jamiat-e-Islami leader, Burhanuddin Rabbani, in Badakshan. There were also skirmishes between the forces of Ahmed Shah Masood and the Ismaili leader Mansur Naderi, as well as the Hizb-e-Wahdat and Jumbish-e-Milli. Dostum encircled Mazar-e-Sharif and was poised to attack the city. The Iranian attempt to cobble together a government in the north was a complete failure. Gulbadin Hikmatyar, whom the Iranians wanted as prime minister, was rejected by Masood and the others—Tehran had hoped that Hikmatyar could be used to stage an uprising in Kunduz, his home province, against the Taliban.

Towards the end of May 1998 fighting between the Taliban and Ahmed Shah Masood erupted but was restricted to Takhar, Kunduz, Baghlan and the northern fringes of Kabul. The Taliban captured Eshkamish in Takhar and encircled Nahrin in Baghlan. Masood's main supply route from the north was thus severed. In desperation, he launched rocket attacks on Kabul. Major commanders in Badakshan also started defecting to the Taliban. The tensions between Dostum and Masood rose to a new pitch as the latter had given refuge to Dostum's arch-enemy Malik.

The steering committee

Burhanuddin Rabbani arrived in Islamabad on 23 December 1997 at the invitation of Prime Minister Nawaz Sharif. This was a landmark event as it was the first such visit to Pakistan by a leader of the Northern Alliance since the capture of Kabul by the Taliban. It established Pakistan's standing and credentials as the only country with contacts with all Afghan groups. In mid-October of that year, Mulla Rabbani also visited Pakistan on a similar invitation from Nawaz Sharif. Since my last meeting with him in June, he had lost weight and looked unwell. There were rumours, which later proved correct, that he was terminally ill with cancer. During a working dinner at the prime minister's residence, he told us that the Taliban would agree to a dialogue with the Northern Alliance on condition that the meeting was held in Islamabad and all the leaders of the Alliance factions participated.

Burhanuddin Rabbani was accordingly informed about this offer. His response was that it would be difficult for the entire leadership of the northern coalition to leave their respective areas for an extended period. We therefore suggested that they need only attend the inaugural and the concluding sessions and that the negotiations could be conducted by their designated representatives who should be vested with full powers. Rabbani accepted this idea though he was visibly uncomfortable with it as he knew that it would be difficult for him to persuade the other Alliance leaders to agree to a meeting with the Taliban in Islamabad.

As a follow-up, foreign secretary Shamshad and I flew to Kandahar where we met Mulla Omar on 28 December. During two-and-a-half hour of talks, we emphasized the need for the Taliban to reach out to other groups. Their inability to do so was isolating Islamabad, which was being unfairly blamed for the prolongation of the conflict. Omar expressed deep appreciation for Pakistan's peace efforts. He reiterated his own commitment to the same objective. However, he voiced serious concern about the Northern Alliance's lack of sincerity as he was convinced that their only objective was to usurp power no matter the cost. Omar said that the warlords of the north should repent for what they had done to Afghanistan and lay down their arms. This was what the Taliban sought to achieve. He then expressed gratitude for Pakistan's generous help which had reached Kabul a few days earlier. This was a reference to the unprecedented move by us to send humanitarian supplies both to the Taliban as well as to the Northern Alliance in Bamyan.

In deference to our desire for a political process, Mulla Omar proposed that the ulema (clerics) from the north and the Taliban-controlled areas should meet on a mutually convenient date to sort out the problems of Afghanistan in accordance with Islamic law. Although the Taliban would prefer the meeting to be held Islamabad, they were willing to consider any other venue the Northern Alliance might suggest. Omar explained that, in Afghanistan, the ulema had traditionally played a vital role in resolving differences as their opinions and decisions had religious sanction.

We emphasized to Omar that, for the talks to be meaningful, a cessation of hostilities was essential. He told us candidly that declaring a cease-fire had serious implications for the Taliban. He explained that they were a volunteer movement and if a cease-fire was announced, his men at the front "would pick up their chadors and return home". In contrast, the opposition had a paid army which would still be intact and, as soon as the Taliban fighters had returned to their villages, the troops from the north would have a free hand to resume military operations. He recalled the massacre of thousands of Taliban in Mazar-e-Sharif a few months earlier. The leaders of the Northern Alliance, he said, were hypocrites and would never honour a cease-fire. To test Omar out, we suggested he should merely declare but not actually implement a cease-fire. He replied without any hesitation: "If I do that, then I too will be a hypocrite like the warlords of the north. I can never stoop to their level. If I announce a cease-fire, I *will* implement it."

It was, therefore, abundantly clear that the Taliban and the Northern Alliance were nowhere near negotiating range. The differences between them were enormous and they totally distrusted each other. Another complicating factor was the disunity and hatred among the component elements of the Northern Alliance which made it virtually impossible for them to adopt a common position for a purposeful intra-Afghan dialogue. This was obvious from Burhanuddin Rabbanni's hesitation about bringing representatives from the north for talks as had been proposed by his Taliban namesake. Therefore, Omar's idea for a meeting of the ulema had merit and could become the starting point of a political process. If the response of the Northern Alliance was positive, the pieces for a negotiated settlement of the Afghanistan conflict could eventually fall into place.

Rabbani, who was still in Pakistan, had a second meeting with us on 30 December before leaving for Mashhad that morning. He was given an exhaustive briefing on our talks with Mulla Omar and, in particular, the ulema meeting. Rabbani said that the Taliban were insincere and did not want a peaceful settlement in Afghanistan. He was told that the Taliban perception of the Northern Alliance was even worse. Mutual recriminations would serve no purpose and it would be better to dwell on the positive. The idea of convening a meeting of the ulema had come from the number one man in the Taliban hierarchy. Its scope could eventually be broadened to discuss the establishment of a future dispensation in accordance with Afghan traditions. Rabbani gave us the assurance that he would send a list of the ulema from the north to the Taliban within two or three days and suggested that the meeting should be held in Islamabad around 20 January 1998. However, nothing more was heard from him for the next three months although the Northern Alliance did send a list of their ulema to the Taliban.

Mulla Rabbani, accompanied by a high-level Taliban delegation which included a minister, seven deputy ministers and senior officials, again visited Islamabad from 23-26 March 1998. He attended the Pakistan Day military parade on 23 March and, through a protocol oversight, was seated next to the Iranian ambassador which the latter refused to believe was coincidental—he told me later that he was convinced we had deliberately done this to embarrass him.

During a breakfast meeting with Prime Minister Nawaz Sharif on 24 March, Mulla Rabbani told us that the list of ulema sent by Burhanuddin Rabbani was a joke. It consisted of military commanders who had fought against the Taliban and others who knew nothing about Islam. Furthermore, from the list sent by the Northern Alliance it was unclear who represented who. We, nevertheless, impressed upon him that it was absolutely essential to move forward with the proposed meeting of the ulema. If the Taliban had objections to the list given by the Northern Alliance, they should think of some way to overcome this difficulty. Rabbani accordingly proposed a steering committee consisting of five to seven members each from the Taliban and the Northern Alliance which should meet in Islamabad to work out the modalities for the ulema conference. He promised to come up with the Taliban nominees within ten days. The Afghan explained that he envisaged the steering committee as a mechanism that would discuss an agreed list of ulema, set a date for the meeting, deliberate upon the possible participation of the Six Plus Two Group (consisting of Afghanistan's six immediate neighbours plus the US and Russia) as well as the UN and OIC as observers, decide on a notional time frame for the completion of the ulema meeting and, sort out its agenda which, in the final analysis, would include the restoration of peace and stability in Afghanistan.

Lakhdar Brahimi, who had been appointed the UN secretary general's special envoy on Afghanistan in the late summer of 1997, was also in Islamabad and had two meetings with Mulla Rabbani. The Pakistan-based UNSMA chief, Norbert Holl, was furious as he would have to take his orders from Brahimi who would be headquartered in New York. Holl had been a disaster. Blunt and ill-tempered, he was disliked by the Afghan parties on both sides of the political divide, scoffed at by the Iranians and regarded with contempt by the Central Asian states, particularly Turkmenistan. As the head of UNSMA, not once did Holl bother to see me from February to June 1997 although I was Pakistan's main Afghanistan coordinator. This raised the important question of what exactly the UN was doing. All UNSMA employees were well paid, they travelled in chauffeur-driven limousines and lived in luxurious air-conditioned houses in Islamabad. This entailed enormous expenditure, which was funded by UN member-states including Pakistan, but for what purpose was this expenditure being incurred if UNSMA was doing nothing about Afghanistan? Mulla Jalil once joked that had the Taliban not been around, Holl and his team would not be "receiving such big fat salaries".

It was only after our shuttle mission had hit the news headlines in Pakistan and had caught the attention of the international media that Holl came out of his hibernation and decided to re-establish contact with the Pakistan foreign office. I was particularly amused by his behaviour after my visit to Kandahar on 13 August 1997 during which I met Mulla Ghaus who, after his disappearance from Mazar-e-Sharif at the end of May, had suddenly reappeared.

When the carnage had started in Mazar-e-Sharif on 27 May because the Taliban had behaved like an occupying power and reneged on their cooperation agreement with General Malik, Ghaus had managed to escape. He had lived with a sympathetic ethnic Uzbek family for three months and had shaved his beard so as not to be identified as a Talib. When the fighting died down, he slowly made his way to Kandahar. Razzaq had also managed to escape and became the interior minister until the fall of the Taliban in 2001. Ghaus was unable to tell us anything about Mulla Ehsanullah, who, he felt, had been killed.

Ghaus's experiences in the north proved that General Malik and other Northern Alliance leaders had been telling us nothing but lies about the peace emissaries. Ghaus then gave an interview to the television team I had brought along with me and this created a sensation because of the Taliban aversion to cameras and photography. Ghaus stated that he fully supported the formation of the political commission proposed by

Qanooni. When this was aired on Pakistan television that evening, Holl panicked because he thought that we had achieved a breakthrough while he had nothing to show for himself. As 14 August was Pakistan's Independence Day anniversary and a public holiday, Holl could not establish contact with me at the office. He therefore dropped in unannounced at my home and ranted against the UN because Brahimi had been appointed the special envoy for Afghanistan. To salvage his tarnished reputation, Holl appeared on Pakistan television the next day and, to our utter disbelief, said that military means was only the second best option for settling the Afghan problem.

In his discussions with Brahimi, Mulla Rabbani urged him to persuade the Northern Alliance to nominate their representatives for the steering committee at the earliest. He said that he would welcome the immediate and comprehensive imposition of an arms embargo on Afghanistan and hoped that the UN and the OIC would put an end to the massive supply of weapons and ammunition by Iran and Uzbekistan to the Northern Alliance.

The first round of the Rabbani-Brahimi talks was devoted entirely to the reported manhandling of UN officials by the governor of Kandahar which prompted the UN to recall their personnel from the city. Rabbani expressed regret at the incident and held out the assurance that it would not be repeated. He, however, told Brahimi that the UN officials were also to blame. They were not only condescending in their demeanour but were consistently rude to Taliban officials. Accordingly, the Taliban and the UN agreed to work out the ground rules for the return of UN officials to Kandahar. Although the vast majority of the UN officials resided in Pakistan, the Taliban attached importance to their presence in Afghanistan as they believed that this lent legitimacy to their rule.

Mulla Rabbani also addressed a widely attended press conference in which he declared that the Taliban wanted a peaceful settlement of the conflict in Afghanistan and repeated what he had told Brahimi about the need for the UN and the OIC to impose a comprehensive arms embargo against Afghanistan. We were embarrassed that he publicly mentioned Iran and Uzbekistan as the main suppliers of weapons to the Northern Alliance. He then announced his proposal on the formation of the steering committee to break the impasse on the meeting of the ulema. He also stated that girls' schools were operational in Taliban controlled areas of Afghanistan and that employment opportunities had not been denied to women. He appealed to the international community to come forward with generous assistance so that more of such facilities could be provided to women.

I spoke to Burhanuddin Rabbani by telephone on 3 April and asked him to nominate five to seven persons to the steering committee. By then, the Taliban had issued a decree assigning Mulla Wakil Ahmad Mutawakil as leader and Mulla Abdul Manan Niazi, Mulla Abdul Raqib, Mulla Abdul Hakim Mujahed and Mulla Jalil as members of their delegation. I sent the decree to Brahimi, who was then in Ashgabat, through Amabssador Tariq Osman Hyder, with the request that he should obtain the list of the Northern Alliance nominees from Rabbani whom he would be meeting the following day.

Brahimi told Hyder that in Islamabad he had discerned excitement about the steering committee idea and was a trifle confused for two reasons. First, in his talks with Mulla Rabbani and with Pakistani officials, it had not been made clear what exactly this committee was supposed to do. The Taliban decree that had been handed over to him also reflected this lack of clarity. Was the steering committee to finalize the list of ulema from both sides or were substantive matters to be discussed? This convinced me that Brahimi was trying to confuse the issue. He had been clearly told when he was in Islamabad that the purpose of the steering committee was to work out the modalities for a meeting of the Afghan ulema which could, in course, discuss the broader issue of a permanent settlement of the conflict. The second reservation expressed by Brahimi was that this proposal would lead nowhere unless it was accompanied by a cease-fire. The indications were that both sides were preparing to resume military operations when the winter snows had melted.

Ambassador Hyder, who unfortunately had not had the time to read the information cable we had sent him on the steering committee proposal, changed the subject and stressed instead the importance of initiating some work on infrastructure development projects in Afghanistan such as the gas pipeline from Turkmenistan, through Afghanistan and onto Pakistan, as an incentive for the Afghans to work towards a peaceful settlement among themselves. Brahimi responded that no investment would be forthcoming for the gas pipeline project in the present circumstances. The UN was repeatedly telling both sides that peace was needed for reconstruction efforts. The Taliban were making it difficult for the UN to operate due to their "silly" ideas about women and their "dismal" human rights track record, while in the north, the UN was hampered by a lack of security. The UN's $200 million budget for Afghanistan could not, therefore, be properly utilized.

Brahimi told Hyder that he had met the Northern Alliance ambassador in New Delhi, Masood Khalili, and Dostum's deputy, Razm, both of whom had been in Ashgabat the previous day. Hyder was informed by an UNSMA official later that Brahimi had also met Dr Abdullah (he later became foreign minister in the Karzai government), who was representing Masood. After consulting with Brahimi, Hyder went to call on the Turkmen Shikhmuradov who was about to leave for the airport to receive Burhanuddin Rabbani. Shikmuradov suggested that they should continue their discussions there. He said that he had wanted Brahimi to also invite the Taliban for the consultations that were about to be held with the Northern Alliance in Ashgabat but was told by UN officials that the authorities in Kandahar would not have accepted the invitation and, as such, Brahimi had not even bothered to broach the idea with them. Shikhmuradov was disappointed as this reflected a bias against the Taliban. He also believed that Brahimi had been dismissive about the gas pipeline project because only the Taliban would benefit from it. President Saparmyrat Niyazov had tried to convince Brahimi that once the project started, the prosperity that it would bring would demonstrate the benefits of peace to the Afghan factions and induce them to lay down their weapons and begin serious negotiations with each other.

Regarding Burhanuddin Rabbani, Shikhmuradov wondered who he really represented. The Northern Alliance was bitterly divided and there had even been skirmishes in Badakshan between Masood and Rabbani loyalists though they both belonged to the Jamiat-e-Islami. Shikmuradov also believed that there were internal divisions among the Taliban but these were not nearly as serious as the differences between and within the various factions of the Northern Alliance. Burhanuddin Rabbani arrived in a military transport plane from Mazar-e-Sharif shortly afterwards and the Taliban decree was given to him. Hyder also reminded Rabbani about my conversation with him the previous day on the need to quickly nominate persons to the steering committee.

In a meeting with Ashgabat-based Six Plus Two representatives that afternoon, Brahimi outlined his discussions with the Pakistan government and with Mulla Rabbani in Islamabad as well as his talks with Mulla Wakil in Kandahar, which he thought was important. He said that although the ulema proposal had come from the Taliban, they had neither provided any list of their own for three months nor had they been willing to accept the list sent by the north. However, there would now be a change and the meeting of the ulema would be preceded by that of a steering committee. The list of the Taliban nominees had been handed over to Burhanuddin Rabbani by the Pakistan ambassador in Ashgabat earlier during the day. He hoped that the Northern Alliance would respond positively and not repeat what the Taliban had done earlier by unnecessarily delaying the nomination of their representatives.

In the meantime, I had briefed Hyder by telephone about the steering committee proposal in some detail. To pre-empt the possibility of Brahimi giving a negative twist to the idea for want of clarity as he had told Hyder earlier, I asked the latter to explain its purpose and objectives to the relevant persons. During the meeting of the Six Plus Two, therefore, Hyder informed Brahimi and the envoys that the steering committee would: discuss the agreed list of ulema for the meeting between the Taliban and the Northern Alliance; work out the modalities, which included the composition and time frame for the ulema meeting; and decide on a notional time frame for the completion of the ulema meeting and sort out its agenda, which would include the restoration of peace and stability in Afghanistan.

Hyder was later told by an UNSMA official that Brahimi had met Burhanuddin Rabbani that morning and had spoken in positive terms about the steering committee proposal despite his own misgivings. Rabbani had asked about the agenda of the committee and was told that this was a secondary issue as it was far more important for the two sides to enter into direct negotiations. Brahimi also stressed the importance of a cease-fire and exchange of prisoners. Rabbani was apprehensive about Islamabad as the venue though he had expressed no such reservations when he had accepted the concept of an ulema meeting in the Pakistani capital during the talks with us on 30 December 1997. Brahimi responded that the Northern Alliance should accept the first round in Pakistan because subsequent sessions could be held in other countries. Brahimi also had individual consultations with the other representatives of the Northern Alliance factions.

On the morning of 5 April 1998, the Northern Alliance team, which had come to Ashgabat, met under the chairmanship of Burhanuddin Rabbani to evolve a common position. Subsequently, they invited Brahimi to join them. He later held a press conference to announce that the Northern Alliance would participate in the steering committee and would soon be nominating their representatives. Brahimi stressed that the best proof both sides could give of the seriousness of their intentions was to declare a cease-fire. The UN and the OIC would now officially convey the response of the Northern Alliance to the Taliban and the Pakistan government.

Search for a political settlement

Ambassador Hyder called on Rabbani that afternoon who felt that the steering committee could be the first step towards peace. The Northern Alliance would send their list of nominees within seven to ten days to the UN and the OIC for transmission to the Taliban and Pakistan. Rabbani, however, was of the view that the agenda for the steering committee had to be broadened to include a cease-fire, formation of a broad-based government, exchange of prisoners and convening of a grand assembly or loya jirga. The Northern Alliance wanted the ulema meeting to take place under the auspices of the UN and the OIC. Rabbani also stated that the Northern Alliance had agreed to Islamabad as the venue for the first meeting but subsequent sessions should be held in other Islamic cities such as Jeddah, Tehran and Ashgabat.

Ambassador Masood Khalili of the Northern Alliance, who was present at the Rabbani-Hyder discussions, requested a separate meeting with the latter. He disclosed that the previous night Ahmed Shah Masood and Rabbani had talked for two hours by telephone as a result of which Rabbani and other northern representatives were given the green light to respond positively to the Taliban steering committee proposal. It was also Ahmed Shah Masood who had formulated the additional elements for the agenda which Rabbani had conveyed to Brahimi and had subsequently disclosed to Hyder. The Hizb-e-Wahdat, during the meeting of the Northern Alliance representatives that morning, had proposed an additional agenda item which was the immediate lifting of blockades on all routes for transportation of food and commerce.

Masood Khalili told Hyder that Afghanistan could never be militarily occupied by any single Afghan group. His own side had tried to do this when it held Kabul but he admitted that it had never succeeded and over time its territorial influence had contracted. He felt that an eventual settlement process could be one of the following three options: a coalition government in which all the Afghan factions would be represented; an interim administration consisting only of technocrats; or the convening of a loya jirga to which both sides would have to hand over power and which would then establish a new government reflecting the ethnic and religious realities in Afghanistan.

The US permanent representative to the UN, Bill Richardson—who was later to become energy secretary and then governor of New Mexico—visited Kabul and Dostum-controlled Shibberghan on 17 April. A jubilant Richardson later announced at a well attended press conference in Islamabad that his visit to Afghanistan had yielded substantial results for which he owed "special thanks" to the Pakistan government. He also acknowledged the leading role played by Islamabad in promoting the peace process.

Prior to his arrival in Islamabad, Richardson gave us a Taliban-specific wish list which included political and social measures that the US hoped they would take. The Taliban agreed to more than 90 percent of the wish list, the immediate consequence of which was the success of the Richardson visit.

The Taliban delegation, which was led by Mulla Rabbani, agreed after more than two hours of talks with Richardson to: (a) schedule the first meeting of the steering committee in Islamabad on 27 April or alternatively on 6 or 7 May (the latter date coincided with 10 Muharram which commemorates the martyrdom of the Prophet Muhammad's grandson, Hussain, in 680 and is observed as a day of mourning particularly by the Shias; it was, therefore, likely to be rejected by the Hizb-e-Wahdat); (b) discuss a cease-fire, exchange of prisoners and the modalities for the meeting of the ulema at the steering committee; (c) refrain from launching any new offensive unless they were attacked; (d) the immediate imposition of a comprehensive UN arms embargo on Afghanistan; (e) open more schools for girls and even a women's university if funds were provided; (f) allow female doctors, medical personnel and teachers to work; (g) prohibit terrorist activities from their soil inside or outside Afghanistan; (h) eradicate narcotics cultivation and trafficking for which they sought international support; and (i) resume negotiations with the UN on 20 April to work out the ground rules for UN operations in Afghanistan.

Richardson's interpretation of the understanding was that the steering committee would meet under UN and OIC auspices. It would also decide the venue for the next meeting. His visit to Afghanistan was the first in twenty years by a cabinet-ranking US official and signified a possible revival of US interest in Afghanistan.

The spadework for the meeting of the steering committee commenced on 20 April. Engineer Abdur Raheem of the Northern Alliance flew into Islamabad from Dushanbe for the preparatory meeting which was held at the foreign office. He and the Afghan ambassador in Islamabad, Abdul Hakim Mujahid, were designated the respective representatives of the two sides for the preparatory discussions. UNSMA and the Islamabad-based OIC representative also attended the meeting. The Taliban conveyed their readiness to participate in the steering committee at a day's notice while Abdur Raheem undertook to obtain the instructions of the

Northern Alliance for the date of the meeting which was tentatively fixed for 25 April. In a separate development, Ahmed Shah Masood, who was not present in Richardson's meeting with the Northern Alliance in Shibberghan, also confirmed that he endorsed the understanding reached with Richardson regarding the steering committee.

On 23 April 1998, James N'gobi, the temporary UNSMA head (Norbert Holl had left), and the OIC representative called on me to say that Lakhdar Brahimi had instructed N'gobi to convey to the Taliban and the Northern Alliance that the UN wanted a letter from them saying that the meeting of the steering committee would be held under UN and OIC auspices. A letter to this effect had been received from the Northern Alliance whereas there was no response from the Taliban. A similar confirmation from the Taliban was "indispensable" if the UN was to play a role.

I told N'gobi that the Taliban and the Northern Alliance had finally agreed to schedule the meeting within the next few days. This was a significant development and the UN was not to derail the understanding by insisting on letters. N'gobi agreed as did the OIC representative. Later that day, Brahimi telephoned N'gobi from Paris to tell him that the meeting was off unless the Taliban also sent a letter. Immediately afterwards, Burhanuddin Rabbani also spoke to N'gobi to tell him that the UN should not obstruct the process for want of a letter. Abdur Raheem of the Northern Alliance also took a similar position during the preparatory meeting. When Brahimi was told about this, he sarcastically observed that "the Afghan ambassador in Islamabad who, after all, was plenipotentiary and had full powers" should himself sign a letter saying that the Taliban accepted the meeting being held under UN and OIC auspices.

Brahimi's insistence on a letter reflected poorly on the UN. In effect, he was trying to unravel all that had been achieved only because he wanted to be at centre stage. The Afghan ambassador adopted a completely reasonable stance during the preparatory discussions. He said that the talks should continue and promised to do his best to obtain a letter from Kabul. The game being played by Brahimi was devious.

By 24 April, the Taliban delegation had still not arrived in Islamabad. Conflicting signals started emanating from Kabul and Kandahar. The latter took a hard line and insisted that the indispensable requirement for their participation was a public declaration by the UN that the only issue to be discussed in the committee would be the composition of the ulema commission. They also foolishly rejected the proposal that the meeting should be held under UN and OIC auspices. The authorities in Kabul, on the other hand, adopted a more moderate stance and this showed that there were differences within the Taliban. Hakim Mujahid held out the assurance that the Taliban delegation would fly to Islamabad the next day. He also sent a letter to UNSMA and the OIC which contained the text of a message addressed to him by his deputy foreign minister, Mulla Syed Muhammad Haqqani, confirming the understanding that the Taliban had reached with Bill Richardson as follows: (a) the meeting of the steering committee should be held by 27 April; (b) the meeting would be under UN and OIC auspices; (c) the first task of the steering committee would be to finalize the list of the ulema commission for which the Northern Alliance delegation should propose their nominees duly endorsed by all the Alliance leaders; and (d) after an agreed list for the ulema commission was finalized, the steering committee would discuss a cease-fire, the exchange of prisoners, the lifting of road blockades and the venue of the next meeting should the first session be inconclusive.

During this period I was in constant contact with Kabul and Kandahar to persuade them to come to Islamabad immediately. I told them that the steering committee was their own idea and they would lose all credibility and sympathy if they derailed it. They would stand out in stark and unfavourable contrast to the Northern Alliance who had already sent their delegation to Islamabad.

The OIC special representative for Afghanistan, assistant secretary general Ibrahim Bakr, flew into Islamabad on the morning of 24 April for the steering committee meeting. In a lengthy discussion with me he was bitter about Brahimi. He described the latter as a pompous individual with a dismally low level of intelligence as was evident from his clumsy handling of the steering committee proposal. He also expressed the view that a mediator had no business to obstruct talks between warring parties by putting forward unnecessary preconditions as Brahimi had done.

I told Bakr that come what may, we must not allow the steering committee meeting to fizzle out. It was imperative that it should get underway at the earliest. We were ready to provide an aircraft to bring the Taliban team to Islamabad. Bakr said that in case it was necessary, I should go to Kabul and Kandahar and he was willing to fly with me. This would demonstrate to the world that the OIC was solidly behind Pakistan in its efforts to promote the peace process.

Bakr's assessment of Brahimi proved accurate. After my meeting with him, I received a telephone call from UNSMA to convey a message from Brahimi that their aircraft had already made two futile attempts to bring the

Taliban delegation to Islamabad and that Pakistan should "chip in" towards the cost of the flights which worked out to US $ 600 per hour. Brahimi was obviously peeved that his ill-advised insistence on a written confirmation from the Afghan parties that the deliberations of the steering committee would be under UN and OIC auspices had been overturned by under-secretary general Kieran Prendergast. I told UNSMA that we would bring the question of payment for their flights to Kandahar and Kabul before the UN's Fifth Committee and demand a thorough review of all expenditure. As contributors to the UN budget, we had every right to demand an audit. We wanted to know what percentage of UNSMA expenditure was allocated to salaries, perks and privileges of its personnel and how much of the budget was actually being spent for promoting the Afghan peace process. This had a sobering effect on Brahimi who did not insist any further that Pakistan should pay for the flights. Fortunately, the Taliban delegation flew into Islamabad on the afternoon of 25 April.

The steering committee, which met from 26 April to 3 May, was inaugurated by foreign minister Gohar Ayub Khan. It brought the Afghan parties together for substantive face-to-face negotiations for the first time in several years. It had involved continuous efforts by us since June 1997 to reach this stage. This had necessitated frequent contacts with the Afghan groups in Kandahar, Shibberghan, Mazar-e-Sharif, Farkhar, Peshawar, Dubai and Islamabad. The meeting of the steering committee was also accompanied by an informal, unannounced halt in the fighting. It was our hope that we would be able to prolong this indefinitely.

The five-member Taliban delegation to the steering committee, which was led by Mulla Wakil Ahmad Mutawakil, the adviser to Mulla Omar, included the governor of Kabul, the interior deputy minister, Ambassador Hakim Mujahid and a senior government official. In contrast, the Northern Alliance was represented by a nine-member team of junior officials. In deference to us, the Taliban neither objected to the disparity in the size of the two delegations nor to the low level of participation from the Northern Alliance.

The meeting got off to a promising start. The Taliban made a significant concession by agreeing that the two sides should prepare their own list of ulema which neither would veto. It was decided that each would propose twenty names. This appeared to be a major achievement and a segment of the sensation-hungry media described it as a "breakthrough".

Thus the primary work of the steering committee had been accomplished and, as agreed earlier, the two delegations started talks on issues such as a cease-fire, exchange of prisoners and lifting of blockades. The

Taliban proposed that a final decision on these issues be left to the ulema commission which should convene in Islamabad as early as possible. The Hizb-e-Wahdat from the Northern Alliance delegation, however, insisted that these questions, particularly the lifting of the blockade of Bamyan, be resolved immediately by the steering committee.

We worked through the night to narrow the differences. Mulla Wakil phoned Omar in Kandahar to persuade him to remove the blockades but the latter insisted that this should be left to the ulema commission which could meet within a few days. In my presence, Wakil yelled at Omar: "May God rid me of you!" The latter, I was told, screamed back over the phone: "May God rid me of you too!" The conversation, if it can be called that, was fascinating to say the least. Here was an official who had no hesitation in reprimanding his supreme leader which the latter accepted because that was the way Afghans interact with each other.

After several more calls to Kandahar, Omar finally agreed to allow humanitarian supplies to Bamyan and Ghorbund. I immediately telephoned Karim Khalili in Bamyan to convey the news to him and to persuade him to wait for a few more days for the ulema commission which would deal with a comprehensive removal of road blockades. However, Khalili would hear nothing of this and insisted on an immediate decision by the steering committee. The other groups within the Northern Alliance delegation told us that they had no problem with waiting for the meeting of the ulema commission but had been unable to convince the Hizb-e-Wahdat.

Wakil left for Kandahar to persuade Omar to be more reasonable and asked Amabssador Hakim Mujahid to continue the talks until he got back. Unfortunately, Wakil did not return and the Northern Alliance boycotted further sessions of the steering committee on the grounds that the Taliban had changed their negotiating team. Appeals to them by the US and Iranian ambassadors in Islamabad to continue the talks were rejected. Instead, they accused the Taliban of derailing the negotiations before the media but appreciated Pakistan's role in promoting the peace process and for hosting the meeting.

The Taliban delegation, on the other hand, stated that they had not walked away from the negotiating table and were still around to resume the dialogue. In his briefing to the press, Hakim Mujahid highlighted the concessions his government had made and the dismissive response of the other side. He also called upon the UN to remove the anomaly of the continued occupation of Afghanistan's seat in the UN by the Northern Alliance.

Subsequently the UN and OIC, as co-chairmen, issued a statement which gave a factual account of the deliberations and emphasized that the meeting was being adjourned by mutual consent of the two Afghan delegations. Abdur Raheem of the Northern Alliance told me in confidence that the Hizb-e-Wahdat, which was acting at the behest of Iran's intelligence agencies, was entirely responsible for the failure of the meeting.

The inconclusive steering committee meeting demonstrated the complex nature of the issues involved—and quick fixes were highly unlikely. However, the first step had been taken in the way of a peace process. An intra-Afghan dialogue had, after many months, been initiated. Sworn enemies had come to the negotiating table and it was vitally important to resurrect the steering committee.

Shortly after the steering committee had been adjourned *sine die*, the US ambassador to Pakistan, Thomas Simons, gave us a letter for Nawaz Sharif from Bill Richardson expressing appreciation for making his visit to "Pakistan and Afghanistan a success". Richardson felt that "a great deal" had been achieved in the way of the Afghan peace process because Pakistan and the US were "working together". He emphasized the importance of maintaining the military stand down and that parallel efforts were needed to reconvene the steering committee.

Simons felt that the agreement on the list for the Afghan ulema conference during the deliberations of the steering committee "was not a mean achievement" which had, unfortunately, been derailed by the obdurate stances adopted by both sides. The insistence of the Hizb-e-Wahdat for an immediate and comprehensive end to the blockade of Bamyan and the Taliban failure to show up for the resumed session after consultations in Kandahar had equally contributed to the inconclusive outcome. The US had not lost hope and Simons felt that it was important to revive the steering committee at the earliest.

In the meantime, we continued to work quietly behind the scenes for an early resumption of the talks and had been in contact with all the Afghan parties. We were considering various permutations and combinations and the course that seemed most viable was a meeting under UN and OIC auspices of a fully empowered representative from each side to decide on the date and venue of the ulema commission. The steering committee would then be dissolved and issues such as a cease-fire, the exchange of prisoners, the lifting of road blockades and the future dispensation could be discussed by the ulema commission. The initial responses we received were positive. Burhanuddin Rabbani had agreed to the idea of only one representative from each side completing the work of the steering committee and promised to get back to us after consulting the other component factions of the Northern Alliance. The Taliban also agreed to the concept in principle.

It had become vitally important to quickly get the ulema commission off the ground. The military stand-down was already beginning to come apart. On 8 May, the Taliban had captured Ishkamishk in Takhar which straddled Ahmed Shah Masood's main supply route from the north. There was bound to be a counter-offensive from Masood and, unless talks were quickly revived, the prospects for peace would receive a serious setback with the onset of the new fighting season.

Our assessment was that for the peace process to succeed three essential steps were needed. These included the immediate imposition of an arms embargo under Chapter VII of the UN Charter, which deals with Security Council action, binding on all UN member states, with respect to threats and breaches of peace as well as acts of aggression; the adoption of the vacant seat formula by the UN to make it that much more credible as a mediator; and, lastly, the commencement of humanitarian assistance to demonstrate the dividends of peace to the Afghan parties. Lakhdar Brahimi, however, felt that if Pakistan and Iran declared that weapons would not be sent to Afghanistan there would not be any need for an arms embargo. This was ridiculous as mere declarations were not enough. A proper mechanism had to be evolved to ensure the end of weapons supplies and to monitor the embargo. This would only be possible through a resolution of the UN Security Council which, for reasons I have never been able to understand, Brahimi was reluctant to promote.

The Pakistan-Iran joint mission

For many months we had been trying to persuade Tehran to work closely and visibly with us towards an Afghanistan settlement. The Iranian response on the several occasions that this was raised with them was always marked by ambivalence and prevarication. It was, therefore, never clear what they really wanted. Their inclination was towards a step-by-step approach through behind-the-scene confidence-building measures such as the exchange of delegations between Kandahar and Tehran, meetings between Iran-based Afghan groups and the Taliban, the lifting of road blockades and the release of Iranian and Pakistani prisoners (in our case civilians) held respectively by the Taliban and the Northern Alliance.

Search for a political settlement

The Iranians finally came round to accepting direct and more open cooperation with Pakistan for promoting the Afghan peace process during the visit of their foreign minister, Kamal Kharrazi, to Islamabad in the first week of June 1998. The probable reason for this change was the disunity among the Northern Alliance which was compounded by the hatred of Iran's protegé, the Hizb-e-Wahdat. The latter, which was detested by Ahmed Shah Masood, Dostum, and Burhanuddin Rabbani alike was too weak to fulfil Iran's Afghanistan agenda by itself. During this period, Dostum's forces had clashed with those of the Hizb-e-Wahadat, tension between Masood and Professor Rabbani had heightened, and Masood had lost ground to the Taliban in Kunduz and Takhar. Added to this was the rivalry between Dostum and Masood for supremacy of the north.

Iran's deputy foreign minister Broujerdi and I came to the following understanding during the Kharrazi visit:

—Pakistan and Iran would nominate a middle-ranking official each who would undertake joint visits to Mazar-e-Sharif and Kandahar

—The Iranians would consult the Northern Alliance and Pakistan would sound out the Taliban to determine whether this would be acceptable to them

—After obtaining the concurrence of the Afghans, our nominee, Ayaz Wazir, would proceed to Tehran at the end of June and, along with his Iranian counterpart Mohyuddin Najafi (a former ambassador to Afghanistan), visit Mazar-e-Sharif and Kandahar to determine precisely what the Afghan parties wanted.

—The results of the joint mission would be examined by Broujerdi and me after which we would recommend future measures to our respective governments.

—The Pakistan-Iran initiative would be played at low key. No formal announcement would be made until the team had left for Afghanistan.

—Simultaneously, Pakistan and Iran would approach the Taliban and the Northern Alliance to nominate a person each, vested with full powers, to resume the steering committee deliberations under UN and OIC auspices.

—At a subsequent stage, Pakistan and Iran would establish joint panels of doctors and narcotics specialists who would visit areas controlled by the Taliban and the Northern Alliance.

In the meantime, a severe earthquake had hit northern Afghanistan. Our minister of state for foreign affairs, Siddique Kanju (he was subsequently assassinated while campaigning during the local bodies elections organized by the Musharraf government), Aziz Khan, Ayaz Wazir and I flew into Mazar-e-Sharif aboard a Pakistan Air Force C-130 transport plane to Bahawalpur with relief supplies on 4 June. In Mazar we met Burhanuddin Rabbani who expressed gratitude for the assistance. He also welcomed the idea of a joint Pakistan-Iran mission. Rabbani was to go to Germany for medical treatment which he postponed on learning that the following day we would be flying two helicopter-loads of relief goods to Faizabad, the capital of his home province, Badakshan.

From Mazar-e-Sharif we took off for Kandahar. On the way we noticed the cockpit crew looking out of the window in all directions. I jokingly told Kanju that they had lost their way. He immediately asked them what was wrong and was told that an unidentified aircraft was following us. It later transpired that it was a Taliban fighter which had apparently—and worryingly—not been able to identify us. In Kandahar, we met Mulla Wakil and Mulla Jalil who were deeply moved to learn that the government of Pakistan had agreed to the Taliban request for food supplies for the internally displaced people of Ghorbund. They were also told that we had decided to provide them 300 million rupees in cash as assistance for humanitarian purposes. Jalil and Wakil also accepted, in principle, the Pakistan-Iran joint mission.

The helicopter flight from Islamabad to Faizabad on 5 June took us three hours inclusive of a refuelling halt at Peshawar. This was a journey that I can never forget. We flew through mountain passes, we passed the towering Trich Mir peak, the Lowari Top and Chitral. The scenery was unbelievably beautiful. At times it seemed we were only a few feet away from the snow-covered mountains. Below us were green fields and rushing torrents. Faizabad was lush green. It was raining as we landed and we were driven to a rest house where Rabbani was waiting for us. Seldom, however, have I witnessed so much poverty as I did in Faizabad. Badakhsan, I was told, was the poorest part of war-devastated Afghanistan. The rest house, which was built a few feet over a river, was the only concrete building that we saw.

I found Rabbani a sad man. He complained about Ahmed Shah Masood who, he said, no longer listened to him and often took an extreme position. During lunch we were told that the fuel for our helicopters which was supposed to have come from Tajikistan had not arrived because of bad weather. Rabbani offered us one of his own helicopters to take us back to Islamabad but by then clouds had set in and more bad weather was forecast along the route. The pilots told us that the flight was dangerous even in good weather and in conditions that prevailed then it was impossible to fly. Rabbani then offered us one of his own war planes, an AN-32. We flew in his helicopter to the airfield where we came across UN relief workers and foreign journalists. The green hills around us, the snow capped mountain peaks at a distance, the crisp cool air reminded me of the Scottish countryside. It was decided that Ayaz Wazir would remain with the helicopter crew until the fuel arrived.

The flight back on the AN-32 was uneventful until we were above Islamabad. We could see the airport several thousand feet below us. The pilot had not made a gradual descent and he decided to dive onto the runway. About two hundred feet above the ground we hit a dust storm and the plane was swept off the runway. We started climbing again for a second attempt. Kanju yelled: "O my God!" Aziz Khan was about to vomit. Luckily we landed safely on the second attempt.

Thus we had obtained the consent of the Taliban as well as the Northern Alliance for the Pakistan-Iran joint mission. We were some-what surprised to see that the leaders of the Northern Alliance were as jubilant as the Taliban on the nuclear tests we had conducted only a few days earlier. These tests were in response to those of India on 11 May 1998, after which Indian leaders made statements that were widely reported by the media as threatening to annihilate Pakistan. The threats stopped immediately after Islamabad also demonstrated its nuclear capability seventeen days later.

Ayaz Wazir proceeded to Tehran where he met Amabssador Najafi on 29 June to prepare for their joint mission to Mazar-e-Sharif and Kandahar. The Wazir-Najafi team left for Afghanistan on 30 June and returned to Tehran on 1 July. In Mazar-e-Sharif, they met a delegation of the Northern Alliance that was led by Burhanuddin Rabbani and included representatives of the Harkat-e-Islami (Mohseni Group), Hizb-e-Wahdat (Khalili and Akbari Groups), Jumbish-e-Milli of Dostum and Hizb-e-Islami of Hikmatyar. After the purpose of the visit was explained by the Pakistan-Iran team, the Northern Alliance made three proposals. The first of these was a meeting of all the leaders of the Northern Alliance and the Taliban led by Mulla Omar; the second was the resumption of the steering committee deliberations in which the representatives of the two sides would have full powers, and, if these two proposals were unacceptable to the Taliban, Iran and Pakistan should come forward with a plan of their own.

In Kandahar, the Taliban delegation led by Mulla Wakil, said that they and the Northern Alliance did not trust each other and, as such, confidence-building measures were required to jump-start any peace process. They proposed the compilation of lists of prisoners held by either side which should be exchanged after the names had been verified. This would be followed by a cease-fire and the release of the prisoners, starting with the sick, the children and the aged. Wakil was of the view that the confidence thus generated would enable Pakistan and Iran to bring the Northern Alliance and the Taliban to the negotiating table.

Ayaz Wazir telephoned me from Kandahar to say that Najafi had sought a separate meeting with the Taliban and that this was against the understanding that Pakistan and Iran would jointly talk to the Afghan groups. I told him not to obstruct the meeting because it was important for the Iranians and the Taliban to have a frank exchange of views. Najafi conveyed Iran's grievances against the Taliban to Wakil who, in turn, said that Tehran was working against the interest of the Taliban by continuing to recognize the Rabbani regime as the government of Afghanistan and providing massive military and economic assistance to the Northern Alliance. Wakil indicated that there were two ways to improve Iran-Taliban relations. The fast track would consist of withdrawal of Iran's recognition of the Rabbani regime and the re-establishment of the Iranian embassy in Kabul. The other option, which was slower, would require Iran's acceptance of the OIC position of non-recognition of either side in Afghanistan, reduction in material support to the Northern Alliance and an end to propaganda against the Taliban. Najafi indicated his preference for the second option. This was the closest that Iran ever came to accepting the vacant seat formula that had been adopted by the OIC in respect of Afghanistan's representation in the organization. The Taliban also allowed Najafi to meet the Iranian prisoners in their custody but did not agree to the request for the release of one or two of the prisoners who could be taken back to Tehran.

On his return to Tehran, Najafi said that he was extremely happy with the visit to Kandahar. The Iranians requested that I reach Tehran by 5 July for a meeting with Alaeddin Broujerdi to discuss the outcome of the joint mission and decide on the future follow-up action.

Ayaz Wazir flew back to Islamabad to brief me in greater detail about the Pakistan-Iran shuttle mission. Shortly afterwards we left for Tehran where we had two hours of useful discussions with Broujerdi on 8 July followed by a brief call on foreign minister Kharrazi. Broujerdi was, with justification, upbeat about the outcome of the Wazir-Najafi mission.

The point that I emphasized to him was that the Taliban had proposed a comprehensive exchange of list of prisoners followed by a cease-fire. This was as encouraging as it was far-reaching. It signified a complete change from their earlier aversion to a cease-fire as was conveyed to Shamshad and to me during our meeting with Mulla Omar in Kandahar at the end of December 1997. Both elements—i.e. an exchange of prisoners and cessation of hostilities—were also acceptable to the Northern Alliance. I stressed that it was important for Pakistan and Iran to work closely together to encourage the Taliban and the Northern Alliance to build upon the initial outlines of a possible compromise that was gradually emerging. The two sides had to be quickly persuaded to prepare their lists of prisoners in preparation for their release so that the cease-fire could be in place. Broujerdi and I would then have to move fast to bring the Afghan groups to the negotiating table.

Broujerdi disclosed that Lakhdar Brahimi had telephoned him when the Pakistan-Iran team was in Afghanistan. Brahimi seemed to be somewhat concerned that the UN had been sidelined. Broujerdi felt that it was important to carry the UN along with us. I agreed with this and said that the OIC should also be associated with the process.

I told Broujerdi that there were reports of contacts between the Northern Alliance and Israel. These meetings were said to have taken place in New York and Moscow after which Israel had sent relief supplies to the quake-stricken victims of northern Afghanistan. Broujerdi said that he too had heard such reports and had checked with the Northern Alliance leadership who staunchly denied any such contact.

Broujerdi and I decided that in order to keep the UN engaged in the peace process, the Pakistani and Iranian permanent representatives in New York would submit a joint report on the Pakistan-Iran peace initiative at the next Six Plus Two meeting. We worked out an agreed text for this presentation. We also decided that the joint mission had to continue and its primary role, at that stage, would be to facilitate the exchange of lists of prisoners so that a cease-fire could be brought about. This would establish an enabling environment for a dialogue between the Taliban and the Northern Alliance. As per our understanding in Islamabad during Kharrazi's visit in June, we decided to expedite the dispatch of doctors and narcotics control specialists to Afghanistan. I undertook to visit Kandahar within the next few days to brief the Taliban leadership about the discussions in Tehran while Broujerdi committed himself to similarly inform the Northern Alliance in Mazar-e-Sharif. We agreed that regular Pakistan-Iran consultations would be held alternately in Islamabad and Tehran.

Although Tehran finally came round to accepting the idea of a Pakistan-Iran joint mission, it failed to understand that its tactical policy of disproportionate support to the Shia Hizb-e-Wahdat could never achieve its strategic objective of supremacy in Afghanistan. This alienated the other ethnic groups and eroded even the semblance of unity in what remained of the Northern Alliance. Iran's acceptance of the joint mission was aimed at buying time to rectify the situation and thereby consolidate its influence in the north. It had not anticipated that the violence that was to breakout in the coming days would transform Afghanistan and its ambitions in that country would receive an irreversible setback.

5
The collapse of the Northern Alliance

THE OPTIMISM that the Pakistan-Iran joint mission to Afghanistan had generated was short-lived. Within a day or two after my return to Islamabad from Tehran, Dostum elements attacked the Taliban across the Murghab river in Badghis. The latter retaliated and, by the middle of the month, captured the Dostum-controlled province of Faryab. Maimena, the capital of the province, came under the control of the Taliban while small pockets of resistance continued around the city. By and large the local commanders surrendered their weapons to the Taliban voluntarily. The Taliban then advanced to Andkhoi, a town at the border with Turkmenistan.

The Taliban also captured a sizeable quantity of weapons and heavy artillery including tanks. Dostum thus became vulnerable and it was speculated that Shibberghan would also be soon taken by the Taliban. The indications were that Dostum might join forces with the Hizb-e-Wahdat, despite his bitter hatred of them, for the defence of Mazar-e-Sharif.

The Taliban also took some eight hundred prisoners about four hundred of whom had been flown to Kandahar. According to unconfirmed reports, some prominent Jumbish commanders including generals Fauzi and Rauf Baqi had been killed. Mulla Omar set up a commission under his information minister to ensure that revenge killings and slaughter did not take place.

On 14 July 1998 Aziz Khan, Ayaz Wazir and I flew to Kandahar to meet Mulla Omar. The purpose was to advise him not to pursue the military option and to allow the Pakistan-Iran joint mission to run its course to bring peace to Afghanistan. I briefed him about my talks in Tehran with Broujerdi and foreign minister Kharrazi six days earlier. I tried to persuade Omar to immediately take the measures agreed upon with the Pakistan-Iran joint mission. His response was that the north had again demonstrated bad faith by attacking the Taliban in Badghis. He could now do nothing because the fighting had started. He speculated that it would all be over in two weeks.

It was during this meeting that I got to know an aspect of Omar's way of thinking that I would never have imagined. The impression we and the world had of him was that he was an incurable religious fanatic. And yet Omar now told me that he had great love for Pakistan which had sacrificed so much and for so long for Afghanistan. He always remembered Pakistan and its people in his prayers even before his own country. Prime Minister Nawaz Sharif was a sensible, pragmatic leader who was good for the Pakistani nation, and the greatest enemies of Pakistan, Omar added, were the religious parties which preached extremism in the name of Islam. Several of these parties claimed to have links with the Taliban which was completely untrue—he had not even met the leaders of most of these organizations including Maulana Fazlur Rahman of Pakistan's Jamiat-e-Ulema-e-Islam.

Omar observed that I had visited Afghanistan often with the aim of promoting peace. He personally felt ashamed of himself because he had been unable to concede much during my several visits to Kandahar. However, the fault was not his. The Afghan opposition was insincere as had been demonstrated yet again by Dostum's military offensive in Badghis.

True to form, the Iranian media again went to town blaming Pakistan for the fighting that had flared up in Faryab. All the wrong conclusions were drawn because of the reverses suffered by the Northern Alliance. The Iranian newspapers even went to the ridiculous extent of insinuating that the government in Islamabad was not in control over policy and that the Pakistan armed forces had their own Afghanistan agenda. I was accused in one write-up of deceiving Broujerdi by promising the continuation of the Pakistan-Iran joint mission to promote an Afghan peace process whereas Islamabad's actual objective was a military settlement in Afghanistan through the Taliban.

Soon after the capture of Faryab by the Taliban, Broujerdi issued a statement regretting the escalation of the fighting in Afghanistan and denouncing the Taliban offensive in Faryab as "fratricide". He added that past experience had shown that the military successes or failures of any of the Afghan parties would not lead to durable peace which could only come through political means. He further stated "the natural reaction to any military attack is defence causing escalation of bloodshed in the Islamic state of Afghanistan".

On 14 July, *Jamhuri-e-Islami*, a paper which had close links to the Iranian supreme leader Ayatollah Ali Khamenei, carried an editorial entitled "the Taliban group is not worthy of trust". It alleged that while the fighting in Afghanistan may appear to be a civil war, in reality it was not that because the conflict was being stoked by outsiders. Saudi Arabia, the United States and Pakistan were the known supporters of the Taliban and the latter were also being assisted by Zionists. The inference drawn by the editor was that the Taliban were the surrogates of the Pakistan armed forces.

Another Iranian newspaper, *Hamshehri*, noted that the Taliban attack in Faryab was carried out at a time when the joint Pakistan-Iran efforts, aimed at the resolution of the Afghanistan crisis, had started and had reached a critical stage. This had generated hopes that the mistrust between the Taliban and the Northern Alliance would be successfully addressed. However, certain countries who did not want peace in Afghanistan were responsible for re-igniting the conflict. Changez Pahlawan, an academic at Tehran University, gave an interview which was prominently carried by the Iranian media with official encouragement, accusing Pakistan of obstructing the restoration of stability in Afghanistan. He commented that whenever there were signs that a peaceful settlement of the conflict was imminent, Pakistan, a supporter of the Taliban, always encouraged the latter to commence hostilities.

On 15 July, Javed Hussain, the new Pakistan ambassador in Tehran, was told by the Iranian foreign office that Broujerdi would be flying to Mazar-e-Sharif as agreed upon between him and me. Hussain accordingly briefed the officials about my discussions with Mulla Omar the previous day and also informed them that, on my return to Islamabad from Kandahar, I had received a message from Mulla Wakil that, despite the escalation of the conflict, the list of Northern Alliance prisoners in Taliban custody was being prepared and would be completed in a few days.

Immediately after returning to Tehran from Mazar-e-Sharif, Broujerdi told Javed Hussain that he had met Burhanuddin Rabbani and other leaders of the Northern Alliance and had apprised them of the outcome of the joint Pakistan-Iran mission. He told them that both Pakistan and Iran had sent a joint report on the mission to the Six Plus Two. The Northern Alliance leaders had complained about the Taliban offensive in Faryab. However, Broujerdi had assured them that the joint Pakistan-Iran peace mission would continue despite obstacles and temporary setbacks. He reminded the Northern Alliance representatives that the conflict in their country had lasted two decades and it was unrealistic to expect Iran and Pakistan to resolve the Afghanistan problem within a few days. He claimed to have said that Pakistan had nothing to do with the Taliban offensive in Faryab and had stressed that Prime Minister Nawaz Sharif was strongly supporting the joint mission.

Broujerdi told Javed Hussain that the Six Plus Two group had welcomed the Pakistan-Iran initiative. He especially quoted US assistant secretary of state Rick Inderfurth as saying that most of the reports coming from Afghanistan were discouraging with the exception of the news about the joint Pakistan-Iran mission. He also said that Brahimi had welcomed the combined efforts of Islamabad and Tehran to promote peace in Afghanistan and had agreed that the UN would also participate in the mission. The Northern Alliance list of prisoners was ready and it was important that this should be quickly exchanged with the one being prepared by the Taliban.

Broujerdi stated that, as agreed upon by him and me, the joint Pakistan-Iran mission should again visit Kandahar and Mazar-e-Sharif. This time the mission would include representatives from the UN and the OIC and could originate from Islamabad. It would proceed first to Kandahar and then to Mazar-e-Sharif. However, if Pakistan had transportation problems, Iran would be willing to provide an aircraft in which case the team could leave from Tehran. He requested Pakistan's views about the timing of the mission.

Hussain took this opportunity to draw Broujerdi's attention to the propaganda blitz against Pakistan in the Iranian media on the fighting in Faryab. The latter gave the expected and unconvincing reply that Tehran had no control on the comments carried by the press which often criticized the Iranian government and, in particular, the foreign office. He nevertheless promised that he would try to remove the media slander against Pakistan.

Three weeks after their advance into Faryab, the Taliban captured the Dostum stronghold of Shibberghan on 2 August 1998. This implied that the Jumbish-e-Milli had been virtually eliminated, leaving only the Hizb-e-Wahdat and the Shura-e-Nazar of Ahmed Shah Masood as the two remaining credible elements of the Northern Alliance.

The fall of Shibberghan to the Taliban came about because of sharp differences between the Jumbish-e-Milli and the Hizb-e-Wahdat. The latter wanted to play the major role in the defence of the city and this was rejected by Dostum. The loss of Shibberghan, which was the main base of the armed forces in the north, meant that concerted military manoeuvres would be more difficult for the Northern Alliance.

Several commanders in Balkh and Samangan again switched sides to the Taliban. The latter initially avoided a frontal attack on Mazar-e-Sharif, and concentrated instead on its strangulation by trying to establish control over the four major supply routes into the city. Almost immediately after the fall of Shibberghan, Broujerdi sent a message to me through Javed Hussain to tell the Taliban to ensure the safety of the Iranian consulate personnel in Mazar-e-Sharif. This was particularly surprising as no one expected Mazar-e-Sharif to be captured by the Taliban anytime soon. I was given a solemn assurance by the Taliban leadership that all citizens, particularly foreign consulate personnel, would be protected by them. They would not stoop to the level of their opponents who had massacred thousands of Taliban the previous year as was proved by the discovery of mass graves. Broujerdi was informed accordingly.

The continuing differences between Mohaqiq and Karim Khalili within the Hizb-e-Wahdat and between Ahmed Shah Masood and Professor Rabbani of the Jamiat-e-Islami further weakened the Northern Alliance. Among its leaders only Mohaqiq remained in Mazar-e-Sharif after the Taliban capture of Shibberghan.

It was widely believed that despite the military success of the Taliban the situation still remained fluid. Much depended on their ability to consolidate their gains in the coming weeks. The last thing that Pakistan had wanted was the resumption of fierce fighting in Afghanistan. Despite our efforts to restore peace, there had unfortunately been no break in the cycle of violence. We were frustrated by the unwillingness of all the Afghan groups to listen to reason. Their battlefield successes or failures meant nothing to us. Our one and only goal in Afghanistan was the restoration of durable peace as Pakistan was the country that had suffered the most from the continuation of the conflict. We hoped that the Pakistan-Iran joint mission on Afghanistan would remain on track.

On 8 August 1998, Mazar-e-Sharif was captured by the Taliban. The initial reports indicated that the city fell with little resistance. It later transpired that this was incorrect. To reach the centre of the city, the Taliban sent in suicide squads. Jeep-loads of Taliban, each following the other after short intervals, were sent into Mazar-Sharif. The first four or five vehicles were blown up by Hizb-e-Wahdat rocket fire but each succeeded in advancing some distance towards the city centre. When this was finally reached, the Taliban ground forces entered the city forcing the Hizb-e-Wahdat to retreat to Bamyan but not without offering fierce resistance.

Although Balkh was Jumbish-e-Milli territory, its capital Mazar-e-Sharif came under the control of the Hizb-e-Wahdat after the defeat of the Taliban in the north in the summer of 1997. This was primarily because bitter hatred between General Malik and Dostum had weakened the Jumbish-e-Milli. Malik had acknowledged Ahmed Shah Masood as his leader and this had further divided the ethnic Uzbeks of the north. Masood, however, preferred to stay in his own provinces in north-eastern Afghanistan and the Hizb-e-Wahdat, which had received massive military and economic assistance from Tehran, became dominant in Mazar-e-Sharif and even in Dostum's stronghold, Shibberghan.

I was later told by ethnic Uzbeks who belonged to the area that Hizb-e-Wahdat control of Mazar-e-Sharif was marked by unparalleled barbarity. Its members, belonging as they do to the Shia belief, had been persecuted alike by the majority Pushtun community as well as by all other ethnic groups and were determined to take revenge. Heavily armed Hizb-e-Wahdat soldiers, many with hand grenades rolled into their long hair like curlers worn by women, patrolled the streets of Mazar-e-Sharif and would extort money at gunpoint from pedestrians. Particularly vulnerable were couples and unescorted women. If they were unable to pay what was demanded, the Hizb-e-Wahdat guards would ask for their marriage documents and the failure to produce these would result in their veils and burqas being ripped away. They were often beaten in public on fabricated charges of immorality for no better reason than venturing out of their homes with a male without documentary evidence of marriage. The resentment of the local population was, therefore, enormous and it was probably for this reason that the only resistance to the Taliban advance into Mazar-e-Sharif was from the Hizb-e-Wahdat.

The fall of Mazar-e-Sharif capped the military offensive that had been prompted by Dostum's attack at Badghis four weeks earlier and had resulted in a stern Taliban response which culminated in the re-establishment of their control of the north. Mulla Omar declared an amnesty for all those who surrendered and his military commanders were under strict instructions to avoid revenge killings for the atrocities that were perpetrated against thousands of Taliban prisoners by General Malik the previous year. The Taliban leadership also announced that their agenda was purely domestic and neighbouring countries had nothing to fear from them.

Despite this, massacres did take place in Mazar-e-Sharif though not on the scale of the one in 1997 in which the Taliban were the victims. This was confirmed to me by Red Cross officials who also said that many of those killed had died in the cross-fire between the Taliban and the retreating Hizb-e-Wahdat forces.

Within hours after the capitulation of the Hizb-e-Wahdat at Mazar-e-Sharif, I received a telephone call from the Iranian ambassador in Islamabad, Mahdi Akhundzadeh, to say that his government had received two reports about their consulate general in the city. The first of these was that the premises had been fired upon and that the Taliban had forcibly entered the building. The second was that the Taliban had entered the consulate without violence.

Akhundzadeh later called on me to say that eleven members of the Iranian consulate had been taken to an unknown destination and that both the Taliban and Pakistan would be held responsible for their safety. I firmly rejected this view and replied that Islamabad was certainly not responsible for what was happening inside Afghanistan. While we would do all we could to ensure the safety of the Iranian nationals, we could not be held accountable for them. In May 1997 we had faced a similar situation—our consulate general in Mazar-e-Sharif was broken into, the lives of our personnel were threatened and the premises was ransacked. We did not point an accusing finger at Tehran and it was surprising that the Iranian government should even think of apportioning blame on us should their nationals be harmed.

I also told Akhundzadeh that we were bitterly disappointed at the manner in which the Iranian media was hurling accusations at Pakistan for the military reverses of the Northern Alliance. This was being done despite Broujerdi's briefing to Amabssador Javed Hussain a few weeks earlier when he had assured the Northern Alliance that Islamabad had nothing to do with the current military offensive of the Taliban. Furthermore it was clear that the Iranian government had not done anything, despite Broujerdi's promise, to dispel the misinformation being churned out against Pakistan by Iran's media. I assured Akhundzadeh that we would do everything possible to ensure the safety of the Iranian consulate personnel—however, he had to realize that what was happening was in another country and not in Pakistan. We did not even have a presence in Mazar-e-Sharif after our consulate general was closed down in May 1997.

After this meeting with Akhunzadeh, we again approached the Taliban authorities in Kandahar at the highest level to ensure the safety of the Iranian nationals. We were informed by them that the Iranian consulate was deserted as its personnel had fled. However, they would be given full protection and would be evacuated to Tehran should any of them fall into the hands of the Taliban. What the Taliban did find, nevertheless, were two Iranian planes loaded with weapons and ammunition at the Mazar-e-Sharif airport.

That night at around 11.30pm Javed Hussain was summoned by Broujerdi to the Iranian foreign office in connection with the security of the Iranian mission in Mazar-e-Sharif and its personnel. Broujerdi said that after entering the city that morning, the Taliban had gone straight to the Iranian consulate general and had broken into it around 11am. They had harassed and maltreated the personnel and had locked them up in a room in the consulate until 2.30pm at which time they were taken away to an unknown place according to some eyewitness reports. Broujerdi again requested Pakistan to use its influence over the Taliban to find the Iranian officials and ensure their safety and release. He added that they were especially worried because they had heard a radio broadcast in which Mulla Omar had stated that there were no Iranians in the Mazar-e-Sharif consulate when the Taliban had entered the city. Broujerdi asserted that this was a lie because Tehran had been in contact with its consulate personnel for some time after the Taliban had gone into the premises. Broujerdi further stated that the Iranian president and foreign minister were personally monitoring the situation closely and, if not properly handled, it could develop into a serious problem between Pakistan and Iran and would, at the very least, derail the Pakistan-Iran joint initiative in Afghanistan.

Hussain told Broujerdi that the Taliban had given us their assurances that the Iranian personnel would not be harmed. He also informed him of my conversation with the new Taliban chargé d'affaires in Islamabad, Mulla Haqqani, earlier that day. Haqqani, a man with a marvellous sense of humour, had assured me that the Taliban had surrounded the Iranian consulate general for its protection and that all the officials were safe.

The next day, director general Mohib Ali of the Iranian foreign office told Javed Hussain that the Iranian government reserved the right to take strong retaliatory action against the Taliban should any of their personnel in Mazar-e-Sharif come to harm. He then expressed the hope that the Iranian nationals captured during the fighting would also be released. Shortly afterwards the Persian dailies *Jamhouri-e-Islami*, *Salam* and *Hamsheri* called for demonstrations at the Pakistan embassy in Tehran to protest against Islamabad's alleged interference in Afghanistan's internal affairs and the assassination of Iranian officials in Pakistan some months earlier.

Separately, Javed Hussain reported that there had been firing from the Iranian side on the Iran-Afghanistan border on 10 August. This was preceded by a visit to the border by the commander of the Iranian Revolutionary Guard Corps (IRGC), Major-General Safvi. The *Tehran Times* in its opinion column of 11 August commented: "The nation expects the government—particularly the armed forces—to shape a sweeping policy to get the Iranian nationals back and safe no matter if they have to cross the border to teach a lesson to the radicals who, in the name of Islam, are committing treason against human beings."

Broujerdi met Javed Hussain the same day to state that what was taking place in Afghanistan should not be allowed to jeopardize Pakistan-Iran relations. He disclosed that the Iranian authorities had reliable information that their eleven Mazar-e-Sharif consulate personnel had been flown from Shindand to Kandahar on 10 August where they were being detained. Pakistan's assistance in securing their release was requested.

Around this time we had helped get nine Iranians who were stranded in Bamyan out of Afghanistan and Broujerdi conveyed the appreciation of his government. However, he expressed regret that the arrival of these Iranian nationals in Peshawar had been given extensive publicity by Pakistan. Javed Hussain, in turn, protested that whenever the two met Broujerdi's office always issued distorted press releases that gave the impression that the Pakistan ambassador had been reprimanded each time. Broujerdi replied unabashedly that this was done to satisfy the Iranian public who wanted the government to take firm measures against Pakistan. Hussain then drew Broujerdi's attention to the planned demonstrations against the Pakistan embassy over the next few days. Broujerdi said that there was a lot of popular resentment against Islamabad because of the earlier assassination of Iranian officials in Pakistan. He would, nevertheless, get in touch with the newly appointed deputy foreign minister, Moshen Aminzadeh, on this matter.

By 11 August, Mazar-e-Sharif was completely calm and the Taliban had succeeded in taking nearly all of Balkh including the border town of Hairatan. They had also captured Taloqan, the capital of Takhar and the second biggest city in the north. The same afternoon Farkhar, where we had met Masood in July 1997, also came under Taliban control. In addition to this, the Taliban dominated all entry points to the Hizb-e-Wahdat stronghold, Bamyan. Furthermore, they had considerable success in taking vast areas of Baghlan that were under the control of Mansur Naderi of the Ismailis. Pul-e-Kumri and Nahrin, both vital supply points to the Panjsher valley, were captured by the Taliban on 12 August.

A campaign of deliberate distortion on the successes of the Taliban was immediately launched by their detractors. It was alleged that their rapid advance would not have been possible without assistance from their "friends"—Iran and Russia were even more direct and mentioned Pakistan by name. The point ignored by those making these allegations was that the Taliban did not need any assistance. There was hardly any resistance to their advances on the ground. In most areas, the local commanders voluntarily surrendered to them. Furthermore, the Taliban had no dearth of men and weapons. In fact, the munitions captured by them were so substantial that they had to send away the surplus to Kandahar which was far away from the theatre of conflict. Around this time, the Taliban captured thirty-two trucks full of arms and ammunition which were being driven by Iranian nationals. There could no longer be any doubt over who was interfering in Afghanistan.

The Pakistan chancery in Tehran was attacked by a mob on 12 August and damage was caused to the premises. The demonstration was held with the approval of the Iranian interior ministry and Javed Hussain protested to Moheb Ali who gave an assurance that measures would be taken for the security of the Pakistan mission. Significantly, he added that once the issue of the missing personnel was resolved, the Iranian government would be willing to deal with the Taliban because they were a reality and could not be wished away. He said that Iran was not concerned whether the Taliban or any other group ruled Afghanistan as it was for the Afghan people to decide who should run their country.

On Pakistan's independence day anniversary on 14 August, between six to seven hundred demonstrators gathered in front of the Pakistan embassy in Tehran after Friday prayers and chanted "Death to the Taliban! Death to Pakistan! Death to America!" They demanded the release of the Iranian consulate personnel who, it was claimed, were under detention in Taliban prisons. In their speeches, the demonstrators condemned Pakistan, the US and Saudi Arabia and asked the Iranian supreme leader for permission to declare a jihad. During the ninety-minute protest, despite efforts by the police to keep the mob at a distance, stones and other projectiles were thrown at the embassy building causing further damage.

Earlier, during his Friday mosque sermon, Hashemi Rafsanjani, the former Iranian president, dwelt upon the situation in Afghanistan. He said that Iran had recognized the Rabbani regime as recommended by Pakistan and in accordance with the agreement arrived at among various Afghan parties in Pakistan. He alleged that Pakistan subsequently withdrew its support from the Rabbani regime and built up the Taliban to oust the former from Kabul. He also called for the release and repatriation of Iranian personnel and an IRNA correspondent, Mahmoud Saremi. He said that Iran would never allow any of its citizens to be held as prisoners in Afghanistan. Iran believed there was no military solution of the Afghanistan problem. It did not favour any particular group. However, the Taliban were giving a bad name to Islam and they wanted to impose their rule through armed conflict.

The same day, the Iranian minister for intelligence, Dorri Najafabadi, addressed the congregation during Friday prayers in Shahr-e-Ray and directly accused Pakistan, Saudi Arabia and "hidden elements" of supporting the Taliban. He said that "the atmosphere of instability and insecurity at the border points in the eastern part of Iran cannot be treated with indifference", and he added that "the government of Pakistan and the Taliban militia are answerable for the consequence of their latest ploys which have become the cause of instability and insecurity at the Iranian border". He concluded that "the Islamic Republic of Iran will, with the full power of its might, appropriately respond to these moves". This was the first time that such inflammatory language was publicly used against Pakistan by a functionary of the Iranian government.

Foreign minister Kharrazi accused the Taliban on 14 August of abducting Iranian diplomats and committing acts of cruelty and genocide. He called upon the Taliban to end their "unlawful acts and yield to the demands of the Afghan people and the international community regarding the formation of a broad-based government". He added that the absence of such a government would perpetuate the conflict in Afghanistan.

Grand ayatollah Sheikh Muhammad Fasel Lankarani, in a statement on 15 August, called on the international community "to liberate Afghanistan from the clutches of the Taliban because of the group's inhumane behaviour". He alleged that "the global arrogance, headed by the United States and its stooge Pakistan, is trying to wipe out Islam from Afghanistan. After completing this task, they will invade neighbouring countries to kill and plunder the Muslims."

Around this time, the Iranian foreign office issued a press release announcing that a senior official of the Indian external affairs ministry, V. Katju, had called on deputy foreign minister Mohsen Aminzadeh immediately after his arrival in Tehran. It was reported by the press that the purpose of the visit was to coordinate Indian policy with Iran on the Afghanistan crisis. An Iran-India-Russia alliance against the Taliban seemed to be emerging.

In addition to the Pakistan embassy in Tehran, demonstrations were staged at our consulates at Mashhad and Zahidan in which slogans of "death to Pakistan" were again raised. Telephone calls were received by the embassy and the consulate in Mashhad in which the personnel were warned that attacks, similar to the terrorist bombings of the US embassies in Nairobi and Dar-es-Salaam on 8 August, would be carried out against the Pakistan diplomatic and consular missions if the Iranian consulate personnel were not released by the Taliban.

Javed Hussain was summoned to the Iranian foreign office by Mohsen Aminzadeh on the evening of 16 August and was told that the Sepah-e-Sahaba, an extremist Sunni religious group, had threatened to stage demonstrations in front of the Iranian missions in Pakistan. This organization was a terrorist outfit and if it was allowed to hold the demonstrations, the reaction of the Iranian public would be extremely adverse and relations between Tehran and Islamabad would be further strained. He expressed the hope that the Pakistan government would take steps to prevent the threatened protests. He also alleged that a member of the Iranian consulate in Peshawar had been kidnapped and beaten up by a group of men on 13 August. The Iranian official was warned that if any more demonstrations were held in front of Pakistan missions in Iran, he and his family members would be killed. Aminzadeh mentioned that from the weapons that they carried and the way they had conducted themselves it appeared that the people who had kidnapped the Iranian official were members of an intelligence agency.

Hussain told Aminzadeh that the points made by him would immediately be conveyed to Islamabad which would undoubtedly take appropriate action to strengthen the security of the Iranian missions and personnel in Pakistan. The incident at the Iranian consulate in Peshawar would also be fully investigated and a report given to the Iranian government. The two agreed that both Pakistan and Iran should deal with the current difficulties in such a way as to avoid the further exacerbation of tensions. Aminzadeh emphasized that since he had taken over as deputy foreign minister, it had been his effort to improve Pakistan-Iran relations. He particularly mentioned that he had intervened with the Iranian interior ministry for the prohibition of demonstrations in front of the Pakistan embassy the previous Friday despite the strong pressure of public opinion. Accordingly, the ministry had withdrawn the permission for the demonstration. Nevertheless, he admitted that "some groups of people" had gathered in front of the embassy and the protest went ahead as had been planned.

Hussain drew Aminzadeh's attention to the statement made by intelligence minister Dorri Najafabadi in which Pakistan had been directly accused of complicity in the internal situation in Afghanistan. To this there was no response on Aminzadeh's part.

Our minister of state for foreign affairs, Siddique Kanju, visited Tehran from 23-24 August during which he met foreign minister Kharrazi and called on President Khatami, to whom he delivered a letter from Nawaz Sharif in which he proposed the stationing of an Iranian in the Pakistan consulate in Kandahar. I had deliberately included this offer in the letter because I thought that it would lessen some of the Iranian pressure on us over the question of their missing consulate personnel. Khatemi's response to the idea was that he would think it over and send a response through Mohsen Aminzadeh who would soon be visiting Pakistan.

Khatami expressed appreciation for Kanju's visit and said that there were "certain elements" and "plenty of common enemies" who wanted to disrupt the friendly relations between Pakistan and Iran. He stressed that, in the short term, the fate of the Iranian consular officials was at the top of the agenda. Everything else was on hold until this problem was settled. As for the long-term perspective, Iran would be willing to exchange views with Pakistan on promoting a durable settlement in Afghanistan in which all Afghan groups could participate. Iran held the Taliban responsible for the safety of its missing personnel and expected Islamabad to use its influence with the Taliban to secure their release.

Kharrazi was far more blunt and told Kanju that Pakistan had not done enough to ensure the safety and the return of the Iranian consulate personnel in Mazar-e-Sharif. Tehran wanted clear and transparent answers on this matter as it had aroused popular emotions which could turn violent. If this problem was not resolved satisfactorily, it would have a very negative impact on Pakistan-Iran relations. Kharrazi was of the view that the proposal on the stationing of an Iranian official in Kandahar was not especially appealing since it implied dialogue between Tehran and the Taliban—the latter were "playing a dirty game" in which Iran did not want to become a party. The satisfactory resolution of the missing Iranian nationals was an indispensable precondition for any talks with the Taliban. Aminzadeh, who was present at the meeting, told Kanju that the Taliban should release at least some of the Iranian prisoners as a gesture of goodwill to defuse the tension.

Tension between Afghanistan and Iran

According to reliable reports, a meeting of the commanders of the Afghan South West Alliance and their supporters was held in the Afghan consulate in Mashhad on 14 August. Till then we knew nothing about the existence of this alliance but were later able to find out that it consisted of pro-Iranian elements in and around Herat. About eight or nine commanders participated in the meeting which was also attended by two generals from the Iranian Revolutionary Guard Corps. The latter told the commanders that fighting against the Taliban was jihad. The next day, as we learnt from other reports, about forty men infiltrated Afghanistan from Iran and moved towards Herat. However, they were intercepted by the Taliban at Ghurian and, after a skirmish in which twenty of the intruders were killed, they were pushed back across the border.

On 17 August Hassan Rowhani, the deputy speaker of the Majlis (Iran's parliament) issued a statement stressing that Tehran had not ruled out anything in order to secure the release of the Iranian personnel from the Taliban and he held Pakistan responsible for their security. He added that "considering the Vienna Convention and the UN Charter as well as the fact that presently no government rules over Afghanistan, Iran considers as lawful any action for the restoration of its rights and also those of its citizens". Similar pronouncements were made—though without mention of Pakistan—by the Iranian president and the secretary of the national security council. The inescapable message was that Tehran was contemplating intrusion into Afghanistan.

In an obviously inspired commentary in the *Tehran Times* the same day, entitled "Probable Scenarios for the Taliban and Pakistan," one of the situations that was portrayed was Iranian military intervention in Afghanistan simultaneously with action by India "to settle the accounts of the last five decades with Pakistan". The commentary, after mentioning the possibility of the Taliban crossing the border with Pakistan to create Pushtunistan, observed: "If there is trouble in North West Frontier Province, if there is trouble along Pakistan's border with India, if there is no peace with Iran, will other states in Pakistan remain loyal to the central government? The days to come and Islamabad's Afghan policy will let us know."

Iranian claims that these were merely the views of the press were totally unconvincing. The media was controlled by the government and it was inconceivable that such an article which actually endorsed an Indian invasion of Pakistan in tandem with Iran's incursion into Afghanistan could have been published without official approval. No less serious was the wishful thinking about the fragmentation of Pakistan. The possibility of a conflict between Iran and Afghanistan loomed large through the autumn of 1998 while tension between Islamabad and Tehran continued to mount. An axis between Tehran, New Delhi and Moscow was fast emerging.

As a special gesture to Iran, we sent Aziz Khan to Kandahar on 16 August where he had discussions with Mulla Rabbani as well as the governor of Kandahar, the deputy foreign minister and other senior Taliban officials on the missing Iranian nationals. He was told that the Taliban had absolutely no information about them. Aziz proposed that, as a gesture of goodwill, the Taliban should consider releasing some of the Iranian prisoners in their custody. He was given the assurance that they would accord due consideration to this proposal and would come back to us within a few days.

I called Akhundzadeh the follow day to brief him on the outcome of the Aziz Khan visit to Kandahar. He said that the issue of the missing Iranian consulate personnel had severely jolted Pakistan-Iran relations. Perhaps his government had miscalculated things. Either it had over-estimated Pakistan's influence on the Taliban or that Pakistan had deliberately decided to ignore Iran's genuine concerns. He recalled that the request for the safety of the Iranian personnel had been made to Javed Hussain well before the fall of Mazar-e-Sharif. I took exception to this and replied that it was patently unfair to blame Pakistan. Akhundzadeh was told that unfounded and unwarranted accusations against us would lead nowhere and would only further vitiate the atmosphere. Furthermore, demonstrations had been held at our embassy in Tehran and damage had been caused to the premises. It was particularly regrettable that these protests were held on the occasion of our independence day despite our request that this be avoided. All this had sent the wrong signals to the people of Pakistan. It was, therefore, important for us to work closely to lower the temperature.

Akhundzadeh was told that the Afghan embassy in Islamabad had informed us that the Taliban had captured people in the north who posed as Afghans but in reality could be Iranian nationals. Though the context in which this information had been conveyed to us was entirely different, i.e. as an example of Iranian interference in Afghanistan, there was a possibility that some of these could be from the Iranian consulate. I therefore asked Akhundzadeh to provide photographs of the personnel along with their other identification details. These particulars were never provided to us, possibly because Tehran wanted to conceal their identities. It later transpired that most of these men were not consular officials but military personnel from the IRGC.

I then told Akhundzadeh that, from the scanty facts available at this time, two scenarios seemed possible. The first, and more logical, was that the personnel would have vacated the premises when the Taliban entered Mazar-e-Sharif as they had a lead time of almost two hours for this purpose. The second was, as the Iranians had claimed, they were in Taliban custody. However, the point that needed to be emphasized was that the Taliban had categorically denied this. It was here that I suggested that Iran should depute an official to Kandahar who would be most welcome to stay at our consulate general from where he would work closely with us in trying to secure more information about the Iranian nationals. Akhundzadeh said that he would seek instructions from Tehran. Kharrazi was to dismiss the proposal during the Kanju visit to Tehran a few days later.

Consul General Amir Imam informed us from Herat that there were indications of a possible move by Tehran to cross the Iran-Afghanistan border and occupy the city. This could not be brushed aside as the Iranian leader Khamenei had publicly used abusive language against the Taliban and had implied that they were the handmaiden of the US and the "Iranian nation, government and armed forces do not tolerate the mischief by the US let alone those of this bunch [the Taliban] of lowly people". The Afghan foreign minister at the time, Mulla Muhammad Hassan, addressed a press conference in Kabul on 19 August during which he stated that he would not even think of repeating the abusive language used by Khamenei which was "truly unbecoming of a so-called spiritual leader". He reiterated his country's resolve to maintain good relations with all its neighbours and added that non-interference in the internal affairs of other countries was a cardinal principle of Afghanistan's external policies. He disclosed that even before the Taliban had entered Mazar-e-Sharif, government-controlled Iranian radio had announced that the city had fallen and that its consulate personnel had been abducted by the Taliban. He also said that Osama Bin Laden was not involved in the bombing of the US embassies in Kenya and Tanzania—Bin Laden had given a solemn undertaking to the Taliban that he would not indulge in such activities. If proof of the Saudi's involvement in terrorism was established, he would be punished under Islamic law.

The next day the US launched cruise missile attacks on Afghanistan and Sudan. Pakistan expressed indignation and outrage at the unilateral military action against the two countries. A statement was issued through the foreign office spokesman that these developments had caused great anxiety and anguish among the people of Pakistan. The government of Pakistan was neither consulted nor given any prior information about US intentions to carry out strikes inside Afghanistan. Pakistan remained fully committed to promoting international cooperation for combating terrorism. It had unceasingly declared its unequivocal and strong abhorrence of all forms of terrorism including state sponsored terrorism. The United States military action against Afghanistan was described as a serious derogation from recognized principles of inter-state conduct and international law. After this statement was issued, the US chargé d'affaires Alan Eastham was called to the foreign office and our concerns were conveyed to him. He was told that the US action also constituted a violation of Pakistan's air space and a strong protest was lodged with him.

Subsequently, Eastham informed us that the US government had contacted the Taliban and had proposed talks. As a follow-up, the American embassy in Islamabad gave a detailed note to the Afghan chargé d'affaires Mulla Saeedur Rahman Haqqani. The major element in the note was an affirmation that the US had no problem with the Taliban. The missile attacks on Afghan territory were not directed against the Taliban but targeted against terrorists and, in particular, Osama Bin Laden. The US had sufficient evidence against Bin Laden and if the Taliban were against terrorism they should extradite him. Eastham requested our help for an early Taliban response to the note.

Throughout this period, the Iranian media continued with hysterical outbursts against Pakistan and the Taliban. Foreign secretary Shamshad Ahmad was constrained to summon Amabssador Akhundzadeh to the foreign office on 26 August and protest about this virulent anti-Pakistan propaganda broadside. Furthermore, the security of Pakistan's embassy premises and personnel in Tehran and its consulates in Iran had repeatedly been threatened and demonstrations had been held, with the encouragement of the Iranian government, in front of the Pakistan missions in Tehran, Mashhad and Zahidan. Akhundzadeh promised to convey these concerns to his government.

Two days later, deputy foreign minister Mohsen Aminzadeh came to Islamabad carrying a letter from Khatami for Nawaz Sharif on whom he called. The discussions focused exclusively on Afghanistan and, in particular, on the missing personnel of the Iranian consulate general in Mazar-e-Sharif. Khatami's letter emphasized the importance of Pakistan-Iran relations and the need to strengthen and consolidate mutually beneficial cooperation. He expressed concern over the situation in Afghanistan and affirmed Iran's right to preserve its security and national interest. The theme of the letter was built around the missing consulate personnel and stressed that their release would assuage Iranian concerns. He requested Pakistan's cooperation for such an outcome.

Aminzadeh's brief was restricted to the missing personnel. After ponderous reiterations of the importance that his government attached to the issue, he proposed that a fact-finding mission headed by the International Committee of the Red Cross (ICRC) be constituted to resolve the problem. The mission would include representatives from Pakistan, Iran and the UN. He requested our endorsement of the proposal and added that the ICRC had agreed to it in principle.

Nawaz Sharif assured Aminzadeh of Pakistan's fullest cooperation. He said that Pakistan had already gone the extra mile to ensure the safety and repatriation of the missing men. However, the point to be noted was that the matter pertained to Iran and a third country on which our influence was more apparent than real. We had, nevertheless, received solemn assurances from the Taliban leadership that should they come across the consulate personnel, they would be protected and repatriated.

As for the specific proposal made by Aminzadeh, Sharif said that we fully supported the idea of an ICRC-led fact-finding mission, the modalities for which needed to be worked out. The first and most obvious step was to secure the approval of the Taliban.

Aminzadeh insisted that Iran had left its personnel in Mazar-e-Sharif after receiving assurances from Pakistan that they would not come to grief. He was told that the insinuation was unwarranted. According to Aminzadeh an estimated eighty-seven Iranian nationals were in the custody of the Taliban. The latter should release these men as a gesture towards Iran. He was told that we had already raised this issue with the Taliban and their response was that Iran should talk to them directly. Aminzadeh was reminded that the Iranian consul general in Jalalabad had already been in touch with the Taliban and had visited Kandahar where he had been given access to the Iranian prisoners. The Iranian consul general had discussed the release of the Iranians in exchange for the Taliban prisoners from Bamyan. Aminzadeh wanted to fudge this issue because the Iranians never felt comfortable with any suggestion that they should talk to the Taliban directly and also for the reason that they did not acknowledge that there were any Taliban prisoners in their custody. It was, therefore, repeated to him that the last contact between their consul general and the Taliban had been on 23 August during which he had accepted that there were Taliban prisoners in Iran

On 1 September Akhundzadeh sought, and was granted, a meeting with Prime Minister Nawaz Sharif to convey the serious concern of his government on a BBC interview by Mulla Omar in which the latter was supposed to have declared that the Iranian personnel had probably been killed. An earlier news clip had indicated that the Iranians were safe. He urged the prime minister to use all the influence available with Pakistan to convince the Taliban to clarify the situation. Nawaz Sharif suggested that minister of state Kanju, accompanied by representatives from Iran, should go to Kandahar and talk directly with the Taliban. Akhundzadeh said that he would consult his government and requested Pakistan to use its influence with the Taliban to release at least some of the Iranian prisoners held by them as a goodwill gesture. This would defuse the inflamed anti-Pakistan and anti-Taliban emotions of the Iranian people. Significantly, he said that Iran would not use this as a precedent to make further demands on us. Thereafter, the ICRC mission as proposed by Aminzadeh a few days earlier could be arranged.

We immediately checked with the Taliban to ascertain what Omar had actually told the BBC. According to them, he had said that the missing personnel were certainly not with the Taliban and, therefore, they were inclined to believe that the men were either with the Northern Alliance or had been killed during the fighting at the time of the fall of Mazar-e-Sharif. The Taliban did not have any concrete evidence that the personnel had been killed and they suggested that the UN should "mediate" between them and Iran to resolve the issue.

To my surprise, I was told the following day by the Islamabad-based ICRC representative for Afghanistan, Olivier Durr, that his organization had never agreed to the Iranian proposal as it was outside their mandate. At the most they would be prepared to provide an aircraft for the mission. They were also willing to facilitate the mission by arranging for experts who would not be from the ICRC. The latter could only play a role if they received a request from family members of the missing personnel. It was against ICRC policy to be associated with other governments on such ventures. We obviously had been misinformed by the Iranians.

On our intercession, the Taliban agreed to the Iranian proposal with the minor modification that the mission should be led by the UN instead of the ICRC. The latter could, however, be included as members of the fact-finding team along with Pakistan and Iran. This was accepted by the Iranians. The Taliban accordingly asked us to request Tehran to nominate officials for the mission. They also approached James N'gobi of UNSMA to seek UN endorsement for the proposal.

Shortly afterwards, N'gobi came to see me to say that Lakhdar Brahimi had given him verbal instructions from Paris to tell us that the UN could consider undertaking such a mission only if formal written requests were received from the governments of Pakistan and Iran. According to N'gobi, the Iranians had not been in touch with UNSMA either on the Taliban proposal or on the earlier Iranian suggestion that the fact-finding mission be headed by the ICRC. I told him that the Iranian government had readily accepted the Taliban proposal when Javed Hussain conveyed it to them and if the UN wanted further confirmation they had better contact Tehran themselves. I also expressed surprise that Brahimi should expect us to approach the UN formally on a request made by the Afghan government. The proposal had been conveyed to N'gobi by the Afghan chargé d'affaires in Islamabad and this should suffice. We had conveyed our agreement to participate in the mission to the Taliban as we had to the UN, so surely, if the UN was at all serious about reducing tension between Afghanistan and Iran, it should not create roadblocks to confidence-building measures that could eventually lead to the stabilization of the Afghanistan situation. It seemed that Brahimi was repeating what he had done just prior to the meeting of the steering committee.

N'gobi fully supported this point of view and said that he would seek instructions from his superiors in New York. He did not have too high an opinion about the manner in which the UN, and in particular Lakhdar Brahimi, was handling the Afghan issue. He thought it ridiculous that the Northern Alliance representative was allowed to make a statement during the Security Council debate on Afghanistan a few days earlier. He seemed to have realized that the continued recognition of the Northern Alliance by the UN and the international community was detrimental to the UN's credibility as a peace broker in Afghanistan.

At about 11pm on 1 September, I was informed by the Taliban leadership in Kandahar that they had also decided to unilaterally release three Iranian prisoners in deference to our intercession and as a gesture of goodwill towards Iran which they hoped would be reciprocated. But these hopes proved short-lived when the Iranian consul general in Jalalabad telephoned Mulla Jalil from Tehran to say that the release of the three prisoners meant nothing and the actual issue was the safe return of the eleven members of their Mazar-e-Sharif consulate. We were, however, able to persuade the Taliban not to go back on their promise. Javed Hussain was instructed to advise the Iranian government to restrain their over-zealous consul general, which they did and which had a salutary effect on the ruffled sensibilities of the Taliban. On 3 September, we decided to send Aziz Khan and Ayaz Wazir by special aircraft to Kandahar to bring back the three Iranian captives. They were accompanied by the representatives of the Afghan embassy in Islamabad as well as the Iranian deputy consul general in Peshawar and a doctor.

That afternoon Mulla Jalil telephoned me from Kandahar. He said that as a mark of respect for Pakistan, the Taliban had released five instead of three Iranian prisoners. This was also a gesture of friendship towards Iran which he hoped the latter would acknowledge. Earlier, I had spoken to Aziz Khan who had reached our consulate general in Kandahar. He told me that the Taliban had gone out of their way to show respect to the two Iranians who had travelled with him. The special gestures included full protocol ceremonies including motorcycle outriders from the airport to our consulate general where Governor Hassan Rehmani was at hand to receive the Iranians. He told the Iranians that the Afghans would never forget the support that Iran had given them during their jihad against Soviet occupation. The Taliban wanted to establish close and friendly relations with Iran and considered all Iranians to be their brothers in Islam.

Formal talks between the Taliban and the Iranians were held at the governor's house. Besides Rehmani, Jalil and Wakil were also present. The two sides presented their grievances against each other in a manner that was as frank as it was cordial. Later, the Taliban showed the vast quantities of Iranian weapons they had captured from the north to the visitors.

On the question of the missing personnel of the Iranian consulate general in Mazar-e-Sharif, the Taliban said that they were not in their possession nor did they know anything about their whereabouts. However, they were ready to extend their fullest cooperation in locating the missing men. The Iranian deputy consul general proposed that Iran and the Taliban should jointly search for the consulate officials. Aziz Khan was subsequently told by Mulla Jalil that the Taliban would prefer the mission to be led by the UN since the Iranians might present a biased picture to the outside world. He also said that it was essential for Pakistan to be involved.

The Iranian delegation requested that they be allowed to see all their detained nationals. This was also readily conceded by the Taliban. At the Kandahar airport just prior to the departure of the delegation and the released Iranian prisoners, Jalil told the Iranian deputy consul general that the Taliban would make another effort to locate the eleven missing members of the Iranian consulate general in Mazar-e-Sharif. If after one week this attempt did not yield results, he proposed a tripartite fact-finding mission consisting of Pakistan, Afghanistan and Iran to investigate the whereabouts of the missing men. The proposal was accepted by the Iranians. Jalil explained to Aziz Khan that there was now no need for the UN to be involved since an understanding had been reached between Pakistan, Afghanistan and Iran. This was a surprisingly rapid turn-around in the Taliban position.

A good beginning had thus been made in defusing the tension between Iran and the Taliban. We had hoped that Iran would grasp the opportunity that had arisen. The Taliban had made a significant gesture and the very least that was expected from Tehran was an acknowledge-ment of this. However, within hours there was a Reuters report from Tehran quoting the Iranian foreign office spokesman as saying that the Taliban gesture was "insufficient".

Despite this unilateral gesture by the authorities in Kandahar, which the Iranians had requested on more than one occasion, there was no reduction in the propaganda against Pakistan and the Taliban in the Tehran media. The Iranian government, besides making threatening statements, amassed troops along Iran's borders with Afghanistan under the guise of exercises. Our initial estimates were that more than three divisions had been deployed along the Iran-Afghanistan border in two major concentrations, namely, in the north at the Turbat-e-Jam sector facing Herat and in Zabul in the south. According to the Iranian author-ities, about seventy thousand troops took part in the exercises involving both air as well as ground forces from 1-3 September. They also declared that the troops would remain in the area indefinitely. A hair-trigger sit-uation had thus been created posing a grave threat to the peace and secu-rity of the entire region. Furthermore, the Iranian government and media also, without any justification, continued to hold Pakistan respon-sible for the safety of the missing consulate personnel.

I summoned Chargé d'Affaires Javed Kazemi of Iran to my office on the evening of 5 September and expressed grave concern about reports that an Iranian attack on Afghanistan was imminent. This had appeared in the *Washington Post* of that day and had also featured on the BBC. Kazemi was told that should this come about, it would have a devastat-ing effect on the security and stability of the entire region. I asked him to immediately convey to his government that it was our hope that Iran would exercise restraint. Should Iran attack Afghanistan, there would be strong public reaction in Pakistan and it would encourage extremists to stoke the flames of sectarian violence. Instability in the region would only invite outside interference and this surely could not be in Iran's long-term interests. The chargé d'affaires was reminded that good progress had been made on establishing a fact-finding mission under UN auspices to locate the missing men of the Iranian consulate general in Mazar-e-Sharif. The recent contact between Iran and Afghanistan had resulted in the release of five Iranian prisoners. It was important to take full advantage of the window of opportunity that was now available to reduce tensions with Afghanistan. Kazemi undertook to transmit the demarche to his government.

On 7 September N'gobi called on me to discuss the establishment of the fact-finding mission on the missing Iranian consular officials. He was under instructions from UN under-secretary general Prendergast to ask us for a letter, like the one Iran had reportedly sent, inviting the UN to participate in the mission. The UN would be willing to be included but would not lead the team. Prendergast sought Pakistan's assistance in establishing contact between the Taliban and the UN for facilitating the mission, providing an aircraft for travelling to Mazar-e-Sharif, as well as ensuring the security and making logistical arrangements for the mission in Mazar-e-Sharif. N'gobi said that he had informed Chargé d'Affaires Haqqani about the UN's willingness to be included in but not to lead the mission. The latter had told him that he did not envisage any problem but would seek instructions from his leadership in Kandahar. N'gobi was unable to have any contact with the Iranian embassy in Islamabad nor was he sure whether the UN secretariat had informed Tehran.

I told N'gobi that, at this point in time, the reduction of tension between Afghanistan and Iran should be of paramount importance to the UN. Pakistan would cooperate fully for the establishment of a fact-finding mission regardless of its composition or who it was led by provided both Afghanistan and Iran were on board. It was for this reason that we had readily agreed to several proposals which included: (a) the Iranian proposal that the ICRC should lead the mission which would include Pakistan, Iran and the UN—contrary to what Mohsen Aminzadeh had told us, the ICRC had not agreed to this as it was outside their mandate; (b) the Taliban proposal that was conveyed by their chargé d'affaires to N'gobi that the team should be led by the UN and include Afghanistan, Iran and Pakistan—this had been subsequently accepted by Iran; and (c) the second Taliban proposal of a fact-finding mission consisting only of Pakistan, Afghanistan and Iran but not the UN. This last suggestion had been made to and accepted by the Iranian deputy consul general in Peshawar when he had accompanied Aziz Khan to Kandahar to bring back the Iranian prisoners released by the Taliban. The Iranian government had subsequently annulled the consent given by their deputy consul general and insisted on a UN-led mission. As a gesture of flexibility this had been accepted by the Taliban.

I also conveyed to N'gobi that the issue basically concerned Afghanistan and Iran. Both had conveyed their respective proposals to the UN (the Taliban to N'gobi and the Iranians to the UN secretary general). We could convey a written assent of our inclusion in the mission. However, it was illogical of the UN to expect us to make a formal request to constitute a fact-finding mission when this had nothing to do with us. Furthermore, we could not be expected to guarantee the safety of the mission in a third country nor provide logistical arrangements inside Afghanistan. We were, however, willing to provide an aircraft for the transportation of the delegation as requested by the UN. Furthermore, we were surprised that Prendergast should ask us to facilitate contact between the Taliban and the UN. What then was UNSMA all about? It was required to establish continuous contact with the Afghan parties. If it could not do this, then it should not expect the international community to pay for its operations. However, this was not the case as UNSMA had been interacting with the Taliban. Norbert Holl, Brahimi and now N'gobi had frequently met officials from Kandahar and Kabul. For instance, UNSMA had been closely involved with the meeting of the Steering Committee and Brahimi had even insisted on a written confirmation from the Taliban and the Northern Alliance that its deliberations would be held under UN and OIC auspices. What devious game was the UN now playing? What was the need for UNSMA if it was reluctant to talk to the group that controlled virtually all of Afghanistan. The UN's insistence that we make a formal request for a fact-finding mission was therefore probably aimed at implicating us as a party to a problem that was of concern only to Afghanistan and Iran. N'gobi did not respond to these comments.

In the first week of September the hair-trigger situation between Afghanistan and Iran became even more precarious. There were ominous signs that Iran might be giving serious consideration to military intervention in Afghanistan at any moment. The Iranian authorities decided not to return the seventy thousand or so IRGC forces to peace time locations after the completion of their military exercise, codenamed "Ashura-3", from the Iran-Afghanistan border. Tehran was thus in a position to intervene militarily in Afghanistan at very short notice, perhaps with the objective of capturing Herat to install the Rabbani regime there. There was speculation in the journalist circles of Tehran that the supreme Iranian leader Ayatollah Khamenei was about to give the green light for military intervention but had been dissuaded by President Khatami from doing so. The Khatami administration, it seemed, was under pressure from the hardliners to launch a full military attack on Afghanistan.

On the morning of 10 September, I received a panicked telephone call from chargé d'affaires Haqqani to say that the Taliban fact-finding mission had completed its enquiries about the missing Iranian consulate personnel and that Pakistan and Iran should immediately send a joint delegation to Kandahar for a full briefing and also to decide on what further action needed to be taken. Accordingly, we lined up a special aircraft that was ready to leave for Kandahar as soon as the Iranian members of the delegation were available. Akhundzadeh, who had gone to Iran for consultations, telephoned me from Tehran to enquire about the programme in Kandahar, the agenda for the talks and whether the Taliban had come across any new information about the missing personnel. I told him that the Taliban had not shared any details with us but would disclose whatever information they had when we reached Kandahar. Akundzadeh felt that it might not be possible for Iran to join the mission and suggested that we proceed without them.

That afternoon Haqqani came to see me to say that Aminzadeh had conveyed a message to Kandahar that in the event that the missing personnel were alive, they should be handed over to Iran. If they were dead, the perpetrators of the crime should be apprehended and punished and a public apology should be rendered to Iran by the Taliban. If these conditions were fulfilled, Iran would hold negotiations with the Taliban to resolve their differences. Haqqani said that his government had decided that the report of their fact-finding mission would be conveyed to the UN secretary general that day through a letter from Mulla Omar. Simultaneously, copies of this letter would be given to the foreign offices of the three countries that had recognized the Taliban government, namely Pakistan, Saudi Arabia and the United Arab Emirates, by the Afghan embassies resident in these countries. The Taliban expected the UN secretary general to convey the contents of Mulla Omar's letter to Iran. Haqqani then revealed that their fact-finding mission had found the bodies of nine of the missing Iranian consulate personnel in a common grave. The fact-finding mission was of the view that the Iranians may have been killed in the heavy fighting in the area without anyone's knowledge that they were consulate personnel. There was also the likelihood that they may have been killed by opposition forces in a bid to smear the Taliban. The fate of the remaining two Iranians was still not known. The Taliban were ready to hand over the bodies of the nine to Iran or to anyone nominated by Tehran. Haqqani also said that although Tehran had started thinning out its troop concentration along its border with Herat, a force of eighteen thousand heavily armed Afghans belonging to the opposition had been amassed at Mashhad for infiltration into Afghanistan. Another force of five thousand had been mustered at Zabul along the border with Nimroz for a similar operation.

Strangely enough, that day we also received a report from a well-connected Iranian national from the private sector claiming that a contact, who happened to be in Mazar-e-Sharif at the time of its fall to the Taliban, had recently returned to Tehran with the report that *all* the Iranian officials in the consulate in Mazar-e-Sharif had been killed. According to this narration of the event, the officials present in the Iranian consulate were actually IRGC soldiers and not foreign ministry officials. When the Taliban entered the premises, the Iranians opened machine-gun fire on them, forcing the Taliban to return fire as a result of which all the personnel in the consulate had died. We were also told that the Iranian government was actually aware of this from the day that it happened.

I summoned the Iranian chargé d'affaires Javed Kazemi to the foreign office to convey our condolences over the deaths of his fellow nationals. He was told that the government of Pakistan had strongly condemned the killings and had called for the punishment of those responsible. I also expressed our deep disappointment that the Iranian government had bracketed Pakistan with the Taliban as being responsible for the tragedy. This unwarranted accusation was firmly rejected. I protested the stoning of the Pakistan embassy in Tehran on the night of 10 September resulting in damage to the chancery building and the mission's cars. Kazemi was asked to approach the Iranian authorities immediately to ensure the safety of our diplomatic and consular personnel. He was reminded that Pakistan had done everything possible to reduce tensions between Afghanistan and Iran. The release of the five Iranian prisoners by the Taliban was cited as an example. We earnestly wanted the early normalization of Iran-Afghanistan ties as only outside powers would benefit from the prevailing stand-off. Kazemi expressed appreciation for the condolences but asserted that, in the Iranian view, Pakistan had not done enough to ensure the safety of its consular officials in Afghanistan. He maintained that demonstrations outside the Pakistan embassy in Tehran were natural because of the inflamed passions of the Iranian public.

Collapse of the Northern Alliance

Regional tensions then rose to an unprecedented level following the statement made by Ayatollah Khamenei on 14 September shortly after the Taliban capture of Bamyan, the stronghold of the Shia Hazara community of Afghanistan. Khamenei announced that the Iranians had received reports from Bamyan that the Taliban were committing even greater atrocities there than what they had done in Mazar-e-Sharif. He went to the extent of saying that Pakistani Air Force planes were "also participating in the killing of the people of Bamyan and the devastation of the area". The Iranian nation, he continued, "in view of the deep anger and unhappiness felt by it, was impatiently waiting for decisive measures on the part of the Iranian authorities". He appealed to all Muslim governments to come to the help of the persecuted Hazaras and other communities in Afghanistan and called upon the "Momineen" ("Believers") of Pakistan not to allow a part of its army to sacrifice the Afghan people for the sake of the Taliban. He beseeched the people of Pakistan not to let the war being waged by the Taliban to take root in Afghanistan and other parts of the Islamic world and to stop the Pakistan army from fighting alongside the Taliban. Khamenei stressed that he had tried to stop "the kindling of the flames of war in the region, which would not be extinguished easily". However, everyone must understand that the danger of this happening was "very serious, all-enveloping and very close". War could only be avoided by persuading the Pakistan army to halt its interference in Afghanistan and by prevailing upon the leaders of the Taliban to accept logic, avoid atrocities and atone for their previous mistakes.

In the meanwhile, arrangements were made through the ICRC to bring the bodies of the Iranians to Tehran. This was done in two installments. The Taliban showed the nine bodies to Iranian forensic experts but the latter could identify only seven, which were brought to Iran on 14 September. Following further examination, only six could be confirmed to be of Iranian officials and their funerals were held in Tehran on 18 September. Six processions were taken out in Tehran alone and at least one each in every major Iranian city. In Tehran, Khamenei himself led the funeral procession. According to independent observers about forty thousand people participated in the funeral procession in Tehran. The usual slogans "Death to Pakistan! Death to the Taliban! Death to America!" were chanted by the mourners.

A resolution was adopted at the end of the funeral which: (i) demanded the release of the Iranians in the custody of the Taliban; (ii) called on the Iranian government to provide the required "facilities" to the

Afghans living in Iran for "fighting against the Taliban"; (iii) warned "Pakistan and other supporters of the Taliban" to stop their assistance to the Taliban; and (iv) appealed to "the Muslim and freedom-loving people of Pakistan" to rise against their "ignorant statesmen" in order to stop them from helping the Taliban.

Khamenei's statement of 14 September served as a green signal for the Iranian officials and the government-controlled media to malign Pakistan and the Taliban with abandon. The bottom line was that Islamabad had betrayed Iran and stabbed it in the back. This government-inspired campaign of slander and vilification added to the security problems of our diplomatic and consular missions in Iran and dealt a crippling blow to Pakistan-Iran relations.

On the night of 16 September, Tehran television showed a member of the Iranian consulate general at Mazar-e-Sharif, Allahdad Shahsavan Ghareh Hosseini, who claimed to be in the building on 8 August when the Taliban allegedly attacked the mission and killed its personnel. Hosseini said that he was merely injured and managed to escape and return home through Herat. He also alleged there was "probably" a Pakistan national among the Taliban who attacked the mission. The following day, the Iranian media reported that another member of the consulate in Mazar-e-Sharif, Hossein Akbari, who was not present in the premises at the time of the Taliban attack on the mission, had also succeeded in returning to Iran via Bamyan.

The *Iran Daily* of 22 September carried the following statement by a certain Ahmad, the father of Muhammad Nasser Nasseri, reportedly an Iranian consulate official who was killed in Mazar-e-Sharif: "My son served the Islamic system since the early days of the revolution and was injured several times during the Iraqi-imposed war." This lent credence to the earlier report we had received that most of the men present in the Iranian consulate on 8 August were actually IRGC soldiers and not Iranian foreign ministry officials because Muhammad Nasser Nasseri was a known IRGC general who had not been heard of in the past several weeks.

Although the Iranians never responded to my request for the particulars of the consular officials, we were able to learn through reliable sources that the eleven officials present in the consulate general in Mazar-e-Sharif on 8 August were Nasser Rigi (Iranian foreign ministry official), Majid Noori (IRGC), Noorullah Norouzi (background not known), Heydar Ali Bagheri (IRGC), Muhammad Nasser Nasseri (IRGC), Hossein Akbari (he returned to Iran), Rashid Fallah (Iranian intelligence), Muhammad Ali Ghiasi (Iranian intelligence), Karim Heydarian (IRGC), Allahdad Shahsavan Ghareh Hosseini (he returned to Tehran), and Mahmoud Saremi (IRNA correspondent).

Ahmed Shah Masood arrived in Tehran on 15 September and stayed until 18 September. There he met with IRGC commanders and intelligence officials as well as Rabbani and Dostum, promising the Iranian authorities that if they destabilized western Afghanistan through guerrilla raids and acts of sabotage, he was prepared to launch parallel attacks on the Kabul and Takhar sectors.

The Afghan chargé d'affaires, Saeedur Rehman Haqqani, called on me on the morning of 5 October to report that the bodies of two more Iranian consulate officials had been found in Mazar-e-Sharif. He had already conveyed this information to the Iranian embassy so that arrangements could be made to collect the remains through the ICRC as on the previous occasion. Haqqani added that the inquiry initiated by the Taliban to investigate the killings of the Iranian personnel was proceeding apace. Mulla Kairuddin Khairkhwa, the acting interior minister and overall in charge of the north had informed Mulla Omar that the inquiry team was close to identifying those who were likely to have been involved in the incident. Khairkhwa had been instructed to complete the inquiry swftly so that the perpetrators of the crime could be brought to book. Haqqani also disclosed that the Iranians had been in direct contact with the Taliban authorities in Kandahar for the release of the forty or so remaining Iranian prisoners. The Taliban had offered negotiations so that these detainees could be exchanged with some eighty Taliban who were taken to Mashhad by the retreating Hizb-e-Wahdat troops before the fall of Bamyan.

The following day, Amabssador Akhundzadeh, who had just returned from Tehran, called on Shamshad Ahmad at his own request to discuss the Afghanistan situation. He zeroed in on the Iranian demands that the Taliban should publicly apologize for the killing of the Iranian personnel in Mazar-e-Sharif, return the remaining dead bodies, apprehend and punish those responsible and release the Iranian prisoners in their custody. He repeated the usual refrain that Pakistan should use its "undoubted influence" with the Taliban to bring this about so that the volatile situation along the Afghanistan-Iran border could be defused, insisting that there could be no military solution to the Afghanistan problem. Significantly, he elaborated that he was implying that Iran would not be launching any military offensive against the Taliban.

Lakhdar Brahimi was scheduled to visit the region around that time and Akhundzadeh asked how we intended to handle the visit. He volunteered the information that the UAE government had provided an aircraft to bring Brahimi to Tehran while Iran would be placing a plane at his disposal to take him to Islamabad. Shamshad responded that we had also offered an aircraft to facilitate the last and most important leg of Brahimi's mission namely, his visit to Afghanistan. The Taliban had extended an invitation to the special envoy through the UN secretariat in New York, via Mulla Wakil when the latter met him in Abu Dhabi, and also through UNSMA. Akhundzadeh asked if the Taliban would send a delegation to Islamabad in the event that Brahimi refused to go to Afghanistan. He was told that we hoped Brahimi would visit Afghanistan as it was vital for the promotion of the "Points of Common Understanding" (it stressed non-interference in Afghanistan, the promotion of an intra-Afghan dialogue and, significantly, the establishment of a multi-ethnic rather than a multi-factional broad-based government in Kabul) reached during the foreign ministers-level meeting of the Six Plus Two on 21 September.

Shamshad told Akhundzadeh that our overarching objective was not to let Afghanistan strain the relations between Pakistan and Iran. This was our foremost priority which we considered far more important than the UN, the Six Plus Two or the developments in Afghanistan. The present stand-off between Afghanistan and Iran merely benefited those powers who were determined to foment conflict among Islamic countries. The great game that was being orchestrated by the extra-regional powers was self-evident and needed no elaboration. It was, therefore, critical to prevent a conflict between Iran and Afghanistan. Akhundzadeh agreed with this assessment. He was told that we were grieved and pained by the baseless allegations that Iran had made about our military assistance to the Taliban. This was completely untrue and the continuation of such unfounded accusations could only have an adverse fall-out—Pakistan and Iran should adopt a joint approach for resolving the Afghanistan problem. In reply, Akundzadeh proposed that the two countries should have a series of exchange of views on Afghanistan. Shamshad said that the starting point should be a frank and structured dialogue insulated from the beaten track of declaratory statements.

On the other issues raised by Akhundzadeh, Shamshad reiterated to the ambassador that the perception that we had enormous influence over the Taliban was erroneous. Furthermore, the Iranians themselves had told us that they had probably overrated our influence after the killing of their personnel in Mazar-e-Sharif. In any case, the Taliban had already repatriated six bodies of the Iranian personnel in Mazar-e-Sharif and two more had recently been found. The Afghans had expressed public regret over the incident and had instituted an inquiry to apprehend the perpetrators of the crime on which some headway had been made. On the question of the Iranian prisoners, certainly we would do our bit but it was important for Iran to make parallel efforts on its own. For instance, the Iranians were supposed to have sent a delegation the previous day to Kandahar but the visit was postponed *sine die* at the last minute by Tehran. Here, Akhundzadeh admitted that they had been in touch with the Taliban for the release of all the Iranian prisoners—however, they were only willing to release five. In response, Shamshad stressed that this was reason enough for Iran to send a delegation to Kandahar. A piecemeal resolution of the problem was far better than no forward movement. Akhundzadeh agreed with this and Shamshad added that the leadership in Kandahar were willing to release all the Iranian prisoners in exchange for the eighty or more Taliban that they claimed had been taken to Mashhad from Bamyan. Akhundzadeh, however, denied there were any Taliban prisoners held in Iran. It was also conveyed to the Iranian ambassador that although the Taliban did not have any problem with the establishment of a multi-ethnic government, they were not willing to deal with warlords such as Dostum, Malik, Ahmed Shah Masood or Burhanuddin Rabbani as they believed that these were the people responsible for the ruination of their country. Akhundzadeh did not dispute Shamshad's assertion that it was important for Iran to come to terms with reality and encourage the Taliban to move towards a multi-ethnic dispensation.

The Russian reaction

After the fall of Shibberghan to the Taliban, the Pakistan ambassador in Moscow, Mansur Alam, was called to the Russian foreign office on 3 August 1998 by Rachit Khamidulin, director of the Third Asia Department. Khamidulin expressed his government's serious concern on the developments in northern Afghanistan. Russia, he said, was particularly surprised by the news that Pakistani citizens and the Pakistan Air Force were assisting the Taliban. If this information was correct, it sharply contradicted Pakistan's continued stance that it only wanted to promote the peace process.

Alam categorically denied this allegation and referred to reports in *The New York Times* and *The Moscow Times* which had contained details of Russia's extensive support to the Northern Alliance. Khamidulin's response was that Moscow would activate the UN in order to "normalize the situation in Afghanistan".

The capture of Mazar-e-Sharif by the Taliban five days after Alam's meeting with Khamidulin intensified the debate in Moscow about the implications of a Taliban-dominated Afghanistan for Russia and the neighbouring Central Asian states. Initially, the Russian foreign office did not make any statement and left the field open to the media which generally gave factual and objective accounts of the fall of Mazar-e-Sharif. But comments by officials and analysts showed growing concern over the potential influence of the Taliban on the internal political and social environment of the neighbouring Central Asian republics and eventually of Russia.

Ample coverage was given by the Moscow media to the remarks of the commander of the Russian border guard contingent in Tajikistan, who declared that his troops were ready to "defend [the Central Asian republics] against any aggression from Afghanistan's Taliban".

An important aspect of the Russian interests in Central Asia was highlighted by the director of the Institute of Diaspora and Integration in Moscow, Konstantin Zatulin, who expressed the view that the Taliban offensive in northern Afghanistan "may strengthen the Commonwealth of Independent States (CIS) from outside". He described the Taliban as "a jinn let out of the bottle by the US and Pakistan in the hope of eliminating any Russian influence not only in Afghanistan but in the entire Central Asian region". Zatulin said that the instability along the southern frontiers of the CIS caused by the military actions of the Taliban could prompt the CIS members to seek Russia's support. However, he felt that Russia should wait until Kazakhstan, Uzbekistan and the other former Soviet republics realize the degree of danger and ask for help and that this help "should not be given disinterestedly but in exchange for firm guarantees of respect for the rights of the Russians in these countries".

The Russian foreign ministry finally issued a statement on 12 August outrightly accusing Pakistan of solidly backing the Taliban. The ministry's spokesman said that "in the current offensive, Pakistan's military experts directly helped the Taliban in planning, conducting operations and providing material and technical supplies". He claimed that "concrete facts" especially "the numerous Pakistani servicemen taken prisoner by the Northern Alliance" proved Pakistan's involvement. Drawing world attention to the Afghan situation, the spokesman said that "massive military assistance from outside encouraged the Taliban's aggressive attempts; fuelling dangerous armed conflict which can exert a negative impact on international peace and security". He urged the international community to take urgent and decisive steps to prevent the expansion of the conflict in Afghanistan and its spill-over into neighbouring countries. In a veiled threat of military intervention in Afghanistan, the spokesman said that Moscow considered the escalating military tension in northern Afghanistan a threat to the CIS southern frontiers and that Russia, together with other CIS countries, had every right to protect its borders.

On 12 August, defence minister Igor Sergeyev and, on the following day, first deputy foreign minister Boris Pastukhov made more specific allegations against Pakistan. The latter said that the Taliban military success had come about because of the "active involvement of Pakistan army units and air force". He also observed that Afghanistan "may turn into yet another seat of international terrorism in the event the Taliban come to power there". He added: "One may suppose that the organizers of several terrorist acts staged worldwide in the past few days were sheltered in Kandahar which has become the centre of the Taliban movement." He went on to urge the world community to do all it could to stop the "ethnic massacre" carried out by the Taliban in Mazar-e-Sharif.

Sergevey in his press conference asserted that the Russian military leadership "is closely following the developments in Afghanistan and is taking measures to strengthen the Russian military contingent based in this region, including the 201st Motorized Infantry Division in Tajikistan". He announced that Tajik President Emomali Rahmonov's proposal on convening an emergency session of the CIS Defence Ministers' Council would be discussed on 2 September during the Joint Russian-Belarussian-Kazakh-Kyrgyz military manoeuvres. At the same time the Russian defence ministry called for invoking the CIS Collective Security Treaty—in particular article 4, which deals with measures to prevent crises and repel aggression against any party to the treaty.

Another prominent Russian, former security chief Alexander Lebed and at the time governor of the Krasnoyarsk Region, who was regarded as a potential future president, strongly criticized Moscow for failing in northern Afghanistan. He said that though he had himself fought against Ahmed Shah Masood, "in this situation, we could have opposed the Taliban using military force". He expressed the fear that the Taliban victory today would mean "Islamic extremism hitting Russia right below the belt".

Thus the Russians were completely unnerved by the Taliban victories of August-September 1998. Mansur Alam was advised by me to impress upon the Russians that their accusations about Pakistan's military support to the Taliban were baseless and completely devoid of truth. The Taliban should be taken at their word—they had said that their agenda was purely domestic and that they did not harbour aggressive designs against any neighbouring country. They had declared an amnesty for those who surrendered and had asked their commanders in the north to desist from revenge killings. Instead of raising the bogey of a non-existent threat to the Central Asian republics, the Russians should encourage the Taliban to adhere to their repeated assurances. Now, more than ever before, constructive engagement with the Taliban was required. Pakistan was ready to work closely with Russia in the interest of peace in Afghanistan. Alam conveyed this to Khamidulin on 19 August and added that UN under-secretary general Prendergast and the president of the Security Council had told our permanent representative in New York that the UN had no independent confirmation about Pakistan's involvement or the massacre of the civilian population by the Taliban.

Khamidulin responded that it was natural for Pakistan to reject the allegations but these were based on concrete facts. For example, the Russians knew the type and number of military planes that were used and the number of military detachments. Prendergast had not been able to confirm this because the UN had left the area. Moscow did not reject contact with the Taliban. It had met them before and was willing to do so now at a higher level in Islamabad or anywhere else. Khamidulin did not think that the time had come to recognize the Taliban. The capture of 90 percent of Afghan territory by them did not mean that hostilities had ended. His assessment was that the fighting was likely to continue. Khamidulin also conceded that the Taliban did not have aggressive designs against their neighbours because they were not in a position to carry out such aggression. The real danger lay in their desire to impose their version of Islam on neighbouring countries since the Taliban threat was ideological rather than military.

When Alam asked whether the Russians really had concrete evidence of Pakistan's military involvement in Afghanistan, Khamidulin replied that they had photographs and the numbers of the units that had taken part in the fighting. When he was asked to show the photographs and to hand over whatever other proof he may have, Khamidulin admitted that no such proof was in the possession of his government.

Collapse of the Northern Alliance

The Russian chargé d'affaires was summoned to the foreign office where I conveyed our bitter disappointment at the baseless allegations about Pakistan's military involvement in Afghanistan. Even his own foreign ministry had conceded that they had no proof. Rather than making provocative statements, Russia should be cooperating closely with Pakistan in stabilizing the situation in Afghanistan. The chargé d'affaires said that a special envoy from Moscow was ready to come to Islamabad to meet senior Taliban representatives. A request for this purpose had been made to his Afghan counterpart in Islamabad. He requested our assistance. He was told that this was the right approach and that we would try to facilitate the meeting.

Towards the end of August, Mansur Alam reported that there were indications that at least some influential Russians were taking a fresh look at the implications of a complete Taliban victory. Ivan Rybkin, the Russian president's representative for the CIS, had taken the lead in describing the Taliban as a threat to the CIS. However, he reversed this position in a radio programme by calling for support to the "choice of the Afghan people" for the sake of "achieving a certain level of stability".

Boris Gromov, the former colonel-general in the Soviet 8th Army in Afghanistan and the last Soviet soldier to leave Afghanistan, was quoted by the Moscow media as saying that as early as two or three years ago he had warned that the Taliban were a serious political, religious and military force and had "urged the government to start a dialogue with the Taliban rather than having relations with the official Afghan government only, which virtually functioned in exile, in order to defend Russia's state and geopolitical interests". However, the Russian leaders either did not take the situation in Afghanistan seriously, or simply relied on their good luck, "whatever the case, they preferred not to make any effort in this regard". He asserted that the Taliban would not be able to wage war against several enemies simultaneously, "even with support from their allies abroad".

Gromov later became deputy defence minister and then chairman of the foreign relations committee of the State Duma. During my own assignment as Pakistan's ambassador to the Russian Federation, I met Gromov, who had become mayor of the Moscow Region, at a luncheon at the Malaysian embassy in early 2001. When we were introduced, he asked me: "Why has your government assigned you here? We know your Afghanistan background and you are a *dushman* [an enemy]!" He added he was only joking and that it was excellent that I was in Moscow as I would now be able to present the correct facts on Afghanistan to the Russian government.

Another Russian, Ruslan Aushev, president of Russia's Ingushetian Republic, who not only fought in Afghanistan but also emerged as a Soviet hero from the war, told the press that Moscow would have to recognize the Taliban's power in Afghanistan. He added: "The Taliban will not cross the border because it is much more important for them to establish their order in the whole territory of Afghanistan."

The English language daily *The Moscow Times* carried a lead article by Leonid Shebarshin, a senior former official in the defunct KGB's foreign intelligence directorate, in which he wrote that: "The greatest mistake Russia can make is to allow itself to be involved in Central Asian conflicts, to pull the chestnuts out of the fire for the sake of [Uzbek president] Islam Karimov, Rahmonov and Rabbani, who is nominal head of the Afghan government. Rabbani is no greater friend and well-wisher of Russia than any Taliban leader." He suggested: "Why not let them fight their own hot and cold wars and take the posture of an interested observer?" Shebarshin ruled out a negative impact of the Taliban phenomenon on Russian interests, and instead predicted that they will "inevitably turn to their Pushtun brethren in Pakistan".

More amusing than serious was a letter written to the Taliban leadership by the publicity-hungry Russian politician Vladimir Zhirinovsky, inviting them to Moscow for consultations with his Liberal Democratic Party "in order to develop constructive interaction". As early as 12 August he called them "true patriots" at a press conference and urged support for them. During my five-year tenure in Moscow from 2000-2005, Zhirinovsky repeatedly tried to visit Pakistan and from there proceed to Afghanistan. On each occasion, I was able to a avoid this potential embarrassment by citing procedural and scheduling difficulties.

The Russian reaction to the collapse of the Northern Alliance in August 1998 was one of shock. The immediate knee-jerk response was to blame Pakistan for its alleged involvement in the Afghan conflict on the side of the Taliban. The Pakistan Air Force planes that were supposed to have bombed Bamyan, the aircraft bringing munitions, the capture of Pakistan's armed forces personnel were just some of the stream of accusations. The ridiculous nature of this was exposed by the Russian foreign office's admission that they actually had no proof despite claiming that they were in possession of photographs and had noted the registration numbers of Pakistan's air force planes in northern Afghanistan.

Russia was nevertheless eager for contact with the Taliban in the hope that some kind of a relationship could be established with the latter but the provocative decision of the Taliban to extend recognition to the

Republic of Chechnya as an independent state had made Moscow their implacable enemy. Russia construed this as a threat not only to its own security and territorial integrity but also to that of the Central Asian republics.

The Northern Alliance which had always been an artificial coalition thus came to an inglorious end after August 1998, though it continued to be regarded by the international community as the legitimate government of Afghanistan. Its leaders, with the exception of Ahmed Shah Mosood, had been defeated and driven away from the areas where they had once been dominant. The Taliban were supremely confident that they would soon be able to capture the remaining 5 to 10 percent of Masood-controlled territory. The Iranians became ever more desperate and stoked the conflict further by continuing to send massive quantities of military hardware, through the neighbouring Central Asian republics, to Masood's Panjsher valley as well as other pockets of Jamiat resistance in Takhar and Badakshan. This was to continue till the fateful autumn of 2001. More Afghan blood was, therefore, unnecessarily spilt.

Few countries, and none in the region, had been indifferent to the emergence of the Taliban. Those with interest in Afghanistan pursued policies that either shaped, or, at least, had an impact on the turn of events in the country and prolonged the suffering of the people. All neighbouring states pontificated about the need to establish a broad-based representative government in Afghanistan while not even a semblance of democracy prevailed in most of these countries. All professed adherence to the sacrosanct principles of interstate relations as enshrined in the UN Charter but interfered in the internal affairs of Afghanistan in violation of these principles. Skewed perceptions of national interests, regional rivalries and unreal threat assessments ensured the continuation of the Afghan turmoil.

6

The interested countries

Iran

THREE PARALLEL elements defined Iran's Afghanistan policy. The first was to enhance its own influence through securing a maximum (disproportionate) representation of the Persian or Dari-speaking Shias in any power-sharing mechanism. The second evolved with the rise of the Sunni-dominated Taliban which Tehran perceived as a threat to its national interests. The third, which was fervently denied by the Iranians, could have been the perpetuation of the turmoil in Afghanistan so that the landlocked Central Asian republics would be denied the most economical trade route through Pakistan and, therefore, forced to rely on Iran as the alternate commercial outlet.

In the absence of a census because of the turmoil, Iran justified the first of these elements by its own version of the ethnic and religious makeup of Afghanistan. If this was accepted, then the Taliban, consisting as they did of mainly Sunni Pushtuns, would have become a minority vis-à-vis the multi-ethnic Northern Alliance. According to a write-up in the Iranian press in the mid-1990s, the ethnic composition of the country in descending magnitude was: 40 percent Pushtun, 25 percent Hazara Shias, 20 percent Tajik (Persian-speaking), 10 percent Uzbek, and 5 percent other small ethnic groups sympathetic to the Northern Alliance. Thus the Taliban represented at most 40 percent of the population (even this was not accepted since not all Pushtuns belonged to the Taliban movement as was conveyed to us during talks with Dostum in Shibberghan on 7 December 1996), while the Northern Alliance represented 60 percent. Therefore, the Tajiks and the Hazara Shias, both Persian-speaking, together outnumbered the Pushtuns.

The Iranian figures were obviously doctored to support Tehran's political ambitions in Afghanistan, central to which was massive assistance to the ousted Rabbani regime. The major part of this aid went to the Hizb-e-Wahdat and was bitterly resented by the other elements of the Northern Alliance.

It was relevant that the Iranians should have relegated the Tajiks, who were the second biggest ethnic group, to third place by more than doubling the actual number of Hazara Shias. This portended Iran-Tajik differences as was evident from the following comment which appeared in the Mashhad-based daily *Quds* in 1996:

> The writer of this article, who is a Shia from Afghanistan, belongs to the Hazara nationality and deplores that Professor Rabbani, when he was ruler of Kabul, did not abide by his promises, which he made to the Shia community of Afghanistan. He was not only against the Jumbish-e-Milli of Rashid Dostum but also launched several attacks against the Shia areas in Kabul as well as in Bamyan, during which a large number of innocent Shia men, women and children were killed. The Afghan Shias will never be able to forget the tragedy of Afshar in Kabul. Now Professor Rabbani has realised that he would not have been pushed out of Kabul so easily if he had meted out better treatment to the Afghan Shias when he was in power.

Despite this, Iran continued to use the Rabbani-Masood-Dostum alliance in conjunction with the Shia groups to bring Afghanistan within its sphere of influence after the emergence of the Taliban.

It is difficult to break a mindset and, in the context of Afghanistan, Iran perceived a threat with the ascendancy of the Taliban. Its counter-strategy was to support the Northern Alliance. The flaw in this strategy was that the Northern Alliance was, at best, only a tenuous coalition of minority ethnic groups. A government built around an ethnic minority could never be stable, while support to such a minority coalition in opposition could have only prolonged the turmoil—which it did, with the strong possibility of fragmentation of the country along ethnic fault lines. The Taliban were seen as an American-sponsored, Saudi-financed, and Pakistan-trained entity for the purpose of undermining the security and stability of Iran. This perception, which verged on paranoia, was reflected in an unbroken strain of media comments with the approval of the government in Tehran especially after the events of May 1997 and August 1998.

Relentless pressure on the Islamic Republic by the United States, which climaxed in the imposition of a trade and investment embargo on 30 April 1995 and the appropriation of a secret fund for operations against Iran, heightened Tehran's fears. This was further compounded at the time by the dismal state of the country's economy: inflation had soared to 30 percent per annum, monetary expansion was substantial, unemployment was high and the external debt reached $25 billion. Though the embargo itself was symbolic and had an insignificant impact on Iran's economy, a number of other US successes—such as keeping Iran out of the Azerbaijan oil consortium, cancellation of the Conoco deal and Japan's withholding of the second instalment of its multimillion dollar credit for the Karoon Dam in 1995—compelled Iran to look for the protection of its political and economic interests elsewhere, i.e. Russia (security), India (economic) and China (economic and security).

In paricular, the low-key approach during Rafsanjani's visit to India in 1995 on Kashmir, Iran's muted reaction to the burning of the Muslim shrine in Charar-e-Sharif by Indian Hindu extremists and the omission of Kashmir in Velayati's speech at the 50th United Nations General Assembly session were indicative of Iranian accommodation of India in an effort to break out of its isolation. The decision to invite India to the regional conference on Afghanistan in Tehran on 29-30 October 1996 was perhaps the most overt expression at that time of Iranian displeasure over Pakistan's Afghanistan policy.

The Iran-US stand-off saw a fall-out in Tehran-Islamabad relations. An insecure Iran saw an attempt by Washington to recruit Pakistan, a traditional ally, in its containment of Iran and Islamic fundamentalism. The emergence and rise of the Taliban could not have come at a worse time for the Pakistan-Iran equation. Already under pressure along its western borders through the US naval build-up, Iran felt that the success of the Taliban was indicative of a US-Saudi plan to exert pressure on its eastern frontiers.

On 8 January 1997—i.e. only three days after the trilateral meeting on Afghanistan in Istanbul of the foreign ministers of Pakistan, Iran, and Turkey during which the three countries agreed to work together to promote an intra-Afghan dialogue—the *Tehran Times* featured a news item entitled: "Taliban Launch Activities to Undermine Iran's Border Security." The report which was hardly newsworthy claimed that the Taliban had abducted some Iranian families living in the eastern province of Sistan-Baluchistan and had mistreated them which demonstrated their hostility towards Iran. Furthermore, Iran-friendly border residents from Nimroz and Farah had been relocated to central Afghanistan and replaced by Pushtuns with the intention of undermining Iran's security in the border regions. The article concluded that US newspapers had confirmed that the Taliban had been fostered by the US to destabilize Iran.

This threat perception induced Iran to extend all-out support (including military) to the Rabbani-Masood-Dostum alliance. Deputy foreign minister Broujerdi visited Afghanistan no fewer than seventeen times in 1995 and 1996, while within Iran itself training camps were established south of Mashhad and along the Afghan border for more than 8,000 fighters belonging to general Ismail Khan who was given about two billion afghanis to buy over Taliban commanders. Within a few weeks after the fall of Kabul on 27 September 1996, Iran sent plane-loads of military assistance to Shibberghan and Mazar-e-Sharif on 16 October, 16 November and 18 December. These flights carried fuel, ammunition, warm clothing and a sizeable number of trained fighters from Herat. This was the mere beginning of massive Iranian assistance to the Northern Alliance which according to one estimate totalled $5 billion in the five-year period from 1996 to 2001.

Tehran also encouraged the establishment of a Mazar-e-Sharif-based parallel government. Under this arrangement, which was announced on 4 December 1996, Rabbani was to become the president, Gulbadin Hikmatyar the prime minister, and Dostum the vice president. The plan did not get off the ground because of Hikmatyar's reluctance to join the coalition and also because of differences among the parties over the allocation of portfolios. Should such a government have come into existence, it would only have accentuated the ethnic polarization of the country and could have led to the fragmentation of Afghanistan. During a meeting with me on 11 January 1997, Amabssador Akhundzadeh claimed that his country had never supported such a move. This, of course, was a blatant misstatement because the *Iran News* of 7 December 1996 went out on a limb in blaming the UN's Norbert Holl for Hikmatyar's change of mind about joining the government.

The Iranian government grasped every opportunity to publicly demonstrate its support for Rabbani whom it considered the legitimate president of Afghanistan. President Rafsanjani met Rabbani at Tehran on 11 November and again on 5 December 1996 although on both occasions the latter was only in transit. At Iran's ill-advised attempt to sponsor intra-Afghan talks on 25-26 January 1996 in Tehran (boycotted by the Taliban) Rabbani was received as the president of Afghanistan.

Towards the end of 1996 we had two frank exchanges with the

Iranians. The first of these meetings was in Ankara on 9 November 1996 and the second in New York on 18 November during the UN conference on Afghanistan. On both occasions it was acknowledged that Afghanistan had cast a shadow on Pakistan-Iran relations and that there was a need for the two countries to hold regular consultations with each other to allay misgivings. The Iranians listed the following grievances:

—The Taliban movement was the brainchild of the United States for the purpose of undermining the security and stability of Iran. It was financed by Saudi petrodollars and trained by Pakistan.
—Iran had evidence that the Taliban forces were being trained and led by Pakistanis. The Interior Ministry, and not the ISI or the Foreign Ministry, formulate and implement Pakistan's Afghanistan policy. (This was surprising because Tehran has consistently blamed the ISI for the turmoil in Afghanistan.)
—The capture of Herat by the Taliban posed a direct threat to Iran. The fall of Jalalabad, Sarobi, Kabul and other provinces had come about through massive bribes to the commanders of the various Afghan groups. The money had come from the US and Saudi Arabia.
—Iran had, time and again, sought to convey its misgivings to Pakistan but to no avail. If Pakistan did not want to cooperate, Iran would be left with no option but to turn to Russia and India. This was the reason for the invitation to India to participate in the Tehran regional conference on Afghanistan on 29-30 October 1996.
—Iran felt that Pakistan wanted Tehran to meekly follow whatever decision was taken in Islamabad. This was unacceptable. The Peshawar Accord was cited as an example when Iran was not consulted on the agreement drafted by Pakistan. (This was also strange because Rafsanjani told Nawaz Sharif when they met in Tehran in June 1997 that Pakistan and Iran had both been responsible for the creation of the Burhanuddin Rabbani regime.)

The Iranian misgivings about Pakistan's Afghanistan policy were particularly acute during the tenure of the Benazir Bhutto government and here again we were reminded of the thoughtless reference to the Taliban as "our boys" by her interior minister, Naseerullah Babar.

With the dismissal of the Bhutto government in November 1996 and the assumption of office by caretaker Prime Minister Meraj Khalid, Iran hoped that there would be a change in Pakistan's policy towards Afghanistan. In the middle of that month, Broujerdi, while responding to a question on the change of government in Pakistan, said that "no doubt if Pakistan adopts a policy of easing tensions and crisis it will produce results" and "the new stance taken by Pakistan provided a ray of hope in the region". Prior to interim foreign minister Sahibzada Yaqub-Khan's visit to Tehran in mid-January 1996, the Iranian media described the visit as a "highly important" event especially "in the light of the cool relations between the two countries because of Iranian concern over Islamabad's role in Afghanistan". Another newspaper article entitled "Islamabad Should Adopt a Realistic Approach to Afghan Crisis" commented: "After the dismissal of former prime minister Benazir Bhutto, the interim government in Islamabad pledged to re-evaluate its Afghanistan policy. However, no concrete measures to this end have been taken so far, nor has Pakistan's attitude towards [the] Taliban been changed to date. Thus the issue continues to be the sticking-point in Tehran-Islamabad ties." The write-up expressed the hope that Yaqub-Khan's visit would open a new chapter in Iran-Pakistan relations and improve Islamabad's regional and international image. It ended with the gratuitous comment: "The above goals will only be attainable if Pakistan re-examines and revises its Afghan policy and adopts a realistic approach to the situation in Afghanistan."

The Yaqub-Khan visit to Tehran resulted in a shallow affirmation that differences on Afghanistan must never be allowed to cause tension in Pakistan-Iran relations. The two countries agreed to consult each other closely in their efforts to promote the restoration of peace and stability in that country. Around this time the Baghram air base fell to the Taliban and the government-controlled Iranian media resumed its vehement criticism of Pakistan. The theme this time was that either Pakistani officials were "lying" about Islamabad's support to the Taliban or the ISI and not the government was in control of policy.

The Iranian newspapers commented editorially on the elections in Pakistan that brought Nawaz Sharif to power for his second term. All the write-ups contained critical references to Pakistan's Afghanistan policy. The *Kayhan International* of 4 February 1997 described Afghanistan as an "irritant" in Pakistan-Iran relations and called upon the new government to resolve the issue. The newspaper alleged that the ISI plays a "permanent and key role" in Pakistan's decision-making process. The editorial in the *Tehran Times* of the same day, entitled "Pakistan's New Government Should Mend Fences with Iran, Promote Regional

Security", criticized Pakistan for its "illusory policy on Afghanistan" and expressed the view that Pakistan, which was engulfed by domestic problems, was incapable of resolving problems in another country. It concluded with the remark: "It is hoped that the new government in Pakistan will adopt a pragmatic approach to the Afghan crisis, paving the way for restoration of peace in that country and stronger ties with Iran." The Mashhad *Quds* of 4 February observed: "It is however not clear whether the fresh elections would be able to determine the course of events in Pakistan, keeping in view the active role the army has been playing in politics especially in regard to the Afghan policy and their wholehearted support for the Taliban."

Nawaz Sharif visited Tehran on 16-17 June 1997 after attending the D-8 Summit in Istanbul. The talks were with outgoing President Rafsanjani while a separate meeting was held with then president-elect Khatami. Afghanistan featured prominently in the Sharif-Rafsanjani talks. Nawaz Sharif outlined Pakistan's perspective the centrepiece of which was commitment to peace and stability in Afghanistan. He emphasized that there could be no military solution. He stated that Pakistan's policy vis-à-vis Afghanistan was even-handed, totally neutral, and based on non-interference. He explained that we had extended recognition to the Taliban after waiting nine months and only when they had reached agreement with General Malik and were in control of most of the territory of Afghanistan. He told Rafsanjani that he had been in continuous contact with the ousted Burhanuddin Rabbani, whom he had met at the ECO Extraordinary Summit in Ashgabat in May 1997, and had also urged the Taliban to reach out to other groups to which they were not averse.

Nawaz Sharif advised Iran to establish contact with the Taliban as well. He suggested that both Pakistan and Iran had to approach the Afghan groups with whom they had some influence and persuade them to come to the negotiating table. He felt that the Central Asian countries neighbouring Afghanistan, i.e. Turkmenistan, Tajikistan and Uzbekistan, should also actively facilitate the peace process. Nawaz Sharif regretted the anti-Pakistan propaganda in the Iranian media which had become even sharper after the Taliban advance to Mazar-e-Sharif and their subsequent rout within a few days. He stressed that Afghanistan must not be allowed to cast a shadow on Pakistan-Iran relations and nor should outside powers be allowed to create misgivings between the two countries.

For his part, Rafsanjani said Iran also believed there was no military solution to the Afghanistan problem. He recalled that Pakistan and Iran had together brought about the establishment of the Burhanuddin Rabbani government and it was even accepted by Saudi Arabia. But then the Taliban had started the war and were perceived to be closer to Pakistan. Iran's position remained unchanged and it was ready to cooperate in any new initiative aimed at facilitating contacts among the Afghan groups in search of a peaceful solution. He said Iran accepted the Taliban as one of the Afghan groups but was not yet ready to accept them as a government. They had no capability or capacity to govern the country and could pose problems for both Pakistan and Iran.

Rafsanjani disclosed that Iran had been in touch with the Taliban and it would review this to see if there was a need to raise the level. He also agreed that the cooperation of the neighbouring Central Asian republics was essential to facilitate the peace process. As for the Iranian media, Rafsanjani maintained it was "free" although he confessed he too was unhappy with its attitude, which was attributable to the "situation in Afghanistan and terrorism in Pakistan". He reiterated that Pakistan-Iran relations were "too valuable" to be affected by the situation in Afghanistan.

To all appearances, the wide-ranging Sharif-Rafsanjani exchange of views seemed to suggest that, despite their differing outlooks, the fundamental interests of Pakistan and Iran on Afghanistan were the same. Both said that they have vital stakes in peace and stability in Afghanistan and agreed that there could not be any military solution. Both committed themselves to the unity and territorial integrity of Afghanistan and shared the belief that there was a need to facilitate an intra-Afghan dialogue by using the influence of the two countries with the various groups. Iran indicated the possibility of reviewing its attitude towards the Taliban and also recognized the role of the neighbouring countries in facilitating the peace process. It was decided that bilateral coordination on Afghanistan would be intensified and, even more important, the Iranians reaffirmed their resolve not to allow the turmoil in Afghanistan to affect Pakistan-Iran relations.

The Sharif-Rafsanjani talks were followed by Broujerdi's visit to Islamabad on 17-18 July 1997. This was at his own initiative and was probably prompted by the shuttle mission I was undertaking at that point in time. This was the first Afghanistan-related visit from Iran to Islamabad after several months and signified a conscious realization in Tehran about the need to coordinate closely with us on the unfolding events in Afghanistan.

I briefed Broujerdi in detail about the outcome until then of the shuttle mission. He expressed appreciation for these efforts and said it signified the determination of the Pakistan government to move swiftly towards a durable settlement of the Afghanistan conflict. I emphasized to Broujerdi that our objective was to bring the protagonists in the ongoing war in Afghanistan within negotiating range and then to convene an intra-Afghan dialogue in Pakistan to which the countries bordering Afghanistan as well as the United States and Russia would be invited as observers or possibly guarantors, should an agreement emerge. Broujerdi was supportive and said that Iran would have no problem of participating in the conference with the United States. He confided to me that the Saudis were playing a subtle mediatory role in bridging the differences between Washington and Tehran.

I told Broujerdi that our assessment from the shuttle mission was that the Taliban and the Northern Alliance did not have any confidence in each other. The Taliban were demanding the release of their unarmed peace envoys, who had been sent to Mazar-e-Sharif on Malik's request in May, as a precondition for agreeing to the establishment of a political commission to discuss a final settlement of the Afghanistan problem. Their demand was perfectly reasonable and Iran should use its influence with the Northern Alliance to bring this about so that the peace process could be initiated. Broujerdi merely took note of this without committing himself.

The deputy foreign minister was also reminded that, despite our recognition of the Taliban, we had maintained contact with the Northern Alliance at the highest level. It was suggested to him that Iran should upgrade its interaction with the Taliban as Nawaz Sharif had proposed to Rafsanjani in Tehran only the previous month. His response was that Tehran would give positive consideration to this idea provided they were convinced that the Taliban wanted to pursue the peace process. Their impression, as of then, was that Kandahar had decided on the military option.

Broujerdi and I decided that we should coordinate our respective Afghanistan initiatives closely and on a regular basis. He suggested that I should pay an early visit to Tehran to continue the discussions. I told him that I was about to embark on the next phase of the shuttle the following day. I would be visiting Kandahar after which we hoped contacts would be established with the Northern Alliance groups individually as well as collectively. When this phase of the shuttle was over I would visit Tehran. I also suggested that, at the appropriate time, Pakistan and Iran should approach the Afghan parties together.

Broujerdi was again in Islamabad from 25-27 November 1997. We had four rounds of discussions, two of which were restricted sessions.

Broujerdi said that Lakhdar Brahimi had suggested to him that the five Islamic countries immediately bordering Afghanistan plus Kyrgyzstan, Kazakhstan and Saudi Arabia should meet to discuss Afghanistan during the OIC summit in Tehran the following month. He claimed to have told Brahimi that he would only be able to respond after he had sounded us out on the proposal

My initial reaction was that the expansion in the number of countries and groups discussing an Afghanistan settlement would only dissipate the focused attention that the problem deserved. The smaller the group the more effective it would be. Saudi Arabia was certainly relevant to any discussion on Afghanistan. However, Turkey also wanted to be associated with the process and its involvement was more justified than that of Kazakhstan and Kyrgyzstan. Furthermore, there was already a surfeit of ideas and proposals from various countries including Turkmenistan, Uzbekistan, Kyrgyzstan and even Japan which had to be rationalized. The Six Plus Two was meeting regularly in New York under UN auspices. The proliferation of such groups and initiatives would only further complicate an already intricate problem. The most important factor was Pakistan-Iran cooperation in bringing about an Afghanistan settlement. All other players were marginal.

Broujerdi agreed with this assessment but felt that we should not categorically reject the Brahimi proposal. Our agreement in principle was conveyed to him on the clear understanding that the group should not become too unwieldy and that it should only include members of the OIC. Broujerdi was told that Brahimi seemed to be contradicting himself because he had insisted in New York that the UN should exclusively deal with Afghanistan peace initiatives.

Broujerdi then said that the Afghan groups were eager to participate in the Tehran OIC summit. As it would not be possible to accommodate them all in Tehran, arrangements had been made for them to meet in Isfahan. Invitations had accordingly been sent to all the Afghan parties including the Taliban. Our impression was that the Iranians hoped the OIC Contact Group on Afghanistan would serve as some kind of a pressure point on the Isfahan intra-Afghan talks. Broujerdi stated that if the Isfahan meeting was inconclusive, the next round could be held in Islamabad.

At the open session of the talks, Broujerdi agreed that the vacant seat formula would be maintained at the Tehran OIC summit. He was visibly uncomfortable when I told him that Iran was to become the post-summit OIC president for the next three years and it was, therefore, important for Tehran to uphold the principles behind OIC decisions in all international forums. Iran should, therefore, join us in persuading the UN to also adopt the vacant seat formula in respect of Afghanistan.

We also decided that the resolution adopted by the OIC foreign ministers during their meeting at the Jakarta ICFM should be approved by the Tehran Summit. Broujerdi suggested emphasis on: (i) affirmation that there can be no military solution and the renunciation of force for settling problems; (ii) reiteration that a political understanding is "the only way out" of the Afghan crisis; (iii) appeal to the international community to provide humanitarian assistance to Afghanistan; (iv) establishment of an OIC fund for assisting the Afghan people; and (v) effective measures to eliminate the production and export of narcotics. We had no problem with any of these elements.

It was also agreed that Pakistan and Iran would support a cease-fire and the imposition of an arms embargo against Afghanistan and that Brahimi's idea of an oil embargo was unacceptable. The two countries would support UN and OIC efforts to promote the Afghan peace process but the UN, as initially insisted upon by Brahimi, could not arrogate to itself the exclusive right to take peace initiatives in Afghanistan. We also agreed that the Uzbek proposal for a trilateral contact group on Afghanistan consisting of Iran, Pakistan and Uzbekistan as well as the Kyrgyz proposal for a regional summit on Afghanistan in Bishkek were untenable. Last but not least, the need for frequent consultations between Pakistan and Iran was stressed.

At the restricted meetings, I told Broujerdi that although the need for Pakistan and Iran to coordinate closely towards an Afghanistan settlement had been repeatedly stressed, the two countries were pursuing policies that were sharply at variance. There was a segment of informed intellectuals in Pakistan who believed that Iran's Afghanistan agenda was altogether different from that of Pakistan's. Their assessment was that Iran wanted to stoke the Afghan conflict for three or four more years in order to consolidate its own trade routes, such as the Tejan-Serakhs rail link, as well as oil and gas pipelines to and from the Central Asian region. They also felt that Tehran would have no problem with the fragmentation of Afghanistan so that its dream of a "greater Khorasan" would be achieved. Under this scenario, Herat would be annexed by Iran and a corridor through Badghis, Faryab, Jowzjan would be established to the Central Asian republics to the north of Afghanistan. The third alternative acceptable to Iran was a unified Afghanistan in which it had a dominating influence. I impressed upon Broujerdi that it was pointless to talk of the affinities between Pakistan and Iran. The reality was that Afghanistan had cast a shadow on our bilateral relationship and the problem had to be faced squarely. Unless we resolved our differences, outside powers would inter-fere in the region to the detriment of both Pakistan and Iran.

Broujerdi turned red in the face and I asked him to tell me frankly what Iran's Afghanistan objectives really were. What were its percep-tions about the composition of a broad-based or multi-ethnic govern-ment? If Iran shared our objective of bringing durable peace to Afghanistan, it should not have any reservations about cooperating closely with us. For instance, we could jointly approach the Afghan par-ties as well as neighbouring countries and those with influence in Afghanistan for promoting a political settlement. Broujerdi evaded a reply to this suggestion and said that Pakistan-Iran cooperation on Afghanistan should be intense but kept at a low profile.

Although the issue was not raised by me in specific terms, Broujerdi was at pains to dispel the notion that Iran's policy was predicated upon promoting the interests of the Shias of Afghanistan. He was of the view that Pakistan and Iran should concert their efforts to encourage an intra-Afghan dialogue which would lead to the formation of a broad-based government. Neither Pakistan nor Iran should suggest any formula on the composition of such a government which should be left to the Afghan parties to decide. Whatever decision was taken by them should be accepted by Pakistan and Iran.

I told Broujerdi, who was becoming increasingly uncomfortable with this one-on-one encounter, that, until now, there had been no forward movement in the intra-Afghan peace process despite our best efforts because the Northern Alliance had refused to take the confidence-build-ing measure of releasing the Taliban prisoners held by them. Dostum had taken such a step a few days earlier unilaterally, and this had result-ed in discussions between the Jumbish-e-Milli and the Taliban on a com-prehensive exchange of prisoners which could, eventually, lead to a polit-ical dialogue. Broujerdi agreed that there was need to encourage, or even pressure, the other groups to come to a similar understanding with the Taliban so that all prisoners belonging to different ethnic groups and nationalities, including Iranians and Pakistanis, could be released.

The talks were generally positive and upbeat. It was obvious that Iran's apparent reasonableness was inspired by its eagerness to convene an intra-Afghan dialogue on the fringes of the Tehran OIC summit the following month. Broujerdi, who was somewhat taken aback by our attempt to have frank discussions, merely reiterated Iran's declaratory policy on Afghanistan.

Afghanistan was discussed extensively and with profit during the

8th OIC Summit in Tehran. Nawaz Sharif effectively took up the Afghanistan issue with the supreme Iranian leader Ayatollah Khamenei and also with Khatami. Both Iranian leaders immediately and without any reservations agreed with Nawaz Sharif that it was of paramount importance for Pakistan and Iran to work together to bring the conflict in Afghanistan to an end. It was decided that Broujerdi and I should meet separately on the sidelines of the summit to discuss the issue in detail. I received a call from the duty officer at the foreign office in Islamabad, at around 4am on 7 December 1997, who conveyed a message that I should reach Tehran that evening. Around 6am foreign minister Gohar Ayub Khan telephoned from Tehran to say that since it would be impossible for me to reach Tehran that day, Shamshad and Broujerdi would initiate the Afghanistan-related talks which I could follow-up within a week or ten days.

In his talks with Broujerdi, Shamshad repeated the proposal I had made to the former about a joint Pakistan-Iran approach to the Afghan parties during our discussion in Islamabad the previous month. He stressed that Islamabad and Tehran would have to move beyond declaratory platitudes and come forward with ideas that were doable within a stipulated time frame. Broujerdi again shied away from this idea and observed that the Taliban seemed to be averse to any kind of a dialogue, and they had rejected the Iranian invitation to participate in the Isfahan meeting. Shamshad bluntly told him that the Taliban did not perceive Iran as a credible mediator because of its support for the Northern Alliance. This had been reinforced by Malik's presence in Isfahan—he had been held responsible for the systematic murder of thousands of Taliban prisoners as had been established by the discovery of mass graves near Mazar-e-Sharif. The Iranians, however, did not allow Malik to speak at the Isfahan meeting probably because this would have discredited their initiative for a dialogue among the Afghan parties on their soil.

Broujerdi proposed incremental confidence-building measures that would facilitate an intra-Afghan dialogue. He envisaged that these would include: an across-the-board exchange of Pakistani and Iranian prisoners held by the Afghan factions within one week; a visit to Kandahar by a delegation of the Afghan representatives who had met in Isfahan; a visit of a Taliban delegation to Tehran; and facilitation of food supplies to Bamyan. These steps, which Broujerdi felt would lead to an intra-Afghan dialogue, could be accompanied by a cease-fire, an arms embargo and the establishment of a political commission to discuss the future dispensation. Shamshad's response was that while the confidence-building measures were alright, the focus of Pakistan-Iran efforts should be to bring the Afghan parties to the negotiating table. The dialogue could be along the pattern of the Tajikistan talks for resolving the conflict in that country and the venue should alternate between Islamabad and Tehran after the inaugural session had been held in Pakistan.

Broujerdi's ideas, as had been expected, never got off the ground. It was clear to us that Iran was merely posturing in order to buy time to unite the Northern Alliance through massive doses of military and economic assistance for an eventual assault on Kabul. Tehran's reluctance to join us in a common and public effort to bring the Afghan parties to the negotiating table was because it would send the wrong signal to the factions in the north and weaken their alliance even further. Within six months, Iran was to realize that it was not possible to forge unity among the Afghan parties. It was only then that Tehran agreed to a joint mission with us which resulted in the Ayaz Wazir-Najafi visits to Mazar-e-Sharif and Kandahar in the summer of 1998. Unfortunately, this again unravelled because of Dostum's offensive against the Taliban in Badghis which was eventually to lead to the collapse of the Northern Alliance in August 1998. The hysterical reaction of Iran to this event almost resulted in a regional conflict.

The Northern Alliance thus existed only in name. The only faction within it which stood in the way of the complete conquest of Afghanistan by the Taliban was the Jamiat-e-Islami, which itself was riven by sharp differences between Burhanuddin Rabbani and Ahmed Shah Masood. The latter became the figure around whom the opposition to the Taliban rallied until his assassination by terrorists barely forty-eight hours before the devastating attacks on the Twin Towers in New York and the Pentagon in Washington on 11 September 2001. Till then, the quantity of Iranian military assistance to the Afghan opposition increased substantially as was demonstrated by the detention of an entire trainload of weapons by the Kyrgyz authorities at the border town of Osh in the late autumn of 1998. This happened because the Iranians had only bribed the Kyrgyz border force but not the customs. The latter, therefore, impounded the train and the extent of external interference in Afghanistan became apparent. The train had originated from Iran and had travelled through Turkmenistan and Uzbekistan with no questions being asked. Ashgabat claimed that it had been deceived by the Iranian authorities who had said that the train was carrying humanitarian supplies while Tashkent was fully aware about the actual cargo and had in fact confiscated, according to reliable reports, two wagons full of weapons for its security contingents.

So eager was the international community to ensure the defeat of the

Taliban that the incident, which violated all norms of inter-state relations, was glossed over. Iran continued to preach that there could be no military solution to the Afghanistan problem and did not relent in its propaganda that Pakistan was militarily assisting the Taliban. Uzbekistan which had told us a few months earlier that all countries with common borders with Afghanistan, had to give a solemn undertaking not to allow their territories to be used for the supplies of weapons to the warring Afghan factions, did not even try to explain the incident. Pakistan had consistently proposed a comprehensive arms embargo against Afghanistan but the international community, and particularly Iran, either merely paid lip service to this or took the plea that such an embargo would be both difficult to implement and also prohibitively expensive.

Russia

Whereas Iran's Afghanistan policy, though cynical, was clear and based on what it perceived as its genuine security and national interests, Moscow's core objectives were undefined for several months after the Taliban had captured Kabul. During discussions with us in Islamabad in January 1997, the US assistant secretary of state Robin Raphel said that Russia was only interested in preventing a Taliban military advance to the north along the borders of the Central Asian republics which it considered its "Near Abroad". Their initial fear was that the Taliban would try to export their ideology to Central Asia. This, according to Raphel, had changed to an apprehension that a Taliban victory would result in the exodus of Afghan Tajiks into Tajikistan and thereby further exacerbate the internal conflict raging in that country at the time.

It was obvious that continued Russian assistance to the Northern Alliance would only prolong the conflict and might even lead to the fragmentation of Afghanistan. However, Raphel felt that this was not Moscow's objective. We told her that if this was true, then the policy objectives of Russia and Pakistan were not in conflict. Both would want a stable Afghanistan that was not dominated by any single group. This could be achieved if the Russians pressured the Northern Alliance towards greater flexibility and a more reasonable negotiating posture. Their demand that the peace process should begin with the demilitarization of Kabul was clearly a non-starter. We expected the US to impress upon the Russians that their stated objectives and those of Pakistan coincided. Moscow needed to move away from its rigid approach and persuade the Afghan opposition to do the same.

It was also explained to Raphel that while the Russians and Iranians had made common cause, their interests were not convergent. The Iranians perceived a threat to their national interests so long as the Taliban controlled the Afghan provinces adjacent to areas in Iran where its Sunni minority lived. They would, therefore, not accept any settlement that left the Taliban in control of those provinces. The Russians, however, should have no such concern and should take the larger view that once a broad-based government emerged the apprehensions of the Iranians would also be addressed. Raphel agreed with this and undertook to convey our assessment to the Russians. She nevertheless believed that enhanced Islamabad-Moscow contacts were also necessary.

I never had any doubt, however, that the Russian threat perceptions from Afghanistan were self-serving and deliberately exaggerated. Its three basic fears of a spill-over of the conflict into Central Asia, the export of extremist ideology and the influx of refugees into Tajikistan never materialized. The Taliban provided a convenient excuse to Moscow to maintain a military presence in the region which it considered its political backyard. For all practical purposes, despite the emergence of the Central Asian republics after the break-up of the Soviet Union, Russia continued to consider its southern borders to be contiguous with Afghanistan. Although Russia was removed from Afghanistan by three international boundaries, it did not hesitate to project the Taliban and their extremist dogma as a threat to its own territorial integrity, particularly after the outbreak of the second Chechen war in 1999 and the Taliban's thoughtless recognition of that republic. The export of the Taliban brand of Islam was projected by decision-makers in Moscow as a threat to the country and, consequently, the twenty million or so Russian Muslims came under increasing suspicion. This was particularly unfortunate because religious dogma meant little to ordinary Russians. I remember being told by a businessman in Moscow that Russian Muslims were so true to their faith that they had even given Islamic names to some brands of Vodka and many of them offered congregational prayers no less than seven times a day.

The Russian reaction to the Taliban takeover of Mazar-e-Sharif in May 1997 and then finally in August 1998, though initially one of panic, was also tempered by realism. Unlike the Iranians, they were always ready to establish some form of contact with the Taliban. This policy did not change even after Kandahar had extended recognition to Chechnya. Until the collapse of the Taliban towards the end of 2001, the Russians remained eager to establish high-level contact with them. After Najmuddin Shaikh's meeting in New York with deputy foreign minister Mamedov during the November 1996 UN conference on Afghanistan, I became closely involved in negotiations with Moscow which began with the visit to Islamabad of Amabssador Konstantin Shuvalov in January 1997.

Shuvalov expressed appreciation that Pakistan had not formally recognized the Taliban as there could not be "two governments" in Afghanistan. When I questioned him about Moscow's continued recognition of the Rabbani regime, he unconvincingly advanced the argument that this had been maintained because any change in Russia's position would exacerbate the turmoil in Afghanistan. He also envisaged a peace process as beginning with the demilitarization of Kabul. I told him that this was unacceptable to the Taliban. They had rightly pointed out that the international community had not insisted on this when the Rabbani regime controlled the Afghan capital even though it had completely lost its legitimacy several years earlier. The talks were unusually frank but inconclusive. It was therefore decided to continue the dialogue in Moscow in either March or April.

I visited Moscow from 2-5 April 1997 for talks with deputy foreign minister Victor Pasuvaluk. He was brilliant and articulated his government's Afghan policy with rare precision and clarity. He chose his words as one chooses flowers from a garden, yet his intellect was never fatal to his wit. We established a friendship that was to last until he succumbed to cancer in the summer of 1999. I explained our Afghanistan policy to him at some length with the emphasis that our objectives were close to those of Russia. Both countries wanted the restoration of durable peace and stability in Afghanistan through an intra-Afghan political process leading to the formation of a broad-based government. As such, there was ample space for the two countries to coordinate their policies in order to achieve this overriding objective. I then made an informal proposal that if the Afghan parties could be brought to the negotiating table in Islamabad, countries with contiguous borders with Afghanistan, namely, Pakistan, Iran, Turkmenistan, Uzbekistan and Tajikistan should participate as observers and even guarantee any agreement that might emerge from this dialogue process. I had not mentioned China because Beijing's involvement and interest were minimal after the Soviet occupation of that country had come to an end. It was made clear to Pasuvaluk that the idea had only occurred to me during our talks and I would have to obtain my government's approval. He was supportive of the concept and added that Russia would be happy to attend such a meeting but there were obvious difficulties along the way. At all events he was emphatic that Russia and the US would also be ready to guarantee any understanding between the Afghan parties. This proposal was later picked up by Lakhdar Brahimi to develop the Six Plus Two mechanism which he unabashedly claimed was his "brainchild".

Pasuvaluk maintained that his country was not "allergic" to the Taliban and considered them "a serious political force" that was destined to play a crucial role in Afghanistan. Russian contacts with the Taliban would, therefore, be initiated and then progressively upgraded for which he hoped to meet them in Islamabad within a month or two. The deputy minister was at pains to explain that Russia was the partner and not the opponent of Pakistan in developing oil and gas pipelines as well as trade routes through Afghanistan. I had explained in some detail earlier that Pakistan had no favourites in Afghanistan and this was appreciated by Pasuvaluk who pointed out that Russia, like Pakistan, was "categorically" against the fragmentation of Afghanistan and also the twin menaces of narcotics trafficking and religious extremism emanating from that country. The policy objectives of Islamabad and Moscow were, therefore, identical. Their differences were only on unimportant nuances.

On the down side, Pasuvaluk believed that the Taliban were in no mood to negotiate and were set on the military option—even if they succeeded in subjugating northern Afghanistan, peace would continue to elude the country as the resistance to their rule would not abate and the entire region would be destabilized. Furthermore, the Taliban did not represent all Pushtuns—and here I could sense what Dostum had told us in Shibberghan in December 1996—and so their exclusive control of Afghanistan would never be accepted by other ethnic minorities such as the Uzbeks, the Tajiks, the Turkmen and the Hazaras. Until the Taliban moderated their policies, foreign businesses would be unwilling to invest in Afghanistan. I told Pasuvaluk that the negative elements that he had identified made it all the more necessary to engage with the Taliban in order to moderate their policies. Isolating them and pushing them against the wall was a self-defeating proposition. The driving force behind all revolutions—and the rapid rise of the Taliban was precisely that—is always initially extremist in nature. However, this eventually mellows and the rhetoric is gradually eroded by pragmatic national interests. This was as true of the Iranian revolution at the end of the 1970s as it was of the Russian and the Chinese upheavals earlier in the twentieth century.

The negotiations with Pasuvaluk resulted in an understanding that: (a) Russia would establish and then upgrade its contacts with the Taliban; (b) Pakistan-Russia consultations would be regularized and Pasuvaluk would visit Islamabad within a few weeks to continue our talks and to meet the Taliban; (c) its reservations notwithstanding, Russia would agree to an intra-Afghan meeting, preferably in Pakistan, to which Afghanistan's immediate neighbours would be invited as observers; and (d) Pakistan's foreign minister would visit Moscow after precise dates had been worked out through diplomatic channels.

True to his promise, Pasuvaluk visited Islamabad from 6-7 June 1997. By this time the Taliban had been routed in Mazar-e-Sharif and the ground situation was more or less the same as when I was in Moscow in April. He met the Afghan ambassador in Islamabad and later told me that Russia had taken our advice and had established discreet contact with the Taliban which would be continued.

In the Islamabad round of talks, I tried to explain that the Russian perception of the threat from the Taliban was exaggerated. Pakistan, Iran and Turkmenistan had long borders with Taliban-controlled areas of Afghanistan and had never encountered any problems. Hence the Russian, Uzbek and Tajik fears about the spill-over of instability to the Central Asian states to the north of Afghanistan were unrealistic—the fact was that the agenda of the Taliban was entirely domestic. While not denying this, Pasuvaluk repeated what he had told me in Moscow that the Taliban had decided on the military option and would never come to the negotiating table. At all events, Russia desired to work closely with Islamabad in developing trade and communication links as well as oil and gas pipelines between Pakistan and the Central Asian republics. Russia was eager to participate in the development of the region and in that sense it was Pakistan's "strategic partner". He told me that foreign minister Yevgeny Primakov was eagerly awaiting his Pakistani counterpart in Moscow and that the former recognized the importance of a dialogue between Pakistan and Russia on regional and global issues. Primakov was also fully committed to removing any "hindrances" in the way of cordial relations between Islamabad and Moscow.

I then provided Pasuvaluk a detailed rundown of the dramatic events in northern Afghanistan a few days earlier. Just prior to the meeting, we received information that Jablus Siraj had been captured by the Taliban and this was conveyed to Pasuvaluk. He took the chance here to comment that Pakistan's decision to recognize the Taliban was premature as it had made them more determined to militarily conquer the whole of Afghanistan. And yet, despite his own reservations about the Taliban, particularly their track record on human rights and narcotics trafficking, he was more than willing to deal with them. He repeated that Russia considered the Taliban "a major and permanent force in Afghanistan" but was concerned by some of their pronouncements. They had, for instance, said that one day the Taliban flag would fly in Samarkand and Bukhara. Aggression by the Taliban against the Central Asian republics would only trigger the defence mechanism of the Collective Security Treaty among the CIS members. He conceded that there had been no cross-border incidents when the Taliban were in the north the previous month and that their rhetoric about Samarkand and Bukhara, damaging though it was, could not be taken seriously.

Pasuvaluk said that his government now considered my proposal to him on an intra-Afghan dialogue with the participation of countries bordering Afghanistan as an "important idea" and Moscow wanted to be included. However, he had heard that Pakistan had reservations about inviting Russia. I assured him that this had never been contemplated and we would welcome Russian participation. The idea was rapidly being endorsed by the concerned countries. Foreign secretary Shamshad Ahmed had discussed the proposal with foreign minister Velayati and Broujerdi in Tehran on 28-29 April and had obtained their complete support. The Turkmen foreign minister had also accepted the proposal during a visit to Pakistan around that time while I had been assured by foreign minister Kamilov of Uzbekistan of his government's participation in such a process. Norbert Holl was no less enthusiastic and had urged us to persevere with our efforts.

The next contact with the Russians was foreign minister Gohar Ayub Khan's visit to Moscow where, on 8 July 1997, he had detailed discussions with Primakov. The Ayub-Primakov talks covered the entire range of Pakistan-Russia relations. On Afghanistan, Gohar Ayub went over the developments since the Soviet withdrawal from that country. At this time, I was in the midst of the shuttle mission. The secret contact with Qanooni had already taken place in Dubai and as Primakov and Ayub met, I was in Kandahar. Gohar Ayub explained the efforts Pakistan was making in narrowing the differences among the Afghan parties so that a purposeful dialogue could start among them. Primakov stated frankly that Pakistan was committing the same mistake which the Soviet Union had made in the past. Pakistan, he alleged, was supporting the Taliban in the hope that they would succeed in gaining control over the whole of Afghanistan which, in his opinion, was not possible. The US too held the same opinion earlier, but had subsequently realized its futility and had distanced itself from the Taliban. It was his impression that in Pakistan's calculation, the Taliban would be the core around whom other groups had to rally to form a government. Primakov said that Russia was not trying to bring either Masood or Malik or any other single party to power in Afghanistan and reiterated that the only solution to the problem was the creation of a coalition government. He did not think that the Taliban would cross into the Central Asian republics but was worried about the spread of Sunni Taliban extremism. This was a cause for concern because Sunnis constituted an overwhelming majority in the Islamic world. In contrast, the Iranian revolution which was Shia in nature did not generate the same worries because the Shias were mostly confined to Iran and constituted an Islamic minority. He was nevertheless supportive of Pakistan's efforts to promote an intra-Afghan dialogue with the participation of Afghanistan's immediate neighbours as well as Russia and the US.

Gohar Ayub's assessment was that it would be difficult to remove Moscow's misgivings about the Taliban and the spread of Islamic extremism to Central Asia. Only a broad-based government in Kabul was likely to allay Russia's fears.

I was to visit Moscow for continuing the talks with Pasuvaluk at the end of May 1998. However the nuclear tests by Pakistan and India that year changed the focus of our attention in the foreign ministry until the dramatic collapse of the Northern Alliance in August 1998.

Despite their frenzied reaction to the recapture of Mazar-e-Sharif by the Taliban on 8 August and the latter's subsequent control of more than 90 percent of Afghanistan, the Russians sent Alexander Oblov, who was designated as special envoy for Afghanistan, to Islamabad towards the end of September 1998 primarily to establish contact with the Taliban and to exchange views with me on the transformed ground realities.

Several months later, towards the end of March 1999, interesting information about Oblov was provided to us by Waheed Mazd'da, the director dealing with Russia and the Central Asian republics at the foreign ministry in Kabul. We were told that Oblov was a well known former KGB operative whose long association with Afghanistan had enabled him to establish close contacts with influential Afghans especially with the communists and their sympathisers. He also had links with leftist Pakistani politicians from the NWFP and Baluchistan.

Oblov had first come to Afghanistan in 1965 when the outlines of a democratic system under ex-king Zahir Shah was emerging and new political parties were being formed despite the monarch's reservations. Oblov had played an important role in the formation of the People's Democratic Party of Afghanistan and, before and during the liberation struggle against Soviet occupation, was often described as the "Afghan

Lawrence of Arabia". The historian, Siddique Farhang, in his book *Afghanistan pa Pinzo Piro Ke* (*Afghanistan in Five Generations*), and another scholar, Sabahuddin Kushkaki, in his *Qanoon-e-Assasi Lasiza* (*Fundamental Laws of the Decade*), held Oblov responsible for the murder of Minhajuddin Gahiz who was respected as one of the founding fathers of journalism in Afghanistan in the 1960s. Another author, General Nabi Azeemi, in his *Fauj au Siyasat-the Dre Lasiza pa Afghanistan Ke* (*Army and Politics during the Last Three Decades in Afghanistan*), which was published in Peshawar, claimed that Oblov had a clear hand in the murder of Mir Akbar Khyber, an Afghan army officer, and that it was this incident which had triggered the coup against Sardar Daud. After the 1979 assassination of Taraki by Hafeezullah Amin, four of the former's close aides, Aslam Watan Jan, Sher Jan Mazdooryar, Asadullah Sarwari (at the time when this information was conveyed to us he was in the custody of Ahmed Shah Masood in Panjsher) and Ghulab Zoi took refuge in the Soviet embassy in Kabul where Oblov was first secretary. Hafeezullah Amin mounted pressure on the Soviets to hand the fugitives over to him but Oblov succeeded in smuggling them out of the country to the Soviet Union. Oblov was declared persona non grata but was able to visit Kabul several times after Burhanuddin Rabbani assumed office to negotiate the re-opening of the Russian embassy. During this period he became particularly close to Ahmed Shah Masood.

Totally unaware of this background, I had two hours of talks with Oblov on 25 September. He stressed that Russia wanted to cooperate closely with Pakistan in promoting a durable settlement of the conflict in Afghanistan. The ground successes of the Taliban in the north the previous month was of concern to all the neighbouring countries and now a lot depended on Pakistan whose influence with the leadership in Kandahar could not be doubted. He stated that he did not intend to imply that Islamabad was involved in the successes of the Taliban but in the next breath contradicted himself by asserting that support from Pakistan had been decisive in their phenomenal gains. This perception was shared by several other countries.

Oblov then said that: (a) it was imperative that Afghanistan should not be fragmented. For this it was absolutely vital to recognize that the country was multi-ethnic and the interests of all groups had to be fully protected; (b) the ability of the Taliban to restore durable peace and stability in Afghanistan was circumscribed by their prejudices and their extremist predilections—they had to get the other ethnic groups on board; (c) the policies of the Taliban were of concern to the international community—their track record on human rights, particularly in regard to women, was dismal and needed to be rectified; and (d) the continuation of the turmoil in Afghanistan had spawned the twin evils of terrorism and narcotics trafficking—this was of concern to the entire world and needed to be seriously addressed.

Oblov repeated that Russia wanted to work closely with Pakistan to bring the Afghan conflict to an end. The cooperation between the two countries should be within the UN framework and, in this context, Moscow attached special importance to the "Points of Common Understanding" that had emerged from the meeting of the Six Plus Two foreign ministers on 21 September in New York. Significantly, he said that Russia was serious about establishing mutually beneficial relations with Pakistan irrespective of the developments in Afghanistan.

I have always felt that the "Points of Common Understanding" were important because the emphasis was on the establishment of a broad-based, representative, multi-ethnic rather than a multi-factional government. This implied a concession to the Taliban who had repeatedly told us that they had no problem with the inclusion of ethnic minorities in any future dispensation but did not want the factions as represented by the Northern Alliance, whom they considered responsible for the turmoil in the country, to have any role in the affairs of state.

The other important element in the "Points of Common Understanding" was the support for a Six Plus Two meeting in Tashkent to which the Taliban as well as the Northern Alliance would be invited. The initial concept of the Six Plus Two, which Pasuvaluk and I had discussed, was that it would be a forum for an intra-Afghan dialogue to which the five countries (excluding China) with common borders with Afghanistan, plus the US and Russia would participate as observers and even guarantors should an agreement emerge among the Afghan parties. Brahimi had, unfortunately, converted this to a meeting of the regional states as well as Washington and Moscow. This group had had all its meetings in New York without the participation of the Afghans. The "Points of Common Understanding" were, therefore, a marked improvement on the previously sterile Six Plus Two deliberations.

I firmly told Oblov that there was no truth in the allegations of Pakistan's military assistance to the Taliban and reminded him that his foreign office had admitted that they had no such proof contrary to what they had previously claimed. I also reminded him that there was no shortage of weapons in Afghanistan and most of these were of Russian origin. For instance, when Shindand was taken by the Mujahideen in

1992 more than a hundred brand-new aircraft from the former Soviet Union came into their possession. These subsequently were passed on to the Taliban. Similarly, when the Taliban captured Torghundi in September 1995 they came across one hundred and fifty Russian tanks which had never been used. Local commanders who joined the Taliban also surrendered their weapons. Huge arsenals had thus been accumulated by the Taliban. With the fall of Mazar-e-Sharif to them the previous month, and subsequently other areas in the north, they had captured so many weapons that most of these had to be sent to Kandahar and other places in the south away from the scene of fighting.

Another point made to Oblov was that such accusations and counter-accusations could continue endlessly. We had already proposed to the Iranians that if they really felt strongly about the inflow of weapons into Afghanistan then a commission of enquiry should be set up to determine where exactly the equipment and military advisers had come from. The Russians were welcome to join the commission so that their suspicions could be set aside once and for all. Nevertheless, there was no escaping the fact that weapons were being continuously sent to Afghanistan, thereby prolonging the conflict, and it was for precisely this reason that Pakistan had insisted at Six Plus Two meetings on the imposition of a comprehensive arms embargo against Afghanistan under Chapter VII of the UN Charter. Paradoxically, those countries that had accused Pakistan of providing military assistance to the Taliban were the most fervent opponents of such an embargo.

Oblov agreed that we should move away from mutual recriminations and focus instead on the positive. Russia wanted to chalk out a joint initiative with Pakistan for restoring peace in Afghanistan. Oblov was told that Pakistan was committed to the Six Plus Two process and fully endorsed the "Points of Common Understanding" of 21 September. Oblov was to meet the Afghan chargé d'affaires later in the afternoon and requested that no publicity be given to his contact with the Taliban.

After the talks, I hosted a lunch for Oblov at the foreign office to which Mulla Haqqani was also invited. The two talked to each other in Dari which Oblov spoke fluently. The conversation was light and embellished with reminiscences, anecdotes and jokes. The apparent cordiality between them gave the impression that two long-lost friends had at last met. Haqqani did not even give the slightest hint that he knew all about Oblov and his past.

The Haqqani-Oblov meeting, after lunch, went off smoothly. Both reiterated their grievances against each other but without rancour. They agreed on the need to move away from the past to a future of mutual understanding and cooperation. Haqqani assured Oblov that the Taliban agenda was purely domestic and they had no intention of interfering in the internal affairs of other countries. It was decided that contact between Russia and the Taliban would continue on a regular basis. The primacy of developing mutual trust and confidence was recognized by both.

Despite the positive outcome of the Oblov visit, official Russian criticism of the Taliban continued unabated. Perhaps this was because they were smarting under the pain of setbacks in Afghanistan and the embarrassment of the train incident at Osh which had taken place in October. Moscow tabled a stern resolution at the Security Council calling for sanctions against the Taliban. On 6 November 1998, foreign office spokesman Vladimir Rakhmaninov described the Taliban as the "main culprits in the ongoing bloodshed in Afghanistan". He also said that "due to the escalation of the armed confrontation by the Taliban, the situation in Afghanistan has sharply deteriorated and turned into an increasing threat to regional peace and security". He continued: "Russia deems it very important to cement the key role of the UN in the international efforts to help with the resolution of the domestic conflict in Afghanistan." He added that these efforts should be built around the Six Plus Two and announced: "Russia is going to push through a new UN Security Council resolution on Afghanistan."

Oblov visited Islamabad again from 19-22 February 1999 and had meetings with me and Haqqani. He repeated the usual Russian refrain about the need for a political settlement for which the Taliban and the Northern Alliance had to come to the negotiating table. His second emphasis was on the proposed Tashkent Six Plus Two and the urgency of finalizing the political document tabled by the Uzbeks for the meeting. Somewhat gratuitously he commented that Pakistan had been obstructing agreement on the question of ending weapons supplies. It was important for the neighbouring countries not to allow their territories to be used as conduits for funnelling weapons to the Afghan factions. I was constrained to remind him of the Osh train affair. Oblov was also told that Russia needed to come to grips with the ground realities in Afghanistan. He kept on referring to the Northern Alliance. I bluntly told him that even at the best of times the alliance had been tearing apart at the seams because of factional rivalries and had imploded after August 1998. The Jumbish-e-Milli, for instance, had fragmented into four factions while the mistrust between Ahmed Shah Masood and Burhanuddin

Rabbani had deepened. Similarly, the Hizb-e-Wahdat was also completely divided. Mohaqiq and Khalili had sharp differences while another leader of the Hizb-e-Wahdat, Ustad Akbari, had joined the Taliban. The emphasis should, therefore, be on encouraging the Afghan parties to move towards a credible multi-ethnic government through an indigenous process as had been envisaged in the "Points of Common Understanding". Oblov, however, insisted that the Northern "coalition" was intact and had united politically and militarily under Masood.

On the Tashkent Six Plus Two, Oblov was told that Pakistan supported the proposal. However, the Central Asians seemed to be having strong reservations. After the attempt in November 1998 by the Uzbek-supported Colonel Khudoybordiev to capture the Leninabad area of Tajikistan, Dushanbe was not in favour of a Tashkent Six Plus Two. Turkmenistan felt that if a meeting was to be held at all, it should take place in Afghanistan. Even the Uzbeks were not too eager to rush into a meeting without adequate groundwork. Oblov's reply, which revealed the extent of Moscow's control on Dushanbe, was that Tajikistan would have no problem with a meeting in Tashkent. He disclosed that he had been appointed ambassador to Afghanistan and that he was anxious to take up his new assignment as soon as the conflict ended. He conveyed an invitation to me from Pasuvaluk to visit Moscow on mutually convenient dates in March. This, however, did not materialize during the suggested period because Pasuvaluk was losing the battle against his cancer and had been hospitalized. Oblov mentioned that on his next visit he would also like to go to Kabul and Kandahar.

The Taliban victories in northern Afghanistan and the pathetic disarray in the ranks of the Northern Alliance seemed to have convinced the Russians that the minority ethnic groups were incapable of sustained military control of Afghanistan and would be marginalized. The Taliban would, therefore, be permanently dominant and this was detrimental to Moscow's core interests. Their extremist ideology would not only impact on neighbouring Central Asia but would also radicalize the already alienated Muslim republics in Russia's northern Caucasus. A political settlement, on the other hand, would at least ensure the representation of non-Taliban factions in the government. In Moscow's view, the inclusion of such elements through a power-sharing mechanism would have a moderating effect on Kabul's policies. The establishment of a broad-based government was, therefore, an issue that Moscow began to take seriously.

The Russians, however, perceived the Taliban as determined to achieve a total military victory in Afghanistan. Moscow believed that Kandahar was not serious about any political dialogue and would never agree to power-sharing unless forced by external pressure. Since the Russian misgivings about the Taliban agenda were also shared by the international community, Moscow was convinced that only punitive UN sanctions would compel Kandahar to establish a government that included the ethnic minorities. Only then would it be possible to ensure that Afghanistan did not come under exclusive Taliban control.

This was the Russian thinking when I revisited Moscow in the second week of May 1999 for talks with Pasuvaluk. It was heartbreaking to see the shape he was in. The piercing eyes that had reflected a razor-sharp intellect barely two years earlier had become dull. He seemed to be perpetually gazing at some invisible object in the distance. The chemotherapy that he had been undergoing had made him completely bald. He told me that he would be going to Berlin at the end of the month for specialized treatment and was not sure that he would come back. He asked me to "pray to Allah" for him. I told him that after his return from Berlin, I would be anxiously awaiting him in Islamabad where we would continue our talks aimed at exploring ways to restore peace in Afghanistan. Unfortunately, Pasuvaluk passed away shortly afterwards.

However, at the formal talks, Pasuvaluk was every bit in command of the situation. He did not allow his illness to prevent him from presenting the Russian position with the same clarity and precision which he had demonstrated when we first met in April 1997. The members of his delegation were taken aback when I told them that I would not be using any papers for the meeting because I wanted a free and frank exchange of views and this would only be possible if the discussions were conducted without briefing notes. Pasuvaluk said that he would have to constantly refer to his brief as his grasp on recent events was not quite so thorough. He reiterated the Russian desire to establish high-level contact with the Taliban and expressed disappointment that during Oblov's last visit to Islamabad he had only met the Afghan chargé d'affaires. A meeting with Mulla Wakil had been expected but the latter had decided not to come to Islamabad at the eleventh hour. Pasuvaluk requested Pakistan's help in arranging Oblov's contact with a person of authority in the Taliban hierarchy. He made it clear that Obolov's next visit to Islamabad would be conditional to such a meeting. It was also agreed that Pakistan and Russia would coordinate their initiatives to promote the restoration of durable peace in Afghanistan.

The starting point of the talks with Pasuvaluk was Prime Minister

Nawaz Sharif's visit to Russia the previous month. Pasuvaluk said that it had redefined Pakistan-Russia relations and had created an enabling environment for closer interaction between the two countries in promoting an Afghanistan settlement. He felt that the opportunity to correct the mistakes of the past twenty-five years in the Moscow-Islamabad equation was at last at hand which both countries should exploit for mutual benefit.

Though the discussions took place against the backdrop of the Taliban recapture of Bamyan, the ambience was relaxed and cordial. There was neither harsh comment nor acrimony as was the case when Mazar-e-Sharif and northern Afghanistan fell to the Taliban in the autumn of 1998.

Pasuvaluk, of course, repeated much of the known Russian position on Afghanistan, but what made the man exceptional was his ability to project events with mathematical, almost uncanny, accuracy. For instance, he told me that even if the Taliban succeeded in capturing all of Afghanistan, peace would not return as the other groups would continue to resist the religious extremism they espoused. Any arrangement that did not take into account the interests of the minority communities and factions was doomed to fail. He cited the example of Kosovo: though Serbian president Slobodan Milosevic controlled territory, he would not be able to maintain such control indefinitely.

Pasuvaluk was also a realist and he agreed with me that the peace process had to be based on ground realities. The Afghan parties to be brought to the negotiating table had to be identified and, in this context, the credible Afghan interlocutors were those that controlled territory. This meant that the first step should be to get representatives of the Taliban and Ahmed Shah Masood to talk to each other. Once they had narrowed their differences, the other Afghan elements could be associated. He also saw reason in the argument that a multi-ethnic rather than a multi-factional arrangement through an indigenous Afghan process was required as had been envisaged by the foreign ministers of the Six Plus Two mechanism in their "Points of Common Understanding".

On contacts with the Taliban, I told Pasuvaluk that I would do my best to persuade Kandahar to send a senior person to meet Oblov. I also informed him that just prior to my arrival in Moscow I had talked to Mulla Wakil who had said that the Taliban were ready to receive a delegation from Russia in either Kandahar or Kabul. At this stage, they did not want publicity to be given to such an event because the Afghan people were still bitter over the devastation that ten years of Soviet occupation had brought to their country. Pasuvaluk felt that the time had come for such an exchange. I also conveyed Wakil's message to him that the relations between Afghanistan and Russia could be normalized if the latter: (a) closed the bases in Tajikistan through which weapons were being supplied to Ahmed Shah Masood; (b) stopped the printing of counterfeit Afghan currency in Russia as that was hurting the common man; (c) paid reparation for war damages; (d) provided the maps for locating the millions of mines planted by the Soviets; and (e) tendered an unqualified apology for the Soviet occupation and destruction of Afghanistan. These steps could be gradual with the easier ones being implemented first.

I shared my assessment with Pasuvaluk that the threat perceptions of the Central Asian republics had undergone a change. They had all established contact with the Taliban, who had sent delegations to Turkmenistan, Uzbekistan and Kazakhstan. The latter was concluding a wheat agreement with Kabul while a Kazakh team was expected in the Afghan capital later in the month to negotiate the terms. It was now the competing ambitions and rivalries among the Central Asian states that was the main cause of regional instability, as was apparent from the attempt by the Uzbek warlord and Dostum loyalist, Mehmoud Khudoybordiev, to capture the Leninabad area of Tajikistan on 4 November 1998. This had prompted retaliatory bomb explosions in Tashkent on 16 February 1999 which had been carried out by Ahmed Shah Masood elements at the behest of the government in Dushanbe.

Pasuvaluk and I also discussed the proposal of ex-king Zahir Shah to convene a loya jirga. The Russian was told that the prerequisites for a loya jirga were that it could only be convened by an accepted leader of the Afghan people, it normally met at a time of national emergency such as an external threat, and it could only be held on Afghan soil. The problem that arose here was to determine who the acceptable leader was and also where in Afghanistan the jirga would be held. What needed to be done was to break both the inertia in the peace process as well as the momentum in the fighting. This should be the focus of the international community. Pasuvaluk agreed with this assessment and also felt that the Zahir Shah proposal was a non-starter.

On my return to Islamabad, I met Chargé d'Affaires Haqqani to convey the Russian request that a senior person from Kandahar should some to Islamabad to meet Oblov. Haqqani's immediate reaction was that Oblov should either visit Kandahar or Kabul because the Taliban were not at the beck and call of the Russians—if Moscow was so very particular about raising the level of contact then they should send someone more senior to Oblov. I explained to Haqqani that Oblov's superior, deputy foreign minister Pasuvaluk, was seriously ill and could not travel. Haqqani conveyed this to the leadership in Kandahar who then decided to send Deputy foreign minister Jalil to Islamabad to meet Oblov on 6 June 1999.

Thus Oblov paid his third Afghanistan-related visit to Islamabad since September 1998. He met me on 7 June and was visibly pleased with his meeting with Jalil the previous day. Jalil had acknowledged that there could be no military solution to the Afghanistan problem and had emphasized that the Taliban wanted to establish a multi-ethnic government. Oblov was also pleasantly surprised that Jalil did not refer, as Haqqani had done in the past, to the damage caused to Afghanistan by the decade-long Soviet occupation of the country. On the contrary, he recalled some of the good things done by the Soviets such as the development of the Afghan infrastructure. Jalil also stressed that the Taliban wanted to develop cooperative relations with Russia, especially in the economic and commercial fields. He asked Oblov to put an end to the printing of fake Afghan currency in Russia and was accordingly assured that no currency was being printed there—the counterfeit notes were, in fact, being manufactured by private German companies hired by the Northern Alliance. Oblov also told Jalil that his country did not differentiate between the Taliban and the Northern Alliance. In fact, Moscow acknowledged the former as the major force in Afghanistan. He emphasized the importance of Taliban participation in the Tashkent Six Plus Two. Jalil responded that they had no problem with this provided that the Taliban were invited as the government of Afghanistan.

On the question of land mines, Oblov said that the Russian government had given forty-five kilogrammes of documents showing the placement of mines to the Rabbani regime. These had apparently been lost. Moscow would, however, be sending duplicate copies, which had painstakingly been obtained, to the UN in about three weeks. This promise was never fulfilled.

However, the Taliban's ill-advised recognition of Chechnya, the alleged presence of training camps for Chechen fighters in Afghanistan and the opening of Chechen offices in Kandahar and Kabul spoilt all chances of the establishment of any relationship between Russia and the Taliban. The Putin administration exploited this to whip up nationalist sentiment over the perceived threat to the Russian federation from Islamic extremism and the Taliban. Intensive consultations were held with the Central Asian countries who fell into line.

On 8 April 2000, Kazakh president Nursultan Nazarbayev declared that any action by hostile elements against Uzbekistan would be construed as an attack on Kazakhstan. His government would do all that it could to oppose terrorism in the Central Asian region, and this included extremists "operating under the cover of religion". The same day, Kyrgyzstan's security council secretary told Russian news agency Itar Tass: "The danger of a new aggravation of the situation in the south of the country and a new attack by international terrorists from outside was real. We know for sure that international terrorists are being trained in special camps in Afghanistan and Pakistan, and some other countries. They are buying weapons and combat equipment including transport means." He called for regional cooperation to "do everything for the physical destruction of terrorists who pose a serious challenge not only to Kyrgyzstan and Tajikistan but to the entire Central Asian region".

On 8-9 April 2000, the secretaries of the security council of Russia, Belarus, Kazakhstan, Kyrgyzstan, Armenia and Tajikistan met in Dushanbe. The secretary of the Russian security council, Sergei Ivanov (subsequently defence minister), told the group that they had to work together to fight the spread of narcotics, illegal immigration and terrorism. He then said that "pre-emptive strikes" against terrorist training bases in Afghanistan could not be ruled out. This was fully endorsed by the president of Tajikistan.

Sergei Yastrazhembsky, the Russian presidential spokesman for Chechnya, with whom I was later to develop a close friendship, also visited Tashkent and Bishkek on 11-12 April. His talks with the Uzbek and Kyrgyz presidents focused on joint measures by the Central Asian states to combat terrorism, religious extremism and drug trafficking. He also linked the fighting in Chechnya to the earlier assassination attempts on the Uzbek and Georgian presidents as well as to the incursion of Islamic radicals into Kyrgyzstan. In both capitals, Yastrazhembsky declared that, as strategic partners and signatories to the collective security pact, Russia would immediately come to the aid of Tashkent and Bishkek in case of another intrusion into these countries by terrorists. According to the foreign ministry in Ashgabat, it was not merely a coincidence that the US FBI director, Louis Freeh, was also in Tashkent on 8-9 April for talks on cooperation in the fight against crime, drugs and terrorism not only in Uzbekistan but also in the whole of Central Asia. The Turkmen assessment was that these visits indicated that Washington and Moscow were preparing the ground for strikes against the Taliban.

Shortly afterwards, on 23 May 2000 Yastrazhembsky publicly threatened preventive air strikes against the Taliban. He was quoted by the

Moscow media as saying that the Taliban were being "strongly supported by the ISI and other fundamentalist religious organizations of Pakistan" that were running training camps in Kandahar, Kunduz, Herat and other areas of Afghanistan under the patronage of Osama Bin Laden. He maintained that the Taliban were in contact with the Chechen leadership and were providing military training to the rebels. Russian intelligence had credible information about Chechen leader Aslan Maskhadov's request to the Taliban for the despatch of a hundred fighters and armaments to Chechnya. Yastrazhembsky claimed that the Taliban were engaged in "militant activities in Kashmir, Bosnia, Chechnya and other parts of the world to escalate tensions between the followers of Islam and other religions" (the Foreign Office in Moscow distanced itself from this by telling us that Yastrazhembsky had no authority to make such statements).

The only exception to this Moscow-inspired Central Asian anti-Taliban hysteria was Turkmenistan. We were told by former foreign minister Shikhmuradov, who was not always reliable and had a tendency to exaggerate, that President Saparmyrat Niyazov had persuaded Russian president Vladimir Putin, during the latter's ten-hour visit to Ashgabat on 19 May 2000, not to be influenced by the "disastrously misleading" Central Asian propaganda against the Taliban. According to Shikhmuradov, Putin stated that he would not support Ahmed Shah Masood or any other warlord despite several suggestions to the contrary. In July, inconclusive talks were held in Ashgabat between Mulla Wakil, who had become foreign minister, and junior officials of the Russian foreign office.

Afghanistan again featured prominently during the Clinton-Putin summit in Moscow from 3-5 June 2000. The two agreed that Afghanistan had become the hub of terrorism which could destabilize not only Central Asia but other parts of the world as well. Putin held the Taliban responsible for the continued conflict in Chechnya and expressed the fear that they may turn the entire region into an "arch of instability". On Chechnya, Clinton advised political dialogue with the Chechens but Putin maintained that Russia was constrained to continue military action because there were no "responsible interlocutors" available. Furthermore, he added, terrorists trained in Afghanistan were returning to Chechnya and this had resulted in the prolongation of the fighting. However, the Russians had no intention to "bomb or invade" Afghanistan unless the Taliban attacked Moscow's Central Asian allies. The Americans reiterated their assessment that Russian military action against Afghanistan would be risky as it could further complicate the turmoil in Chechnya and result in a spill-over of the conflict into Georgia.

It was against this background that my tenure as ambassador to the Russian Federation began on 27 August 2000. I tried to explain, with little success, to the Russians that there were, of course, differences between Islamabad and Moscow on Afghanistan but these were not insurmountable. Both wanted durable peace in that country but differed on their respective perceptions of the Taliban. Pakistan's policy was based on the acceptance of the Afghan ground realities whereas Russia and other countries wanted to change these realities by interfering in the internal affairs of Afghanistan. There was also a refusal to recognize that the Taliban agenda was purely domestic because they had neither the intention nor the capability to destabilize the neighbouring countries. Pakistan was no less against religious extremism than Russia and the Central Asian states because, with its low literacy rate, it was far more vulnerable. Furthermore, Russia was insulated from the events in Afghanistan by three international boundaries and its threat perceptions were, therefore, exaggerated . If instability in the Central Asian republics was of special concern to Moscow, then it must understand that the cause was, not the Taliban, but the indifference of the dictatorial leadership of these states to the plight of their own people as well as their distrust of each other.

I was under no illusion that my frankness was resented. First deputy foreign minister Vyacheslav Trubnikov, who was appointed ambassador to India in 2004, told me in mid-September 2000 that relations between the Russian Federation and Pakistan could never be normalized until we changed our Afghanistan policy. Afghanistan had become a breeding ground for terrorists. Russia was concerned because Chechen fighters were being trained in camps being run by the Taliban. Pakistan had recognized the Taliban and had provided them military assistance. There were reports of Pakistani nationals, its armed forces and Arabs fighting alongside the Taliban during their ground successes in the Jablus Siraj area in the summer of 2000. Pakistan had enormous influence on the Taliban and should persuade them to desist from giving shelter to terrorists. Russia was not alone in its grievances against the Taliban. The US, China, Iran and other countries had similar complaints. The Russians and the Americans had discussed the Afghanistan situation and they had decided to impose further UN sanctions against the Taliban. Furthermore, there were Chechen militants in Pakistan and this was a major irritant in Pakistan-Russia relations. The same sermon was repeated to me by former prime minister Yevgeny Primakov the following month. I was no less blunt in my response.

Many similar bruising meetings were held with Russian officials and parliamentarians. Deputy foreign minister Alexander Losyukov who was responsible for Asian affairs and later became ambassador in Tokyo, told my colleagues in the diplomatic corps on numerous occasions that "the most difficult job in Moscow is that of the Pakistan ambassador!" There were several demonstrations outside my residence with the encouragement of the local authorities in Moscow. On one occasion we received a phone call threatening a rocket attack on the embassy. On another occasion demonstrators protested the shameful desecration of the Buddha statues in Bamyan by the Taliban although Pakistan had been the only country to intercede at ministerial level to try and persuade the authorities in Kandahar not to go ahead with this sacrilege. It was only after 9/11 when Pakistan emerged as a front-line state in the fight against global terror that the demonstrations stopped.

I was able to prevail upon Yastrazhembsky to visit Islamabad in September 2000 which he described later as an important development in Pakistan-Russia relations. He told me that he had briefed Putin on his return and that there was now a better understanding in Moscow about Pakistan's "historic concerns" vis-à-vis Afghanistan. In turn, Islamabad also had a more accurate assessment of the Chechen problem. He said that he had come back convinced that Pakistan and Russia were against religious extremism and their attitude towards Islam, which was a moderate religion, was the same.

The Russian government appreciated, according to Yastrazhembsky, the assurance of chief executive Pervaiz Musharraf (he assumed the title of president in June 2001) that the alleged presence of terrorist camps near the Pakistan-Afghan border would be looked into and if such camps existed remedial measures would be taken. If this was done, it would demonstrate Islamabad's sincerity and put Pakistan-Russia relations back on track. Yastrazhembsky said that Russia did not have any information about the presence of training camps for Chechen fighters in Pakistan but welcomed the assurance of foreign minister Abdul Sattar (he initially became foreign minister after Nawaz Sharif's ouster in October 1999) that if ever Moscow had any information about the existence of such camps, these could be jointly investigated by the intelligence outfits of the two countries.

I proposed that a meeting of the interior ministers of Pakistan, Russia, Uzbekistan, and Tajikistan should be held to develop a joint approach towards illegal boarder crossings. Yastrazhembsky felt that this was a good idea and suggested that Kyrgyzstan should also be included. Unfortunately, this proposal never materialized because of foot-dragging by the Russian interior ministry.

US under-secretary of state Thomas Pickering met with Trubnikov in Moscow on 17-18 October 2000 to discuss Afghanistan. Significantly, both understood Pakistan's limitations vis-à-vis the Taliban and agreed that Islamabad was not in a position to deliver all that they wanted. Nevertheless, they felt that Pakistan was not doing enough. It was decided that Moscow and Washington would continue to engage with Islamabad on this issue. During the meeting it was also recognized that elements from Pakistan were fighting alongside the Taliban but the Pakistan government could not be blamed for this. Appreciation was also expressed for the success of Pakistan's anti-narcotics programme. This contrasted sharply with what Trubnikov had told me the previous month.

The first session of the Russia-India Joint Working Group on Afghanistan (established during Putin's visit to India in October 2000) was held on 20-21 November in New Delhi. The delegations of the two countries were led respectively by foreign secretary Lalit Mansingh and Trubnikov. The latter also met foreign minister Jaswant Singh and national security adviser Brajesh Mishra. According to the Russian foreign office, Trubnikov, despite his complaints to me, emphasized that Islamabad could not be blamed for the extremism of the Taliban. Russia sought to deepen its dialogue with Pakistan which could not be held hostage to the Moscow-New Delhi equation.

Trubnikov said that Moscow was currently awaiting concrete action by Pakistan on some of the grievances spelt out by Yastrazhembsky during his visit to Islamabad regarding the presence of terrorist training camps along the Pakistan-Afghanistan border. Significantly, he elaborated that Russia realized that it was impossible for Pakistan, as indeed for any country, to completely seal its borders "with its neighbours", especially Afghanistan.

However, the Russians and the Indians agreed that the Taliban continued to provide sanctuary to terrorists and had done nothing to close down training camps located in the areas controlled by them. This posed a danger for all neighbouring countries and, in particular, Russia and the Central Asian republics. It was also agreed that Taliban-dominated Afghanistan was the world's primary source of narcotics. The Taliban had not taken any measures to curb the production and trafficking of drugs and were, in fact, benefitting from the trade.

Trubnikov said that Russia was prepared to talk to the Taliban. Initial discussions had been held in Islamabad between junior officials of the two embassies. However, the Taliban were not interested in continuing the dialogue. Russia would not beg for the resumption of the talks.

Throughout the rest of my stay in Moscow, until the fateful events in New York and Washington on 11 September 2001, the Russians fully exploited the stupidity of the Taliban in extending recognition to Chechnya. What is interesting is that I was told privately by foreign ministry officials in Moscow on numerous occasions that Osama Bin Laden was an American problem and that Russia, despite what it said in public, had no proof of his direct involvement in Chechnya. Their only grievance against the Taliban was that the latter had given shelter to and were training Chechen separatists. Russian officials also conceded that it would not be possible for the Taliban to derecognize Chechnya but they should at least take measures such as closing down Chechen offices in Kandahar and Kabul. I was asked, time and again, to help in promoting contact between the Taliban and the Russian ambassador in Islamabad. The problem, as in the past, was the venue. Ambassador Zaeef of the Taliban, who had just assumed his new responsibilities in Islamabad and was to receive considerable media attention after 9/11, insisted that his Russian counterpart should come to the Afghan embassy for the talks. By July 2001, the two were moving towards a meeting at a neutral place. However, this was overtaken by the events of 11 September.

The foreign ministry in Moscow kept alleging that there were Pakistani army officers in Afghanistan to help the Taliban in their military operations. One such officer, a general from the ISI, was supposed to be headquartered at the Tajbek palace near Kabul. Russian intelligence had obviously not done its homework properly because the palace had been destroyed in the fighting several years earlier. Similarly, we were given the names of twelve Pakistan army personnel who had supposedly been killed in the fighting after the collapse of the Northern Alliance in August 1998. This again proved to be totally incorrect as all the men were alive and had not set foot into Afghanistan for several years.

After 11 September 2001, Moscow became more vociferous that Osama Bin Laden was involved in the violence in Chechnya contrary to what I had been told by Russian foreign ministry officials in confidence. Immediately after the assassination of Ahmed Shah Masood, the Russians organized a regional meeting in Dushanbe which was attended by intelligence and foreign ministry officials from Russia, Tajikistan, Uzbekistan, Iran and India. The purpose was to evolve a post-Masood strategy and to meet his successor, General Faheem. The Russians knew that Masood had been killed on 9 September but deliberately withheld the news until they had consulted their close allies on the future strategy against the Taliban. When Masood's death was finally made public two or three days later, Moscow announced that it would give full support, including military assistance, to Burhanuddin Rabbani who was "the legitimate President of Afghanistan". The common effort would be to defeat the Taliban and their Osama Bin Laden-sponsored terrorist network.

Before the US-led attack against the Taliban began on 8 October 2001, there was considerable debate among the authorities in Moscow about the extent and type of support Russia and its CIS partners would give to the international coalition against terrorism. The day American planes started bombing Taliban positions in Afghanistan, the influential chairman at the time of the State Duma Foreign Relations Committee, Dmitry Rogozin, was lunching with me at my residence. He commented that this signified the beginning of the end of Russian influence in Central Asia. For Moscow, the important question was whether US bases should be allowed in the Central Asian states. However, it could do nothing to prevent this. During the US-Russia Joint Working Group meeting on Afghanistan in Washington on 8 February 2002, Trubnikov was sceptical about the assurances of under-secretary Richard Armitage that the US had no intention of remaining in the region a moment longer than was absolutely necessary.

After the ouster of the Taliban at the end of 2001, there was a substantial improvement in Pakistan-Russia relations. Besides the normal bilateral consultations at the level of deputy foreign ministers (equivalent to Pakistan's additional foreign secretary), the two countries established mechanisms for regular structured consultations on counterterrorism, Afghanistan, as well as between their respective audit chambers to deal with such issues as money laundering. President Musharraf paid a landmark visit to Moscow on 3-5 February 2003. His scheduled thirty minute meeting with Putin extended to two-and-a-half hours plus three hours of further talks in which the respective delegations of the two countries also participated. After their *tete-a-tete*, when Musharraf introduced me to Putin as "my ambassador" the latter quipped "you're wrong Mr. President, he is our ambassador."

Turkmenistan

Turkmenistan, unlike Tajikistan and Uzbekistan, prudently adopted a posture of neutrality towards the conflict in Afghanistan in 1996 and emphasized that it had no problems with the Taliban. The rationale was based on the practical reality that Afghanistan and Pakistan provided the most economical outlet for Turkmen exports.

Ashgabat did not join the other Central Asian republics in the 1992 collective security arrangement and never sent troops to Tajikistan. It fully supported the December 1996 decision of the 24th Islamic Conference of Foreign Ministers in Jakarta to keep Afghanistan's seat vacant in the Organization of the Islamic Conference, but did not take any initiative for a similar move by the UN. It boycotted a CIS meeting of defence ministers attended by Russia, Kazakhstan, Kyrgyzstan, Tajikistan and Uzbekistan at the end of February 1997 to discuss the situation along the Tajik-Afghan border. While establishing good working relations with the Taliban it also kept its channels of communications with Dostum open until May 1997. The purpose was to secure its eight hundred and fifty kilometre border with Afghanistan.

However, after the events in Mazar-e-Sharif in May 1997, Turkmenistan, despite its neutrality, began to tilt towards the Taliban. Shikhmuradov flew into Islamabad aboard a special plane on 7 June 1997 and expressed complete understanding of Pakistan's decision to recognize the Taliban. He said that President Niyazov had asked him to inform us that Turkmenistan was also going to recognize the Taliban government but was waiting for the situation to become more clear. At all events, the Turkmen government was "moving forward towards recognition". In practical terms, Shikhmuradov said, Turkmenistan recognized the Taliban. He, however, reiterated his country's neutral stance in the conflict in Afghanistan and drove home the point that Turkmenistan had refused to be drawn into any anti-Taliban alliance propounded by Moscow, Tehran and some of the Central Asian republics. He said that a few days earlier, the commander of the Russian border guard had visited Ashgabat. The latter was flatly told that Turkmenistan did not perceive any threat from the Taliban and nor did it foresee a large influx of refugees into Central Asia from Afghanistan. As such, it would not participate in any collective security meeting against the Taliban. Shikhmuradov claimed that Turkmenistan had been in close contact with General Malik and said that the latter was amenable to cooperation with all other groups in order to establish a central government. Turkmenistan regarded the Taliban as the major political force and the most important ethnic element. Shikmuradov also met the Afghan ambassador during the visit and was told by the latter that his government was willing to talk to General Malik at any time.

After the collapse of the Northern Alliance, our minister of state for foreign affairs Siddique Kanju had an hour and a half long meeting with Niyazov in Ashgabat on the morning of 26 August 1998. The latter opened the talks by stating that he fully understood Pakistan's position on Afghanistan because of its long border with that country. The Turkmen president underlined the need for the Taliban to moderate their policies. He then made the revealing comment that the Taliban need not bring about a radical transformation but their overall image had to undergo a cosmetic change. This would encourage other countries to soften their attitude towards them and help in the recognition of their government. If they failed to demonstrate moderation and continued to act in isolation then within one year anti-Taliban Afghan groups and foreign forces would join to destabilize the country. It was, therefore, imperative for the Taliban to play "a more civilized and active role in international relations". Niyazov also stressed the need for the Taliban to repeatedly affirm their resolve not to cross international borders and to form a broad-based government with representatives of other ethnic groups to ease the fears of the regional countries and the international community.

Niyazov held Russia responsible for the troubles in Afghanistan and maintained that it was Moscow which was influencing countries like Uzbekistan and Tajikistan to remain in conflict with the government in Kabul. He said that although Iran had concerns about the welfare of the Shia minority in Afghanistan, it was not averse to establishing contact with Kabul. It was afraid of the powers that it perceived to be backing the Taliban, such as the United States and the Arabs but not Pakistan.

Niyazov also confided that a Russian diplomat was caught in Ashgabat a few days earlier on suspicion of inciting the Afghans residing in Turkmenistan against his government's policy of working with the Taliban. Kanju informed him that the Russian government had requested us to help them establish contact with the Taliban. Niyazov's response was that he was not surprised as Moscow had also made a similar request to him but wanted these contacts to remain secret. This was not acceptable to Turkmenistan because it followed a policy of open engagement.

President Niyazov observed that the Russian press had downplayed the gas pipeline project to Pakistan. He commented: "For the present we have to lie low. The situation in Afghanistan will clear up soon and we will be able to lay the foundation stone in the beginning of 1999." He confided that President Khatami had told him confidentially that Moscow had contacted Tehran not to allow the export of Turkmen gas through Iranian territory.

Subsequently, on 29 August 1998 Shikhmuradov took Amabssador

Babar Malik, who had replaced Tariq Osman Hyder, aside during a reception at the Uzbek embassy in Ashgabat and confided that Ahmed Shah Masood's representative, Dr Abdullah Abdullah, who was to become foreign minister in the interim administration of Hamid Karzai in December 2001, had called on him earlier in the day. He said: "Ahmed Shah Masood is happy with his friends and confident of facing the Taliban challenge." Shikhmuradov further added that Masood was not contemplating surrender.

Two weeks later, Shikhmuradov told Babar Malik that there was a great deal of pressure on Turkmenistan to invite Burhanuddin Rabbani to Ashgabat for an official visit. The Iranian government was also insisting on this but President Niyazov had instructed him to use some pretext to put the visit off.

Shikhmuradov visited Pakistan from 25-27 January 1999 primarily to continue the Afghanistan related discussions that had been initiated by us. Sartaj Aziz, the new Pakistani foreign minister, told him that Islamabad and Ashgabat had to get their thinking straight about the political document envisaged by the Uzbeks at the proposed Six Plus Two meeting in Tashkent. It was important to guard against such a document being used to foreclose our own initiatives to promote an Afghan settlement. As for the proposed Tashkent Six Plus Two, our approach had to ensure that: (a) only those Afghan groups who control territory were to be invited to the meeting; (b) as previously agreed in the 21 September 1998 "Points of Common Understanding," the UN should immediately set up enquiry commissions to investigate the killings in the north in May 1997 and August 1998; (c) the formation of a multi-ethnic government through an indigenous Afghan process was not impeded; (d) an immediate end to weapons supplies to the Afghan parties was enforced; and (e) generous contributions for reconstruction and rehabilitation programmes in Afghanistan were committed.

Shikhmuradov expressed the view that any approach towards an Afghanistan settlement had to be predicated on the existing situation. This entailed acknowledging that the Taliban were the dominant Afghan reality and the Northern Alliance, which even in the best of times was riven with dissension, had virtually ceased to exist. With the exception of Ahmed Shah Masood, none of its leaders controlled territory and, as such, could not be taken seriously. Unlike the other parties, the Taliban could not be treated as an Afghan faction. They represented an ideology to which the overwhelming majority of the population subscribed. A viable way to promote sustainable peace in Afghanistan would be to bring about conciliation between the Taliban and Masood. While we agreed with this in principle, we felt that the idea would have to be preceded by a series of confidence-building measures as the two just did not trust each other.

Shikhmuradov disclosed that Dr Abdullah Abdullah had spoken to him a few days earlier and had told him that Pakistan was now following a more balanced policy on Afghanistan and that Masood wanted to establish contact with Islamabad. Although Masood had been receiving weapons and money from Iran, he was certainly not a puppet that Tehran could manipulate. Our own thinking was that there could be some truth in this because Masood had always resented the disproportionate manner in which Iran had built up the Hizb-e-Wahdat. Shikhmuradov felt that the military council that had been set up only days earlier by the defunct elements of the Northern Alliance with Ahmed Shah Masood as its head was a clear indicator that Burhanuddin Rabbani had been sidelined.

Shikhmuradov was of the opinion that Uzbekistan, which had been blatantly interfering in Afghanistan, was the least qualified to host the Six Plus Two meeting. If at all such a meeting was to take place in the region, it should be held in Kabul. He said that the point to be kept in mind was that Uzbekistan and Tajikistan were bitter enemies and were fighting turf wars inside Afghanistan through the respective ethnic Uzbeks and Tajiks of Afghanistan. It was not the Taliban who were interfering in Central Asia, rather it was the converse. The Russians were hand-in-glove with Uzbekistan and Tajikistan. Unlike these two Central Asian states, Turkmenistan considered the ethnic Turkmen population of Afghanistan as Afghans. The term "Turkmen Afghans" was not in his government's lexicon. This is what Uzbekistan and Tajikistan had to learn otherwise they would continue interfering in Afghanistan under the pretext of protecting different ethnic groups. Shikhmuradov said that Turkmen consulate officials had been asked to work on expanding trade and economic relations with Afghanistan. A Turkmen team would visit Kabul after which his government planned to reopen its embassy in Afghanistan. The future government in Afghanistan could only be decided by the Afghan themselves. Outside parties had no say in this matter. Shikhmuradov met Mulla Wakil who flew into Islamabad from Kandahar for this purpose.

This was the changed political reality in which the Taliban occupied centre stage. It was publicly enunciated by Shikhmuradov when he and assistant secretary of state Rick Inderfurth were jointly invited by the Central Asian Caucus to a seminar in Washington on 21 April 1999. Responding to a question on social and economic rights of women in

Afghanistan, Shikhmuradov said that Turkmenistan believed in respecting rights of all citizens of Afghanistan. However, Afghanistan was a country where a "standard approach" did not apply. It was therefore crucial that the local customs, traditions and aspirations of the people should be taken into account. In response to another question, Shikhmuradov said that international community, and particularly the countries in the region, should treat Afghanistan as a unified entity and not view it through the prism of ethnic diversity. Moreover, outsiders should respect the aspirations of the Afghan people who wanted a dialogue between the "real forces" inside Afghanistan.

During the rest of the seminar, Shikhmuradov forcefully presented his country's viewpoint on Afghanistan, pointing out that the incorrect notions about the Taliban in the West were due to disinformation and lack of knowledge about Afghan traditions. He also made a veiled criticism of the UN stating that an active involvement of the UN was needed to carry forward the peace process.

In the autumn of 1999, the Turkmen assessment was that the Northern Alliance knew their strength lay in making their sympathisers and supporters vociferously criticize the fundamentalist and obscurantist policies of the Taliban especially at times of difficulty. Shikmuradov told us: "In order to cover their weaknesses, the Northern Alliance accuse the Pakistan army of fighting alongside the Taliban to attract more assistance from Russia, India, Iran and the West. Their voice was not only the loudest but its echo obscured the actual facts." He reiterated that Turkmenistan's Afghan policy was dictated purely by peace dividends which would be enormous in economic and political terms not only for Ashgabat but also for the entire region. He thought that a Pakistan-Turkmenistan joint initiative to promote peace in Afghanistan would yield results. This would be all the more effective if China could be persuaded to join.

In April 2000, the Russians sent a message to Ashgabat that Turkmenistan's perception of the Afghanistan problem was flawed and that the Northern Alliance was not weak. Around this time, Dostum and Malik signed an agreement in Mashhad under which they undertook to cooperate closely with each other in order to defeat the Taliban. In the third week of the month, Malik was in Ashgabat and met Shikhmuradov who claimed to have told him that his entry into Turkmenistan would be "banned for ever" if he joined hands with Dostum. Shikhmuradov informed us that Malik, who was a frequent visitor to Ashgabat where he had a mistress, had readily agreed to this. Thus, from a position of even-handed neutrality in 1996 when Turkmenistan kept its channel of communication with Dostum open, this represented a radical change in its posture. The reason most certainly was not Turkmenistan's love for the Taliban but the belief that the latter controlled more than 90 percent of Afghan territory which the Northern Alliance would be unable to reverse.

A few days later, on 30 April, Dostum arrived in the Turkmen border town of Charjeu from Tehran en route to Tashkent. Shikmuradov had told us earlier that President Niyazov had "absolute hatred" for Dostum and had given instructions not to ever allow him into Turkmenistan. After repeated requests from Dostum, Shikhmuradov had agreed to grant him a transit visa without informing Niyazov in order to determine the reason for his visit to Tashkent. A "special team" was sent by Shikmuradov to Charjeu "to look after him during his overnight stay".

Alcohol apparently got the better of Dostum who revealed in a drunken outburst that he was to meet a very important visitor from Moscow in Tashkent after which he would go to Russia for follow-up discussions (Shikhmuradov presumed this "very important visitor" to be President Putin who was due in Tashkent on 19 May). Dostum also told his Turkmen hosts that Ahmed Shah Masood was despised by the Russians who considered him a traitor and a trouble-maker because they thought he was supporting the Tajik opposition against Russia, and they also believed he had established secret links with the Taliban. Furthermore, the Russians were furious because Masood had refused to become a party to the Dostum-Malik agreement that had been signed a few days earlier in Mashhad. Accordingly, they had decided to terminate military supplies to him.

The following morning, Dostum spoke to Shikmuradov by telephone and referred to the Iranians as "bastards" for restricting his movement in Mashhad. He was no less abusive of the Tajiks. Dostum also cursed Masood and tried to advance the argument that a conflict between the Turkic and the Persian-speaking Afghans was inevitable. He attempted to convince Shikmuradov that Masood's ultimate aim was to eliminate Afghans of Turkic origin and, therefore, Ashgabat should throw its weight behind the endeavour to dislodge Masood. He then bragged that he was the natural leader who could solve the problems of Afghanistan and "sort out Masood and his cronies".

On his return to Mashhad from Tashkent two weeks later, Dostum was again given permission to transit Turkmenistan. As on the previous occasion, Shikhmuradov sent his people to Charjeu where Dostum spent the night. After several glasses of vodka, he revealed that his visit to

Tashkent had been sponsored by President Islam Karimov and that he had been the guest of the Uzbek intelligence chief. As it was not possible to meet Putin, he had left a six-page note for the Russian president explaining the situation in northern Afghanistan. Dostum claimed that the loyalties of important Taliban commanders in the north, with whom he had been in touch, could be bought. Putin was requested to pressure Ahmed Shah Masood to join the Turkic-speaking group against the Taliban and also to provide weapons and financial assistance for this purpose. Dostum said that after Karimov had spoken to Putin about this plan, the Uzbek president would visit Ashgabat to persuade Niyazov to come on board.

Shikmuradov felt that Dostum was being manipulated by Karimov who wanted to play the dominant role in the region. He was also of the view that Moscow was playing a dubious role in Uzbekistan and Tajikistan. It was exploiting the vulnerabilities of presidents Karimov and Rahmonov to opposition elements within their respective countries in order to keep them on their toes and dependent on Russia. Dostum, according Shikhmuradov, fitted into the Russian game plan. He had been given a compound in Tirmiz built by the former Soviet Union where several of his commanders were living and, with Moscow's ostensible approval, had been assigned the task of neutralizing opposition groups inside Uzbekistan and Tajikistan. Intelligence circles in Moscow knew only too well that this would be extremely difficult especially because of the latent tensions between Tashkent and Dushanbe but it served the purpose assuring Karimov and Rahmonov of the Kremlin's solidarity with them. About a hundred and fifty Afghan-Uzbeks were trained for this purpose in which the Uzbek intelligence chief was also involved. But Dostum, as was to be expected, was also trying to find a place for himself inside Afghanistan and had been sending some of his commanders across the Amu Darya (Oxus) at night for the purpose of storing weapons and ammunition and also to bond with Afghan-Uzbeks in Balkh and Jowazjan for an eventual uprising against the Taliban. Shikmuradov seriously believed that Dostum would first try to neutralize the Tajik and Uzbek opposition and then, with support from Tashkent, make incursions into Afghanistan on the pretext of a threat of Islamic extremism.

Uzbekistan

Uzbekistan considered itself the heavyweight among the Central Asian republics who resented this and suspected their neighbour of hegemonic ambitions. On Afghanistan, its policy had been built upon support for the ethnic Uzbek minority and, particularly, Dostum. In the autumn of 1996, President Farouk Leghari of Pakistan met his counterpart Karimov in Tashkent. The latter expressed reservations about the Russian designs in the region and agreed that a divided Afghanistan was not in his country's interest. The Uzbek also reiterated the usual declaratory mantra that the turmoil in Afghanistan was its internal affair and could only be resolved by the Afghans themselves without outside interference. He promised to use his "limited influence" to persuade Dostum to remain neutral. However, this was at a time when the Taliban had taken Kabul but were nowhere near Afghanistan's northern borders.

I visited Tashkent in June 1997 after the Taliban and been pushed out of Mazar-e-Sharif for talks with foreign minister Abdul Aziz Kamilov. He was critical of our recognition of the Taliban and bluntly told me that Pakistan could no longer pretend to be pursuing a neutral policy towards Afghanistan. For its part, Uzbekistan would not establish official contact with the Taliban. Kamilov said that the only way to stabilize Afghanistan was for the neighbouring countries to solemnly affirm that they would not allow their territories to be used as conduits or even transit routes for weapons supplies to the warring factions. He thought my proposal to Pasuvaluk about an intra-Afghan dialogue in which countries with contiguous borders with Afghanistan would participate as observers was a good idea but then added that the other Central Asian states were unimportant. To emphasize this point he commented contemptuously that Kyrgyzstan had been "making noises about hosting a regional conference on Afghanistan but the Kyrgyz president does not even know who the leaders of the Northern Alliance are". The only countries that really mattered were Uzbekistan, Iran and Pakistan, and they should embark on a trilateral effort to bring the Afghan groups to the negotiating table. This concept was repeated time and again by Tashkent but was politely brushed aside by us as well as by the Iranians. The collapse of the Northern Alliance in August 1998 compelled the Uzbek leadership to then rethink their Afghanistan policy. In order to emphasize that it was the most important Central Asian state, Uzbekistan focused all its energies towards hosting a meeting of the Six Plus Two in Tashkent. This was approved by the foreign ministers of the group and incorporated into their "Points of Common Understanding" of 21 September.

In the first week of November 1998, I accompanied minister of state Kanju to Tashkent for talks with Kamilov. Since my meeting with him in the summer of the previous year, there had been a dramatic shift in the Uzbek policy towards Afghanistan inasmuch as Tashkent had come to terms with the new ground realities. They now wanted to engage with the Taliban whereas previously they were allergic to any formal contact with the latter. I could not resist the temptation of reminding Kamilov about his insistence in June 1997 that the neighbouring countries should not allow their territories to be used for weapons supplies to Afghanistan and yet an entire trainload of Iranian military equipment for Ahmed Shah Masood had been allowed to pass through Uzbekistan only to be intercepted by the Kyrgyz authorities at Osh just a few days earlier. Kamilov was visibly discomfited and responded unconvincingly that the Uzbeks had been told that only humanitarian assistance was being sent and, as such, the consignment was not checked. As I did not wish to embarrass him further, I decided not to remind him that one or two of the carriages had been impounded by the Uzbek security authorities for their own use. Kamilov said that he would visit Pakistan towards the end of the month.

As indicated by him, Kamilov was in Islamabad from 25-26 November 1998 primarily to discuss the Afghanistan situation. Through our good offices, he met Mulla Wakil who flew over from Kandahar specifically for this purpose.

Kamilov had visited Tehran prior to his arrival in Islamabad and he told us that the Iranians felt that the Tashkent Six Plus Two should only be held if there were cast-iron guarantees that it would be purposeful and result oriented. In contrast to our position that the Taliban should be encouraged to evolve a multi-ethnic government, the Iranians were still talking in terms of a multi-factional Afghan dispensation consisting of the warlords of the past. Tehran also wanted the leaders of these factions to participate in subsequent meetings of the Six Plus Two. We told Kamilov that this was a recipe for failure. Insistence on the inclusion of the factional leaders would not allow the proposed Six Plus Two meeting in Tashkent to get off the ground. A multi-ethnic government in accordance with the wishes of the Afghan people had been accepted by all including the UN. Instead of raking up the past, the focus should be on the positive. According to Kamilov, the US was insisting on an early Tashkent Six Plus Two. However, he felt a cautious approach was required and that progress towards the Tashkent meeting should be through a gradual step-by-step process. There was no need to fix dates and deadlines which could not be met.

Kamilov said that Uzbekistan had come to the realization that the prevailing realities in Afghanistan had to be recognized. To our surprise, he added that Uzbekistan did not want to see a change in the ground situation which implied that Tashkent wanted the Taliban to remain in control of the north. This remark was significant particularly when factored into his meeting with Mulla Wakil. The impression we had was that he was distancing himself from Tajikistan and the weapons that were being channelled through that country to the Afghan Tajiks led by Ahmed Shah Masood. This clearly reflected the differences and tensions among the Central Asian republics. Kamilov also emphatically opposed any further expansion of the Six Plus Two and observed, in an off-the-cuff manner, that accepting new members would allow India to claim membership of the group. Subsequently, on 7 April 1999, a four-member Taliban team led by Maulvi Raqib, minister for refugees and martyrs (he was of Uzbek origin), held discussions with the Uzbek authorities in Tirmiz. The delegation also included Mulla Abdur Rahman Zahid, deputy foreign minister, Waheed Mazd'dah of the foreign office, who had provided us the information about Oblov's past, and Mulla Qasim Jan Hashmi, the foreign office representative in Mazar-e-Sharif. They were received by the Uzbek deputy ministers of power, interior and foreign affairs as well as the mayor of Tirmiz. There was no pre-planned agenda for the meeting, which was held at Tashkent's initiative. The situation along the border between the two countries was discussed in order to reduce tension. It was also decided that the talks would be continued on cooperation in such areas as the supply of Uzbek electricity to Mazar-e-Sharif and combating narcotics trafficking and currency racketeering.

Kamilov again paid an Afghanistan-related visit to Islamabad on 31 May 1999 and proceeded to Kandahar the following day for his first-ever meeting with Mulla Omar. This marked a watershed in the relationship between the Taliban and the Central Asian republics. Only Tajikistan had not established direct contact with Kandahar at the highest level. In contrast to what he had told us in November, Kamilov now wanted the Six Plus Two meeting in Tashkent at the earliest. This was his main emphasis in his talks with us as well as with Mulla Omar who again assured him that the Taliban agenda was purely domestic and they posed no threat to any neighbouring country.

Kamilov also conveyed the Uzbek assessment to us that Tajikistan was hand-in-glove with Russia to further stoke the conflict in Afghanistan. Uzbekistan had spoken vociferously against a new military base that Tajikistan had permitted the Russians to establish on its territory. The bomb blasts in Tashkent in February 1999 had been instigated by Ahmed Shah Masood at the behest of the Tajik president. We were also told that Dostum was no longer relevant and Kamilov was at pains to emphasize that his government had not been in contact with him for the last two years.

Tajikistan

The ground successes of the Taliban towards the end of 1996 and their capture of Kabul in September of that year were received with anxiety in Dushanbe. The electronic media had been regularly projecting slanted stories about Pakistan's alleged involvement in Afghanistan relying mostly on statements made by Rabbani and Masood. However, the Tajik government itself had refrained from making adverse comments about Islamabad. We hoped that the peace accord between the opposition and the Tajik government, though fragile, would result in a more balanced Tajik position on Afghanistan.

In December 1996, Tajikistan became the first country to establish a consular post in Taloqan, the Rabbani-Masood headquarters at the time. While this decision may have been motivated essentially for keeping a watch on the Tajik opposition and for arranging the return of refugees to Tajikistan, it also reflected the growing warmth between Dushanbe and Burhanuddin Rabbani.

Minister of state Kanju and I flew into Dushanbe on 5 November 1998 for a four-hour visit during which we met foreign minister Talbak Nazarov and later had a working lunch with deputy foreign minister Rehmatullayev. Nazarov was dishevelled in his appearance as though he had just come out of bed after a sleepless night. He had reason to be worried. The previous evening colonel Mehmoud Khudoybordiev, an Afghan Uzbek commander loyal to Dostum, had captured an area of northern Tajikistan. According to the Pakistan ambassador in Tashkent at the time, the late Shahryar Rashid, the Uzbek rebel forces entered Khojand from a fifteen kilometre-long underground tunnel connecting an old Soviet uranium mine inside Tajik territory (Yeschlof) in the Leninabad region to a processing area in Uzbekistan. The rebels crossed the border in small vehicles through this tunnel. They were able to obtain some heavy weapons from the armouries of the Tajik forces after crossing over. It was widely believed that the rebels were trained in northern Afghanistan and Uzbekistan and were given logistic support by Dostum. The Tajiks claimed that two hundred and seventy persons died during the fighting while four hundred were injured.

Without naming Uzbekistan, Dushanbe accused a "neighbouring country" of providing assistance to Khudoybordiev. Quoting government sources, the state-controlled radio announced that Tajikistan had "undeniable evidence" of the location of training camps in that country and that many of the rebels were loyal to Dostum. The Tajik authorities also said that the "neighbouring country" had provided weapons and had helped the rebels to cross into Tajikistan.

The Uzbek government initially refrained from responding to the implied Tajik allegations but later issued statements dismissing any connection with the incident. To clarify the Uzbek position, foreign minister Kamilov announced that the Tajik president had called Karimov immediately after the outbreak of the violence to exchange views on joint measures to "improve the situation" and that the Tajik militia had been permitted to pass through the Uzbek town of Bekabad to the troubled area. There were unconfirmed rumours that Dostum was seen in the Khojand region. Similarly, there was talk that the Uzbeks first encouraged him to participate actively in the takeover bid but then decided against this. The Uzbek rebels had expected sympathetic uprisings in other parts of Tajikistan but these failed to materialize. Interestingly, the Muslim "fundamentalist" elements in Tajikistan supported the government in resisting the rebels, perhaps because the Uzbeks had persistently rejected overtures from the Islamic dissidents in Tajikistan.

Tashkent resented the inclusion of the economically prosperous Leninabad region in Tajikistan and also the marginalization of the dominant Uzbek Khojandite clan in the area. The Khojandites had been used by it in the past as a pressure point on the leadership in Dushanbe. After Dostum's defeat, Uzbekistan's Afghanistan ambitions received a severe setback and it then focused its attention on Tajikistan where it sought to increase its influence. The Khudoybordiev incident was a reminder to the leadership in Dushanbe that they needed to give the Khojandites a larger representation in government otherwise the country would remain in turmoil and vulnerable to interference by Uzbekistan. From Taskhent's perspective an unstable Tajikistan would ensure its continued dependence on Uzbekistan and also discourage the large ethnic Tajik community in southern Uzbekistan from anti-state activities with the help of their kinsmen across the border.

It was against this background that Kanju and I met Nazarov. The latter reiterated the hackneyed line that there was no military solution to the Afghan problem. The recent successes of the Taliban would turn out to be short-lived. Their gains would unravel within weeks unless they came to the negotiating table for establishing a broad-based government. Nazarov said that the Taliban owed their success to outside support. They had gone on the rampage and there were reports of mass killings and ethnic cleansing. The international community could not remain indifferent to such blatant violations of human rights. The Taliban were a blot on the good name of Islam. They had discredited the religion. Their attitude towards women and policies towards other ethnic groups were deplorable. The twin menaces of drug trafficking and terrorism could be traced to the Taliban. The turbulence in Tajikistan was being stoked by elements in Afghanistan. Nazarov urged Islamabad to realize that if the Taliban succeeded in consolidating their hold in Afghanistan, Pakistan would be the next victim. The spectre of Pushtunistan would raise its head again and religious extremists would destabilize the country.

Kanju responded that whereas Pakistan held no brief for the Taliban, the blame for the continuing tragedy of Afghanistan could not be placed at their doorstep alone. There had undoubtedly been outside interference. The Osh train incident was an eye-opener. Furthermore, five of Masood's pilots who had defected a few days earlier to the Taliban along with their AN-32 had admitted undertaking no less than thirty-five sorties in the previous weeks to deliver weapons to the Northern Alliance from Kulyab in Tajikistan. This had been continuing for several months and it was certainly ironic that these very weapons had been used by Khudoybordiev against Tajikistan. As expected, Nazarov vehemently denied that his country was being used for military assistance to Ahmed Shah Masood.

In the luncheon with Rehmatullahev, I emphasized the need for Pakistan and Tajikistan to work together towards an Afghanistan settlement. The Six Plus Two format was all very well but something else had also to be done. Pakistan and Tajikistan should evolve a "one plus one" mechanism in which the two countries would exchange views and ideas on bringing peace to Afghanistan. Perhaps they could approach the Afghan parties together. A significant outcome of the visit was that the Tajiks agreed to establish contact with the Taliban and to work closely with us independent of the other Central Asian republics to promote the Afghan peace process.

Nazarov visited Pakistan and had detailed Afghanistan-related talks with foreign minister Sartaj Aziz on 23 December 1998. He stated that the key to an Afghanistan settlement lay with the Afghans themselves. The role of its neighbours could only be that of facilitators. He felt that the situation in Afghanistan had undergone a radical change and, unexpectedly, added that the transformation was for the better after the Taliban had taken control of the north in August 1998.

Sartaj Aziz told Nazarov that a permanent end to the conflict in Afghanistan had to be based on the existing political realities. The Taliban were the dominant force and had demonstrated their staying power. They had been ascendant for the last four years and were in control of two-thirds of the country including the capital for well over two years and 90 percent of the territory since August 1998. Somewhat bluntly, Sartaj Aziz added that the principal reason for the continuation of the conflict was external interference. The Osh train affair should leave no doubt as to who was stoking the conflict and why. Unfortunately, Tajikistan had become a conduit for the supply of weapons to the Northern Alliance. The Kulyab airport as well as ground routes were being used with abandon for this purpose. It was strange that the weapons intended for the Northern Alliance had eventually been used against Tajikistan as demonstrated by the Khudoybordiev incident the previous month. Dushanbe had to seriously ask itself where the threat to its security really emanated from. Did it come from the inward-looking Taliban, who had repeatedly stated that their agenda was purely domestic, or from some other quarter? Several top leaders of the defunct Northern Alliance, for instance, Ustad Akbari of the Hizb-e-Wahdat, Nasim Mahdi of Dostum's Jumbish-e-Milli and many commanders of Karim Khalili's Hizb-e-Wahdat had already joined the Taliban. Rabbani, who was an ethnic Tajik and the so-called president of Afghanistan, had himself been in contact with the Taliban leadership. There were clear indicators that the process for the formation of a credible multi-ethnic government had started. The discarded and discredited factional warlords of the past no longer had any relevance. At this critical juncture, it was important for Afghanistan's immediate neighbours to engage with the Taliban because there was a real possibility of restoring sustainable peace in the country through the establishment of a multi-ethnic government.

A befuddled Nazarov at first rejected the accusation that his country had been a weapons' conduit for the Northern Alliance but eventually conceded, especially when reminded of the Khudoybordiev uprising, that such transhipments had taken place through Tajikistan's long and porous borders with Afghanistan although without the approval or knowledge of his government. He was obviously bluffing but Sartaj Aziz had the grace not to embarrass his guest any further.

Nazarov wanted to avoid meeting the Taliban because he did not have the authorization of his government which, in turn, took its instructions from Moscow. He was reminded that the Taliban had repeatedly stated that their policy was one of strict non-interference in the internal affairs of other countries particularly their neighbours. It was, therefore, important to reassure them that Tajikistan would not allow its territory to be used for the supply of weapons to the Northern Alliance. If they perceived that other countries were interfering in their internal affairs, they might be constrained to react. Nazarov eventually met Chargé d'Affaires Haqqani at a dinner hosted for him by Sartaj Aziz the same evening.

Nazarov agreed that the factional leaders of the past had no place in Afghanistan. He was bitterly critical of Dostum who, he said, no longer had any right to play a role in Afghanistan as he had abandoned his people and had taken refuge in Turkey. He also agreed that the Afghans should be encouraged to work towards the formation of a multi-ethnic, rather than a multi-factional, government.

The United States

Washington's position on Afghanistan changed from one of sympathy for the Taliban to that of bitter condemnation because of human rights violations, particularly those of women, and the refuge given by them to Osama Bin Laden.

At the November 1996 UN conference on Afghanistan, assistant secretary of state Robin Raphel took a clear line in favour of the Taliban stressing that they controlled more than two-thirds of the country and were an indigenous movement which had demonstrated staying power. Significantly she added: "The reasons they have succeeded so far have little to do with military prowess or outside military assistance. Indeed when they have engaged in truly serious fighting, the Taliban have not fared too well."

Even on the adverse international perception of the Taliban's track record on human rights, especially gender discrimination, Raphel commented: "If we want them [the Taliban] to moderate their policies we should all engage with them." Later that month she telephoned Pakistan's permanent representative to the UN in New York and informed him that the State Department had received a letter from Mulla Ghaus which was "full of sweetness and drafted in the most excellent English".

This brief period of support for the Taliban changed radically by the time Madeleine Albright became US secretary of state. During her confirmation hearing in January 1997, Senator Christopher Dodd said that he intended to table a resolution on the Taliban in the near future because of their "reprehensible and disgusting" treatment of women. Albright's response was: "We are all deeply troubled by what we have heard that the Taliban were doing. The whole situation in Afghanistan is one that is deeply troubling. There are factions that for years have been unable to get together. What we would like to see is a government that is a unity government of some kind." By the time Albright visited Pakistan in November 1997 she expressed her dislike of the Taliban with considerable venom and described them as "despicable" while addressing Afghan women at the Nasir Bagh refugee camp in Peshawar.

The following three fundamental elements were discernible from the declaratory US policy towards Afghanistan:

—Support for Afghanistan's territorial integrity. Afghanistan should be a country which is at peace within its borders which neither threatens nor is threatened by any of its neighbours.
—Support for an independent, sovereign Afghanistan which is not a political and military battleground for outside interests. No outside power should aspire to dominate Afghanistan.
—Support for an Afghanistan which seeks to cooperate with all its neighbours to advance mutually beneficial interests such as economic development and trade.

In the transformed post-Cold War world in the 1996-97 period, and four years before the 11 September 2001 terrorist incidents in the US, Afghanistan was barely of peripheral interest to Washington. Its initiatives had been few and far between and those too, initially, at a relatively junior level. For instance, meetings were held in Mazar-e-Sharif in 1997 between the deputy chief of mission at the US embassy in Islamabad and Dostum, Masood and Rabbani during which the American official advised them against forming a parallel government. As for the Taliban, the main US concern then was shifting from human rights issues, particularly gender discrimination, to narcotics trafficking and training camps for terrorists. On narcotics, US embassy officials told us that Washington would come down heavily against the Taliban if it could be conclusively established that they were encouraging poppy cultivation or were being financed by the drug mafia.

Later US contacts with the Afghan groups were aimed at promoting a negotiated end to the conflict. Washington leaned towards the monarchists and sponsored conferences in Europe mainly attended by émigrés. The Americans also realized that a durable settlement would have to be based on the Pushtun majority and the idea of "a second Pushtun option" built around educated Afghans rather than the Taliban gradually emerged.

With the capture of Mazar-e-Sharif by the Taliban on 8 August 1998 and their virtual control of 90 to 95 percent of Afghan territory a short while later, the US policy on Afghanistan gravitated to the single issue of Osama Bin Laden. Several unproductive meetings were held between senior US diplomats and the Taliban leadership on the extradition of Bin Laden to a place where he could be brought to justice. On 20 August, the US carried out missile attacks against Bin Laden's training camps in Khost which were prompted by the terrorist bomb blasts at the American embassies in Tanzania and Kenya. Subsequently, after 11 September 2001, Afghanistan became the first battleground in the US-led coalition against terrorism.

China

China continued to recognize the Rabbani regime primarily because the latter occupied Afghanistan's seat at the UN. Beijing's Afghanistan policy, and in particular, its attitude towards the Taliban was never very clear. In large measure, China's worries stemmed from its fear of the export of both fundamentalist ideology and weapons from Afghanistan to Islamic militants in Xianjiang (populated mainly by Muslim Uighur Turks). Beijing established informal contact with the Taliban through its embassy in Islamabad and subsequently decided to send a foreign office delegation to Kabul in August-September 1998. This, however, was postponed until the following year due to the fall of Mazar-e-Sharif.

The *China Daily* of 11 August 1998 carried a rare, but detailed, comment by the official Xinhua news agency that the ground successes of the Taliban in and around Mazar-e-Sharif were probably only temporary as had been demonstrated by the pattern of the conflict in Afghanistan. The resumption of fighting in the north had all but derailed the peace efforts of the international community and, particularly, the Pakistan-Iran joint mission.

In September 1998, some overseas Chinese institutions received letters from a previously unheard of organization which called itself the "European Taliban Islamic Center" and threatened bomb attacks. The Chinese government took up this matter with the Taliban, who firmly denied any involvement with or knowledge of the group and reiterated their desire to maintain good relations with Beijing. However, reports continued to filter in about the presence of a number of Xianjiang separatists in the Taliban-controlled areas of Afghanistan.

We were told the following month by senior Chinese foreign ministry officials that Beijing had noted Kandahar's repeated affirmations of friendship with all countries and the purely domestic nature of its agenda. For its part, China hoped to establish friendly and cooperative relations with the Taliban. We were also told that the Taliban diplomats in Islamabad were "very friendly" towards China, as the latter had helped the Afghan people both during the Soviet occupation of their country and later in times of natural disasters. Beijing, nevertheless, continued to believe that the Taliban were involved in the killing of the Iranian personnel in Mazar-e-Sharif, as well as in exporting "Talibanism", although the central Taliban leadership was not accused of being involved in this. On the US air strikes against Afghanistan and Sudan, the Chinese foreign office spokesman said on 21 August 1998 that Beijing condemned all kinds of terrorist activities and "the international community should strengthen cooperation in fighting against international terrorism, in order to eradicate the causes of terrorism and safeguard world peace and stability". He added that the bombings in Kenya and Tanzania should be handled in line with the UN Charter and the norms established by international law. Later, on 1 September, China in an indirect criticism of the US action said: "We insist that the international community make joint efforts to fight against terrorist activities in accordance with the principles of the UN Charter and international rules, and on the basis of respect for a country's sovereignty and territorial integrity."

An editorial in the *China Daily* of 2 September noted that the "compelling evidence" the US had referred to for its 20 August missile attacks on alleged terrorist-related facilities in Sudan and Afghanistan turned out to be less than convincing. Tit-for-tat retaliation was not what the international community was looking to in its fight against terrorism. There was no doubt that the US attacks constituted a transgression of other countries' sovereignty. There was also speculation in the diplomatic circles in Beijing that the Chinese military was interested in "having a look at the cruise missiles which had landed in Afghanistan unexploded", and that this might warm up China-Taliban ties to some extent.

The Chinese eventually sent their foreign office delegation to Kabul from 31 January to 2 February 1999 in order to see the three buildings of the Chinese embassy and to assess the damage they had undergone as well as to meet representatives of all "warring groups" either in Islamabad or in Kabul. In Islamabad, the Chinese embassy had arranged meetings with representatives of the Northern Alliance. The delegation met Mujaddadi, representatives of Dostum and Karim Khalili, Pir

Gillani's son and Professor Amin of the Afghanistan Study Centre. The Chinese were told that all the parties wanted a peaceful solution to the Afghan conflict and although the Taliban could not control Afghanistan militarily, they had decided on the military option. The conflict could only be brought to an end if the Taliban showed flexibility and a willingness to talk to the other groups.

In Kabul, the Chinese delegation met deputy foreign minister Abdur Rahman Zahid and other members of the government who assured the visitors that the Taliban would not allow Afghan territory to be used by the Uiygur extremists in Xianjiang and this was appreciated by the Chinese. Zahid then repeated the standard Taliban refrain that they controlled 95 percent of the country where peace and stability had been restored. The Taliban interpretation of a peaceful settlement of the conflict, however, was the surrender of the opposition to them. Furthermore, they claimed that a multi-ethnic government was already in place and there was no question of including people like Masood, Dostum, Khalili and Malik in it as they had been rejected by the Afghan people. Thus, as in May 1997, the Taliban made it abundantly clear that they were in no mood to enter into peaceful negotiations to bring the conflict to an end. They obviously refused to learn from their past mistakes and were convinced that they would be able to militarily defeat their opponents.

The Chinese response was characteristically cautious and confined to bland observations such as the need for the Taliban to interact with the international community and to improve their image. They emphasized the advantages of a negotiated settlement which could only emerge from the Afghans themselves. The Taliban already controlled 90 percent of Afghanistan and, therefore, further territorial expansion was unnecessary. Their focus should instead be on consolidation and, in this context, a lesson could be learnt from the collapse of the Soviet Union.

The Taliban had a genuine respect for Beijing. They told me on several occasions that China was the one country in the Six Plus Two group against which there were no allegations of interference in Afghanistan.

India

In 1996, the assessment of the main Indian intelligence outfit, the Research and Analysis Wing (RAW), was: "If the Taliban consolidates its position, it would leave India at a distinct disadvantage . . . it would diminish India's manoeuvrability not only with regard to Afghanistan but also as far as India's strategy towards Central Asia is concerned, future Indian interests which demand that transport routes to Central Asia be kept [open], lie threatened . . . Above all, Afghanistan will enhance Pakistan's diplomatic manoeuvrability in the region. Right from 1979, when Soviet troops intervened in Afghanistan, it has been New Delhi's consistent policy to thwart Pakistan's attempts to install a puppet regime in Kabul. India has lost the covert battle to have a friendly regime in Afghanistan. It is no secret that the Rabbani regime was propped up mainly due to the overt support lent by Russia and the covert support given by India."

While India had, in the past, gone out of its way to advertise its good relations with the Rabbani regime, it was significant that New Delhi should have disclosed (through planted stories in the media) that it had also "established direct contacts with General Dostum". It was clear to us that India was trying to signal to the international community that, by virtue of being the largest country in the region, it had a definite role to play in Afghanistan. This was encouraged by Tehran and Moscow. The Indians also let it be known that an emerging military relationship between New Delhi and the anti-Taliban forces could not be ruled out. Press reports which were clearly based on official briefings disclosed that a delegation from Dostum, led by "an air force officer known only as General Hafiz", spent nearly a week in Delhi towards the end of 1996.

The Indians assured Dostum both political and military support. They tried to establish a consulate in Mazar-e-Sharif and asked Dostum to open an office in New Delhi. Efforts were are also made to start weekly flights of Balkh Airlines and Air India between Mazar-e-Sharif and New Delhi on a reciprocal basis. During our visit to Shibberghan on 7 December 1996, we were told by Dostum that the Indians would not be allowed to open a consulate at Mazar-e-Sharif.

Two officials of the Indian ministry of external affairs, Vivek Katju, joint secretary in charge of Iran, Pakistan and Afghanistan and Alok Prasad, the joint secretary responsible for the Americas, visited Washington in the first week of September 1999 for discussions on Afghanistan. The objective was to put across India's views on cross-border terrorism, an excuse the country has used to repress the people of Jammu and Kashmir in their struggle for self-determination as promised to them by the international community through several resolutions of the UN Security Council. In particular Katju and Prasad sought to emphasize alleged links between the Taliban and the ISI and the phenomenon of narco-terrorism. India had long been stressing links between the ISI, the Taliban, Pakistan-based Islamic extremism, Osama Bin Laden, the Kashmiri freedom struggle and narco-terrorism.

The interested countries

The US Embassy in New Delhi told our High Commission officials that the Indian arguments had received a boost since the Kargil crisis which had almost resulted in a full-fledged Pakistan-India conflict during that period. Furthermore, according to the US mission in New Delhi, there was a greater Western sympathy for India's portrayal of Pakistan as a state sponsor of terrorism. Many in the State Department and the National Security Council shared the Indian concern that Pakistan was fast becoming a hub of religo-terrorist activities. The US intelligence community gave Secretary Albright a briefing on terrorism which focused mainly on Afghanistan and Pakistan.

The Indian leadership maintained that the Kargil operation had been launched by the Pakistan army with the involvement of the Taliban and Osama Bin Laden. External affairs minister Jaswant Singh said at a press conference on 1 September 1999 that reports of Osama Bin Laden's involvement in Kargil were being compiled and would be released at an appropriate time. However, the promise was never fulfilled for the simple reasons that there was no evidence.

The State Department subsequently informed us that the Katju-Prasad visit was on India's initiative. New Delhi had taken positive action by suspending Ariana flights to Amritsar at US request. This action demonstrated that US-India interests were congruent as both countries had similar perceptions on terrorism and instability flowing from Afghanistan. On the Taliban, the US and the Indians held somewhat differing views at the time. While the US objected to the Taliban's "behaviour," the Indians believed that the Taliban were "fundamentally a destabilizing phenomenon" in the region.

*

The policies of countries with interest in Afghanistan thus evolved with frequent and dramatic changes in the ground situation. All professed the need for a political settlement of the conflict, the establishment of a representative multi-ethnic government (which a majority of the neighbouring countries did not themselves have), and the end of weapons supplies to the warring factions but unfortunately, in most instances, their operational initiatives were far removed from these pious pronouncements.

The Taliban and their opponents were no less self-serving. Each expected outside assistance for the furtherance of their narrow political ambitions; each was falsely self-righteous—the Taliban believed that they and they alone represented the will of God while their opponents donned the mantle of religious tolerance and liberalism; and each lacked the vision to bring true peace and stability to Afghanistan.

Through all this, the UN was largely ineffective. It sought the exclusive right to promote an Afghanistan settlement but did little to bring about such an outcome. In effect, it became a passive bystander as the Afghan tragedy continued.

7
The United Nations

SOON AFTER the Taliban capture of Kabul on 27 September 1996, there was a brief burst of activity by the UN—after which it went into hibernation. The UNSMA chief, Norbert Holl, shuttled between Mazar-e-Sharif and Kandahar but was never able to meet Mulla Omar. The purpose of his mission was to arrange a cease-fire between the Taliban and the Northern Alliance. On his return from Kandahar on 30 October 1996, he told us that the Taliban and Dostum had agreed, in principle, to a military disengagement around Kabul, the exchange of prisoners of war and a twelve-member commission to monitor the cease-fire. There were differences on where the troops should withdraw to. The Taliban were willing to move back to Charasiab, Kargah, Pul-e-Charki, while Masood had agreed that his forces would withdraw to Panjsher and Dostum's to Mazar-e-Sharif. The latter, however, insisted that if he was to withdraw to Mazar-e-Sharif, the Taliban should go back to Kandahar and, at the very least, the forces of the two sides should be equidistant from Kabul.

According to Holl, there was also agreement for a neutral police force to be deployed around Kabul but disagreement on its composition. The Taliban wanted one hundred persons from each province but Dostum was adamant, with good reason, that the representation should be in proportion to the population of the provinces. He made the ridiculous claim that the Taliban were in twelve provinces and an equal number were under his control while both the Taliban as well as the Northern Alliance were in six provinces.

Shortly, after I assumed charge of Afghanistan affairs, Mulla Ghaus visited Islamabad where he had his first, somewhat comical, meeting with foreign minister Sahibzada Yaqub-Khan. Holl availed of the opportunity of Ghaus's presence in Islamabad and persuaded him to meet Dostum's representative in Pakistan, General Paindah on 7 November 1996. Paindah was a gentle, unassuming person and the exact opposite of Dostum. I doubt whether he had ever seen conflict and his military rank was of no consequence because non-Taliban Afghans had the propensity to give titles such as "general", "engineer", "professor", etc to whoever wanted them. Whereas there were many "commanders" and "generals" in Afghanistan, I have never come across any lieutenant, captain, major, colonel or brigadier. The meeting between Ghaus and Paindah was a non-starter as neither had the authority to conduct negotiations. It was this initial progress made by Holl that we tried to build upon during our visit to Shibberghan and Kandahar on 7 and 8 December of that year.

Norbert Holl convened working level inter-Afghan talks in Islamabad on 13-15 January and 24-26 February 1997. From the Taliban side the meeting was attended by Mulla Muhammad Sadiq, a member of the central shura, Mufti Masoom Afghani, who was then ambassador designate to Pakistan, and Haji Fazl Muhammad. General Paindah from Dostum's Jumbish-e-Milli and Rasul Talib of the Hizb-e-Wahdat (Khalili group) represented the Northern Alliance. The representative of Ahmed Shah Masood could not attend due to travel problems.

As in the past, the Taliban insisted that the peace process should commence with the exchange of prisoners whereas the Northern Alliance were equally adamant that it should begin with the demilitarization of Kabul. There was no progress in the talks and the only understanding that was reached was on the exchange of fifty prisoners from each side through the ICRC.

Holl told me later that the Taliban appeared to be confident of military success and that was the reason for their insistence on the exchange of prisoners which they considered as the only element that needed to be addressed for a final settlement. He had, therefore, decided to abandon the working level format and had proposed to the Afghan parties that future talks should be held at the political level. The idea, according to him, was not rejected by either side. Holl planned to convene the political level talks in mid-March 1997 in either Islamabad or Ashgabat to which Pakistan and Iran would be invited as observers. He hoped to be able to persuade Mulla Rabbani and Dostum to send their representatives for the meeting. To promote the idea, he intended to visit Mazar-e-Sharif and Kandahar. Unfortunately, the meeting never materialized and Holl was seldom seen or heard from until our own shuttle mission was in an advanced stage by mid-August 1997.

One of the reasons for UNSMA's inability to effectively carry out the mandate entrusted to it under UN General Assembly resolution 50/88 was its reluctance to come to terms with the dominant realities in Afghanistan. Burhanuddin Rabbani's representative continued to occupy

Afghanistan's seat at the UN despite the categorical assertion by the secretary general's special envoy, Mehmoud Mestiri, during the donors' conference in Stockholm on 2 June 1995 that the Rabbani-Masood regime represented only the ethnic Tajiks and excluded the Pushtuns, the Uzbeks and the Hazaras. His efforts to facilitate the transfer of power and the formation of a transitional council had foundered because of Burhanuddin Rabbani's intransigence. The minority regime in Kabul, whose writ extended to only four or five of the thirty-two provinces of Afghanistan, was dismissive of any proposal for an equitable sharing of power. Rabbani's claim to represent the government of Afghanistan emanated only from his control of Kabul. De facto legitimacy, if at all arising from nominal control of state structures should have been deemed to have terminated with the collapse of the Rabbani regime on 27 September 1996. The UN's credibility as an impartial mediator was, therefore, severely compromised by its recognition of a single ethnic entity as the government of Afghanistan. While the question of legitimacy was for the people of Afghanistan to decide, the UN should not have been seen as partisan in its approach especially in the fulfilment of the mandate stipulated in the UN General Assembly resolution 50/88 of 19 December 1995 under which UNSMA was required to continue to facilitate national reconciliation and reconstruction in Afghanistan. An example had been set by the OIC, which had decided to keep Afghanistan's seat vacant until such a time as a government acceptable to the Afghan people emerged. The vacant seat formula could have easily been adopted by the UN.

Although the Northern Alliance continued to receive massive military and economic assistance from its external supporters, the front-lines north of Kabul and in western Afghanistan were stable and reflected a military stalemate. Active and sustained UN involvement was, therefore, desperately needed. UNSMA's early efforts to bring the Afghan parties within negotiating range had demonstrated the difficulties in promoting an intra-Afghan dialogue. The prospects for achieving durable peace, if that was what the Afghans really wanted, could have been significantly advanced through the UN-generated sequential settlement proposal. The interim administration that the Taliban had set up in Kabul could have, if properly handled by the UN, become a first step towards establishing a broad-based government acceptable to the Afghan people. With twenty provinces under its effective control at the time of the UN conference on Afghanistan in November 1996, the Taliban were uniquely placed, with the support of the UN, to draw upon the immense goodwill of the people and local commanders, which they subsequently lost, for launching a credible intra-Afghan political process for restoring peace and national reconciliation.

Through its resolution 1076 (1996) of 22 October 1996, the Security Council had already reaffirmed the UN's strong commitment to the sovereignty, independence, territorial integrity and national unity of Afghanistan. It was necessary for the Security Council to follow this up by the immediate imposition of a mandatory arms embargo on Afghanistan under Chapter VII of the UN Charter. This would have been wholly consistent with its appeals to all states to respect the principles of non-intervention and non-interference in the internal affairs of Afghanistan as well as respond to the exigencies of the prevalent situation.

However, the UN drifted into a slumber from March to July 1997 and did little to promote an Afghanistan settlement. In the intervening period, Mazar-e-Sharif had been taken and lost by the Taliban and we tried to bring the Afghan groups to at least talk to each other through our shuttle mission. Its main purpose was to supplement and not supplant the progress achieved by UNSMA on the sequential settlement proposal. Holl was removed from his post—to the combined relief of the Northern Alliance, the Taliban and the neighbouring countries. Lakhdar Brahimi was now appointed the UN secretary general's special envoy for Afghanistan. However, he decided to base himself in New York and visited the region only occasionally. He adopted my proposal to Pasuvaluk for an intra-Afghan dialogue with the participation of countries with contiguous borders with Afghanistan and established the Six Plus Two mechanism. The difference was that the original idea envisaged negotiations among the Afghan groups in which outside countries would only play a marginal role while Brahimi's Six Plus Two ignored the most important element namely, the Afghan parties. The only time they were invited was to the special session in Tashkent in the summer of 1999.

The Six Plus Two group thus met regularly at the ambassadorial level and at times that of foreign ministers in the comforts of far away New York while Afghanistan continued to be ravaged by conflict. During these meetings, the Taliban were rightly criticized for their human rights track record as well as narcotics production and trafficking (the issue of terrorist training camps emerged later). However, the criticism was one-sided because the Northern Alliance was no less culpable. Both sides were equally guilty of violating human rights and both had benefited from the drugs trade which predated the emergence of the Taliban as the major political force in Afghanistan. The Six Plus Two countries also reiterated the need for a peaceful political settlement ad nauseam while four of them either provided or served as conduits for military supplies to the Northern Alliance. Our position, which was built around the imposition of a comprehensive arms embargo against Afghanistan, was consistently ignored by the group.

The UN's arms embargo concept

In February 1998, Brahimi circulated a paper on an Afghanistan-specific arms embargo among the Six Plus Two UN ambassadors. The paper, as was to be expected, highlighted the problems for adopting such a measure. Our own views which were communicated to Brahimi was that a weapons embargo was neither as difficult to implement nor as expensive as it had been made out to be. What was essentially needed was the will, sincerity and determination to reduce, if not altogether eliminate, the level and intensity of the fighting which was being abetted by foreign interference. This would necessitate the establishment of an efficient mechanism for monitoring weapons and ammunition shipments to Afghanistan. Brahimi was reminded that UN monitors had performed reasonably well in the nine-month period that the Geneva Accords on Afghanistan were being implemented in 1988-89.

Bennon Savon, who resigned from the UN in 2005 over the Iraqi oil-for-food scandal, was initially the overall in-charge and fulfilled his responsibilities from Islamabad with remarkable efficiency. The primary focus then was to oversee the withdrawal of Soviet forces and to investigate the violation of the armistice. The number of personnel involved was not large and the task was successfully completed. The primary responsibility of the arms monitors, who would be neither peacekeepers nor peacemakers, would merely be to report the flow of weapons and munitions into Afghanistan. An embargo was certainly possible though, given the rugged terrain of land-locked Afghanistan, its implementation had to be broad, preventive and observatory in nature. A one hundred percent embargo was neither possible nor required because large quantities of weapons supplies could only be sent through a limited number of routes and not through the dirt tracks that were used for illegal crossings and the narcotics trade. Therefore, if the objectives of the embargo were kept limited, there would be no need to employ a large number of UN monitors and the expenditure would be minimized.

The UN paper, which was obviously not intended as a serious proposal but as a study to highlight the problems in implementing an embargo, dwelt unnecessarily upon the use of satellite imagery, remote-controlled pilotless vehicles (drones), electronic sensors and signals intelligence (sigint). We told Brahimi that, in the context of Afghanistan, such sophisticated devises were not needed. Effective monitoring could best be achieved through physical means.

In the past, Pakistan had repeatedly and openly said that we would never agree to a fuel embargo as that would hurt the Afghan people. We had not stopped the flow of petroleum to Afghanistan even when the country was controlled by regimes that were hostile to Pakistan and would certainly not agree to any such measure in the future. This position had been accepted by the UN secretary general during a meeting with foreign secretary Shamshad Ahmad in December 1997. We were, therefore, somewhat surprised that the paper circulated by Brahimi attempted to include the supply of petroleum, oil and lubricants in an arms embargo.

The paper deliberately played down the main sources of weapons transfers to Afghanistan. Mere lip service was done, probably at the behest of Russia, to the flow of weapons from Uzbekistan and Tajikistan to the Northern Alliance in formulations such as "supplies to Afghanistan could hypothetically be arranged from southern Tajikistan". The factual position was that the airfield in Kulyab (Tajikistan) had virtually been leased out to the Northern Alliance whereas Tashkent and Tirmiz had become major terminals for supplies from Uzbekistan. If there was any doubt about the main suppliers of weapons to the Northern Alliance, it was removed by the Russian foreign office spokesman's statement, on the occasion of Iranian foreign minister Kamal Kharrazi's visit to Moscow on 4-5 April 2002 that "Russia and Iran have heavily contributed to the fight against the extremist Taliban".

The UN document went into various options ranging from monitoring at the level of three thousand tons of supplies per month which would "bite" but would also be prohibitively expensive, to transfers of heavy weapons and supplies of between ten thousand and fifty thousand tons per month. Our opinion was that the latter was more doable and could be implemented by monitors from the neighbouring countries who would be stationed at the main entry points under the supervision of the UN or by international teams who would oversee the work of local monitors. Both implementation mechanisms were cost-effective and required only a small international staff.

We did a detailed study on the mechanism for the imposition of an arms embargo which was sent to Brahimi. Our finding was that there were approximately three hundred and sixty-two ground supply routes to

Afghanistan. The terrain along these routes varied from mountainous to dry plains as in Pakistan, Iran and Turkmenistan and river crossings as in Uzbekistan and Tajikistan. The monitoring of all ground routes was, therefore, difficult and we felt that a more practical course would be to have mobile monitoring teams based in the major Afghan cities near the entry and exit points. It was primarily these points that had to be monitored. This would have substantially reduced though not altogether eliminated the supply of weapons. The main entry points for the countries bordering Afghanistan (China was not included in our assessment because it only has a seventy-six kilometre border with Afghanistan) were Peshawar-Torkham-Kabul and Quetta-Chaman-Kandahar for Pakistan, Mashhad-Islam Qila-Herat and Zahidan-Zabul-Zaranj (Nimroz) for Iran, Ashgabat-Mary-Khushka/Torghundi for Turkmenistan, Guzar-Shirabad-Tirmiz-Hairatan for Uzbekistan, and Dushanbe-Kurgan-Sher Khan Bander as well as Dushanbe-Darwaz-Faizabad for Tajikistan.

In addition, because a substantial amount of military supplies was being airlifted, our recommendation was that monitors should be stationed in the airfields at Kabul, Jalalabad, Kandahar, Herat, Mazar-e-Sharif, Taloquan, Shibberghan, Faizabad, Ishkasham, Khawajaghar and Kunduz. Brahimi's paper only mentioned the placement of monitors in six unspecified airfields. Furthermore as weapons were also being sent into Afghanistan across the Amu Darya by boats we felt that monitors should be placed at Dali-Shor and Pakhar-Moskovskiy in Tajikistan.

Our proposal envisaged that the monitoring units, which would be based in Jalalabad, Kandahar, Herat, Hairatan, Shibberghan, Mazar-e-Sharif and Taloquan should only be tasked to report incidents of weapons and ammunitions flows into Afghanistan to the UN secretary general. For this check-and-report function, they needed to be authorized to verify each incident , take photographs where required and communicate their findings to their headquarters in Kabul. No more than twenty-seven men were required for the headquarters which would be headed by an officer of the rank of major general or brigadier and include a staff of eight officers and eighteen men (divers, maintenance crew, telephone operators, clerks and a general duty staff). The equipment and transport required were one fixed wing aircraft, a helicopter, two cars, four jeeps and communications equipment. For the monitoring units all that was needed was two officers of the rank of lieutenant colonel or major and an eight-member staff who were to be provided with three jeeps and a pick-up plus communications equipment. In addition, three helicopters were to be allocated to each zone.

The total cost of the operation for a two-year period worked out to no more than $28 million. This inexpensive and easy to implement plan was ignored by Brahimi and the flow of weapons to the Northern Alliance, as was demonstrated by the Osh train incident of October 1998, increased. All Six Plus Two member states routinely reiterated, as did the international community, the need for a peaceful political settlement in Afghanistan but did nothing to end or even reduce the intensity of the fighting which only an arms embargo could have ensured.

The arms embargo that the UN eventually imposed on Afghanistan through Security Council resolution 1333 of 19 December 2000 was one-sided and applied only to the Taliban. Thus the world body, whose primary responsibility was the promotion of regional and global peace, had become partisan in a conflict which it had been mandated to bring to an end.

The Brahimi-Omar meeting

On the margins of the Tehran OIC summit in December 1997, Shamshad Ahmad had a meeting with Brahimi. The latter was despondent and conceded that the Northern Alliance had become virtually non-existent. Its components were more divided than ever whereas the Taliban were intransigent and "behaving like spoilt kids". He was at a loss as to how to move forward and disclosed that Broujerdi had told him that Pakistan and Iran had decided to work together for an Afghanistan settlement. He welcomed this and added that he was always there to be of any assistance. Shamshad replied that we wanted the UN to be actively engaged, however, it was important that it should establish its credibility as an impartial mediator by adopting the vacant seat formula. Brahimi was also told that unfortunately the UN's Afghanistan track record had not been up to the mark. Holl had not only been totally negative but had been misinforming the UN Secretariat. For instance, in May of that year he had wrongly informed the UN headquarters in New York that the authorities in Karachi had held up the World Food Programme's consignments for Afghanistan. The following month he told Shikmuradov in Islamabad that he did not believe there had been any agreement between the Taliban and Malik although both had acknowledged that there was a written understanding between them. Holl was also vehemently critical of Pakistan and strongly felt that Islamabad was not the appropriate venue for intra-Afghan talks which should be held, instead, in Ashgabat. Shikmuradov was furious and told us later that instead of bringing countries neighbouring Afghanistan closer towards a minimum agreed position, Holl was playing a divisive role.

In a way one felt sorry for Brahimi at the time. Our initial reaction was to welcome his appointment as anyone would have been more effective than Holl. Furthermore, Brahimi, as a Muslim, would be more acceptable to the Afghan groups and we felt that his experience as a diplomat (a former foreign minister of Algeria) made him suitable for the job. The expectation was that he would be able to jumpstart and promote an intra-Afghan peace process. However, his mission got off to a bad start because, like Holl, he had not been able to meet the reclusive Mulla Omar and dealt with only second-rank Taliban representatives. Brahimi, as I was able to gather from my several meetings with him, was totally under the influence of Washington. He considered Rick Inderfurth, who had replaced Robin Raphel, as the fount of all wisdom. The problem with this was that the initial US enchantment with the Taliban was over. The latter had stupidly squandered whatever international goodwill they had initially generated.

The feminist lobby in the US ended any sympathy that the administration may have had for the Taliban who could have been used to keep Iran on its toes. Washington thus moved away from the ground realities in Afghanistan and tried to build upon the second Pushtun option as an alternative to the hated Taliban. In hindsight it was ironic, almost amusing, that the Taliban had enacted a diplomatic miracle by bringing Washington and Tehran together as partners on an Afghanistan settlement. Both wanted to get rid of the Taliban for which even Iran privately conceded that a future dispensation would have to be built around the Pustuns but in which the Persian-speaking minorities would have a disproportionate role. Thus, in a sense both Washington and Tehran were not averse to the idea of a second Pushtun option. This, however, was easier said than done because an imposed settlement would never be acceptable to the fiercely independent Afghan people. Brahimi met people like Haji Qadeer, Abdul Haq, Pir Gillani as well as several educated and enlightened Pushtuns but the problem was that these people, whom the US was trying to promote, not only had unsavoury reputations but were of little consequence in the transformed Afghanistan.

Pakistan was the only country that had allowed all Afghan groups irrespective of their political persuasions to set up offices on its territory. Thus representatives of the Jamiat-e-Islami, Hizb-e-Wahdat, Jumbish-e-Milli and practically every other faction were in Peshawar, Islamabad, Quetta, Karachi as well as in other cities despite their hatred for Pakistan. This was resented by the Taliban who claimed that we were sheltering their enemies, many of whom, they said, had carried out terrorist attacks in Kabul, Kandahar and other towns of Afghanistan. The presence of these groups, however, had the advantage of enabling us to keep in constant contact with all Afghan parties. It should have also put an end, which it did not, to the propaganda that we were the blind supporters of the Taliban.

For the UN, the presence of these factions was useful as it enabled its officials to hear different views on Afghanistan. What added to Brahimi's difficulties was that the US had gone out on a limb to advertise the virtues of people like Haji Qadeer and his brother Abdul Haq. We were forced to expel Qadeer from Pakistan in early 1997 and this had upset Washington. Raphel told our ambassador in the US that Qadeer was a "valuable leader" who could have had "a stabilizing influence" in Afghanistan. The facts, however, were altogether different.

Our policy was not to allow Afghan groups and leaders who resided in Pakistan to pursue their factional fights from our territory. If they wanted to settle scores with their rivals they were at liberty to do so inside their own country. Haji Qadeer had been told ten times in the three months prior to his expulsion to desist from such activities while in Pakistan. He ignored this advice and even fomented trouble within our borders. He was, therefore, asked to leave even though we could have taken more severe measures against him by pushing him into Afghanistan or declaring him persona non grata. The former course of action would have resulted in his capture and probable death at the hands of his opponents. The second alternative available to us was also an extreme measure which we wanted to avoid and, therefore, he was asked to quietly leave Pakistan. Soon afterwards, Raphel told our ambassador in Washington that Haji Qadeer's son had been killed by the Taliban and his body mutilated and put on public display in Kandahar. The factual position was that he was alive and in the custody of the Taliban.

It was difficult to understand Washington's partiality for Qadeer and Abdul Haq whom we had known since 1978. Qadeer was essentially a small time smuggler who had accumulated substantial wealth through drug trafficking. During his tenure as governor, Nangarhar had become a major production and processing centre for narcotics. This had enabled his family to acquire valuable real estate in the Gulf region and Europe. Even during the Afghan struggle against the Soviet occupation forces, Qadeer had concentrated more on building his personal fortunes. He became the head of the powerful Pushtun Eastern Shura or council which included the provinces of Nangarhar, Kunar, Laghman and the region of Nuristan. Such shuras exist in various parts of Afghanistan and their numbers vary. Qadeer was able to become the leader of the Eastern Shura mainly due to his talent as a communicator and his proclivity for intrigue. The actual power in the area was, however, with the family of commander Shomali who was assassinated on the instructions of Haji Qadeer in 1993. Since then Qadeer had been living in fear and this was the primary reason for his fleeing Jalalabad without firing a shot against the Taliban when they captured the city. This was providential for him since the assassin and seventy-four of his followers were killed by Shomali's brother in September 1996. Abdul Haq, whom I knew well and was fond of, was also killed in October 2001 when he went into Afghanistan, despite the advice of his well-wishers, to instigate a tribal rebellion against the Taliban.

In spite of their considerable wealth and local influence, the Haji Qadeer family could have only raised at the most about one thousand five hundred men from their Jabbar Khel, Ahmadzai tribe and this hardly qualified him as a major player who could have had "a stabilizing" anti-Taliban influence in Afghanistan. Since his arrival in Pakistan in early 1997, Qadeer had received substantial economic help from the Iranians who were also trying to build him up as an alternate Pushtun force. Brahimi's frustration when he met Shamshad in Tehran in December 1997 was, therefore, understandable. The Taliban were as rigid in their views as ever and did not take him seriously, the so-called educated and enlightened Pushtuns were nonentities, and the components of the Northern Alliance hated each other almost as much as they feared and despised the Taliban. The Six Plus Two group continued to meet in New York and made all the right noises but failed to take any ground initiative.

Despite Brahimi's negative attitude, the meeting of the Steering Committee was held in Islamabad and got off to a good start. Its subsequent derailment by the Hizb-e-Wahdat was taken by UNSMA in stride and no serious attempts were made by it to get the Afghan groups together until after the capture of the north by the Taliban in August 1998. With the fall of Mazar-e-Sharif to the Taliban and the rout of the Northern Alliance, the Iranian government and media went into a frenzy bordering on hysteria. Although Iran had massed about seventy thousand troops along its border with Afghanistan there was no visible attempt by the UN to defuse the situation for several weeks. By that time, it had been confirmed that the Iranian consulate personnel in Mazar-e-Sharif had been killed and a hair trigger situation was thus generated.

Popular outrage in Iran on the fate of the consular personnel was so intense that an Iranian invasion of Afghanistan seemed likely. This would have had disastrous consequences and indefinitely destabilized the entire region. The UN was shaken out of its slumber and the foreign ministers of the Six Plus Two met in New York in the third week of September to adopt the "Points of Common Understanding" which called for the establishment of a broad-based multi-ethnic government, dealt with Iran's grievances, enumerated measures to be taken by the Taliban on human rights and narcotics trafficking and provided the framework for Brahimi's re-involvement in Afghanistan.

By mid-October significant progress was made by Brahimi towards defusing Afghanistan-Iran tensions. He had an unprecedented three-hour meeting with Mulla Omar in Kandahar on 14 October 1998. Other than with us and a few Saudis, this was to be Omar's first official contact with foreigners and Brahimi was ecstatic. On his return to Islamabad the same evening, he addressed a crowded press conference and declared: "I am delighted to announce, first of all, that the supreme leader Mulla Muhammad Omar has authorized us to tell you that all Iranian nationals who are still in detention in Afghanistan will be released immediately." The previous month we had been able to persuade the Taliban to release twenty-five Iranians, albeit in installments, and an equal number were still in their custody. Brahimi thus succeeded in removing one of the major causes of regional tension. The Taliban expected that their own men who, they claimed, were taken to Mashhad from Bamyan would also be similarly released. Brahimi undertook to ensure a reciprocal gesture from Tehran and promised the Taliban that he would persuade the Iranians to thin out their military presence along the Afghan border.

Brahimi also managed to secure a written response from the Taliban to the "Points of Common Understanding". The latter committed themselves to: (a) release all Iranian prisoners and expected that their own men who were taken by Iran and Tajikistan would also be set free; (b) complete the return of the bodies of the Iranian personnel killed during the fighting; (c) accept inquiry commissions to investigate the killing of the Iranians as well as previous mass killings; (d) apprehend and punish those responsible for killing the Iranian personnel; (e) eradicate poppy cultivation, although the plant provided livelihood to thousands of small farmers in rural Afghanistan. If a ban was to be imposed the growers would be deprived of a major source of income. Funds were, therefore, required to enable them to cultivate other crops. The Taliban accordingly requested financial assistance for this purpose; (f) fully protect human rights, particularly those of women, and; (g) condemn terrorism in all its forms.

In Kandahar, Brahimi was almost overpowered with emotion when he was shown the bodies of some six hundred Taliban retrieved from the mass graves in the north. He was told that about three thousand had already been buried. These were the bodies, as Brahimi acknowledged in his press statement, of Taliban killed the previous year by the Northern Alliance. He told the journalists "It was extremely sad and extremely moving. There should be no more of this in Afghanistan. Let us work to establish lasting peace in Afghanistan."

Brahimi was also shown massive quantities of weapons and ammunition of Iranian origin which had been sent to Kandahar from the north after the defeat of the Northern Alliance. During his meeting with Omar, the latter alluded to the Osh train affair which had taken place only a few days earlier. The Taliban also told Brahimi that they were willing to hold talks with the Iranians which could be either under UN auspices in New York, OIC sponsorship in Jeddah or any other mutually acceptable place.

In private discussions with us, Brahimi was almost apologetic when he referred to the formation of a broad-based government in Afghanistan and accepted the logic that the future dispensation in Kabul would have to be multi-ethnic rather than multi-factional. He also acknowledged that the defeated and discredited warlords, responsible for Afghanistan's tragedy, could not be imposed on the Afghan people again. For their part, the Taliban claimed that they already had a multi-ethnic government and again reiterated that they had no reservations whatsoever about further broadening the representation of the ethnic minorities. Brahimi felt that such people should be selected at a grass-roots level instead of being appointed by the Taliban. Our own view was that a mechanism would be required for such a process and could only be decided upon by the Afghans themselves in accordance with their traditions. It was, therefore, important to engage with the Taliban so that a genuine multi-ethnic dispensation could emerge.

Brahimi's attitude towards the Taliban had thus undergone a complete change. He felt that they had made the required gestures towards Iran but feared that the latter would keep shifting the goal post by making further demands. Brahimi confided to us that he had come under fire because of his press statement after his meeting with Mulla Omar and he was being accused by the UN secretariat, mainly at the prompting of Russia and Iran, of a pro-Taliban bias.

Brahimi stayed in Pakistan for almost two weeks and then proceeded to Iran and the Central Asian republics before finally returning to New York where he convened another meeting of the Six Plus Two group to evaluate the outcome of his visit to the region and to decide on follow-up measures. He acknowledged while briefing UN agencies and Western diplomats in Islamabad that the positive outcome of his mission was due to the "massive but quiet" support given by Pakistan.

The tensions between Iran and the Taliban were thus defused and the latter consolidated their control of more than 90 percent of Afghan territory. The only opposition to their harsh rule came from Ahmed Shah Masood who was mainly confined to the Panjsher valley, Badakhshan and parts of Takhar. The Northern Alliance had thus ceased to exist and its leaders fled the country. The implication of this was that any future intra-Afghan dialogue would have to be initially confined to Masood and the Taliban since only they controlled territory. The new head of UNSMA in Islamabad was Andrew Tessoriere, a British foreign service officer who understood this only too well and kept close contact with Masood and the Taliban. He eventually succeeded in getting representatives from both sides together in Ashgabat where talks were held on 10 February 1999. The Taliban sent one of their deputy foreign ministers for the meeting but were disappointed at the low level of participation from the opposition. Masood's delegation did not even have a negotiating brief and consequently the meeting had to be adjourned.

The build-up to the second Ashgabat meeting from 11-13 March was also fraught with uncertainty as the Taliban were reluctant to participate after their experience in the talks the previous month. We had to intercede with them in support of the UN's efforts and eventually they decided not only to attend the meeting but also appointed Mulla Wakil as the leader of their delegation. Consequently, Masood decided to send Younis Qanooni as his chief negotiator.

In the intervening period, Shikhmuradov, who was involved in peace efforts of his own, flew into Kandahar and met Mulla Omar on 3 March. This was the first ever visit by a cabinet minister of a foreign government to Taliban-controlled Afghanistan. Not even Pakistan, which had extended recognition to the Taliban, had sent a full-fledged minister to Kandahar until then. The only visit from Islamabad was that of Siddique Kanju who was only a minister of state. Shikhmuradov told Omar that Masood wanted to know what his status would be in a future government, whether the Taliban would use the services of Afghan expatriate technocrats and whether adequate representation would be given to other ethnic groups in a future dispensation. Omar's response was that the Taliban were willing to accommodate Masood in government, but not necessarily as defence minister, and they also had no problem with the inclusion of technocrats as well as more representatives from the ethnic minorities.

Significant progress was achieved in the second round of talks in Ashgabat. The Taliban and Masood delegations agreed to: (a) set up a combined judiciary, legislature, and executive; (b) discuss a cease-fire and other issues in a subsequent meeting which would be held in Afghanistan at a place to be determined later; and (c) release twenty prisoners each as a goodwill gesture.

The international media exaggerated the results of the Ashgabat meeting which it described as a "breakthrough". What had happened was that a broad understanding had been reached and the two sides had yet to address intricate and critical issues such as the mechanism for power-sharing as well as demilitarization and the collection of weapons. It was important at this juncture for the UN, especially because of the accident-prone history of previous accords among Afghan groups, to quickly build on its initial success and set in motion an irreversible peace process. The Ashgabat talks had demonstrated that only those Afghan parties who controlled territory were competent to conduct negotiations and this entailed coming to terms with the ground realities. However, nothing was done by the international community to end the anomaly of the UN's recognition of the defunct Northern Alliance as the government of Afghanistan and this made Brahimi's work even more difficult.

It was, in fact, surprising that the Ashgabat agreement should have emerged at all. Brahimi, who was unimpressed by the apparent success of UNSMA's Tessoriere, rushed to Kandahar where he had another meeting with Omar on 24 March. The latter told him that a day prior to the Ashgabat talks, Ahmed Shah Masood had telephoned him and had stressed the need for lasting peace but had almost immediately afterwards launched a three-pronged attack on Ghorbund, Bamyan and Sar-e-Pul which had resulted in eighty-five Taliban deaths. Thus Masood had again demonstrated bad faith and could not be trusted. A resumption of the Ashgabat process would, therefore, only be possible after Omar had consulted his key commanders, shura members and important ulema. Omar also told Brahimi that he was willing to talk with the opposition, if the UN could guarantee that Masood would cooperate with the Taliban in restoring peace in Afghanistan and implementing the sharia.

The Tashkent Six Plus Two meeting

This phase of the UN's efforts to promote an Afghanistan settlement was built around the eagerness of Turkmenistan and Uzbekistan to be seen as important regional players. The former had already hosted two rounds of talks in Ashgabat and the latter was anxious to occupy centre stage by holding a meeting of the Six Plus Two group in Tashkent to which the Afghan parties would also be invited.

Mulla Omar, however, told Abdulaziz Kamilov during their meeting in Kandahar on 1 June 1999 that the Taliban had already met representatives of Masood in Ashgabat and had reached an understanding on power sharing. However, this had been undermined by Masood's military offensive against the Taliban. It was, therefore, pointless to meet him or his representatives again. Seeing the disappointment on his visitor's face, Omar made a concession by telling Kamilov that the Taliban would participate in the Tashkent Six Plus Two if they were invited as the government of Afghanistan and not as one of the factions. Kamilov responded that he personally had no problem with this but he would have to sound out his leadership before he could make any commitment.

Uzbekistan had earlier circulated a political document for adoption by the Tashkent Six Plus Two. It had been deliberated for quite some time by the representatives of the group in New York and had undergone several alterations. The text as modified until 26 May was examined by me and the Uzbek foreign office expert, Director General Yusupov Kadirjan Ibrahimovich, who had accompanied Kamilov on his visit to Pakistan and Afghanistan. Yusupov agreed that all Taliban-specific criticism be deleted from the text if they were expected to attend the Tashkent meeting. The draft document was, however, again revised by the Six Plus Two and all the adverse references against the Taliban were reintroduced, mainly on the insistence of Iran. It was, therefore, uncertain whether the Taliban would agree to participate in a meeting which had decided in advance to castigate them.

Foreign minister Sartaj Aziz told Kamilov that the Afghanistan situation had undergone a complete change and it was imperative that this should be factored into any initiative whether at the Tashkent Six Plus Two or any other forum. The factional leaders of the past had been rejected by the Afghan people and could not claim to represent any ethnic group. The determinant regarding the Afghan parties to be associated with the Six Plus Two should be the control of territory. It was pointless to involve factional leaders of the past such as Dostum, Malik, Khalili and others. The inescapable reality was that only the Taliban and

Ahmed Shah Masood mattered as they controlled territory. The UN-sponsored Ashgabat talks had also adopted this criteria for a dialogue among the Afghan parties. A multi-ethnic, rather than a multi-factional settlement, through an indigenous process, was the only way to end the Afghan turmoil. Kamilov agreed with this assessment in its entirety. In effect he was conceding the loss of Uzbek influence in Afghanistan by acknowledging that Dostum no longer mattered and that only the ethnic Tajik Masood was relevant. This was all the more surprising because in early April the Uzbek ambassador in Islamabad had told Chargé d'Affaires Haqqani of the Taliban that he had received a telephone call from President Karimov to inform him that the Uzbeks did not hold the Taliban responsible for the bomb blasts in Tashkent earlier in the year. Six culprits—two in Kazakhstan and four in Kyrgyzstan—had been arrested and it had been established that they were all ethnic Tajik Afghans who had been trained by the Jamiat-e-Islami of Burhanuddin Rabbani and Ahmed Shah Masood. This had apparently been done at the behest of the president of Tajikistan who wanted to settle scores with Tashkent for the Khudoybordiev incident of November 1998.

All this was interesting inasmuch as it demonstrated the undercurrents of suspicion and even outright hostilities at play in the relationship among the Central Asian states. It also showed that these former Soviet republics were gradually overcoming their fear of the Taliban. Both Shikmuradov and Kamilov had visited Kandahar and met Omar, Taliban delegations had visited Uzbekistan and Kazakhstan while Turkmenistan had become a fervent supporter of the Taliban. In Almaty, the Taliban delegation was received by the Kazakh commerce minister and then taken by special aircraft to the country's new capital, Astana, where an agreement was concluded under which wheat was to be provided to the Taliban at an extremely low price.

As the date for the Tashkent Six Plus Two, 20-21 July, drew closer, the Taliban persisted with their insistence on being invited as the Afghan government. The only concession they made was to allow the opposition the same status. The invitation finally sent to them fell short of this and they decided not to attend. To the foolhardy leadership in Kandahar, the text of the draft Tashkent declaration, weighted so heavily against them, mattered little. Their primary concern was status which they were also willing to share with the opposition. Or was this a subtle comment on UN resolutions and declarations—verbose, saturated with stereotyped phraseology that typify multilateral diplomacy and full of pious intent seldom to be taken seriously?

As the Tashkent Six Plus Two was at the level of deputy foreign minister, I led our delegation, which included Aziz Khan and the Pakistan ambassador in Tashkent. Aziz reached Tashkent in advance as I first went to Ashgabat for consultations with Shikhmuradov. The latter went straight to the point and said that he was delighted the Taliban had decided not to attend because the meeting was a farce. The "so called Tashkent declaration," he said, was shameful because the Taliban alone were being blamed for all the ills of Afghan society. While the Taliban were not the type of people one would want to invite to dinner, they were certainly better than the "criminals of the north" who alone were responsible for the destruction of Afghanistan. The Taliban treatment of females was not above reproach but at least women were no longer raped and molested as they used to be when the warlords controlled Afghanistan. Furthermore, narcotics trafficking predated the Taliban, so why should they alone be blamed for this evil? All this and much more, Shikmuradov said, had induced President Niyazov to decide that Ashgabat would not attend the Tashkent meeting. On my insistence he finally agreed to Turkmen participation but at a junior level. Later that day I was informed by Islamabad that the Taliban had decided at the last minute to attend and would be sending their minister of information, Mulla Muttaqi, to the Six Plus Two. Shikmuradov was taken aback when I conveyed this to him during a banquet hosted by Niyazov for foreign minister Igor Ivanov of the Russian Federation.

The banquet was memorable for all the wrong reasons and demonstrated the power wielded by President Niyazov. He was seated at the centre of rectangular main table along with the chief guest and a few ministers of the Turkmen government. The others—who included Ashgabat-based ambassadors, important Turkmen officials and myself—were at several small circular tables for six or seven persons. A protocol official welcomed foreign minister Ivanov from a rostrum and then announced that I was also present. Shortly afterwards, each ambassador was asked to make a short speech extolling the virtues of Niyazov and Turkmenistan. When this was over, women danced to popular Turkmen melodies played by an orchestra whose musical accomplishments were unremarkable.

Shikmuradov, seated at one end of the head table, was summoned by Niyazov who whispered something to his minister who promptly walked over to the women and started dancing with them. The message was clear: when Turkmenbashi so wished it his ministers danced. Foreign minister Ivanov was also not spared the ordeal and soon joined

Shikhmuradov on the dance floor as did other functionaries of the Turkmen government. Niyazov was now alone at the table and each of the dignitaries who had been asked to dance returned but sat on the floor in front of the Turkmen president and proposed toasts to his health. I was asked to join them and Niyazov welcomed me and conveyed his regards to the president and prime minister of Pakistan. I left for Tashkent accompanied by a junior official from the Turkmen foreign office the next day.

The Six Plus Two thus met under Brahimi's chairmanship and, for the first time ever, the Afghan parties representing the Taliban and Ahmed Shah Masood participated. The document adopted at the end of the meeting was critical of the Taliban and called for a sequential settlement beginning with a cease-fire, a comprehensive exchange of prisoners, and a dialogue among the Afghan parties for the establishment of a broad-based, representative, multi-ethnic government.

Turkmenistan refused to sign the Tashkent Declaration because of its bias against the Taliban. Pakistan agreed to go along with the text for the reason that the adverse reference to the Taliban in the context of terror-ism had already been incorporated in the "Points of Common Understanding" of 21 September 1998. What made the meeting inter-esting was that Mulla Muttaqi told Kamilov that his government would try to persuade Turkmenistan to sign the document despite its criticism of the Taliban.

The Tashkent Six Plus Two would have been no different from the previous meetings of the group in New York without the participation of the Afghan parties. Both sides were invited as Afghan factions even though a majority of countries recognized the defunct Northern Alliance as the Afghan government. Whereas the Northern Alliance had no problem with this and agreed to attend the meeting, the Taliban refused as they insisted on being invited as the legitimate government of Afghanistan. The die was thus cast for the failure of the meeting until we were able to prevail upon Mulla Omar to send a delegation.

Muttaqi and his delegation were received by President Karimov, who thus became the first head of state, other than that of Pakistan, to invite the Taliban to his country and then have an exclusive meeting with them. He was told by Muttaqi that the Taliban wanted to establish the best of relations with all its neighbours so that the entire region could prosper. This was deeply appreciated by Karimov who gave the assurance that his country would resume power supplies to northern Afghanistan and also broaden bilateral cooperation.

I was received separately by Karimov who expressed gratitude for Pakistan's successful efforts to ensure Taliban participation in the meeting. He also said that Islamabad's insistence that the ground realities in Afghanistan had to be taken into account had been vindicated and this implied that only the Taliban and Masood were relevant. He reminded me that this was what he had included in his inaugural address and the implications for continued recognition by the international community of the Rabbani regime were obvious. Kamilov was also present at the meeting and kept nodding his head to every word and sentence uttered by his president, when we were both taken aback by Karimov's next remark. In the same way that Turkmenistan's Niyazov had made his foreign minister dance in public, Karimov suddenly informed me that "Kamilov knows nothing about diplomacy" and that I should give him "a few lessons" on the intricacies of inter-state relations. I was as embarrassed as the unfortunate Kamilov, who had turned red in the face but dutifully nodded again. I quickly responded that I had met the Uzbek foreign minister on several occasions and admired his acumen and diplomatic skills.

That night I reflected upon the events of the past few days in my hotel room in Tashkent. All the Six Plus Two countries had been repeatedly calling for the establishment of a broad-based, representative, multi-ethnic government in Afghanistan and yet a number of them had anything but democratic governments themselves. I had interacted with the presidents of Turkmenistan and Uzbekistan during the week and had been able to see for myself the extent of personality cult that surrounded these two leaders. Neither tolerated any opposition and both presided over countries that were manifestations of the Soviet paradigm of totalitarianism. Initially, when he came to power in 1989, Karimov had allowed the Birlik ("Unity") and Erk ("Freedom") parties to exist as opposition movements. However, by the middle of 1992, he came out in his true colours and both parties were suppressed. Similarly, Niyazov, who appeared on the scene in 1985, was soon styling himself "Turkmenbashi" ("Leader of the Turkmens") and his portrait, despite the frequent changes of hair colour, became an indispensable feature of all Turkmen institutions alongside the slogan *"Khalq, Vatan, Turkmenbashi!"* ("People, Homeland, Turkmenbashi!"). The Paris-based *Reporters Without Borders* (*Reporters sans Frontières*) commented in November 1997: "Turkmenistan and Uzbekistan are still states where the rule of law is unknown . . . These two countries remain the most isolated countries . . . and press freedom is no more than a mirage."

Subsequently, in December 1999, the Turkmen parliament, Halk Maslahaty, gave Niyazov the "exclusive right to exercise the powers of head of state without restriction in time". Less than two weeks later, Karimov was re-elected for a second seven-year term with 92 percent of the vote and, in an unprecedented election accomplishment, his only opponent, Abdulhafez Jalalov, first secretary of the Central Council of the People's Democratic Party, also voted for him.

A day after the Six Plus Two meeting in Tashkent, Aziz Khan and I flew back to Islamabad, and Brahimi proceeded to Kabul where he was treated to doses of heavy rocket attacks from Ahmed Shah Masood's forces. This signalled the end of the UN-sponsored Ashgabat and the Tashkent processes. Lakhdar Brahimi was despondent yet again, as he had been when he met foreign secretary Shamshad during the Tehran OIC summit in December 1997, amid rumours that he no longer wanted to be associated with Afghanistan.

A meeting of the Six Plus Two was held over lunch at the initiative of Uzbekistan on 22 September 1999 in New York. The foreign ministers of Uzbekistan, Turkmenistan and Pakistan were present. Iran was represented by deputy foreign minister Jawad Zarif, the US by Inderfurth and Russia by a senior foreign ministry official. China and Tajikistan participated at the level of their permanent representatives to the UN while under-secretary general Kieran Prendergast filled in for the UN secretary general. Though Masood had initiated the fighting after the Tashkent Six Plus Two, as he had following the second round of the Ashgabat talks in March, the blame for the continuation of the hostilities was placed on the Taliban. What the participants said at this meeting summed up their subsequent approach to the Afghanistan problem so long as the Taliban were in control of the country.

Prendergast stated that Brahimi, who was recuperating in Paris after having undergone two operations (he did not specify for what), was sceptical about the future of the Six Plus Two, because he felt there was a mismatch between the declarations by member countries and what was happening on the ground. Tajikistan felt that Brahimi should continue his efforts and that the approaching winter, when the so-called "fighting season" ended, would provide an opportunity for the Afghans to negotiate.

Iran shared Brahimi's disappointment on the Six Plus Two's performance and, while continuing to send weapons to Masood, stated that the members of the group were not in tune with the position of the Security Council and of the secretary general. As such, said Zarif, the Taliban were receiving mixed signals and their summer offensive was a blow to the credibility of the Six Plus Two. Furthermore, Iran also had information that more military action by the Taliban was in the offing. The Six Plus Two should, therefore, condemn the Taliban for defying the will of the international community and also take them to task on forced internal displacements as well as for increased narcotics production and terrorism in the areas controlled by them.

The United States agreed with Iran as well as Brahimi's views as conveyed to the group by Prendergast. Inderfurth felt that the Six Plus Two should either consider dissolving itself or expanding its membership by admitting other relevant countries. Pressure had to be applied on the Taliban to come to the negotiating table and action needed to be taken against them for the plight of women as well as on the drugs and terrorism issues. Inderfurth also proposed Security Council sanctions against the Taliban. He, however, noted that Pakistan had been encouraging the Taliban to resume a dialogue and more such steps were needed. The reference was to our unproductive meetings shortly after the Tashkent Six Plus Two with Qanooni in Dushanbe and the Taliban in Kandahar to somehow revive talks between the two. On the drugs issue, Inderfurth noted that Iran was closing off the drug routes out of Afghanistan. Similarly, Islamabad was trying hard to stop the exponential increase in drug addicts in Pakistan. He felt that the neighbouring countries of Afghanistan should coordinate closely to choke the drugs trade.

The Russian representative expressed understanding on Brahimi's frustration but noted that all members of the group were no less disappointed with the lack of movement towards peace in Afghanistan. Despite this, the disbandment of the Six Plus Two" would be a grave mistake because the group provided a useful forum to discuss possible initiatives in the future. Russia was speaking to representatives of both sides of the Afghan political divide but had not discerned any change of heart in the Taliban. They were still hoping for a military victory and should be told what the world thought of them. He felt that a clear signal should be sent by the Security Council to the Taliban. He noted with appreciation steps by Pakistan to bring the two sides to the negotiating table.

Shikmuradov stated that it was premature to discuss changes in the Six Plus Two mechanism. The member states should instead review the performance of the group and give it a new impetus. He noted that the military action immediately after the Tashkent Six Plus Two came as no surprise because no firm action had been taken by the international community to bring the conflict to an end. The Afghan situation therefore required delicate handling.

Kamilov stated that too much was being expected from the Six Plus Two group. It was the only international mechanism available and Uzbekistan was convinced that the group must continue to function since there was no viable alternative. Uzbekistan preferred the step by step approach approved at Tashkent. There should be a cessation of hostilities, followed by intra-Afghan negotiations. Uzbekistan was also closely following the efforts of Pakistan to facilitate negotiations between the two sides and was eager to hear Islamabad's assessment.

Foreign minister Sartaj Aziz shared Brahimi's annoyance. However, he stated that the group must continue to function, and should maintain its present membership. Pakistan had been disappointed by the summer fighting and had intensified its efforts to promote a dialogue. Islamabad was not mediating in the conflict and had no proposals of its own. It was working for the implementation of the Tashkent Declaration. It had conveyed to both sides that it was merely facilitating the holding of a direct dialogue between the Taliban and the opposition. Sartaj Aziz noted that the defunct Northern Alliance did not enjoy any greater legitimacy than the Taliban and the two should find a formula for power sharing. The basic issue was the lack of trust between them. He also stated that any signals from the Six Plus Two should be balanced. If the signals were one sided, the Northern Alliance would be encouraged to continue its intransigence. If, however, the Six Plus Two were even-handed, the forum would be seen as objective by both sides and would retain its credibility. Sartaj Aziz stated that on the issue of human rights, there was not much difference between the Northern Alliance and the Taliban. He pointed out that the statement on the situation of women issued by the UN Special Rapporteur for violence against women to which Inderfurth had referred, contained a number of positive elements in favour of the Taliban. The Pakistani foreign minister underlined that sanctions against the Taliban would be counterproductive and would not promote peace. They would merely increase the misery of the Afghan people. He suggested that the international community must provide funding for the rehabilitation and reconstruction of Afghanistan. This would nudge the two sides towards peace. For Pakistan, peace was most important as it was still hosting 1.8 million registered refugees and had suffered the fallout of drugs, gun-running and ecological degradation. Afghan refugees would not go back in the present circumstances since food prices in Afghanistan were extremely high and no jobs were available. He expressed the view that the position of the

Northern Alliance was more unreasonable than that of the Taliban. The Northern Alliance wanted to be brought back to Kabul by the Six Plus Two. This clearly was impossible.

The Chinese permanent representative underlined the central role of the United Nations in any political solution. He also felt that the international community should exert influence on both sides and that an arms embargo should be imposed on Afghanistan. China had a positive assessment of the Tashkent meeting and of the Six Plus Two, which was the most appropriate mechanism for a political solution. Beijing was not in favour of sanctions. However, it felt that some pressure should be exerted on both sides to persuade them to abandon military ambitions and to negotiate with each other. The Six Plus Two should, therefore, continue its dialogue and engagement with the Taliban. Extreme measures would be counterproductive.

After these initial statements, there was an exchange of views, during which calls to cut off supplies of weapons, fuel and personnel were made by Prendergast, the US and Iran. Prendergast reiterated that the political will was lacking among the members of the group to find a solution. He also noted that all principal suppliers of weapons to the two sides were none other than the members of the Six Plus Two.

Prendergast suggested that a meeting of the Six Plus Two at the permanent representatives level be organized, at which the Taliban and the Northern Alliance could be represented. Pakistan supported the proposal as did the United States. However, the Iranians were not in favour of the idea since, according to them, the Taliban were not recognized by the United Nations. Iran also noted that the cause of the continuing conflict in Afghanistan was the mentality of the Taliban and their determination to achieve a military victory. They had to be restrained through the imposition of punitive sanctions or by any other means. Jawad Zarif also made a reference to the volunteers from madrassas going into Afghanistan in large numbers to fight alongside the Taliban. The response of the Secretariat was that the UN did not recognize the Turkish Republic of Northern Cyprus but maintained contacts with its leadership. It was agreed that a way would be found to associate the Taliban with the discussions.

Thus the Six Plus Two continued to hold sickeningly meaningless meetings without involving the Afghan parties and that was all that the UN had to show for itself. Whatever little progress that was achieved in Ashgabat and Tashkent was never built upon and Brahimi all but disappeared from the scene until the post-Taliban Bonn accord which resulted in the installation of the Karzai administration.

The ground situation remained unchanged and the Taliban became increasingly convinced of their invincibility and ultimate triumph. This made them even more rigid and repulsive as demonstrated by their sacrilegious destruction of the ancient Buddhist statues in Bamyan and, shortly afterwards, their edict that Afghan Hindus should wear arm bands to set them apart from the rest of the population. Although the Taliban had de-weaponized the areas they controlled and had brought relative stability, ordinary Afghans, struggling to survive in their destroyed country, were deprived of basic rights. Masood's assassination under mysterious circumstances on 9 September 2001 opened the way for the Taliban to capture the remaining 5 to 10 percent of Afghan territory until the fateful and tragic events in New York and Washington on 11 September 2001 intervened. Historically, Afghanistan had never been ruled by mullas and there were no regrets on the subsequent ouster of the bearded fanatics of Kandahar, though the consequences for some of the neighbouring countries were entirely different from what they had hoped for or expected.

The UN's inability or reluctance to objectively assess the situation in Afghanistan and to take the needed initiatives encouraged the warring factions to pursue their narrow ambitions and resulted in the virtual control of the entire country by the Taliban after 8 August 1998. The latter's ouster by the end of 2001 brought long-term US presence into the region and undermined, perhaps irreversibly, Russian and Iranian ambitions. Moscow saw its influence in its Central Asian "near abroad" sharply reduced. It had exploited the imagined fear of Taliban extremism spilling into the region in order to maintain a military presence in Central Asia, particularly Tajikistan. It had never expected that political liberalism and not obscurantist religious dogma would threaten and even replace the entrenched dictatorships in the former Soviet republics. The subsequent "rose" and "orange" revolutions in Georgia and Ukraine which brought pro-US governments to power and the abrupt change of regime in Kyrgyzstan made the autocratic rulers in the Central Asian states nervous and apprehensive about the future. Islam Karimov's decision in the summer of 2005 to ask the US to close its air base in Uzbekistan was probably no more than a tactical ploy to generate a nationalist upsurge in support of his regime which had been shaken by earlier internal disturbances resulting in several deaths. The same wave of freedom affected Azerbaijan and large scale demonstrations were held in the country's capital Baku in September 2005.

Similarly, Tehran, which perceived the Taliban as the only impediment in the way of its hegemonic ambitions in Afghanistan, sent massive quantities of weapons to the Northern Alliance. The UN turned a blind eye to these infusions. Despite what the Ayatollahs of Tehran claimed, the inward-looking Taliban could never have posed a serious threat to Iran. The collapse of the harsh Taliban regime brought prolonged Nato presence and US influence into Afghanistan. Tehran was thus confronted by a real security challenge in the face of the Ahmedinejad government's continued defiance of the West over its uranium enrichment programme and its outlandish pronouncements about Israel.

The consequences of UN inaction in Afghanistan during the five years that the Taliban controlled the major part of the country were, therefore, far-reaching. Engagement with the warring factions could have pre-empted the massacres of May 1997 and August 1998 in which thousands lost their lives and many more were maimed. In addition, the skirmishes, which occurred almost daily, also took a dreadful toll. After their defeat of the Northern Alliance, the Taliban had a freehand to enforce their absurd interpretation of Islam even more rigorously. Afghanistan had virtually become an isolated failed state and a haven for terrorists

8
Islam and
the Taliban

THE SPEED with which the Taliban secured control of Afghanistan convinced them that their success owed itself to divine will. I was told by many of them that after they had taken Kandahar, the natural course for the movement would have been to head north towards Kabul and the Pushtun-dominated eastern provinces but Mulla Omar was said to have had a vision directing him towards Herat. Its capture set alarm bells ringing in Tehran and, as we were told in informal discussions with Iranian foreign ministry officials, this touched a raw nerve in their policy-making circles.

The capture of Kabul and two-thirds of Afghanistan by the end of September 1996, removed all doubt, if any existed, in the mind of Omar, that God was on his side and nothing could stop him from the accomplishment of his mission which was to impose the Taliban interpretation of Islam on the long-suffering people of Afghanistan. The farce was given legal shape by the ulema shura which pronounced Omar the amir-ul-momineen, commander of the faithful, but not the "khalifah", leader of the community. This was no different from the decision of the Turkmen parliament declaring Niyazov the head of state without any time limit which was justified as being in line with early Islamic polity. In its time, this system was more advanced than the absolute monarchies that prevailed in the then known world because the khalifah had to emerge through consensus and not hereditary right. In this sense, monarchies are alien to Islam.

However, whereas there was political evolution in the West and the divine right of kings was gradually eroded by the transfer of power to parliament, the Islamic political structure witnessed no such change. The main transformation in several Muslim countries during the second half of the twentieth century was the replacement of absolute dynastic rulers by autocratic republican regimes. Only a few are now emerging as democracies. All of them, whether republics, monarchies or quasi-democracies, have to contend with extremist or, at best, obscurantist religious forces.

Mulla Omar, like Turkmenistan's Niyazov, thus became the supreme leader of his country without any time limit. The ground successes of the Taliban despite their first rout in Mazar-e-Sharif in May/June 1997, which they were able to reverse in August 1998, spawned a messiah complex in Omar and convinced him that he and he alone was the saviour of his people. He saw his mission as the enforcement of Islam in a godless warlord-dominated Afghanistan.

The religious philosophy of the Taliban was "village Islam" which was heavily influenced by "Pakhtunwali", the traditional Pushtun code of honour. The Islam of rural Afghanistan, where the overwhelming majority of the people live, had little to do with the actual teachings of the religion and when enforced by the state, it became oppressive. Thomas Jefferson spoke of the "loathsome combination of church and state" and it was in Taliban-controlled Afghanistan where its impact was at its worst. Although the Quran clearly states that "there shall be no coercion in matters of faith", the Taliban, and particularly the hated Amr-bil-Maroof, or religious police, set about with a vengeance to enforce their version of Islam. *Dawn*, a mass-circulation English newspaper in Pakistan, carried an article on 13 May 2000 entitled "Danger from the North" in which the author described the Taliban as "the spiritual descendants of the Brown Shirts of Hitlerite Germany, Stalin's youth brigades and the Black Shirts of Mussolini". Such was the image that the Taliban had created for themselves and it resulted in their international isolation.

The Taliban thus disgraced themselves and tarnished the image of Islam which was perceived as a harsh and intolerant religion that could not co-exist peacefully with the rest of the world. Muslim scholars feel that this assessment of their religion is biased and prejudiced because peace, non-aggression and tolerance are integral to Quranic teachings. This is probably correct. Nevertheless, it is also true that Muslims are themselves to blame for the image their religion has acquired because they have been unable to achieve its social, economic and political ideals. For instance, Islam lays stress on education but, according to one estimate, 6 out of 10 Muslims are illiterate. Although Islam believes in a welfare state, there are none in the Muslim world. Furthermore, Muslims, who account for 22 percent of the world's population, produce less than 5 percent of global GDP. Even though Islam does not countenance totalitarianism there are only a few democracies in the Islamic world. Western criticism of Islam is, therefore, often based on the acts of Muslim extremists such as the Taliban who are far removed from the spirit of the religion. What then is the actual Islam? What is its motivating impulse? How does it differ from modern concepts and from other major monotheistic religions, particularly Judaism and Christianity?

The collapse of the Soviet empire and the concomitant political transformation of Eastern Europe dealt a crippling body-blow to the communist ideal. In his controversial essay "The End of History", Francis Fukuyama interpreted this as "an unabashed victory of economic and political liberalism" and "the end point of mankind's ideological evolution and the universalization of Western liberal democracy as the final form of human government".[1] Such reasoning is common in affluent secular states which confine religion to the inner world of the individual. Religion, in these societies is often considered irrelevant or even an impediment to progress and political stability. The spiritual and the temporal aspects of human existence are, therefore, entirely separate.

Islam, as several scholars believe, does not accept the separation of church and state. The Kingdom of Caesar and the Kingdom of God do not exist as unrelated entities—they are one. According to Ashraf Jehangir Qazi, a Pakistani diplomat who subsequently became the UN secretary general's special envoy for Iraq, the will to political expression in the form of public law, political authority and state structure constitute the fundamental element of a truly Islamic society. When this is denied, the Muslim community becomes a mere group of individuals without a clear-cut sense of direction. Islam is more than a personal faith. It envisages a political community which provides the framework for the fulfilment of divine will on earth. To Muslims it is Islam, and not the economic and political liberalism of the West that is the "end point of mankind's ideological evolution". A practical example in the last century of the Muslim will to political expression was the movement in the South Asian subcontinent which resulted in the emergence of Pakistan in 1947.

As against this, Jehangir Qazi believes, that the Jewish faith is based on moral, ethical and juridical principles in the form of the Laws of Moses. Yahweh's initial covenant with this "Chosen People" promising them the land of the Canaanites lent the religion an apparent political dimension. However, the covenant was restricted to the Hebrew tribal confederacy and, in this sense, Yahweh was only a tribal deity. Later Israelite prophets transformed Him into a universal being but, by then, they were only preaching against the moral decay that had blemished society. They called upon their people to return to the Laws of Moses.

These prophets strove to redeem souls rather than build the basis for a political structure. The Zionist movement which led to the emergence of Israel drew more of its strength and substance from the prevalent political realities than from the Hebraic scriptures.

Early Christianity was even more categorical in the belief that the religious and the political existence of man were separate. There was no relationship, no linkage between the two. Man's redemption lay in an almost ascetic form of devotion to the Divine. There was no political content in the message of Jesus. Christianity confined itself to moral principles. Subsequent attempts by the church in Europe to acquire political power came too late and resulted in the Reformation. In England absolute monarchs, who believed that they ruled by divine right, claimed that they were the supreme head of both church and state. This was vigorously resisted by the clergy in their attempt to safeguard their power, privileges and prerogatives. Leo XIII, who was elected Pope in 1878, was later to speak about "the fatal theory of the separation of church and state" but eventually the church was relegated to the political backwaters with the emergence of nation states.

The unity between the spiritual and the secular that is endemic to Islam has been both a blessing and a bane. It brought stability and glory to early Islamic societies whose leaders were guided by the true spirit of the religion. In later history, it caused incalculable harm to Muslim countries that were led by those who sought self-aggrandisement rather than the benefit of the community. The post-colonial era saw the emergence of several Islamic nations where autocrats tried to perpetuate themselves under the garb of religion. In the process Islam acquired the image of a religion that was aggressive and had no compunctions about violating human rights as was the case in Taliban-dominated Afghanistan. A determination whether this assessment is correct can only be reached by examining the actual political philosophy of Islam.

In history Muhammad was one of the few prophets who wielded both spiritual and temporal power. This, more than all else, emphasizes the point that an Islamic society is essentially a political community. The dividing line between the secular and the spiritual did not exist in the eventful life of the Prophet. He neither lived the life of a recluse nor sought to spread his message through miracles. In Medina, where he assumed political authority, he administered the new-found community, dispensed justice, led military campaigns in defence of his people, negotiated treaties, conducted diplomacy and laid the socio-economic structure for an Islamic state.

The Quran, which was revealed piecemeal over a period of twenty-three years, spans two distinct phases of the Prophet's life. The earlier revelations in Mecca laid down the basic principles of the religion while the later ones in Medina dealt also with political, economic and social issues.

The Quran is specific that the leader of the community should be a person of unquestionable probity and that society owes him complete fealty so long as he does not resort to persecution or violate the tenets of the religion. However, the holy book of the Muslims is silent on how the leader is to be chosen, the duration of the tenure, the method of succession and whether women can become the chief executive. In such situations, guidance is derived from the acts ("sunnah") and the sayings ("hadith") of the Prophet. When even the sunnah and the hadith are silent on any particular issue, then consensus ("ijma") among people of learning forms the basis of policy. The problem that arises is that not all Muslims agree that the compilations of the hadith are faithful records of the sayings of the Prophet. They have no such reservations about the Quran which they consider to be the most authentic scripture. Unlike the Bible, there is only one version of the Quran which all Muslims, regardless of sect, accept in totality. The difficulty lies in their interpretation of Quranic injunctions. The Quran states that some of its verses are clear in and by themselves whereas others are allegorical. It even predicts that none other than those who profess to be Muslims will give distorted interpretations to the allegorical verses and misrepresent the true teachings of the faith. This was as evident in Taliban-controlled Afghanistan as it is in the acts of extremists.

Distinct principles of polity and of statecraft emerged as an integral part of Islam during the Prophet's lifetime. His assumption of political authority in Medina with the unanimous and complete support of his people, highlights the point that the leader should emerge through consensus. This casts doubt on whether hereditary monarchies are acceptable in a truly Islamic society. The popular perception is that women are relegated to a secondary position in Islam. This is incorrect: the Prophet was once the paid employee of a woman and the first convert to Islam was a woman as was its first martyr. In recent times, Benazir Bhutto of Pakistan, Khalida Zia and Hasina Wajid of Bangladesh, Tansu Ciller of Turkey and Megawati Sukarnoputri of Indonesia have been prime ministers and president of their respective countries. These nations collectively represent more than two-fifths of the Islamic world's population.

Although Islam believes in strong central authority, it does not countenance totalitarianism. The powers of the head of state are circumscribed by the sharia or the laws of Islam. He does not have the option to deviate from the injunctions of the Quran. There can be no Hitler or Mussolini in a truly Islamic society. According to the French orientalist Oliver Roy: "There can be no such thing as totalitarianism [the reduction of civil to political society] in Islamic countries, in as far as in Islam the development and interpretation of laws does not depend on the state. By definition, a return to the shariat can neither be fascist nor totalitarian."[2]

Similarly, the powers of the legislature are also limited. Islam does not accept the complete supremacy of parliament. No legislature can promulgate the profane or prohibit what is lawful. There can be no question of a parliament in a Muslim society legalizing homosexuality or curtailing the fundamental human rights that are inherent to Islam. However this does not restrict the competence of parliaments to legislate because only about 190 of the Quran's 6,200 verses deal with personal, penal and civil laws as well as jurisprudence and testimony. Therefore, there is no impediment in the way of Islamic legislatures enabling them to enact laws in line with modern values. However, Taliban-controlled Afghanistan did not have a legislature while their shuras and the ulema had neither the vision nor the ability to break the dreadful hold of obscurantist tradition.

Islamic laws have been criticized as harsh and perhaps they are. However these laws prescribe the maximum punishment. No court can exceed the limit but a judge has the discretion to award lesser sentences. Furthermore, Islamic jurisprudence is built on mutual obligations between the individual and the state. The latter can only award punishment for certain crimes if it has fulfilled its obligations. For instance, punishment for habitual theft can be given only if the state has delivered on its part of the social contract by providing employment, housing, security, education, health care and other amenities to its citizens. The Taliban were unable to provide any of these facilities and therefore not competent to award punishment for this crime. This, however, did not deter them from amputating the hands of habitual thieves.

Moreover, punishment can only be given if guilt has been conclusively established. This is often difficult because the Islamic laws of evidence are stringent to the extreme. Adultery, for instance, can only be proved on the solemn testimony of four first-hand witnesses. The Quranic punishment for this, in the unlikely event that guilt is established, is not stoning to death, as the Taliban believed, but lashes which were to be administered lightly—the objective being to shame and not to hurt the individual.

The Taliban rigorously enforced the Islamic punishment for murder. The Quran prescribes capital punishment unless the immediate relative of the victim agrees to reduce the sentence by accepting financial compensation. Under Taliban rule, the murderer was always executed in public and often by the nearest of kin to the deceased even if the relative happened to be a woman. In the late summer of 1999, I had gone to Kandahar for a meeting with Mulla Omar and, as we were entering the compound where his office was located, the Pakistan consul general showed me a field on the opposite side of the road. He said that he was passing by the place the previous day and noticed a sizeable crowd which he joined out of curiosity. Shortly afterwards a man with his hands tied behind his back was brought from a nearby building and made to kneel on the ground. A few minutes later a four-wheel-drive vehicle arrived and a burqa-clad woman got out. She was given a Kalashnikov by a man who had to have been a law enforcement official since the Taliban had deweaponized their society and only the police and security personnel were allowed to carry firearms. She walked with confidence towards the kneeling man and then fired a short burst from the weapon killing him instantaneously. Two or three days earlier, it was reported, the executed man had murdered her husband and she had insisted on carrying out the punishment herself. Taliban justice was as swift as it was severe.

The Taliban ruthlessly implemented what they believed to be the teachings of Islam. They ignored fundamental Quranic precepts such as the renunciation of compulsion in matters of faith. Though there has never been any inquisition in Islamic history, the religious police of the Taliban behaved like the inquisitors of post-Reformation Europe and persecuted men, women and children alike in the name of religion.

Unlike either Judaism or Christianity there is no priesthood in Islam—no bedrock on which the foundations of an ecclesiastical hierarchy can be built. The individual does not need an intermediary to seek God's forgiveness or to solicit His benevolence. No one is required to confess sins of either commission or omission before a priest. Any believer is competent to lead a prayer congregation, conduct marriage or funeral rites and perform all the functions that are assigned to the clergy in Judaism, Christianity and several other religions.

Islam believes in a stable world order. War is permitted but only in self-defence, treaties and international obligations are considered sacrosanct and have to be implemented in letter and spirit, persecution is strictly prohibited. Racism is anathema to Islam whereas its world view is one in which there is no chosen race and mankind can live in harmony.

This is clearly brought out in the Prophet Muhammad's last sermon: "The white has no preference over the black. The Arab has no preference over the Persian. There is no distinction of race and colour or of birth amongst you."

Many analysts share the assessment that "with the death of the Soviet empire, some Western policy makers are concerned whether Islamic fundamentalism—a term rejected by Muslims as a misnomer—may shape up the next millennial threat, to liberal democracy."[3] But before comment is made on the perception of Islam as a potential threat, the term "fundamentalism" needs to be put in its proper perspective.

Fundamentalism essentially implies a return to the basic tenets of a religion. In his informative study of the Afghan resistance against Soviet occupation Olivier Roy writes:

> For fundamentalism it is of paramount importance to get back to the scriptures, clearing away the obfuscation of tradition. It always seeks to return to some former state; it is characterized by the practice of re-reading texts, and a search for origins. The enemy is not modernity but tradition or rather, in the context of Islam, everything which is not the tradition of the Prophet (the sunnat). This is true reform. In itself fundamentalism sits uneasily within the political spectrum, for the return to first things may take different forms. First, there is return to strict religious practice, found most frequently in émigré circles. A return to the carrying out of the injunctions of the scriptures (the study of the Quran and the hadith) is the fundamentalism of the madrassa; while a return to religious laws, to the practice of the shariat, is the fundamentalism of the Ulema.[4]

If Roy's definition of religious fundamentalism is accepted then, in the context of Islam, fanaticism and acts by extremists cannot be equated with Islamic fundamentalism. Fanaticism is repugnant to Islam. The religion emphasizes reason and moderation. Toleration is one of its guiding principles. This, in turn, implies the acceptance of other creeds and systems. For instance, a Christian delegation from Najran visited Madina shortly before the Prophet Muhammad's death. When the time came for their prayers, he offered them his own mosque to carry out their religious obligations. In a *Time* magazine article, James Walsh commented: "At bottom, the Prophet Muhammad's revealed word is among the most egalitarian of religions. Certainly one of Islam's strongest appeals down the centuries was to people who felt victimized, and deprived of worth in God's eyes, under the social hierarchies sanctified by some other faiths. In theory, with an ethic that allows merit to be rewarded, Islam ought to serve as a solid platform for political flexibility and economic growth."[5] Walsh also conceded that the political upheavals, which are often marked by anti-Western rhetoric and impulses, in certain parts of the Islamic world are unrelated to religious doctrine.

In the absence of a priesthood, Sunnis who constitute the overwhelming majority of Muslims, have never had a clergy-led government. Until the emergence of the Taliban, it was only Shia Iran that witnessed the rule of clerics, but even there the initial revolutionary rhetoric is fading and attempts were made during the Khatami presidency to pursue more liberal policies.

In Sunni societies self-appointed clerics also exist. Although they wield influence in some of these countries at the social level, their political clout, when measured by the yardstick of winning at the ballot box, has always been marginal. In Pakistan, for instance, never have religious political parties won more than a handful of parliamentary seats in elections. In the local bodies elections which were completed in August 2001, religious elements secured no more than two percent of the popular vote. The strong showing of religious parties in the parliamentary elections in 2003 is an aberration and was probably a reaction to the events in Iraq.

In this sense the Taliban movement in Afghanistan was also an aberration and a reaction to the prevalent anarchy caused by the warlords. The Afghans have always looked down upon mullas and never in their history have the bearded men from the madrassas and mosques controlled the country. A little known fact is that Omar, who was declared amir-ul-momineen by the ulema shura, does not even qualify to be a mulla since he was unable to complete his religious education. Furthermore, the Taliban movement is said to have been actually started by the more moderate Mulla Rabbani and reportedly also by Mulla Ghaus but as it grew in strength Omar was appointed the leader for the simple reason that he belonged to a bigger and more influential tribe.

The basic elements of Islamic political philosophy make it both liberal in spirit and modern in outlook. Yet the image of the religion continues to be shaped by events that are completely at variance with its true teachings. The unschooled, semi-literate Taliban were never able to grasp the true spirit of their faith. Neither did they have any idea about how to run a government. They punished ordinary Afghans in the name of religion and imposed their tribal values on a people that were ignorant of the rights that the Quran had given them. The Amr-bil-Maroof behaved like the Gestapo of Nazi Germany. Even members of the Pakistan embassy in Kabul and the consulate general in Kandahar were not spared. On more than one occasion our diplomats and consular officials were arrested and taken to the police station for no better reason than the short length of their beards. This caused enormous embarrassment to the Taliban leadership who apologized for the misconduct of their religious police and took disciplinary action against those responsible. On another occasion, Pakistan's defence attaché in Kabul was dragged to prison because he was out in the streets without identification papers. Again firm action against the over-zealous religious police was taken by senior Taliban officials on instructions from Mulla Omar. But it was the Afghan people, particularly women, who suffered the most from the rigours of religious extremism.

Women

In the Taliban's Afghanistan, stories abound on the plight of women, especially widows, who were deprived of educational as well as employment opportunities. *The New Yorker* of 15 May 2000 carried a piece entitled "Letter from Afghanistan" by William T. Volkmann in which he describes how a beggar woman in Jalalabad came up to a young man and wept: "Don't you recognize me?" She turned out to be his teacher when he was in elementary school. So overpowering was the emotion felt by the young Afghan that he too burst into tears and gave her whatever little money he had. Thousands of women, some educated and previously employed and others simple housewives, either became beggars or prostitutes because their husbands, brothers and fathers, all breadwinners, had died in the fighting. Peshawar and several Pakistani cities acquired notoriety for prostitutes from Afghanistan.

The international community did nothing to save these women—who did not have the good fortune to be registered as refugees—from the dreadful but avoidable circumstances in which they were placed. There was condemnation of the Taliban almost without exception by foreign governments, human rights groups, the UN and its affiliated bodies, non-governmental organizations and influential lobbies but none of them came forward with any meaningful assistance for these non-refugee Afghan women. Instead of engaging with the Taliban, as the Americans had initially envisaged, the world decided to shun and isolate them long before terrorism became the main issue. Even worse, those UN organizations that interacted with the Taliban and had a more objective assessment were reprimanded by their headquarters. For instance, the Islamabad-based Afghanistan office of the United Nations High Commissioner for Refugees (UNHCR) organized a seminar on the legal aspects of repatriation in Kandahar in the last week of September 1997 as a follow-up to a Taliban amnesty for returning refugees. The Taliban leadership, including the governor of Kandahar, the president of the Council of Ulema, members of the Afghan Islamic Council as well as ranking officials agreed to let a female UNHCR expert, Sathu Suikkri of Finland, deliver the key note address in front of an all-male audience. As some of the commanders objected to this, Suikkri agreed to speak from behind a curtain. However this prompted a protest walk-out by the representatives of the UNICEF, UNOCHA and UNDP. The three were later asked to leave Afghanistan by the Taliban administration for their lack of respect for Afghan customs and traditions.

The UNHCR was severely criticised by the other UN agencies for agreeing to the Taliban request. In their view, the precondition that Suikkri should speak from behind a curtain militated against the rights of women. They justified the walk-out on the grounds that it was in accordance with the spirit of the UN secretary general's instructions that UN agencies should not shift their headquarters to Afghanistan so long as the Taliban continued to discriminate against women. However, the UNHCR felt, as did Suikkri, that the Taliban had made an unprecedented gesture by agreeing to listen to a speech from a woman and a European at that. Far from appreciating this, it seemed that the UN had already made up its mind to ignore Afghan sensitivities and was determined to impose social norms that were at variance to the values of a traditional people.

To their surprise, the UNHCR officials and Suikkri were later taken to a secondary school for eighty girls and sixty boys. They were told that such schools existed in every village outside Kandahar. They were also informed by the governor of Kandahar that the UN could set up any number of schools for girls. He asked them to start income-generating programmes for women. Suikkri and her colleagues were given access to more than eight hundred male prisoners and were able to talk to about thirty of them. Their impression was that the prisoners were being treated well.

Suikkri's address to the male audience in Kandahar, her meeting with the prisoners and the Kandahar governor's request for programmes for women were indicators that the Taliban policies were more moderate than was generally believed. It was certainly strange that instead of commending the UNHCR for persuading the Taliban to listen to a lecture from a lady, its representative should be reprimanded for nothing more than respecting the culture and the traditions of the Afghan people.

Almost immediately after the UNHCR seminar in Kandahar, the total lack of respect for Afghan sensitivities was again demonstrated and this time by the European Union. Emma Bonino, an Italian and at that time the European Union Commissioner for Humanitarian Aid, was on a visit to Kabul. I received a panic call from the Italian ambassador in Islamabad who said that Bonino and her delegation which included eminent Western journalists from the print and electronic media had been taken to a Kabul police station. I was later told by the Taliban that Bonino and her delegation were detained at the police station for about three hours. Their version of the incident was that the journalists accompanying Bonino took photographs and video films during a visit to a women's hospital in contravention of Afghan customs and traditions. The hospital staff brought this to the notice of the religious police who asked Bonino and her team to accompany them to the police station. When the journalists were asked to give the films to the police, they deceptively only handed over blank reels and this further increased the annoyance of the jail authorities. The Taliban deputy minister of health reached the police station about half an hour after Bonino and her delegation were taken there. After lengthy deliberations, he was finally able to prevail on the police to release the visitors.

Subsequently, the Taliban deputy ministers of foreign affairs and health met Bonino and apologised profusely over the incident. During her meeting with us in Islamabad, Bonino described the event as unfortunate and said it would not be allowed to prejudice her report to the European Commission. She conceded that there were some extremely reasonable persons among the Taliban while there were others who were insufferable. She also said that the Northern Alliance was no better, as was evident from the looting of the UN and NGO offices in Mazar-e-Sharif around that time. A few weeks later, UN assistant secretary general Angela King told me that Emma Bonino's visit to the hospital with the team of camera wielding journalists was unscheduled and probably designed to "provoke" the Taliban. In effect, King said, without even bothering to obtain the approval of the local authorities, women were photographed in deliberate disregard of Afghan sensitivities. The consequence, which even the meanest intelligence could have anticipated, was blown out of proportion by the sensation-hungry international media.

The Japanese ambassador in Islamabad visited Kabul a few days after the Bonino incident. He was taken to the same women's hospital and, to his surprise, the Taliban escorts accompanying him said that he was at liberty to take photographs. The ambassador told me that he declined the offer out of respect for Afghan culture to which his hosts responded that, as an Asian, they had expected this reply from him which was in contrast to the cultural arrogance of the Europeans who merely wanted to impose their own values on others. Mulla Wakil asked me around this time whether Bonino would have behaved in a similar manner had she been visiting Saudi Arabia where the rules concerning women were no less strict? He replied the question himself by observing that such an incident would not have occurred because the West was dependent on Saudi oil. "It is only us poor Afghans that are singled out for such kind of treatment," he added as an afterthought.

There seems to be some truth in Wakil's comment. I was told by Sri Wijeratne, a Sri Lankan lawyer who was at the time the Islamabad-based UNHCR chief of mission for Afghanistan, that the Taliban had agreed to open the first "formal" girls' school in Kandahar and that it was supposed to have been inaugurated by the UNHCR deputy high commissioner who was to have flown over from Geneva for this purpose on 8 March 1998. All preparations had been made for the ceremonial opening when, at the last minute, the deputy high commissioner decided to cancel his visit and the occasion, which coincided with international women's day, was used to malign the Taliban for gender discrimination. As a result the school was never opened because the UN thought it more important to castigate the Taliban rather than address the problem of educational opportunities for Afghan women. Similarly, when Bill Richardson visited Kabul the following month an understanding was reached with the Taliban that an equal number of educational institutions would be opened for girls as well as boys for which funds were promised but never provided.

Furthermore, the UN adopted a policy under which some of its humanitarian projects for Afghanistan could only be implemented if 50 percent of the work force employed were women. This would have been difficult to implement even in countries with far more liberal norms than traditional Afghanistan. As if this was not enough, UN agencies responsible for Afghanistan were asked to headquarter themselves in Pakistan until such time as the Taliban agreed to let women work in UN offices. In effect, UN agencies were under instructions to continue living in posh air-conditioned houses in Pakistan, go about in chauffeur-driven limousines and benefit from duty free privileges while the Afghans and particularly the women of that country suffered. It was for precisely this reason that I was constrained to ask Brahimi, when he insisted that Pakistan should pay for the air transportation of the Taliban from Kabul and Kandahar for the meeting of the steering committee what percentage of the UN budget was being spent on the Afghan people. During her meeting with me, even Angela King described the criteria for the employment of Afghan women in UN offices and UN-related projects as "absurd".

While doing little to help Afghan women, who had the misfortune of living in a country ravaged by a senseless war that had lasted so long, human rights groups in the West at times went to a ridiculously irrational extent in their enthusiasm to criticize the unacceptable behaviour of the Taliban towards women. foreign secretary Shamshad Ahmed kept a neatly packed piece of blue cloth mesh that had been taken from a burqa worn by Afghan women on his desk throughout his tenure. It had been given to him during a visit to the United States by a women's rights organization. He was told that the rule requiring Afghan women to wear a burqa posed a health and a traffic hazard as it obstructed vision when they ventured out of their homes. Shamshad, who could barely suppress a grin at the absurdity of this observation, replied that in his own family, as in thousands of others, women had worn similar burqas because of local traditions (the Quran does not prescribe such a dress code) and not once had there been a report of an accident because of the apparel. Furthermore, in the war-devastated Afghanistan of the Taliban era there were hardly any vehicles and hence the chance of an accident was remote. Women in Afghanistan continue to wear the burqa, as they have through the centuries, even though the country has been liberated from Taliban oppression.

The bias was obvious. Facts were distorted. The Taliban were rightly criticized for their despicable conduct and particularly that of their religious police but some of the positive measures they had taken were ignored. Hardly a mention was made that the UNHCR had come to learn that many girls' schools existed in Taliban-controlled Afghanistan (similar findings by a Swedish NGO were ignored), that the Taliban had agreed to set up an equal number of schools for girls and boys, that the governor of Kandahar had requested help for providing vocational education to women. The pitiable state of Afghan women was because the Taliban uncompromisingly enforced the tribal traditions of their country which were often far removed from the teachings of Islam. However, in the period that the Burhanuddin Rabbani regime controlled Kabul, the plight of females was even worse. Rape and other forms of violence against them were commonplace despite the Pushtun code of honour that women and the elderly were never to be harmed. Pushtun tribesmen often said: "If you want to be safe, walk with a woman or an old man." The sexual crimes against female Afghans only ended after the warlords had been defeated.

Many of the Taliban leaders I have met readily conceded that the Quran gives absolute equality to men and women and, in some respects, females actually have an advantage over males. For instance, the husband, no matter how poor, has to provide for his wife even though she may be well off. He has no right over her property and earnings and the responsibility for the maintenance of the family is entirely his.

The veiling of women and confining them to their homes has more to do with local customs and traditions than the injunctions of the Quran. All that Islam requires is that both women as well as men should dress and behave with modesty. This is a mere social guideline and no punishment is prescribed if it is violated. Yet women were publicly beaten by the over-zealous religious police of the Taliban and even by some of Mulla Omar's ministers, such as the hated minister of justice Mulla Turabi.

Furthermore, the Taliban did nothing to alleviate the dismal social conditions under which Afghan women lived and died during their five-year rule. Much has been made about the denial of employment opportunities for women. However, this was also partly for the reason that there were no such opportunities available even for men in war-devastated Afghanistan and this was what had prompted the governor of Kandahar to request UNHCR assistance in providing vocational education for women. The few women who had managed to secure employment were, like the men, either underpaid or received no salary at all.

Had the Taliban been encouraged to implement Islamic injunctions in respect of marriage many war widows would not have become destitute. The Quran restricted and set conditions on the plurality of marriages and allowed a person to have more than one wife only under special circumstances: "And if you fear that you cannot do justice to orphans, marry such women as seem good to you, two, or three, or four; but if you fear you will not do justice, then [marry] only one."[6] This conditional permission to marry a maximum of four women is further explained in another verse, "And they ask thee a decision about women. Say: 'Allah makes known to you His decision concerning them; and that which is recited to you in the Book is concerning widowed women, whom you give not what is appointed for them, while you are not inclined to marry them, nor to the weak among children, and that you should deal justly with orphans'."[7]

The first of the two verses was revealed after the battle of Uhud (625 AD) in which seventy of approximately seven hundred men in the Prophet Muhammad's army lost their lives. Their widows and children faced complete destitution. The conditional permission to marry more than one woman was designed to secure widows and their children their rights and not for any other reason. Arabs had, until then, been reluctant to marry widows, particularly those with children, in order to avoid the contractual obligation for their welfare and upkeep. According to some commentators, with the revelation of this verse, a Muslim who wanted to marry again could do so on condition that his other three wives were widows or orphans. Even this is on condition that he deals equitably towards his wives and if this is not possible then he is permitted to have only one wife. The second verse makes it clear that the contents of the first verse regarding polygamy refer to widows and their children: "That which is recited to you in the Book is concerning widowed women."

Under Afghan and Pushtun tribal traditions, however, a man is required to make a payment either in cash or in kind to the family of the woman he intends to marry. The amount involved is often unaffordable. This contributed in considerable measure to the destitution of widows and orphan girls in war-devastated Afghanistan. As opposed to these tribal traditions, the Quran requires that a dowry whether large or small must invariably to be paid to the bride and not to her family. Thus a woman acquires property rights through marriage over and above what she inherits under Quranic injunctions. Had the correct Islamic principles been applied, Afghan males seeking a second wife would have had to marry widows on the obligatory payment of a mutually agreed dowry to the woman. Unfortunately no effort was made to educate the tribal Afghans about the actual marriage laws of the Quran. At the least this could have saved thousands of Afghan women from humiliating poverty and destitution.

Terrorism

After the bombings of the US embassies in Tanzania and Kenya in August 1998, terrorism became the main international concern in respect of the Taliban. By then they had squandered whatever initial goodwill there was for them because of their atrocious human rights track record which stemmed, in large measure, from their absurd interpretation of Islamic doctrine. The Americans claimed that the Taliban were giving sanctuary as well as providing training and assistance to terrorists. If this was correct then others must have been involved because the unschooled mullas of Kandahar had neither the resources nor the expertise to render such help. At the most they could allow their territory to be used for this purpose in return for monetary benefits.

The foremost American demand became the extradition of Osama Bin Laden. On 20 August 1998 US naval vessels in the Arabian Sea fired cruise missiles on Khost in an abortive attempt to eliminate Bin Laden. Although the Tomahawks flew over and violated Pakistan airspace, we were informed about it only after they had been launched. Even this information was probably shared with us because of the fear that Pakistan might have mistakenly believed that the missiles were Indian and this could have triggered a conflict between the two nuclear-armed neighbours—missiles fired by either country would take no more than five minutes to hit targets in the other. The American decision to withhold information from us about their attack on Khost until the very end was, therefore, a gamble which could have had disastrous consequences.

An initial report filed by a junior official of the North West Frontier Province indicated that one or two of the cruise missiles had hit our tribal areas bordering Afghanistan and had resulted in a few deaths. This generated public resentment and violent anti-US demonstrations were anticipated. Without waiting for the final report from the NWFP administration, Prime Minister Nawaz Sharif issued instructions that a strongly worded protest be made to the American embassy in Islamabad. Washington immediately expressed deep regret on the reported deaths. However, it later transpired that the interim information was inaccurate as there had been no Pakistani casualties. Nawaz Sharif was embarrassed and reacted by sacking the NWFP chief secretary, Rustam Shah, who had played so important a role in our shuttle mission. It was Rustam Shah who had arranged the Farkhar meeting with Ahmed Shah Masood in July 1997 and had also been responsible for my earlier contacts with Younis Qanooni in Dubai.

Osama Bin Laden and his terrorist network thus became the one point agenda in Washington's Afghanistan policy. The erroneous perception in the US was that Pakistan wielded considerable influence on the Taliban and enormous pressure was exerted on Islamabad to convince the authorities in Kandahar to hand Bin Laden over to the Americans or extradite him to a place where he could be brought to justice. Several of my subsequent meetings with Mulla Omar were, therefore, Bin Laden-specific.

Mulla Omar told us that the Taliban were in a bind. They wanted to get rid of Bin Laden but did not know how. Under Afghan traditions it was not possible to surrender a person who had sought asylum. He told us on several occasions that if he extradited Bin Laden there would be a nationwide uprising which he would not be able to control. There was some truth in this. Under the Pushtun code of honour, refuge seekers have to be protected no matter what the cost. Afghan men, women and even children, according to Omar, would rather die than dishonourably surrender a fugitive.

Mulla Haqqani, the Afghan chargé d'affaires in Islamabad, once told me that soon after the Second World War twelve Nazi generals had requested and were granted asylum by the Afghan government of the time. The victorious allied powers demanded their extradition and this was summarily rejected by Kabul. Stringent sanctions were then imposed which lasted for several months and resulted in severe famine. The price of wheat, the Afghan staple, soared and the people faced starvation. The crisis was resolved through a loya jirga convened by the king and it was decided that the Nazis would only be handed over to the Allied Forces if a binding undertaking was given that they would not be executed.

I am unsure how accurate this account is but a few people—mostly non-Afghans who were aware of the story—believe that comprehensive UN sanctions may have resulted in Bin Laden's extradition if a face-saver could have been agreed upon by a loya jirga. This simplistic view ignores the indispensable requirement that a loya jirga can only be convened by a leader acceptable to all Afghans—and, as was obvious, no such leader existed in the country.

Mulla Omar also repeatedly conveyed to us that Bin Laden had been made ineffective as his means of communications had been confiscated. In one of these meetings he also claimed with ill-disguised glee that Bin Laden had a serious aliment and was not expected to live long.

To resolve the problem, Omar proposed that a small group of ulema from Afghanistan, Saudi Arabia and a third Islamic country should meet to decide what should be done with Bin Laden. If the ulema advised that he should be extradited or punished, the Taliban would comply. However, the proposal was rejected by the Saudis and the Americans.

Subsequently, the Taliban also set up a committee headed by their chief justice, to receive evidence about Bin Laden's complicity in acts of terrorism. They gave a solemn commitment that he would be punished under their laws if concrete evidence was received establishing his guilt.

The US, they claimed, had merely given them a copy of the indictment. Until the Bin Laden issue was resolved they were willing to allow the Organization of the Islamic Conference to monitor his movements.

Through this period Washington applied incremental pressure on us to persuade the Taliban to extradite Bin Laden. Our response was that we would play a discreet but helpful role though our leverage with the Taliban was limited. Furthermore, Osama Bin Laden was a problem between the US and the Taliban and should be sorted out by them bilaterally. The US subsequently took a much tougher stance and decided not to talk to the Taliban any more. We were bluntly told that Washington would act to get Bin Laden with or without our cooperation.

Through resolution 1267/99 the Security Council imposed Osama Bin Laden-specific sanctions under Chapter VII of the UN Charter on the Taliban. Its provisions froze the latter's funds and confined their planes to Afghan airspace. The sanctions were to remain in force until such time that Bin Laden was extradited. We tried to make the Taliban realize that the sanctions were likely to increase in severity causing further hardship to the Afghan people. We seemed to talking to the deaf.

The US under-secretary of state Thomas Pickering visited Pakistan from 25-28 May 2000, and during his meeting with President Musharraf he stated his country's appreciation of Islamabad's concerns as a neighbour of Afghanistan. However, he insisted that Pakistan had to also take into account the emerging Afghan realities over the last six months. The Taliban were facing internal opposition. Furthermore, they were impervious to any suggestion of conciliation with the other Afghan groups. The Northern Alliance was equally divided. The US, nevertheless, recognized that the Taliban were the strongest force in Afghanistan. It also appreciated Pakistan's appeal to the leadership in Kandahar to announce a cease-fire.

Pickering stressed that a satisfactory resolution of the Osama Bin Laden issue was of paramount importance for the US. Washington was disappointed that Mulla Razzaq, whose uncompromising attitude had cost the Taliban dearly in Mazar-e-Sharif in May 1997 and who had become interior minister, had, during a visit to Pakistan a few days earlier, merely repeated Kandahar's three Bin Laden-related proposals which were: a decision by the ulema; action through their chief justice; and the monitoring of Bin Laden's movements by the OIC. Conclusive evidence had been provided earlier, Pickering said, to Pakistan's interior minister by the FBI director and to the authorities in Kandahar through other channels about Bin Laden's terrorist activities. Despite this, the Taliban had done nothing to address US concerns.

Furthermore, they had been lying because Bin Laden had not even been restrained and continued to act against US interests. Washington expected Pakistan to use its undoubted influence with the Taliban to resolve the problem. If there was no forward movement on the issue, then more stringent UN sanctions could be imposed against the Taliban. These might include travel restrictions on the Taliban leadership, impounding all their bank accounts, and a Taliban-specific arms embargo. The US declared it would even use force if it felt that its security was in jeopardy. It would act decisively and firmly against terrorists.

Eventually, the UN imposed the more stringent sanctions indicated by Pickering. This meant, among other the things, that a one-sided arms embargo was implemented against the Taliban while the defunct Northern Alliance was free to acquire all the weapons it needed. The implication was that the international community was even willing to accept a military settlement of the Afghan problem if that was the only way it could rid itself of the hated Taliban. In this sense, Norbert Holl was not that far off the mark when he told television viewers in Pakistan after my return from Kandahar on 13 August 1997 that a military solution was "the second best option".

Musharraf told Pickering that the perception about the extent of our influence with the Taliban was exaggerated. However, we had been speaking firmly to them on our concerns especially terrorism and training camps. We had also taken up the Bin Laden issue with them on several occasions. The most recent was our ISI director general's meeting with Mulla Omar in Kandahar. There had been some progress. The Taliban had taken action to close down the Rishkore training camp near Kabul and had warned religious extremists from Pakistan to wind up their training activities, failing which they would not be allowed to remain in Afghanistan. This clearly demonstrated that it was important to engage with the Taliban. Isolating them would not solve any problem. Furthermore, the UN sanctions would only hurt the Afghan people who had suffered enormously in the last twenty years. We wanted the return of durable peace to Afghanistan and were urging the Taliban to reach out to other ethnic groups.

Musharraf also said that on the Bin Laden issue, it would be a good idea for the US not to reject the Taliban proposals, particularly the ulema commission, because our assessment was that Mulla Omar wanted to be rid of this problem. Pickering accepted this and, despite the earlier US decision about not talking to the Taliban, unexpectedly asked us to arrange a meeting for him with a senior representative from Kandahar. He also wanted Pakistan to participate in the deliberations. We agreed to be present as observers.

Accordingly, a night meeting with deputy foreign minister Mulla Jalil was arranged in the ministry of foreign affairs on 27 May. Pakistan's interior minister, Moinuddin Haider, ISI representatives and I attended. Pickering told Jalil that the Taliban could convene the ulema commission or revive their judicial enquiry, as that was what they had proposed earlier. Whatever method they chose the outcome had to be Bin Laden's extradition to a place where he could be brought to justice in accordance with Security Council resolution 1267/99.

Moinuddin Haider, who should have kept quiet because our participation in the meeting was in an observer capacity, butted in to say that the US government had provided him conclusive evidence about Bin Laden's terrorist activities. Pickering was visibly delighted by this unexpected intervention.

Jalil did not lose his cool and responded that no concrete evidence had thus far been given to the Taliban. All that they had received from the US was a copy of the Bin Laden indictment. If there was further information, it should be shared with his government so that, if warranted, action could be taken against Bin Laden. He then thanked Pickering for the support extended by the United States to Afghanistan during the jihad against Soviet occupation and then subsequently for the assistance given to the Afghan refugees. He also expressed appreciation for the American donation of $500,000 for the drought-stricken people of Afghanistan.

Pickering responded that the US was concerned about the presence of Osama Bin Laden in Afghanistan. It considered this a hostile act on the part of the Taliban. There was now concrete evidence that he had been carrying out terrorist attacks against the United States. A few days earlier, an Al Qaida operative, who had been arrested in Jordan, had confirmed this. Similarly, an Algerian national who had crossed over from Canada to the US in a car loaded with explosives had been arrested by the US authorities and was being interrogated. He had admitted that he was a part of Bin Laden's network. He had also disclosed that a number of other Arabs were being trained in Afghanistan for terrorist acts.

Pickering then gave Jalil a copy of a document containing evidence about Bin Laden's involvement in the bomb blasts in Tanzania and Kenya. He said that it was the product of exhaustive investigations and contained the following main elements:

—Al Qaida's role as a terrorist organization and its declaration of jihad against the US on 23 August 1996 on the ground that the latter had violated the sanctity of the two holy mosques in Saudi Arabia by its presence in the kingdom.

—In February 1998, Bin Laden had given full support to a fatwa given by the Afghan ulema to kill Americans wherever they were found.

—Muhammad Rashid Daud Al Mahali, Khalid Al Fauz and Muhammad Sadiq Al Oudiah of the Al Qaida were responsible for the bombing of the US Embassy in Kenya. The operation had been conceived as early as 1993-94. The planning included the transfer of money for the purpose of renting cars, houses, hotel rooms, manufacture of explosive devices and for their daily activities from 1-8 August 1998 when the bombings occurred.

—Several of Bin Laden's close associates in London had accepted responsibility for the bomb blasts in Kenya and Tanzania.

Pickering continued that the Bin Laden issue had been discussed with the Taliban many times. They should now study the new evidence carefully. He emphasized that the US wanted the faithful implementation of UN Security Council Resolution 1267/99 by the Taliban. This meant that Bin Laden had to be handed over to the US or sent to a place were he could be arrested and brought to justice. Unfortunately, there had been no clear and adequate response from the Taliban. The UN was ready for further sanctions if Resolution 1267/99 was not honoured. The Taliban were on a collision course with the international community. They should quickly resolve the Bin Laden problem, end training of terrorists and close all camps. Not only the US but also other countries had complaints against Afghanistan on this score. This was also a grievance of the Russians who had reserved the right to carry out bombing attacks against Afghanistan. He hoped that the Taliban understood that the US had every right to defend itself and its people in any manner it deemed fit.

On the subject of training camps, Jalil said that Afghanistan would not allow its soil to be used against any other country. There were no training camps. Such camps were not allowed in Afghanistan. He invited the US to come and see for itself whether such outfits existed. He said that if these camps were shown to the Taliban they would immediately close them. Pickering said that he had noted Jalil's statement that Afghan soil would not be allowed for terrorist activities against any other country. However, the evidence was to the contrary. He was told yesterday that Pakistan had also made its concern in this regard known to the Taliban. There was no need for the US to go into Afghanistan to identify training centers. This could easily be done through satellite photography. The Taliban claim that they controlled 90 percent of the territory and yet did not know about the existence of training camps was absurd.

As for Bin Laden, Jalil, said that he had come into Afghanistan long before the emergence of the Taliban and had participated in the jihad against Soviet occupation. Several persons from other countries had also taken part in this liberation struggle. After the Soviet retreat from Afghanistan they went back to their own countries as did Bin Laden. It was the regime of Burhanuddin Rabbani that had brought him back to Afghanistan. Nobody had asked for Bin Laden at that time nor had any request been made to restrict his movements and activities. According to Afghan traditions, it was difficult to extradite him. Other groups were making full use of Bin Laden's name. The Taliban were ready to share the particulars of such groups with the Americans. All of Bin Laden's assets had been impounded by the Saudi government. It was, therefore, impossible for him to carry out the activities for which he was being accused.

Mulla Jalil said that there were many others, not only Bin Laden, who had declared jihad against the US. For example, the imam of the Holy Mosque in Madina had also called for jihad against the United States. The Taliban had no intention of siding with Bin Laden but they wanted to apprise the US about the factual position. The US was far away from Afghanistan. The Taliban had severe problems of their own. How could they possibly be hostile to the United States? The Taliban did not support Bin Laden and they did not want him in their country. The US should understand their constraints. They had even requested Bin Laden to leave Afghanistan of his own accord, and when he did not comply, his means of communication had been confiscated. This meant that he did not have the ability to perpetrate terrorist attacks on a global scale as that would have required coordination. The Taliban had decided to restrict him even more. Clearly, Afghanistan was also a victim of terrorism. The evidence provided by the US would be studied. Kandahar was ready to reactivate the commission headed by their chief justice if there was proof of Bin Laden's terrorist activities.

The Jalil-Pickering talks were frank but inconclusive. The Taliban resorted to their usual tactic of giving evasive replies on issues on which they had already made up their mind. Pickering was merely told that the new evidence against Bin Laden would be studied by the authorities in Kandahar and a response would be forthcoming. They had no intention to reply because they had already decided that Bin Laden would not be extradited. Furthermore, Jalil was either lying about the non-existence of training camps inside Afghanistan or was ignorant about what was happening in his country. The reason for the Taliban's refusal to deliver on the Bin Laden issue was probably because they were afraid of the backlash since protection of refuge seekers was sacrosanct to their tribal traditions. Another likely reason could have been that Bin Laden was providing them substantial financial help.

The interesting point that Jalil did make was that Bin Laden had been brought back to Afghanistan by the Burhanuddin Rabbani regime when they controlled Kabul. The Northern Alliance were, therefore, as much to blame for his presence in Afghanistan as were the Taliban.

Another element that cannot be ignored is that the US itself was responsible for bringing some 20,000 Arabs, including Bin Laden, into Afghanistan to fight the Soviet occupation forces. They were indoctrinated in madrassas in Pakistan about the evil of communism, provided military training in camps and given money and weapons. After the Soviet defeat in Afghanistan, the US and its allies ignored the region. The monster they had created thus had a free hand to destabilize first the region and subsequently threaten world peace and security.

Several months earlier, the Saudis had also demanded, probably on American urging, that Osama Bin Laden be handed over to them in accordance with an undertaking supposedly given to their intelligence chief, Prince Turki, by Mulla Omar. I was unaware that the two had met nor was I informed about their agreement on Bin Laden. What transpired in that meeting was to emerge later. It was in this context that Turki visited Pakistan in the autumn of 1998 and met Nawaz Sharif. I received a phone call the same evening from the prime minister's office to tell me that I was to accompany Turki to Kandahar the following morning. Accordingly, ISI officials and I met Turki at the same Chaklala air force base from where I had undertaken the first of my several flights to Afghanistan on 7 December 1996. However, this time we travelled in style aboard the Pakistan prime minister's Boeing. It was bright and sunny in Kandahar when we landed and we were taken without delay to Mulla Omar.

Turki congratulated Omar for the ground successes achieved by the Taliban against the Northern Alliance and, after these preliminaries, said that he had come to take Osama Bin Laden back with him as per Omar's commitment three months earlier. Omar replied that he had made no such commitment to which Turki responded that he had. Turki insisted that Omar should redeem his pledge on which the latter went out into the courtyard in front of us and poured a bucket of cold water over his head and then rejoined the talks. Turki kept insisting that Omar had promised to hand over Bin Laden within three months. Omar again replied that he had given no such undertaking and there could have been a mistake by the interpreters. Turki then told Omar that he should learn Arabic to avoid such misunderstandings.

The latter's response was immediate: "I know Arabic but you should learn Pushtu. I am not a liar. If I had told you that I would give Bin Laden to you I would have fulfilled my promise. You are putting pressure on me at a time when the Iranians have massed thousands of troops along our borders. Let me tell you we will not be pressured. If Iran makes the mistake of attacking us, we will fight back and shortly thereafter the white flag of the Taliban will be flying in Tehran. Are you in league with Iran? "

"We are not," replied Turki. "Now hand over Bin Laden."

Omar responded: "You are a hypocrite, your king is a hypocrite and so are your ulema. God has given you everything but yet you cannot defend yourselves against puny Iraq and therefore you invited the Americans into your country to protect you and to fight your battles. Learn from us how to fight. If you are scared of Iraq then let us defend you."

This was too much for Turki. He stormed out of the meeting and we headed for the airport to fly back to Islamabad. Shortly afterwards, Saudi Arabia withdrew its chargé d'affaires from Kabul and relations between the Taliban and Riyadh remained strained.

The Taliban and Osama Bin Laden were blamed for the 11 September 2001 terrorist attacks in New York and Washington. However, several months later, Burhanuddin Rabbani gave an interview to Russia's *Izvestia* which was published on 15 April 2002 in which he said that he did not believe that Osama Bin Laden was responsible for 9/11. He commented: "I personally don't understand it that such a complex, thoroughly planned and technically well organized operation, which the US September 11 attacks were, could have been organized and carried out by a small bunch of bandits located in the lifeless Afghan mountains—however, anything is possible. But none of the people who knew him has told me that Bin Laden is a great man. On the contrary, everyone who knew him speaks of him as an ordinary warlord, a totally ordinary man. Bin Laden spent a long time in the mountains. You don't rule the world from there. Other people were and probably are behind Bin Laden, and I would like to know who they are."

Rabbani's comments raise fundamental unanswered questions. Pinning 9/11 on Bin Laden and his Al Qaida network is simplistic. Since then terrorist violence, mainly by those professing Islam, has and is continuing to destabilize the world. The problem is that the enemy is amorphous. There is no structured organization that can be identified, targeted and eliminated. Terrorism is the symptom of a malaise that feeds on perceived political and economic inequities. Till the causes are redressed the symptoms will keep reappearing with or without Al Qaida and similar outfits, with or without persons such as Osama bin Laden and his likes. It is the idea, therefore, that has to be vanquished.

Although violence and aggression are anathema to Quranic doctrine, the question arises how extremist claiming to be Muslims justify terrorist acts. The answer probably is that they consider themselves victims of aggression because their territories have been occupied through war and, therefore, they believe that jihad is justified to remedy the wrong done to them. Approximately three years prior to 9/11, Bin Laden had issued an appeal entitled "Declaration of the World Islamic Front for Jihad against the Jews and the Crusaders" in which he declared that "to kill Americans and their allies, both civil and military, is the individual duty of every Muslim who is able, until the al-Aqsa mosque [in Jerusalem] and the Haram mosque [in Mecca] are freed from their grip, and until their armies, shattered and broken-winged, depart from all the lands of Islam." Though the US presence in Saudi Arabia was with the acquiescence of the Saudi government, it had also been objected to by Mulla Omar during his altercation with prince Turki.

Harvard professor Samuel P. Huntington's article "The Clash of Civilizations?", which appeared in the summer 1993 edition of *Foreign Affairs*, provoked more discussion, according to the journal's editors, than any article since the 1940s when George F. Kennan, using the pseudonym "X," wrote his seminal essay, "The Sources of Soviet Conduct," which was to result in the US Cold War doctrine of containment. Huntington tried to analyse whether "the fault lines between civilizations" would replace "the political and ideological boundaries of the Cold War as the flash points for crisis and bloodshed". He quoted M. J. Akbar, a Muslim from India, who observed: "The West's next confrontation is definitely going to come from the Muslim world. It is in the sweep of Islamic nations from the Maghreb to Pakistan that the struggle for the new world order will begin."

Richard Nixon in his tenth and perhaps most controversial book *Beyond Peace*, published posthumously in 1994, agreed with Huntington that conflict between the West and Islam was not necessarily inevitable but could become a self-fulfilling prophesy if the West continued to be indifferent to conflicts in which Muslims were the victims. Nixon elaborated:

It is an awkward but unavoidable truth that had the citizens of Sarajevo been predominately Christian or Jewish, the civilized would not have permitted the siege to reach the point it did on February 5 [1994], when a Serbian shell landed in the crowded marketplace. In such an instance, the West would have acted quickly and would have been right in doing so.

Extremists in the Islamic world have exploited such incidents, where double standards are obvious, to develop their warped concept of jihad. Indiscriminate violence, including suicide bombings, to achieve political ends was thus justified. To the Taliban, Osama Bin Laden was a freedom fighter and a Mujahid who had helped them in the past, with the encouragement of the West, to liberate their country from Soviet occupation and had returned to assist them in their fight against their "godless" enemies in the north. It is no mere coincidence that their one remaining opponent, Ahmed Shah Masood, should have been assassinated by suicide bombers (till then uncommon in Afghanistan) just two days before 9/11. Less than a month later the US began intensive aerial bombing of Taliban-controlled areas of Afghanistan and the Northern Alliance forces were able to enter Kabul by the end of 2001. A military solution was thus imposed by the international community.

Postscript

Thus ended the era of the Taliban. During their rule, Pakistan and the international community had stressed the need for a broad-based government but what initially emerged from the Bonn Agreement was a dispensation dominated by the Tajiks and, among the Tajiks, the Panjsheri elements. Faheem, who in May 1997 had been nominated by the late Ahmed Shah Masood to negotiate an honourable surrender with Mulla Obaidullah of the Taliban, became the strongman in Karzai's interim administration. The Panjsheris who, at the best of times, controlled no more than 10 percent of Afghan territory, now called the shots. The government in Kabul was as narrow-based as any dispensation could be. The majority Pushtuns, the Uzbeks and the Hazaras had little say in the affairs of state. Warlord zones reappeared and Afghanistan was again at the mercy of ambitious, avaricious men eager to establish their own fiefdoms. The Taliban had deweaponized Afghan society but now weapons were no longer in short supply. Several ministers and high government functionaries were assassinated and even Karzai's bodyguards consisted of non-Afghans because he could not trust his own nationals, having narrowly survived two attempts on his life in 2002 and again in 2004.

The international community had rightly condemned the Taliban for the violation of human rights and particularly gender discrimination. Such oppression had been the dominant element in the tragic history of the country. The atrocities against the Afghan people by their leaders through the previous decades and centuries no longer seemed relevant to the post-Cold War world which sincerely believed in the final triumph of political liberalism and the free market system. The policies of the Taliban contrasted starkly with this wave of freedom.

The Taliban were also severely criticized for narcotics production and trafficking although the problem predated their rule. In 1997, the Taliban signed an agreement with the United Nations Drug Control Programme (UNDCP) through which they undertook to reduce poppy cultivation if funds were provided for crop substitution. According to the UNDCP, narcotics production in Afghanistan more than doubled in 1998 to 4,600 tons compared with 2,100 tons in 1997. In this period there was a 43 percent increase in the area under poppy cultivation with 97 percent located in places under Taliban control. In their report the UNDCP ignored the ground reality that in 1998 almost the entire country was dominated by the Taliban. Under international pressure, Mulla Omar eventually issued an edict banning poppy cultivation and, according to experts, the production of the crop ended though there was no significant reduction in trafficking because of abundant poppy stockpiles. Unfortunately the international community failed to grasp the opportunity that had suddenly presented itself. Economic assistance for crop substitution was urgently needed but was never provided. In 2004 Hamid Karzai turned down a US proposal which involved the aerial spraying of herbicides to end poppy cultivation because he dared not alienate certain powerful warlords on whose support he depended. By 2005 Afghanistan became the world's major source of narcotics production and trafficking for which the international community is also culpable.

Under Taliban rule most of Afghanistan was secure and stable. But in the absence of freedom, it was the security of a prison. The Bonn-generated interim government of Hamid Karzai brought relative freedom but this unfortunately also resulted in initial instability. Disappearances, killings and factional fighting occurred with alarming frequency. However, these were not sponsored by the state though many believed that Faheem himself had instigated some of the violence. The main cause was probably weak governance which is inherent in minority dominance of society. A part of the problem was also because the majority Pushtun community, unlike the other ethnic groups, did not have a recognized leader. The urbane Karzai, though a Pushtun, did not enjoy a mass following. After the Soviet withdrawal from Afghanistan he had served as a minister in Burhanuddin Rabbani's regime, and then, in the early stages of the Taliban ascendancy he supported them but later became disillusioned with the movement as he suspected that they had links with Pakistan. This, however, did not deter him from living in Quetta where he, along with his family members, actively strove for the return of ex-king Zahir Shah. After the assassination of his father on 14 July 1999, which Karzai believed was carried out by the Taliban, he vowed to avenge the murder by working to oust them. He thus became an important element in the so-called "second Pushtun option" which the US and a number of European countries were trying to promote.

However despite the obvious shortcomings of the Bonn Accord, it offers the best hope for the establishment of lasting peace in Afghanistan. A loya jirga was convened and after the presidential election on 9 October 2004, Karzai emerged as a more credible leader. By winning in twenty-one Afghan provinces and defeating twenty-two of his opponents he became, in effect, the first democratically elected president of Afghanistan. His government took measures to provide employment and education opportunities to women but the dreadful hold of obscurantist tradition was the impediment: most Afghan women still preferred to wear the burqa and few ventured outside the security of their homes.

The stabilization of Afghanistan could have been achieved much earlier had the international community engaged with and not isolated the Taliban. The Afghans need strong leadership. This was what the British and the Russians understood only too well as they competed with each other in the nineteenth century. Pakistan with the support of the major powers could have played an important role. Positive pressure on the Taliban was required. A strong leadership was already in place. Ethnic minorities, but not the leaders of the factions, had been included in the administration. Economic assistance would have provided job opportunities and resulted in the stabilization of Afghan society. Gender discrimination could have been substantially reduced. The narcotics problem and the spectre of terrorism could have been squarely addressed. The 9/11 tragedy might not have happened and other acts of terrorist violence could have been averted. The opportunity was squandered.

*   *

*

Clockwise from top left: The author with Ahmed Shah Masood (12 July 1997, Farkhar Valley); the one-legged governor of Kandahar, Mulla Hasan Rahmani (right), with Ambassador Aziz Khan and the author (Governor's House, Kandahar); Burhanuddin Rabbani (Northern Alliance headquarters, Mazar-e-Sharif); Ahmed Shah Masood (interview with Pakistan TV); Rustam Shah, Aziz Ahmad and Ayaz Wazir; Rashid Dostum; General Malik, leader of the rebellion against Dostum in May 1997; Younis Qanooni.

Images of key players

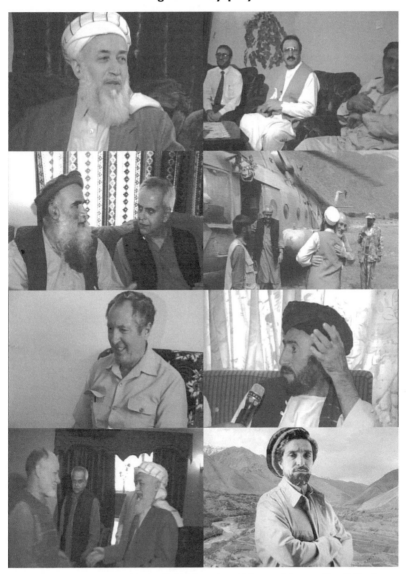

Clockwise from top left: Burhannudin Rabbani; Ayaz Wazir in Mazar-e-Sharif; Prof. Sayyaf of Northern Alliance with the author (Sayyaf was instrumental in bringing Osama Bin Laden back to Afghanistan); alighting from Ahmed Shah Masood's helicopter in Farkhar Valley; Norbert Holl of UNSMA; foreign minister Mulla Ghaus giving first ever Taliban television interview on 13 August 1997, Kandahar (he had escaped a month earlier from Mazar-e-Sharif); Aziz Khan greeting Burhanuddin Rabbani; Ahmed Shah Masood in the Panjsher Valley.

Appendices

Text of Mulla Omar's letter to President Clinton

All statements and the few letters written by the Taliban were spontaneous and often ill-thought-out reactions to events—for instance, their rhetoric that the Taliban flag would be hoisted in Bukhara and Samarkand, or Mulla Muttaqi's assurance to Uzbek foreign minister Kamilov after the Tashkent Six Plus Two that he would try to persuade Turkmenistan to sign the conference declaration which in fact was weighted heavily against the Taliban. The background of Omar's letter is the increasing US pressure on the Taliban over their links with international terrorism and that they should hand over Osama Bin Laden. Note that the Taliban's inexperience meant that they did not have the ability to draft formal documents.

In the name of Allah who is Kind and Merciful

6 September 1999

His Excellency Bill Clinton
President of the United States of America,

Excellency,

Please accept our greetings and well wishes.

I want to express my view regarding your attitude towards the Islamic Emirate of Afghanistan. I would like to say that whatever you do and whosever enemy you become, please do not become an enemy of Islam. When you say that the Taliban are fundamentalists or they are strict Muslims and that is why you are against them, it means that you are against Islam, although you may say that you do not have any animosity towards Islam. If you look at the history of thousands of years, anyone who has become an enemy of Islam has gained nothing instead of harming himself. Whatever we are—even if we are as you say fundamentalists—we are far away from you and we do not intend to harm you and cannot harm you either.

Ours and your Almighty God has obligated us to serve our religion. We are not mad nor are we in love with power. We are in the service of God and that is why we are strict in our position. If you have any objection to anything we do, you should look at our deeds in the light of Islam (whether they are according to Islamic principles) and if they are in accordance with Islam—you should know that that is why we have to follow this path, how indeed could we change it? Please be a little fair.

Much is going on in the world. And it is possible that your strict position regarding us might be flawed. So let me bring another point to your attention and it is this: if we were overthrown, there would be major chaos and confusion in the country and everyone including every single oppressed individual would blame you for it.

Furthermore, if we are overthrown, Afghanistan would be used by Iran. And Iran is such a harmful terrorist nation that there is no other nation like it in the world. As it is, despite what you think, even now we have posed no problem for you as has Iran. So, if despite these clarifications, you still say that we are to be blamed and you consider that you are right, what can we say except that God alone knows who is really to be blamed and may God punish the guilty with storms and earthquakes.

Mulla Muhammad Omar
Amirulmumineen of the Islamic Emirate of Afghanistan

Chronology of events up to the fall of Kabul

1994

End August — Mullah Omar Akhund sets out with 45 followers from a local madrassa in Maiwand, Kandahar, to punish a commander for molesting a local family. Thereafter the movement gathers momentum.

Mid-September — The Taliban start negotiations with local commander for the take-over of Kandahar. In the first week of October, they take control of the main road to Kandahar excluding the Spin-Boldak check post. The following week the check-post is captured with seven casualties.

5 November — The Taliban capture Kandahar after fierce fighting with local Afghan commanders Amir Lalai Mansoor, Sarkatib and Ustad Halim, who had detained a Pakistani trade convoy of 30 trucks en route to the Central Asian republics. A Taliban spokesman rejects allegations that they were backed in the fighting by the Pakistan Frontier Constabulary or that the ISI was supplying them weapons. The Taliban start moving towards Helmand.

15 November — The Taliban reach Dilaram from where they move towards Ghazni. In the third week of November, Zabul falls to the Taliban without any opposition.

24 December — The Taliban restore complete order in the province of Kandahar. Journalists visiting the area are taken to all military bases and the places captured from Mujahideen commanders. They are briefed about the fair treatment meted out to commanders who have surrendered to the Taliban and also about the improved law and order situation in the province.

Mid-December — The Taliban enter Ghazni.

1995

31 January — The Taliban seize power in the provinces of Paktia and Paktika. They claim that government forces surrendered following the launch of successful separate attacks. However, according to some reports the governors of the two provinces voluntarily handed over power to the Taliban.

10 February — The Taliban capture Maidan Shehr, 30 kilometres outside Kabul, after defeating Hizb-e-Islami forces of Hikmatyar. (Until now Rabbani has supported the Taliban against Hikmatyar).

11 February — The Taliban seize the strongholds of Kolangar and Burki in Logar from the Hezb-e-Islami (Hikmatyar).

Chronology

13 February — The Taliban capture three more towns: Pule Alam, Khoshi and Kolangar in Logar.

14 February — Charasiab (25 kilometres south of Kabul), the headquarters of the Hizb-e-Islami, is taken by the Taliban. Hikmatyar and his forces flee to Sarobi leaving behind a large quantity of arms and ammunition.

15 February — The Taliban capture another Hizb-e-Islami controlled province, Khost.

16 February — The forces of the Rabbani regime partially withdraw from the southern fringes of Kabul, leaving Rishkor to the Taliban.

20 February — The talks between the Taliban and the UN mediator end in deadlock. The terms put forth by the Taliban include: a) the control of Kabul should be handed over to a neutral security force, b) one representative from each of the thirty provinces should be included in the new setup, c) all those becoming part of the new administrative mechanism should be pious Muslims with a clean record.

25 February — An ulema delegation representing the Kabul regime contacts the Taliban to end the fighting. The Taliban leadership assures the delegation that they are not in favour of war and want a peaceful settlement.

27 February — Talks are held in Maidan Shehr between a delegation of the Kabul regime, led by Ahmed Shah Masood, and the Taliban, led by Maulvi Muhammad Rabbani. There is no breakthrough.

28 February — The Taliban establish Shariah courts in the provinces under their control.

8 March — Taliban forces attack various positions southwest of Kabul. They capture several positions held by Hizb-e-Wahdat troops. Wahdat troops surrender their weapons voluntarily.

11 March — The Rabbani regime recaptures some Taliban-held positions around Kabul. Ahmed Shah Masood retakes the Darulaman palace.

13 March — The Hizb-e-Wahdat leader Abdul Ali Mazari is killed in a gun battle with the Taliban.

14 March — After five days of fierce fighting Taliban forces capture strong defence lines in Farah from commander Ismail Khan, the governor of Herat. However, he is able to retake Farah the following day.

19 March — Rabbani forces recapture Charasiab. About 100-150 men of the Taliban militia are killed.

21 March — The Taliban launch a successful counterattack on the Rabbani forces and capture a district in Logar which is the power centre of Muhammad Agha.

28 March — The Taliban capture the Shindand air base controlled by Ismail Khan (Shindand was the second largest air base of the Soviet occupation forces during 1979-89).

5 April — The Taliban claim the capture of Badghis from Ismail Khan. A representative of the Taliban, Mullah Eid Muhammad, announces that the administration of Badghis has surrendered peacefully.

11 April — The Taliban take Farah and Farah Rud where opposition groups who have fled from Helmand and Kandahar are being armed by General Ismail Khan. Aab-e-Kurima, which is close to Shindand is also captured.

20 April — After three days of bloody clashes with the forces of commander Ismail Khan, the Taliban retreat from Shindand.

28 April — The Taliban are pushed further back from Herat by Ismail Khan's troops.

15 May — Troops of the Rabbani regime recapture a key town, Zaranj, in Nimroz. The Taliban suffer heavy casualties.

16 May — After victories in Farah and Nimroz, forces of the Rabbani regime penetrate Ghor and capture the main centre of the Taliban in the Dehak area.

21 May — Ahmed Shah Masood captures Kotal-I-Takht, a strategic position 35 kilometres south of Kabul, from the Taliban.

30 May — The Taliban capture Sayyaf's central base in Paghman. Maulana Abdul Rehman Zahid of the Taliban declares that besides taking important Ittehad-e-Islami positions such as Qila Haider Khan, Baghi Daud, and Qara, they have also captured substantial quantities of sophisticated weapons. Maulem Toor, a prominent Ittehad-e-Islami commander is killed in the fighting.

10 June — As a result of mediation by M. Khan Sherani of the Jamiat-e-Ulema-e-Islam, the Rabbani regime and the Taliban agree on a 10-day cease-fire in order to hold peace talks.

11 June — As a goodwill gesture, the Kabul regime releases six Taliban prisoners who are handed over to the Pakistani mediator. The Taliban reciprocate by releasing eight prisoners of the Kabul regime the following day.

12 June — Former Mujahideen commanders from the southwestern provinces form a "jehadi shura" against the Taliban. A spokesman of the shura, Maulvi Ghulam Muhammad, announces at the press club in Quetta that the Taliban have failed to restore peace in the provinces where the Mujahideen have laid down their weapons voluntarily.

27 June — Talks are held between the Taliban and General Dostum for forging an alliance against the Rabbani regime.

6 August — A Russian Ilushin-76 from Tataristan is force-landed by the Taliban at Kandahar. Akhtar Muhammad, commander of the Kandahar air base, announces that the plane was carrying 3.4 million rounds of AK-47 ammunition and two crates of ammunition for Zikoyak anti-aircraft guns. The seven-member Russian crew are taken as prisoners.

13 August — A meeting is held between Russian Embassy officials and the Taliban to negotiate the release of the Russian crew. The Taliban demand a list of Afghans who have been taken to the former Soviet Union as a precondition for beginning the negotiations.

August — Ismail Khan temporarily pushes the Taliban out of Farah Rud and Dilaram. The latter retaliate by taking Girshik on 21 August and recapturing Farah Rud and Dialaram on 29 August.

Chronology

31 August — The Taliban position themselves at Aab-e-Kurima and in the night between 2-3 September enter the Shindand air base unopposed.

5 September — The Taliban enter Herat unopposed. Ismail Khan takes refuge in Iran.

6 September — The Taliban capture Ghor. With this, their control of 14 out of 32 provinces is established.

19 September — The Taliban ask Islamic and other friendly governments to close embassies, consulates, trade offices and banks operated by the Rabbani regime in their countries. Ambassador Mehmoud Mestiri visits Kabul for talks with the regime.

20 September — The Taliban spokesman in Peshawar, Maulvi Gul Hashim, gives an ultimatum to Rabbani to step down within five days or face an attack on Kabul. He also warns India not to interfere in Afghanistan.

21 September — The Taliban hijack an Afghan airliner, forcing it to land at Kandahar.

10 October — Taliban jets, for the first time, bomb the Kabul regime positions in the Paghman area north of the capital.

11 October — Charasiab falls to the Taliban after fierce fighting.

14 October — After a heavy gun battle, the Taliban enter the Paghwan province, the headquarters of Sayyaf.

15 October — Taliban militia capture Islam Qila near the Iranian border.

17 October — The forces of the Kabul regime launch a massive attack and recapture two districts in Paghwan.

18 October — The Taliban and the Shura-e-Ham Ahangi agree to launch a joint attack on Kabul. No agreement is signed as there are differences about the future setup in Afghanistan.

22 October — Two Taliban aircraft bomb Kabul for the first time.

14 November — Mullah Rocketi and five of his commanders are killed in an armed clash with the Taliban in Maidan Shehr.

16 November — Mehmoud Mestiri announces in Islamabad that Rabbani has agreed to transfer power to a 28-member council representing the various warring factions. Those to be included in the council were agreed on during talks between Mestiri, Rabbani, Masood and Dostum on 14 November. The peace formula is rejected by the Taliban on 17 November on the grounds that it protects the Kabul regime.

22 November — The Taliban spokesman, Najibullah Irfan, annouces to the *Frontier Post* in Peshawar that the Taliban have captured Pul-I-Charki, the eastern gateway to Kabul.

4 December — The Rabbani regime captures a strategic mountain pass at the border of Logar province from the Taliban.

28 December — Rabbani offers peace talks to all the warring factions, including the Taliban. The offer is made during a gathering of the ulema in Kabul on the occasion of the 16th anniversary of the Soviet invasion of Afghanistan. This is rejected by the Taliban the following day.

1996

3 January — Twenty civilians are killed and 48 injured as a result of a rocket attack on Kabul by the Taliban.

18 January — Mehmoud Mestiri visits Kabul and appeals to the Taliban to come to the negotiating table. He insists that they will not be able to seize power through military means.

22 January — The Kabul regime offers a unilateral cease-fire to mark the beginning of Ramadan. This is rejected by the Taliban the following day. They declared that they cannot trust Rabbani and that the offer is merely a ploy to buy time.

6 February — Ahmed Shah Masood repulses a Taliban offensive on Rishkor.

11 February — The Taliban threaten war on Iran for its interference in Afghanistan and bomb cities controlled by Ismail Khan.

14 February — Troops of the Kabul regime enter Herat and seize some areas of the province from the Taliban.

17 April — The Taliban reject a mediation offer from Iran (Alaeddin Broujerdi suggested Iran-Taliban talks in Tehran).

18 May — The Hizb-e-Wahdat and the Taliban agree to resolve their differences and form an alliance against the Rabbani regime. The two parties undertake to reopen roads between the areas under their control, recapture areas from the Rabbani forces, and establish a commission to investigate the killing of Abdul Ali Mazari.

24 May — Radio Kabul announces that Rabbani and Hikmatyar have signed an agreement to jointly defend the country. Under the accord, the two sides decide to explore ways to establish a truly Islamic government in Afghanistan and set up a national Islamic army. Hikmatyar's Hizb-e-Islami are to be given the prime ministership and the ministries of defence and finance. The purpose of the agreement is to launch a combined attack on the Taliban, recapture areas under their control and setup a joint government.

27 May — The Taliban invite four Afghan factions for talks aimed at forming a new alliance against Rabbani. The leaders invited to Kandahar are Muhammad Nabi Muhammadi of the Harkat-e-Inqilab-e-Islami, Younis Khalis of the Hizb-e-Islami (Khalis group), Ahmad Gillani of the Mahaz-e-Milli-e-Islami, Sibghatullah Mujaddadi of the Jubba-e-Nijat-e-Milli and the heads of the supreme coordination council which also includes the Jumbish-e-Milli, and the Hizb-e-Wahdat.

30 May — The Taliban capture the strategic western province of Ghor. Their control up to this point in time of Kandahar, Zabul, Urzgan, Paktia, Khost, Farah, Logar, Wardak, Badghis, Nimroz, Herat and Ghor is firmly established.

6 June — In an interview, Rabbani offers negotiations with the Taliban for power sharing in Kabul. At the same time he promises peace talks with Dostum. The Taliban reject the offer and describe the Rabbani regime as "corrupt and un-Islamic".

14 June — Mujaddadi visits Kandahar for talks with the Taliban. In a joint state-

ment, Mujaddadi and Mulla Omar urge all Islamic Afghan groups to continue their struggle to force "the usurper Rabbani regime to submit to the
will of the people so that peace and stability can be restored". The Kabul
regime is described as illegal and unconstitutional and the root cause of
Afghanistan's problems.

26 June — The Taliban spokesman in Peshawar, Maulana Ahmed Jan, ask foreigners, citizens, journalists and politicians not to attend the oath taking
ceremony of Hikmatyar in Kabul. A Taliban rocket attack subsequently
kills 61 and injures a hundred people during the ceremony.

6 July — Fifteen people are killed in a rocket attack on Kabul during the cabi-
net's swearing-in ceremony. The following ministers are inducted by
Hikmatyar: Wahidullah Sabawoon (Defence), Hadi Arghandiwal
(Finance), Qanooni (Interior), Ahmad Shah Ahmadzai (Education),
Qaimuddin (Information and Culture), Syed Ali Javad (Planning), and
Samiullah Najabi (Martyrs and Disabled). Hikmatyar calls on the Taliban
to stop fighting. This is rejected by Mulla Omar.

17 August — The seven Russian crew members captured on 6 August escape
from the Taliban in their own aircraft and land at Sharjah.

22 August — After fierce clashes, the Taliban capture an important military post
of the Hizb-e-Islami (Hikmatyar) in eastern Paktia. The Hizb-e-Islami
representative in Peshawar confirms the fall of Paktia.

26 August — The Taliban capture Azra, a strategic military base of Hikmatyar
in Logar. Kabul jets bomb Taliban positions in Wardak, Logar, and Paktia
but fail to repulse the Taliban.

11 September — Jalalabad is captured by the Taliban after fierce fighting.
Seventy people are killed including the acting governor. All leading roads
to Kabul are cut off as a result of the fall of Jalalabad.

14 September — The Taliban take control of Kunar after the province's pro-
regime leadership surrender.

16 September — After the Taliban successes, Dostum joins the Kabul forces and
sends two thousand troops to help the regime. Aziz Murad, a Rabbani
spokesman, urges Pakistan to "recall its militias". The allegation is denied
by the interior minister Naseerullah Babar.

23 September — The Taliban capture Dara Patch, a town in Badakshan.

25 September — The Taliban enter the suburbs of Kabul and capture vital government bases including Sarobi, Pul-I-Charki, Gumruk, Lataband Pass,
and Mahipur.

26 September — The Taliban enter Kabul's eastern residential district and take
Pul-I-Charki prison and the military academy.

27 September — Kabul falls to the Taliban. Dr Najibullah, his younger brother,
Ahmadzai, and his bodyguard, Jabseer, are hanged. Mulla Muhammad
Rabbani is named chief of the ruling council.

Afghan personalities

Abdali, Ahmad Shah. Founded kingdom of Afghanistan in 1747. Died in 1773.

Abdul Wali. Cousin and son-in-law of ex-king Zahir Shah. Commander-in-Chief Central Forces until 1973. Imprisoned by Daud, 1973-76. Deported and lived in Italy since 1975.

Abdullah Abdullah. Belongs to Jamiat-e-Islami. Foreign minister in the Karzai administration.

Abdur Rahman. Amir from 1880-1901. Known as the "Bismark of Afghanistan."

Akbari. A leader of the Shia Wizb-e-Wahdat. He had sharp differences with Karim Khalili.

Amanullah Khan. Third son of Habibullah Khan. King of Afghanistan from 1919 to 1929. Forced to abdicate.

Amin, Assadullah. Nephew and son-in-law of Hafizullah Amin. Became head of Hafizullah Amin's secret police. Was killed with his father-in-law in 1979.

Amin, Hafizullah. US-educated member of PDPA (Khalq faction). After abolition of monarchy was active in party affairs. Became vice premier and foreign minister in 1978 in the first cabinet of the Democratic Republic of Afghanistan, prime minister and foreign minister in April 1979, president in September 1979 after Taraki's ouster and subsequent murder. Killed on 27 December 1979 when the Parcham faction took over.

Daud, Muhammad. Cousin of ex-king Zahir Shah. Prime minister 1953-63. Overthrew monarchy in 1973 and established the Republic of Afghanistan. President 1973-78. Killed in PDPA coup on 27 April 1978.

Dost Muhammad. Amir of Afghanistan from 1826 to 1839 and, after a brief period of exile, ruled form 1843 to 1869.

Dostum, Abdul Rashid. Powerful ethnic Uzbek warlord from Jowazjan. Began career as a worker in a gas field near Shibberghan. Joined communist party and then entered army where he was trained by the Soviets. Organized his own militia in northern Afghanistan. Became Najibullah's most important militia commander. Head of the Jumbish-e-Milli faction (Uzbek) of the Northern Alliance.

Ehsanullah, Mulla Ehsan. Taliban governor of the State Bank. Killed in Mazar-e-Sharif in 1997.

General Malik. Ethnic Uzbek. Dostum's deputy who led rebellion against him in 1997.

General Faheem. Ahmed Shah Masood's deputy. After Masood's assassination in November 1991, Faheem became the most powerful element in the Northern Alliance and also in the earlier part of the Karzai administration.

Ghaus, Mulla Muhammad. Taliban foreign minister until mid-1997.

Gillani, Pir Syed Ahmad. Pushtun. Born 1933 in Jalalabad. Migrated to Pakistan after 1978 PDPA coup. Formed the moderate pro-monarchy Mahaz-e-Milli party in 1979.

Habibullah Khan. Son of Abdur Rahman. Amir of Afghanistan form 1901 to 1919.

Haqqani, Saeedur Rahman. Taliban envoy to Pakistan.

Hassan, Mulla Muhammad. Taliban foreign minister in 1997 and later first deputy Council of Ministers. Reported to have spoken to Reuters from an undisclosed destination in May 2003.

Hikmatyar, Gulbadin. Pushtun. Born 1946 in Kunduz (northern Afghanistan). Dropout from Engineering Faculty at Kabul University. Founded the Muslim Students Organization. Jailed in 1972 for murder of Maoist student. Fled to Pakistan after his release in 1974. Founded the Hizb-e-Islami which became one of the main parties resisting Soviet occupation. Named prime minister under the Islamabad Accord of 1993. Associated off and on with the anti-Taliban Northern Alliance.

Ismail Khan. Tajik. Born in 1942 in the Shindand district of Farah. Played a key role in the fight against the Soviet occupation forces. Joined Rabbani's Jamiat-e-Islami. Given the rank of general by Mujadaddi and was made in charge of Afghanistan's south-west. Fled after the Taliban capture of Heart.

Jalil, Mulla Abdul. Taliban deputy foreign minister. Whereabouts not known.

Kabir, Mulla. Taliban governor of Nangarhar.

Karmal, Babrak. Born 1929 in Kabul. Became Marxist in the early 1950s and adopted pen name Karmal ("friend of labour") in 1954. Imprisoned in 1953 but freed by Daud in 1956. Member of PDPA Founding Congress. 1974. Led PDPA Parcham faction. After 1978 coup vice chairman of Revolutionary Council and deputy prime minister. Succeeded Hafizullah Amin in December 1979. President and secretary general PDPA 1980-86.

Karzai, Hamid. President of Afghanistan after the ouster of the Taliban.

Khalili, Karim. Leader of the anti-Taliban Hizb-e-Wahdat (Shia).

Khalis, Younis. Pushtun. Born 1919 in Nangarhar province. Head of his own faction of Hizb-e-Islami which was established in 1979. Most of the fighters from this resistance group joined the Taliban.

Masood, Ahmad Shah. Persian-speaking commander of the Panjsher Valley. Head of the military wing of the Jamiat-e-Islami. After the Soviet invasion of Afghanistan he led resistance in Panjsher Valley but negotiated truce with the Soviets in 1983. Became the most important person of the Northern Alliance from August 1998 until his assassination on 9 November 2001.

Mazari, Abdul Ali. Head and co-founder of Hizb-e-Wahdat. Captured and reportedly killed by the Taliban in March 1995.

Mohseni. Shia resistance leader.

Muhammadi, Muhammad Nabi. Pushtun. Born 1921 in Logar province. Member of parliament for four years during Zahir Shah period. Jailed during Daud regime but released for want of evidence. Fled to Pakistan after PDPA coup in 1978 and formed the resistance party Harakat-e-Inqilab-e-Islami. The party included Uzbeks and was considered moderate.

Mujadaddi, Sibghatullah. Pushtun. Born 1925 in Kabul. Masters in Islamic Jurisprudence from Al Azhar University, Cairo. Imprisoned for four years in 1959 for anti-Soviet activities. Formed the underground anti-communist Jamiat-e-Ulema-Muhammadi. Shifted to Pakistan after 1978 PDPA coup and established the moderate resistance party Jubba-e-Nijat-e-Milli.

Mujahid, Mulla Abdul Hakim. Taliban envoy to UN.

Mutawakil, Mulla Abdul Wakil. Taliban foreign minister. Current whereabouts not known.

Muttaqi, Mulla Amir Khan. Taliban minister of culture and information. Whereabouts unknown.

Nadir Shah, Muhammad. Born 1883. King of Afghanistan from 1929 until his assassination in 1933.

Nadiri, Syed Agha Mansur. Leader of Ismaili Hazaras. Cooperated with Dostum to topple the Najibullah regime in 1992.

Najibullah, Muhammad. Pushtun. Born in Kabul. Joined PDPA (Parcham). Exiled by Taraki 1978. Director General Khad (intelligence agency) 1980-85. General secretary PDPA and president of Watan Party 1986-92. President of Afghanistan1987-92. Refuge in Kabul UN office until he was killed by the Taliban in 1996.

Obaidullah, Mulla. Taliban defence minister. Current whereabouts not known.

Omar, Mulla Muhammad. Reportedly born in 1962 in Uruzgan province. Fought the Soviets as a commander of Nabi Muhammadi's Harakat-e-Inqilab-e-Islami. Spearheaded the Taliban movement from Kandahar in 1994. Declared the supreme leader of the Taliban with the title Amirul-Momineen in April 1996. Ousted as a result of US-led military action against Taliban after 9/11. His present whereabouts are not known.

Qadeer, Haji Abdul. Governor Nangarhar. Fled to Pakistan with the approach of the Taliban.

Qanooni, Younis. Member of Jamiat-e-Islami. Minister of interior in Karzai administration. Fought presidential elections against Karzai. Currently an opposition leader.

Rabbani, Burhanuddin. Ethnic Tajik born in Badakshan in 1940. Masters in Islamic Philosophy from Al Azhar University, Cairo. Escaped arrest for Islamic activities in Kabul and fled to Pakistan. Became president under the Peshawar Accord and kept on having his term extended until his government was ousted by the Taliban in September 1996.

Rabbani, Mulla Muhammad. The Taliban Chairman of the Ruling Council, Head of the Council of Ministers. Died of liver cancer in Pakistan in April 2001.

Rahman, Dr Abdur. Important member of Burhanuddin Rabbani's Jamiat-e-Islami.

Rahmani, Mulla Hassan. Taliban governor of Kandahar.

Rasul Pehlawan. Powerful ethnic Uzbek warlord and brother of General Malik. He was murdered by Dostum in 1996.

Razzaq, Mulla Abdul. Taliban interior minister. Captured by Afghan forces in April 2003. His high-handed behaviour was largely responsible for the uprising against the Taliban in Mazar-e-Sharif in May/ June 1997.

Sayyaf, Abdul Rab Rasul. Pushtun from Paghman in Kabul province. Studied at Al Azhar University, Cairo. Imprisoned by Daud regime but released in 1979 through a general amnesty accorded by Karmal. Fled to Pakistan in 1980 where he formed the resistance group Itehad-e-Islami. Allied with Burhanuddin Rabbani in 1993.

Sharq, Dr Muhammad Hassan. Non-communist prime minister appointed by Najibullah.

Tanai, Shahnawaz. Pushtun from Paktia. Chief of army staff, 1986-88. Defence minister 1988-90. Staged abortive anti-Najibullah coup 1990, subsequently fled to Pakistan.

Taraki, Nur Muhammad. Pushtun from Ghazni. Born 1917. Leader of PDPA Khaq faction. President of Afghanistan, April 1978. Murdered in September 1979.

Turabi, Mulla Nooruddin. Taliban minister of justice. Captured by US forces.

Zahed, Mulla Abdul Rahman. Taliban deputy foreign minister. Current whereabouts not known.

Zahir Shah, Muhammad. King of Afghanistan 1933-73. After he was ousted by Daud lived in exile in Rome.

Glossary

Aimak: Minority Persian-speaking ethnic group found mostly in Ghor, central Afghanistan.

Al-Aqsa: The name the Quran gives to the Temple Mount in Jerusalem and to the Temple of Solomon (also called al-Bayat al-Muqaddas). The Aqsa Mosque is one of the most important in Islam.

Alim (Plural: ulema): Religious scholar. A person who has successfully obtained a higher degree from a madrassa.

Amir: A title taken by several Afghan kings. It also means leader. Some warlords also used the title for instance Ahmed Shah Masood.

Burqa: A shuttlecock like over-garment worn by Afghan women and by some in Pakistan, India and Bangladesh. It covers the entire body and face. The eyes are covered by a net cloth allowing the woman to see. This type of dress is not prescribed by the Quran.

Chapter VII Sanctions: Binding Security Council sanctions under Chapter VII of the UN charter which deals with action with respect to threats to the peace, breaches of the peace, and acts of aggression.

Commonwealth of Independent States (CIS): A confederation or alliance of 11 former Soviet republics: Armenia, Azerbaijan, Belarus, Georgia, Kazakhstan, Kyrgyzstan, Moldova, Russia, Tajikistan, Ukraine and Uzbekistan. Turkmenistan discontinued permanent membership as of 26 August 2005.

D-8: The Developing Eight Economic Group (D-8) was launched in Turkey on 15 June 1997, at a summit in Istanbul. The D-8 countries are Egypt, Iran, Pakistan, Bangladesh, Nigeria, Malaysia, Indonesia and Turkey.

Durand Line: The 2,450 km (1,519 mile) border between Afghanistan and Pakistan. The Durand Line was established in 1893 and is named after Sir Mortimer Durand, the foreign secretary of the British-India government.

Greater Khorasan: A Persian province which once included parts of today's Afghanistan (Herat, Kabul, Ghazni and Balkh), Turkmenistan, Uzbekistan and Tajikistan.

Hadith: Sayings and traditions of Prophet Muhammad, compiled some 150 years after his death.

Hanafi: One of the four schools of Sunni law. It derives its name from Abu Hanifa (d. 767).

Harakat-e-Inqilab-e-Islami: A Pushtun moderate party founded by Muhammad Nabi Muhammadi in 1978.

Hazara: Shias of central Afghanistan, found mostly in Bamyan but also in parts of Ghazni, Oruzgan, Ghor, Jowazjan, Balkh, Samangan, Bhaglan, Parwan and Wardak.

Hizb-e-Islami (Hikmatyar): Pushtun-dominated fundamentalist party led by Gulbadin Hikmatyar.

Hizb-e-Islami (Khalis): A fundamentalist Pushtun splinter group from Hikmatyar's party led by Yunis Khalis. Its fighters later joined the Taliban.

Hizb-e-Wahdat: The Shia party of the Northern Alliance. Its agenda includes maximum autonomy for provinces, inclusion of Jafferia school of thought as one of Afghanistan's religious doctrines, and one-third Shia representation in all branches of government.

Ijma: Consensus among learned believers to interpret laws on which the Quran, Hadith and Sunnah are silent.

Iranian Revolutionary Guard Corps: The IRGC, also known as Pasdaran-e-Inqilab, was established by Khomeini on 5 May 1979 and entrusted the task of guarding the Iranian revolution. By 1986 its numbers rose to 350,000.

Islamic Conference of Foreign Ministers (ICFM): A part of the OIC mechanism. It meets annually to make recommendations to the summit and to review the implementation of OIC decisions. The ICFM decided during its Jakarta session in 1996 to keep Afghanistan's seat vacant in the OIC until a government acceptable to all Afghans was formed.

Ismaili: A Shia sect that considers the seventh Imam as the hidden Imam as opposed to orthodox Shias who regard the twelfth as the hidden Imam.

Itehad-e-Islami: A Pushtun fundamentalist party founded in 1980 by Sayyaf.

Jafferia: A Shia School of Law based on the teachings of Jafar as-Sadiq (699-765).

Jamiat-e-Islami: Ethnic Tajik party formed in 1970. Anti-Pushtun and led by Burhanuddin Rabbani, it became a key element of the Northern Alliance.

Jihad: The word carries the basic idea of endeavour towards a praiseworthy aim and has many shades of meaning in the Islamic context. It may express a struggle against one's evil inclination or exertion for the sake of Islam. It also implies a holy war against aggression. The Quran permits war only in self-defence.

Jubba-e-Nijat-e-Milli. A moderate Pushtun party founded by Mujaddadi in 1978.

Jumbish-e-Milli: The ethnic Uzbek component party of the Northern Alliance. The party is led by Dostum.

Kaaba: The large cubic stone structure at the center of the Grand Mosque of Mecca. It is towards the Kaaba that Muslims orient themselves in prayer.

Khalq ("Masses"): A PDPA faction after the party split. It provided the first two leaders of the revolution (Taraki and Hafizullah Amin).

Loya Jirga: An Afghan grand assembly

Madrassa: A seminary imparting higher religious education.

Mahaz-e-Milli: A Pushtun monarchist party formed in 1979 by Pir Gillani.

Majlis: Iranian parliament. The word also means a gathering, an assembly, a ruling council, a parliament.

Momineen (Singular Momin): Believers.

Muharram: The first month of the Islamic calendar, the first ten days of which are a period of mourning by Shias for the martyrdom of the Prophet Muhammad's grandson Hussain who was killed on the 10th of Muharram.

Mujahideen: A holy warrior.

Mulla: A title accorded to religious scholars.

Murid: A disciple in a Sufi order.

Murshed: A spiritual guide.

Organization of the Islamic Conference (OIC): Set up in Rabat, Morocco on 25 September 1969 in reaction to an arson attack on the Al-Aqsa Mosque in Jerusalem on 21 August. Includes 57 mostly Islamic nations and aims "to promote solidarity among all member states" on the political, "economic, social, cultural, scientific and other fields of activity". Its summits are held every three years.

Parcham ("The Flag"): A PDPA faction led by Babrak Karmal.

Pushtun: Pushtu-speaking tribesmen of Afghanistan where they are the largest ethnic group, and in Pakistan where they are a minority and live in the North West Frontier Province. They are also known as Pathans in Pakistan, India and Bangladesh. They are Sunni Muslims.

Pushtunistan: A separatist movement of the 1950s and 60s among some Pushtuns of Pakistan's Tribal Areas in the North West Frontier Province to establish a homeland of their own. It was encouraged by Afghan governments.

Shia: One of the two main branches of Islam comprising 10 percent or less of the total of all Muslims. Shias themselves are divided into three principal groups. They regard Ali, Prophet Muhammad's cousin and son-in-law, as his true successor as leader of Islam.

Shura: Consultation. Council. A consultative assembly.

Shura-e-Aali-e-Difa-e-Afghanistan: The Supreme Council for the Defence of Afghanistan, more commonly known as the Northern Alliance. It consisted mainly of minority ethnic groups who, despite their deep-seated hatred and suspicions of each other, came together to oppose the Taliban.

Shura-e-Nazar: The military wing of Burhanuddin Rabbani's Jamiat-e-Islami. It was led by Ahmed Shah Masood.

Sunni: The largest group of Muslims often known as "the orthodox," who recognize the first four Caliphs, attribute no special religious or political function to the descendants of Prophet's son-in-law Ali, and adhere to one of the four Sunni schools of law.

Notes

Chapter 1

1. G. P. Tate, *The Kingdom of Afghanistan: A Historical Sketch*, Asian Educational Services, New Delhi, 2001, p.111.
2. Sir Thomas Holdich, *The Indian Borderland*, Methuen & Co, London, 1901, quoted in J. C. Griffiths' *Afghanistan: Key to a Continent*, p.20.
3. Ludwig W. Adamec, *Afghanistan, 1900-1923: A Diplomatic History*, University of California, 1967, pp. 4 & 10.
4. John C. Griffiths, *Afghanistan: Key to a Continent*, Waterview Press, 1981, p.16.
5. Richard S. Newell, *The Politics of Afghanistan*, Cornell University Press, 1972, p.48.
6. Griffiths, *op cit*, p.66.
7. Newell, *op cit*, p.185.
8. Griffiths, *op cit*, pp.66-67.
9. Griffiths, *op cit*, p.68.
10. Griffiths, *op cit*, p.125.
11. M. G. Aslanov, E. G. Ghaffarbeg, N. A. Kisliakov, K. L. Zadykhin & G. P. Vasliyeva, "Ethnography of Afghanistan, a Study", translated by Mark & Greta Slobin in *Afghanistan, Some New Approaches*, Center for Near Eastern and North African Studies, University of Michigan, Ann Arbor, 1957.
12. Aslanov et al, *op cit*, pp. 44-45, 69-77.
13. Aslanov et al, *op cit*, pp. 44-45, 69-77.
14. Vartan Gregorian, *Emergence of Modern Afghanistan: 1880-1946*, p.34.
15. Holdich, "Gates of India", quoted in Gregorian, *ibid*.
16. Newell, *op cit,*, p.33.
17. Major H. B. Lumsden, "Mission to Candahar," quoted in Tate. op. cit. p.154.
18. Interview with *Middle East Journal* (winter 1952).
19. *Afghan News*, May 1995, published by the Jamiat-e-Islami of Burhanuddin Rabbani.
20. The ECO was established in 1985 by Pakistan, Iran, and Turkey as a successor to the Regional Cooperation for Development. It was expanded in 1992 to include Afghanistan, Azerbaijan, Kazakhstan, Kyrgyzstan, Tajikistan, Turkmenistan and Uzbekistan.
21. Speech at the Afghan Support Group meeting in Stockholm, 2 June 1995.

Chapter 2

1. All Taliban ministers were designated "acting ministers" because they maintained that their government was interim and that permanent ministers would be appointed when the permanent dispensation was in place.

Chapter 3

.1. Francis Fukuyama, "The End of History?", published in the summer 1989 issue of the *National Interest.*

2. Olivier Roy, *Islam and Resistance in Afghanistan*, Cambridge University Press, 1986, p.5.

3. *Time*, 15 June 1992, article by James Walsh.

4. Olivier Roy, *op cit*, p.3.

5. Walsh, *op cit.*

6. *Quran*, 4:3.

7. *Ibid*, 4:27.

Select bibliography

Adamec, Ludwig W., *Afghanistan, 1900-1923: A Diplomatic History*, University of California, 1967.

Ahmed, Rashid, *The Resurgence of Central Asia: Islam or Nationalism?*, Oxford University Press, 1994.

Ahmed, Rashid, *Taliban: Islam, Oil and the New Great Game in Central Asia*, I .B. Tauris, London 2000.

Anwar, Raja, *The Tragedy of Afghanistan: A First-hand Account*, Verso, London, 1988, (trans. from the Urdu by Khalid Hasan).

Armstrong, Karen, *Islam: A Short History*, Weidenfeld & Nicolson, London, 2000.

Aslanov M. G., N. A. Ghaffarbeg, K. L. Kisliakov, G. P. Vasilyeva & K. L. Zadykhin, *Ethnography of Afghanistan: A Study*, trans. Mark & Greta Slobin in *Afghanistan, Some New Approaches*, Center for Near Eastern and North African Studies, University of Michigan, Ann Arbor, 1957.

Cordovez, Diego, & Selig Harrison, *Out of Afghanistan, The Inside Story of the Soviet Withdrawal*, Oxford University Press 1995.

Dupree, Louis, *Afghanistan*, Princeton University Press, 1980.

Fukuyama, Francis, 'The End of History?', *National Interest*, Summer 1989.

Gall, Sandy, *Afghanistan: Agony of a Nation*, Bodley Head, London, 1988.

Goodwin, Jan, *Caught in the Crossfire*, Macdonald & Co, London, 1987.

Griffiths, John C., *Afghanistan: Key to a Continent*, Waterview Press, 1981.

Haleem, M. A. S. Abdel, *Understanding the Quran: Themes and Style*. I. B. Tauris, London, 1999.

Holdich, Sir Thomas, *The Indian Borderland*, Methuen & Co., London, 1901.

Huntington, Samuel P., *The Clash of Civilizations and the Remaking of the New World Order*, Simon & Shuster, New York, 1996.

Maley, William (ed.), *Fundamentalism Reborn? Afghanistan and the Taliban*, Hurst, London, 1998.

Marsden, Peter, *The Taliban: War, Religion and the New Order in Afghanistan*, Oxford University Press, 1998.

Matinuddin, Kamal, *The Taliban Phenomenon: Afghanistan 1994-1997*, Oxford University Press, 1999.

Munir, Muhammad, *From Jinnah to Zia*, Vanguard Books, Lahore [2nd edn., 1980].

Newell, Richard S., *The Politics of Afghanistan*, Cornell University Press, 1972.

Nixon, Richard, *Beyond Peace*. Random House, New York, 1994.

Roy, Olivier, *Islam and Resistance in Afghanistan*, Cambridge University Press, 1986.

Rubin, Barnett R., *The Search for Peace in Afghanistan: From Buffer State to Failed State*, Yale University Press, 1995.

Tate, G. P., *The Kingdom of Afghanistan: A Historical Sketch*, reprinted by Asian Educational Services, New Delhi, 2001.

Index

Index

Index